200
-65.-/Seg

POLITICAL MAGIC

POLITICAL MAGIC

BRITISH FICTIONS OF SAVAGERY
AND SOVEREIGNTY, 1650–1750

CHRISTOPHER F. LOAR

Fordham University Press New York 2014

Copyright © 2014 Fordham University Press

All rights reserved. No part of this publication may be reproduced, stored in a retrieval system, or transmitted in any form or by any means—electronic, mechanical, photocopy, recording, or any other—except for brief quotations in printed reviews, without the prior permission of the publisher.

An earlier version Chapter 3 was previously published as "How to Say Things with Guns: Military Technology and the Politics of *Robinson Crusoe*," *Eighteenth-Century Fiction* 19, nos. 1–2 (2006): 1–20; and an earlier version of Chapter 5 was previously published as "The Exceptional Eliza Haywood: Women and Extralegality in *Eovaai*," *Eighteenth-Century Studies* 45, no. 4 (2012): 565–84.

Fordham University Press has no responsibility for the persistence or accuracy of URLs for external or third-party Internet websites referred to in this publication and does not guarantee that any content on such websites is, or will remain, accurate or appropriate.

Fordham University Press also publishes its books in a variety of electronic formats. Some content that appears in print may not be available in electronic books.

Library of Congress Cataloging-in-Publication Data
Loar, Christopher F.
 Political magic : British fictions of savagery and sovereignty, 1650–1750 / Christopher F. Loar. — First edition.
   pages cm
 Includes bibliographical references and index.
 ISBN 978-0-8232-5691-4 (cloth : alk. paper)
 1. Political fiction, English—History and criticism. 2. English fiction—17th century—History and criticism. 3. English fiction—18th century—History and criticism. 4. Politics and literature—Great Britain—History—17th century. 5. Politics and literature—Great Britain—History—18th century. 6. Politics in literature. 7. Authority in literature. 8. Aliens in literature. I. Title.
 PR858.P6L83 2014
 823'.509358—dc23
                                                                    2013037283

Printed in the United States of America

16 15 14   5 4 3 2 1

First edition

For Barbara

Contents

Acknowledgments ix

Introduction: Magical Government 1

1. Enchanting the Savage: The Politics of Pyrotechnics in the Cavendish Circle 33

2. Fire and Sword: Aphra Behn and the Materials of Authority 66

3. Talking Guns and Savage Spaces: Daniel Defoe's Civilizing Technologies 104

4. *Doctrines Détestables*: Jonathan Swift, Despotism, and Virtue 142

5. Savage Vision: Violence, Reason, and Surveillance in Eliza Haywood 181

Coda: Enemies 217

Notes 229
Bibliography 285
Index 319

Acknowledgments

In the decade I spent working on this book, I received aid and comfort for which these words of thanks are but a paltry recompense. This work could never have been completed without the extraordinary mentoring and support I received as a graduate student at UCLA. Felicity Nussbaum patiently supervised this project in its early stages and has continued to offer advice and criticism in the intervening years. I owe an infinite debt to her for her relentless erudition and her boundless patience. During my first year of graduate study, I was lucky to take a seminar with Helen Deutsch; her class first triggered my interest in the eighteenth century, and the habit of energetic and creative reading she instilled has changed my life. Her support for this project has been unfailing and very, very welcome. I am also very grateful to Christopher Looby and Margaret Jacob for their sage counsel. Allison Harvey, Nicole Horejsi, James Masland, Manushag Powell, and Melissa Sodeman read with patience the earliest versions of these pages; I am as grateful for their bracing criticism as for the warmth of their friendship. Thanks as well to Robert Sterner and Molly Hiro for reading Adam Smith, Thomas Hobbes, and Jean-Jacques Rousseau with me, and to boon companions Royce Dieckmann, Kevin Cooney, Andy Fleck, Christopher Flynn, Anthony Galluzzo, David Long, Julia Lee, Andrew Rosenblum, and Anne Stiles.

Most of this book was rewritten during my years at UC Davis, and to my colleagues there I also offer hearty thanks. I was fortunate enough to receive outstanding guidance and mentorship from three skilled department chairs: Margaret Ferguson, David Robertson, and Scott Simmon. Margaret Ferguson also read and commented on major pieces of the manuscript, as did Kathleen Frederickson, Alessa Johns,

John Marx, Timothy Morton, Catherine Robson, and David Simpson. Many thanks to them for their suggestions great and small. Extra thanks are due to John Marx, who helped me wean myself from a dangerous preoccupation with forts. Frances Dolan and Gina Bloom provided astute hints and advice at key moments. Perhaps just as important was the generous friendship of Nathan Brown, Seeta Chaganti, Joshua Clover, Gregory Dobbins, Elizabeth Freeman, Desirée Martin, Elizabeth Miller, Matthew Stratton, and Michael Ziser. I also learned much from students in my graduate seminars, whose creative and intellectual energies were a constant inspiration.

Farther from home, I have benefited from the counsel of many other generous and gifted scholars. Marc Redfield and Jill Benton encouraged me at an important and early stage in my career. I welcomed acute critiques and suggestions from Arne Bialuschewski, Nicholas Hudson, Jayne Lewis, Rivka Swenson, and Cynthia Wall, as well as the anonymous reviewers for my previously published articles on Defoe and on Haywood. Many thanks to the editors of *Eighteenth-Century Studies* and *Eighteenth-Century Fiction* for permission to reprint portions of those articles here. Faculty at my new institutional home, Western Washington University, asked probing and helpful questions as the book neared completion. I was blessed with two sensitive and brilliant referees for my manuscript, Elliott Visconsi and Laura Rosenthal. I am also grateful to my editors at Fordham University Press—Helen Tartar, Thomas Lay, and Eric Newman—who have steered this work from manuscript to book with keen eyes and steady hands.

Research for this project was supported by funds from the English departments at UCLA and UC Davis and by an Andrew W. Mellon Foundation Fellowship at the Huntington Library. Important research for this project was conducted at the Huntington and at the William Andrews Clark Memorial Library. Many thanks to the able staff at these libraries for their assistance.

It might go without saying that this book would never have existed without the loving encouragement of my family. Thanks to my mother, Patricia Loar, for instilling in me a deep love of the written word. Thanks to my father, Darrel Loar, for showing me how to have the courage to make bold and life-changing decisions. Thanks to all my siblings for their faith and encouragement. Barbara Lehman may, at times, have wished that this book had not required so much of my attention, but she has never been anything other than supportive. To her this book is dedicated. Honorable mention goes to Micah Lehman-Loar, who has never lived in a world in which his father was not trying to write this book. Not until now, anyway.

Can a savage, remaining a savage, be civil? Were not we ourselves made and not born civil in our progenitors' days? And were not Caesar's Britons as brutish as Virginians? The Roman swords were best teachers of civility to this and other countries near us.

—Samuel Purchas, marginal note in
William Strachey's *True Reportory* (1610)

At first it frighted them to the last degree, and I may well say it frighted them out of their wits, for they that were near it started so violently that they fell down and lay speechless for some time; those that were farther off ran away as if it had been some new kind of lightning and thunder . . . but when they saw the two creatures fall down dead out of the air, and could see nothing that flew up to them to kill them, they were perfectly astonished, and laid their two hands on their breasts and looked up to heaven as if they were saying their prayers in the most solemn manner imaginable.

—Daniel Defoe, *A New Voyage Round the World* (1724)

Introduction: Magical Government

Samuel Purchas is startlingly frank in his depiction of the role of violence in producing the civility that undergirds modern forms of government. For Purchas, there is no categorical distinction between "savage" peoples in the New World and the ancient inhabitants of the British Isles, who themselves required an armed conqueror to subdue them and fashion them into civil subjects. The modern English subject is separated from the wild Virginian more by temporality than by skin color. While most later British advocates of efforts to bring civility to savages would try to obscure colonialism's violence, Purchas highlights the brutal fact of conquest as a fundamental and inevitable moment in the transition from lawless savagery to civility. This book argues that for some writers, Rome's civilizing project in England never ended: British fictions of empire in the century following Charles I's execution are centrally concerned not only with conquest, conversion, and slavery but also—even primarily—with reimagining fundamental political categories of the "civilized" world such as sovereignty, liberty, and civility.

Examining fictional narratives of cultural contact in the century following the publication of Thomas Hobbes's *Leviathan* (1651), I argue that these narratives redeploy tropes from histories of contact and exploration to explore the question of how sovereign powers might best harness violence and human irrationality as techniques of government, instilling reason, order, and a sense of duty into an increasingly complex and dynamic political community. Focusing in particular on narratives by Margaret Cavendish, Aphra Behn, Daniel Defoe, Jonathan Swift, and Eliza Haywood, I argue that these fictions link ongoing crises of political authority in the century following the English Civil War with two other developments: shifts in British imperial thought and practice, and the much-heralded eclipse of belief in magic by a culture of reason. Restaging moments of cultural contact, when "savages" witness the power of European technology for the first time, these fictions transform technological devices such as guns into something like fetishes: technologies that appear to "savages" as magical, godlike, or mystically animate. From the perspective of the savage, guns speak and magnifying lenses produce fire from nothing. In deploying these ambivalent objects, at once technological and magical, contact narratives focus attention on a foundational political moment, often an instant of astonishment that establishes the superiority of European modernity and inaugurates a civilizing project. These imperial acts are also, however, meditations on the foundation and maintenance of the political and legal order of the "civilized" European world. Belief in magical objects in this period is associated not only with "savages" but also with the vulgar multitude, whose superstition, it came to be thought, made them vulnerable to misleading magical displays. During this period of Britain's transition from absolutism toward a liberalized constitutional monarchy, the difficulty of conceptualizing a legitimate authority that escapes the Scylla of tyranny and the Charybdis of mobocracy is reworked in these fictions of violence and deceit. This study examines fictional portraits of savagery and contact that reimagine sovereignty in this crucial transitional period in British politics, when older clashes between "English liberty," republicanism, and divine-right monarchy began to give way to new tensions internal to something recognizable as liberalism. The narratives that are my primary interest repurpose colonial scenarios to imagine ways in which political power might be intensified without giving way to the dangers and temptations of tyranny.

Critics of the long eighteenth century have trenchantly argued for the significance of non-Europeans in British cultural and political life during the long eighteenth century.[1] This book supplements these studies by reading colonial fictions of the Restoration and early eighteenth century as explorations not just of colonial theory but of the nature of the political community and its relationship to violence and law. I am particularly interested in their explorations of sovereignty—the final locus of political power and authority that underwrites law and sustains the political community of the nation-state.[2] In this period, sovereignty is variously ascribed to the monarch, to Parliament, or to "the people," whatever that term is taken to mean. The sovereign also bears responsibility for sustaining the political community through periods of crisis and emergency, operating outside the confines of the law. For this reason, sovereignty also flirts with extremes of lawlessness: kings and ministers may grow into tyrants, and the people may degenerate into its disorderly double, the mob or the rabble. Efforts to represent and explain these relationships are rife during this period in which Britain is developing a new understanding of the relationship between sovereignty, people, and political community. Most political writers of this era understood the *demos*, though free, as incapable of wielding political authority. For some writers, particularly those influenced by theories of natural law, "the people" may register as the ultimate source of legitimate political authority—what contemporary political theorists often call *constituent power*, the authority of a political community that lies outside and beyond established political institutions.[3] Humanist scholarship followed a parallel track during the seventeenth century, developing the theory that English political institutions and common law are "rooted in a fabric of immemorial custom" and founded on the construction of a citizen who "rules and is ruled."[4] However, both theories of this political collectivity generally excluded a large portion of the population—women, the landless, and religious minorities, among others.[5] Thought in this period repeatedly grapples with these paradoxes. Is there a single locus of political authority? If so, what is its relationship to the law? How are the boundaries of the political community and those who may participate in it to be defined and policed?

One attempt to answer these questions is found in fictions of cultural contact between "civil" and "savage" peoples in Africa, the Caribbean, North America, and the Pacific and Indian Oceans. In these narratives, colonists or explorers bring civility to the "uncivilized" human: the African, "Indian," Pacific Islander, or Tartar who belongs to a different political moment: not yet modern, not yet civilized, not yet subject to sovereignty or law.[6] Significantly, the civilizing process in these fictions is repeatedly produced through acts of deferred violence: technologically enhanced performances of simulated divinity or mysterious powers to kill at a distance. Technological devices such as guns play a key role in the imagining of colonial sovereignty. But these fictional savages are not merely Britain's Others; they are also figures for the prelegal or prepolitical subject or multitude who also appear in the form of the rogue, the vagabond, or the mob inside Britain's own borders. These texts, by seeking something like a universal politics, tend to collapse distinctions between the colonial periphery and home. One of sovereignty's tasks has always been the need to transform violence against bodies into a force that can direct them; though the sovereign holds the power of life and death, corpses make poor subjects. This is a problem that intensifies after 1660 as Britain seeks to cultivate a political community that does not need strong applications of violence to keep it ordered; more authoritarian writers sought to amplify sovereign power through wonderful displays and more effective use of deception, while those drawing on liberal and republican thought needed models to imagine how a free people might be governed without undue restraint. Colonial fiction imagines one solution to this problem. If the display of technological prowess and simulated divinity can astonish and instill habits of obedience in prelegal savages, bringing them into the sphere of civility and law, then some similar deployment of terror, wonder, and the supernatural might have similar effects on unruly subjects at home. These foundational moments produce obedience and subjection, which in time lead to civility, which is the precursor to the early development of a governmentality that provides the context for these texts.

In the sections that follow, I discuss these issues in more detail. I first briefly discuss what I call the *first gunshot topos*, a recurring moment of technologically produced wonder. I then offer a brief discussion of seventeenth- and eighteenth-century political theory and the narratives that suffuse it. In response to the persistent social and political instability that dominated the Restoration and earlier eighteenth century, political theorists repeatedly created fictions of political origin to explain and justify the existence of political community and its obligations. The texts I examine are in part responses to and critiques of these theorizations of sovereignty, rights, and obedience. I then discuss the figure of the savage and the idea of civility, underscoring the languages of technology and magic that recur in colonial fictions. I close with a brief description of the chapters that follow.

The First Gunshot Topos

Guns feature prominently in the fictions I examine here. When savages encounter gunfire (and sometimes other technological displays) for the first time, they are astonished and amazed, often paralyzed or almost swooning. This trope appears early in ostensibly nonfictional narratives of encounter, but the fictions I examine heighten and emphasize its role to highlight their interest in sovereignty and violence. Drawing on a long history of ambivalence about gunpowder's potency, muskets and cannons in these texts signify not only raw power but also a superiority that scans to the "savage" as divinity or magic—a divinity that is ascribed to the gun wielder and his (or, less commonly, her) civilization. By imputing a supernatural power to the forces of colonialism, narratives that emphasize technology's power to terrify without killing allow writers to imagine nonviolent points of origin to political and legal orders. However, the boundary is porous between these magical performances and more alarming states of tyranny and illegitimate violence. Disproportionate technological power can also figure this problem: gunpowder is associated not only with civilizing displays but also with devastating violence and atrocities. Gunpowder frequently figures a lawmaking or civility-making violence that shapes the anarchical power of the constituent multitude into a free but quiescent political community. However, it also repeatedly emerges as a figure for states of emergency in which sovereign violence goes beyond instituting or reaffirming law and instead unleashes massacre and devastation. Thus gunpowder, like the term *war* itself, is an unstable signifier.[7] Gunpowder's ability to represent political violence in forms both strategic and uncontainable makes it a potent figure for sovereign power as I seek to understand it: it is law forging and law destroying, divine and satanic all at once.

This tension is visible in Defoe's tableau of encounter. The sailor-merchants in the epigraph that precedes this introduction encourage the savages they meet to believe their guns to be enchanted or animated, thereby claiming a divine authority for themselves. Defoe's scene draws on travel narratives that appeared in the great collections of voyages produced in the early modern era by Richard Hakluyt and Samuel Purchas, as well as in later collections by John and Awnsham Churchill and others, to suggest that civility might be instilled without swords, without violence, and without conquest, through spectacular displays of technology.[8] Unlike a Roman sword, this show of force does not immediately make the savage into an enemy. Instead, this moment of contact represents itself as an intercultural and political friendship, as Defoe's mariners direct their technologies against the natural world to establish themselves as bearers of sacred or of supernatural power—a power that leaves the savages speechless with wonder, terrified but tractable and obedient. To assuage their fear, Defoe's narrator offers them gifts and shows them "all the Kindness and Tenderness imaginable."⁹ These voyagers present themselves not as conquerors but as messiahs.

But the potentially civilizing authority they establish over these islanders remains grounded in violence and fear. This gunshot "gave them terrible Ideas of us," the narrator notes.[10] This terror is also integral to the sailors' performance; Defoe alludes to gunpowder's longstanding connotations not only of technological prowess but also of a terrible destructive power. Gunpowder is able to figure not only as an element in a tactical sovereign performance but also as pure violence detached from order, law, and reason. The fear that sovereign violence once unleashed will refuse to be contained reappears in these narratives as massacre and apocalyptic destruction, often augmented by the same fetishized technologies that initially strike awe rather than death. This figuration draws on a different colonial archive that represented the dark underside of civilizing violence: the Spanish conquest of the Americas. Many Anglophone readers knew this story directly or indirectly from Bartolomé de las Casas, whose litany of colonial horrors appeared in several English translations from 1583. His narrative depicts naive and benign savages who initially treated their Spanish enslavers as though "they had been sent from Heaven."[11] The folklore of conquest has long held that the Spanish victories relied heavily on the astonishing force of their modern weaponry; Robert Boyle, for example, praising modern technological sophistication, suggests that "the poor Indians lookt upon the Spaniards as more than Men, because the knowledge they had of the Properties of Nitre, Sulphur and Charcoale duly mixt, enabled them to Thunder and Lighten so fatally, when they pleased."[12] Had the Spaniards been forces for Christianity and civility, they might have redirected this power to civilize and convert. But since the Spaniards opted for tyranny, Cortez and his guns embody only the dark side of colonial sovereignty, eviscerating and depopulating the land.

The Spanish conquest is of course part of a longer and wider tradition that treats Roman Catholicism as a tyrannical and persistent threat to British liberty. Spanish or papal tyranny is commonly linked to both massacre and gunpowder, not only in the context of the New World but also because the indelible memory of 1605's Gunpowder Plot, intended to restore Catholicism to England. Consider the conjoining of gunpowder to tyranny in this nightmarish vision, penned by the radical Whig Charles Blount in 1679, at the height of the hysteria surrounding allegations of Jesuit conspiracies known as the Popish Plot. Blount's pamphlet envisions London in the wake of a successful conspiracy to place the Roman Catholic James, the Duke of York, on the throne:

> First, Imagine you see the whole Town in a flame. . . . Fancy, that amongst the distracted Crowd, you behold Troops of Papists, ravishing your Wives and your Daughters, dashing your little Children's brains out against the walls, plundering your Houses, and cutting your own throats, by the Name of Heretick Dogs: Then represent to your selves the Tower playing off its Cannon, and battering down your Houses about your Ears.[13]

What is striking here is not simply the familiar litany of Catholic atrocities or even their similarities to the savage violence of cannibals and barbarians (the smashing of infants' brains is of course familiar from writings from the American frontier). It is also an evocation of tyranny as such; it is regal violence escaping its boundaries and destroying all signs of civility in its path. Here sovereignty itself is figured by the Tower of London and its guns; this architectural emblem of royal power, so long in tension with the city that surrounded it, is in Blount's dystopian vision armed to the teeth, annihilating the civilized urban and domestic spaces that Blount's readers inhabit.[14] And this threat is not merely external to Britain; absolutist horrors lurk within, too, most obviously in the figure of the Catholic Duke of York, soon to ascend to the throne himself.

Fictions of Obligation, Fictions of Contact

Gunpowder, then, has associations not only with war but with magic and performance and with domestic insurrection and existential threats to the political community. This role is highlighted in fictions of contact, when colonists or explorers inaugurate modernizing projects that bring law or civility to savage spaces. These fictions critique and compete with other fictions of political origin, which frequently traced political obligation from its source in primordial acts of assent that surrender rights to a sovereign. Narratives from the natural-rights tradition of Hugo Grotius, Thomas Hobbes, and John Locke, in particular, linked a conception of fundamental natural rights to well-ordered political systems.[15] These narratives presented a number of problems, to be sure; Grotius and Hobbes arrive at authoritarian systems all the more oppressive for their grounding in primordial acts of consent, while Locke's liberalized model remains problematic for the propertyless and for women, in particular. But the most compelling problem these narratives present is what William Connolly has called the paradox of sovereignty: how can a prepolitical, uncivil person become sufficiently civil to enter into an agreement about government?[16] This paradox was later given its most influential formulation by Jean-Jacques Rousseau, whose theorization of popular sovereignty requires a *demos* to bring legitimate government into being—a *demos* that itself is the product of that law and discipline it institutes.[17] This was hardly an abstract question for British thinkers in the long eighteenth century. As Victoria Kahn has argued, the years of civil war and unstable government provoked intense disputes about "the violence and artistry required to fashion the contracting subject."[18] These crises of the seventeenth century were only one facet of a long-term challenge to established order. By the mid-seventeenth century, individuals near the bottom of Britain's socioeconomic hierarchy had become less tightly bound to traditional forms of deference, authority, and obligation, part of the long-term disintegration of social hierarchies associated with medieval forms of land tenure and with an increasing emphasis on the individual ultimately stemming from the Protestant Reformation.[19] These historical shifts are the conditions of possibility for the emergence of liberal thought and practice.[20] The ungoverned person, the mob, or the rabble possess the British birthright of liberty, free from tyrannical or arbitrary violence, but few considered them worthy of an active voice in their government. This exclusion for most writers applied to women as well; as Carole Pateman has demonstrated, Locke implicitly assumes a "sexual contract" that subordinates women prior to the later compact that institutes government.[21] This exclusion was quite clearly noticed by many women writers in this period; as I discuss later, many of them explore and exploit this exclusion from government to fashion new arguments about the topology of sovereignty or explore the relationship between the uneducated woman and the uncivilized savage.

While some thinkers hoped to restore traditional forms of patriarchal sovereignty, the dominant tendency during this period is toward imagining a looser style of government, suitable for a modernizing and commercial society that requires subjects to be docile and productive but that cannot monitor each of them individually. Following Foucault, I understand this theory of the practice of government as an early form of liberal governmentality, which in some degree occludes sovereignty as political theory and practice from the eighteenth century onward. Foucault's conception of governmentality is of a form of power that governs bodies and populations in order to achieve optimal outcomes, rather than seeing obedience itself as the primary objective of politics. The concept of governmentality allows Foucault to understand developments in liberal thought not simply as a universal system of rights but as an economics of government, maximizing order and productivity in a population with minimal inputs from the state.[22] The writers that are my object of interest are concerned in the production of the subject who is obedient and yet free; the subject of governmentality occupies a valuable place in the social order without being forced to do so. To be clear, I do not claim that these fictions offer a full-fledged model for later developments in political economy; they are primarily transitional texts and, with the possible exception of Haywood, have no conception of a population in this sense. They are, however, exploring the production of the self-governing subject who can inhabit such a social order. These texts are transitional in imagining the cultivation of subjects who can govern themselves without continuous oversight, but in also assigning a critical role to sovereign violence in producing and sustaining the forms of obedient subjectivity that sustain that liberty.[23] These narratives, however, are ambivalent, uneasy, and often well aware of their own contradictions and instabilities—acknowledging the dependence of the political on violence and magic, on force and fraud. Even writers most clearly associated with liberalism, such as Daniel Defoe, manifest in their fictions of colonialism a powerful interest in sovereign violence as a necessary precursor and sustainer of other forms of government and governmentality.

These fictions find that they cannot represent an absolute boundary between a civilized and liberalized polity and savage anarchy; they imagine a continuing need for sovereign acts of coercion that occur within or border on the quotidian legal order. Twentieth-century political theorist Carl Schmitt posited the role of the sovereign as a maintainer of the normal; this idea is already embedded, however, in much early modern political thought and practice.[24] In these texts, sovereign acts are not limited to founding moments. Even for Whigs concerned with liberty, the possibility that sovereignty will reenter the political sphere remains ever present. In moments of external crisis or internally driven emergency conditions—war, rebellion, civil unrest, or simply a deterioration of civility—even most liberal theorists and writers agreed that a centralized power (monarch or parliament) retained the ability to suspend normal operations, procedures, and rights. Such decisions also establish the boundaries of the political community, determining who is able to make determinations about public matters and who is entitled to the law's protections. Moira Fradinger has argued that societies produce narratives of political origin with particular intensity at moments of democratization, when the boundaries of the political community are uncertain and the identification of the Other assumes greater importance.[25] I here adapt this thesis to the somewhat different political culture of Stuart and Hanoverian Britain, not moving toward democracy so much as toward a liberalized but regularized form of government. Many British writers deploy a democratic rhetoric, but it is not a language that suggests that the lower orders ought to have a voice in matters of public interest; Parliament speaks on their behalf but not in their voice. To govern a nation of free subjects without excessive violence, however, a state must have a multiplicity of tactics at its disposal. The colonist's technological superiority and the ambivalence of gunpowder offer figures for the problems of government that are at stake in these narratives.

The political thought developed by radical republican Algernon Sidney illustrates the tension internal to these nascent forms of liberalism. Sidney's fusion of elements of natural rights, republicanism, and common-law nativism powerfully influenced later theories of government and liberalization, as did his secular martyrdom in his dubious trial and execution for treason.[26] Sidney is often remembered for his staunch defense of rights of resistance and rebellion, but as Jonathan Scott notes, he was also significant in envisioning a positive role for the state as a molder of virtuous subjects rather than as a mere restraint of evil.[27] Sidney's *Discourses Concerning Government* (in draft, 1683; published posthumously in 1698) understands political subjects as "rough pieces of timber or stone, which 'tis necessary to cleave, saw, or cut: this is the work of a skilful builder, and he only is capable of erecting a great fabric, who is so. Magistrates are political architects."[28] Sidney's language describing ungoverned multitudes echoes descriptions of savages, criticizing "the fierce barbarity of the loose multitude, bound by no law, and regulated by no discipline" as intrinsically ungodly and productive not of a happy piety but of "perpetual anxiety" (2.1, 83). Sidney's favored republics are godly republics, free from tyranny. As political communities, however, they emerge and develop historically, often under the tutelage, rough or gentle, of a legislator or lawgiver. Ancient Rome provides his key example; following Livy's account of Rome's origins, he notes that Rome at its founding was by no means prepared to govern itself. "If a popular government had been set up in Rome immediately upon the building of the city," he writes, the "unruly" folk there would have ruined themselves; "herdsmen, fugitive slaves, and outlaw'd persons" have no capacity for republican self-government. Instead,

> that boisterous humour being gradually temper'd by discipline under Romulus, or taught to vent its fury against foreign enemies, and soften'd by the peaceable reign of Numa, a new race grew up, which being all of one blood, contracted a love to their country, and became capable of liberty, which the madness of their last king, and the lewdness of his son, gave them occasion to resume. (3.25, 462–63)

Sidney here is not so much disavowing the rhetoric of liberty that he so strongly proclaims; he is contending that while no people is required to submit with docility to a tyrannical king, neither is it true that all peoples are capable of making good use of liberty. A brutish people must be subject to sovereign discipline and the stresses of combat if they are to develop the capacity to exercise a just, orderly, and virtuous liberty. Sidney's republicanism here anticipates the uneven and inconsistent treatment of rights under liberal regimes. As Laura Doyle has argued, Anglo-Atlantic rhetorics of liberty are not generally appeals to a universal right, but are tied closely to the mythos of the Anglo-Saxon nation.[29] Sidney insists on the need for a powerful sovereign to soften and tame the intractable, which reminds us that at the core of his argument is the idea that personal liberty emerges historically within a state or society. If Sidney is indeed an influential and radical defender of freedom, as Jonathan Scott, Annabel Patterson, and Elliott Visconsi have persuasively argued, his writings also reveal tensions and contradictions internal to the ideals of liberalism and republicanism—in particular their complex stances on sovereignty and political community.[30] Though a scourge to monarchs, Sidney acknowledges the existence of "bestial men" who "being incapable of governing themselves, fall under the power of such as will take the conduct of them" (2.8, 122–23). He also echoes Purchas's colonial logic: bestial men must be disciplined by an outsider; their political community must be shaped by a sovereign who is "in nature different from those he takes the charge of" (2.8, 123). A community's first law must come from elsewhere.

The political poetry of Daniel Defoe similarly highlights the tension between assertions of popular right and a reverence for ungrounded sovereign power. Defoe in the early eighteenth century established himself as a political poet and pamphleteer; his writings from these years proclaim the priority of constituent power and inveigh against doctrines of extralegal monarchy. Yet his invocations of popular right also simultaneously envision a sovereignty that must oppose and constrain the multitude. Defoe's early career—including, probably, involvement in Monmouth's Rebellion and, certainly, fomenting popular agitation against the Tory House of Commons during the crisis surrounding the Kentish petition—might seem to paint him as a radical democrat, since he strongly argued for the reservation of ultimate constituent power to the people. "All power must centre somewhere," Defoe wrote in 1701, and it is the people, not political institutions, who have this authority. In Defoe's writings from this period, the *vox populi* is the *vox Dei*. But Defoe's "people" are freeholders, not "the vulgar or mixt multitude," in Tyrrell's phrase.[31] Freeholders harbor the country's other inhabitants only as guests or "sojourners."[32] Women and landless workers must apparently get by on hospitality. In his first well-known poem, *The True-Born Englishman* (1701), Defoe describes his country folk as a rebellious and unreasoning crowd who will brook no law:

> *Restraint from ill, is Freedom to the Wise;*
> *But* Englishmen *do all Restraint Despise.*
> Slaves to their Liquor, Drudges to the Pots,
> *The Mob are Statesmen and their Statesmen Sots.*
> Their Governors they count such dangerous things,
> That 'tis their Custom to affront their Kings:
> So jealous of the Power their Kings posses'd,
> They suffer neither Power nor King to rest.[33]

If the English people are, alternately, a *vox populi* and a mob, then some external force must restrain, regulate, and limit that power. This force may, in fact, derive from conquest, since law follows property, and property follows war: "Conquest, as by the moderns it is expressed / May give a title to the lands possessed" (line 1.265). Laws, by definition, protect holdings originally claimed prior to their advent.[34]

Defoe's late poem *Hymn to the Mob* (1715), written in response to Jacobite riots that followed the accession of George I, crystallizes these issues: identifying the ungoverned mob as the source of all political authority, it also lambasts London's contemporary mobs as mad and easily deluded.[35] This mob, the wellspring of legitimacy, must also be tamed by an external sovereign power. The primal mob, he writes, is the "Parent of Nations, Spring of Government":

> Power began with thee,
> And was but lent to guard thy Liberty;
> If when 'tis misapply'd, we grant it true,
> The Re-assumption has been thought thy Due. (lines 63–66)

The mob here figures the constituent power; it understands the people to be the ultimate source of law's legitimacy, preceding and authorizing political institutions. Yet the London mob's apparent support for high-church and authoritarian doctrines seems to have nonplussed Defoe; mobs in practice cannot be trusted to know what rights to defend or how to defend them. The mob's primordial authority is terrifying and unruly; it is subject to fits of blindness and victim to unscrupulous demagogues. Though the poem offers hope that the mob will return to reason of its own accord, it may also may need to be tamed with sovereign violence: "Persuasion must attempt to make them still, / and if persuasion won't, the gallows will" (line 689). The gallows here, representing the power of the sovereign over the unruly body—the power to make die, in Foucault's terms—remains in a paradoxical relationship to this primordial constituting power. Defoe's political community, like Sidney's emergent republic, needs a supplementary form of violence that threatens to undo it, a sovereign violence that restrains and reshapes the populace in times of madness or, we might say, of emergency. Sidney's writings and Defoe's political poetry both pose recurring and different questions about political practice: what techniques might the wielder of sovereign authority use in the ambiguous space between persuasion and the gallows? Answering this question also allows us to understand why colonial encounters so readily figure practices of sovereignty as they steer between the violence of conquest and the doubtful powers of mere persuasion.

These colonial fictions participate in a wider project that Elliott Visconsi has called "imaginative originalism"—writings that represent the origins of law, responding to the challenges and paradoxes posed by a liberalizing polity. Fictions of origin populate the pages of canonical works of political theory as well as lesser-known tracts throughout the period I am discussing. These fictions respond to and challenge other narratives of origin, probing problems and paradoxes inherent to the imagining of the governmental production of free subjects, capable of entering into contracts and exchanges or of functioning as autonomous subjects of a liberal legal order. Colonial fictions form a paratradition to what was to become the canonical eighteenth-century realist novel. Novelists such as Samuel Richardson, Henry Fielding, and Jane Austen have been enshrined in a canon that highlights individual autonomy and membership in a national community, celebrating liberation and nation.[36] Colonial fictions, while also explorations of liberty, are less sanguine about the relationship of the free subject to the political sphere; all evince concern about the creation of subjects able to exercise liberty properly and lawfully. They also investigate the possible fate of unlawful subjects who cannot be fit into a liberal political community and consider the crises these subjects may provoke. While this desire to contain and harness popular power is visible in various modes and genres, it is fictions of colonialism that offer the most capacious imaginative space for its exploration. The fictionalized and refracted travel accounts and colonial fictions I examine all narrativize and heighten the moment of contact, clarifying and simplifying categories of otherness that in the rawer narratives they draw from remain ambiguous, unclear, and sometimes perplexing to readers as well as to those in the thick of the action. Fiction restructures contact, creating a literary savage that permits a stripping away of ambiguities, clarifying and focusing attention on the distinct boundaries between the modern colonist/sovereign and the temporally belated savage/subject. Jonathan Elmer has noted that literary texts can represent contradictions in order to highlight them, emphasizing the capaciousness of literature to register ambivalence.[37] This spaciousness is particularly salient in the generically loose fictions of the late seventeenth and early eighteenth centuries; its open-endedness is striking in comparison with, for example, the more constrained formal demands of heroic tragedy.[38]

Savage Subjects

In the political imaginary of the seventeenth and eighteenth centuries, the savage often appears as a figure for the human or protohuman who lives before or outside of modern sovereignty. Though Hobbes and Locke were cautious about equating their prepolitical contracting subjects with contemporary inhabitants of Africa or the Americas, others were not so subtle. Algernon Sidney describes the "bestial barbarity" of Africa, the Americas, and parts of Asia, suggesting that it reveals the natural human condition, "if it be not improved by art and discipline." For Sidney, to improve human nature is the task of politics, a natural course of progress not dissimilar from architecture, shipping, and modern armaments—other signs of modern and civil life (3.7, 357–58). Sidney's political opposite, the flamboyant Tory Charles Leslie, pilloried the idea of the contract in the state of nature, in a dialogue between two of his political enemies and a South African "hottentote," who defends the idea of a state of nature and the rule of the strongest—that is, until he unmasks himself as, in fact, a resident of a kingdom established on principles of patriarchal monarchy.[39] The savage is not simply the Briton's Other, however, for there are domestic savages as well: criminals, rebellious dissidents, unruly apprentices, vagrants, and others to whom the law's reach extends only partially and tentatively. Women, too, could be understood as metaphorically akin to savages; "covered" in English law by husbands and fathers, they were sometimes represented as outside the jurisdiction of the legal order, governed by patriarchal masters rather than kings or courts. This exteriority derives from the commonplace analogy that linked husbands to monarchs and wives to subjects.[40] Comparisons between women and slaves were not unusual in protofeminist writings from this period; Mary Astell famously asks, "If all men are born free, how is it that all Women are born Slaves?"[41] Hilda Smith suggests that Astell's consciousness of her status as an outsider to law and politics fueled her larger critique of liberal thought; this book will argue that other women writers similarly found methods to use that exteriority as a tool for alternate political narratives. There is also the persistent possibility that the civilized person, or even an entire community, might slide backward temporally into more savage conditions. Richard Helgerson, Elliott Visconsi, and Debora Shuger have all noted the threat that the idea of "Gothic barbarism" and degeneracy posed to early modern thought; eighteenth-century writers expressed similar fears, though they were perhaps more likely to make reference to savagery.[42] Most theories of savagery required some account of degeneracy; since all humanity descends from Noah's family, it is clear that some sort of falling away from civility and into savage ways must have occurred. Bernard Mandeville notes that this degeneration can easily recur in the absence of good government: "Mankind will always be liable to be reduced to Savages."[43]

The presence of domestic savages troubles the prospects for political liberty and governmentality; in effect, it requires that the sovereign must not only shape the original polity but must also reproduce, reconstruct, and refurbish it by maintaining subjects in a state of obedience. When threats to the community overwhelm the norms of law, extraordinary measures may be necessary. In the twenty-first century, this tension is often described using the language of emergency: sovereigns who perceive existential threats to the nation from within or without are permitted to suspend, at their discretion, the normal legal order. Exceptional sovereign powers, however, can easily bleed into the normal course of business; stabilizing the boundary between the normal and the exceptional situation is difficult.[44] The fraud and coercion that pave the way for law and civility are not firmly anchored in a distant past but perpetually threaten to come unmoored, drifting into the present moment, particularly during times of political crisis. This constant shadow of that founding moment—a moment that anticipates our current interest in states of exception and extralegality—makes the protections of law sometimes appear gossamer thin, particularly to those whose standing in the political community is uncertain: the laboring classes, religious minorities, and political dissidents. The savage is thus not just a figure for the political subject: the savage is what that subject legally becomes vis-à-vis sovereignty.

The state contrary to savagery in this period most commonly goes under the term *civility*. Like savagery, civility is a complex and imprecise concept, but it is a necessary precondition of liberal governmentality. Without it, government must of necessity be by force rather than autonomous obedience. Defoe describes civility as involving "the Manners, the Morals, the Politics, and even the Tempers and Dispositions of the People"; it encourages the "Practice of Virtue" and "true Methods of Living." It is crucially involved with traditions and lifeways that combine kind feeling and politeness with a fondness for "Regularity of

Life" and is based on "Clemency, Humanity, Love, and Good Neighbourhood."[45] Some uses of this term highlight the close relationship between the production of civility and the sovereign creation and preservation of lawful subjects. Samuel Johnson's dictionary entry (1755–56) for the term *civil* offers a striking parallel between the condition of the "savage" and the political subject. Johnson defines the term *civil* by negation: his definitions tell us that the civil is "not wild," "not barbarous," "not military," "not in anarchy," and "not natural." The distinction between the wild and the civil, and the civil and the military, will concern us in the pages to come, but first let us linger on the "natural" that is the opposite of civil. Johnson clarifies what he means in the second half of this definition: "as, a person banished or outlawed is said to suffer *civil*, but not *natural* death." Johnson here anticipates Giorgio Agamben's *homo sacer*; the human living under the ban, excluded from and marking the boundary of civil society, is reduced to natural life, deprived of civility.[46] To be civil is also, of course, to possess "politeness" and "elegance"—to be courtly.[47] But to *civilize*, as Johnson defines it, is primarily "to reclaim from savagenesse and brutality; to instruct in the *regular arts of life*." These "regular arts" are what the extralegal savage has not yet internalized.[48] Thus Johnson's rough definition of civility connects this term both to law and to lifeways. In the narratives I examine, this connection is vital: the savage is civilized by extralegal action on the part of the voyager or colonist and thus made *ready* for law by acts that are lawgiving and, also, culturally transformative. The civility of the savage brings him or her into the sphere of law. But that civilizing act is not, in these texts, itself lawful, operating instead in anomic zones outside the control of law.

Johnson's savages and those discussed in this book are not quite those defined by David Hume, Adam Smith, and Adam Ferguson, among others, who in the later eighteenth century attempted a more rigorous theorization of savagery and barbarism. These stadial histories belong to a later moment that is not my concern here.[49] Savages in this earlier period, whether found in West Africa, the Pacific, Central Asia, the Arctic Circle, or the Americas, were defined much more loosely but were generally understood to share certain "uncivil" features: lack of legitimate legal authority (though they might have "chiefs" or "kings" of a despotic or arbitrary sort); living without permanent architecture (most common in representations of allegedly nomadic North Americans); a taste for human flesh (less common but always a concern when encountering unknown peoples); an absence of certain key technologies (particularly of metalworking, of mechanics, of optics, of shipbuilding, and of gunpowder); a proclivity for violence; and, crucially, an absence of monotheism, which is replaced by the worship of idols, demons, or fetishes.[50] Mandeville writes of savages as having no "orderly way of proceeding" and governed by gusts of passion: "The Passions must be boisterous and continually jostling and succeeding one another; no untaught Man could have a regular way of thinking or pursue any Design with Steadiness."[51] Seventeenth-century traveler Gemelli Careri similarly describes the "first inhabitants" of New Spain, in what is now Mexico: "The first Inhabitants of *New Spain* were a sort of wild People, since they kept on the uncouth Mountains, without Tilling the Land, without Religion, without any Form of Government, and without Cloaths; living after a disorderly Manner like Beasts; feeding upon what they kill'd." A similarly savage people still inhabited the Mexican interior, Careri notes. "The *Spaniards* have not been able to Subdue them, because it is in vain to look for them, who hide themselves in thick Woods, where they have no settled Place of Abode; and to endeavour to Fight them would be no other than hunting of wild Beasts."[52] This account, appearing in Italian in 1699 and in the Churchills' widely read translation in 1704, depicts a "wild" people who live without technology, agriculture, government, or even clothing. Their depiction as "wild beasts" alludes not only to their animal-like habits in dress and economy but also to a proclivity for anarchic and unfocused violence.[53] It also, of course, encodes a complex of attitudes a colonist or sovereign might take toward them; beasts may be tamed or killed with impunity.

But fictions of contact go to great lengths to suggest means for governing savages without killing them like beasts. How and why this is—why the primordial gunshot is so often directed away from the savage instead of toward him—is the work of the next section to explain.

Political Fetishes

All things that were able to do them hurt beyond their prevention, they adore with their kinde of divine worship; as the fire, water, lightning, thunder, our ordinance, peeces, horses, etc.
—John Smith, *A Map of Virginia* (1612)[54]

They not only seem to think there is an Intelligence in those material Things that are of immediate Good or Hurt to them, but also the

Fetish-Men to have Conversation, and by it to be acquainted with their most private Affairs at any distance, which preserves Awe and Regard.   —John Atkins, *Voyage to Guinea* (1723)[55]

Smith and Atkins write in very different contexts, but their assessments of savage worship are strikingly similar. Not only do Indians and Africans tend toward naiveté, superstition, and idolatry; they are also easily manipulated by those with a more cynical stance toward those objects. Smith's colonists associate their tools of war with fire and lightning to encourage "divine worship" and strengthen their authority; in this they are like the West African fetish-man who also uses "material things" to "preserve Awe" by persuading the gullible that he knows their private affairs. In the travel narratives and fictions I explore, we find many sequences in which colonists, in particular, take advantage of this superstitious tendency by performing wondrous feats with technical expertise—"juggling" performances, easy for them to understand but difficult for their naive counterparts to avoid fearing and worshiping. In many representations of "savage" politics, that politics is organized around the fear of supernaturally cathected objects. Many observers suggested that this fear was organized and manipulated by despotic figures who use savage fear to establish and sustain their rule. It is to these models that, I suggest, the political fictions I examine make an unexpected turn: perhaps a sovereign might learn to turn British superstitions to advantage, supplementing the limitations and possible injustices of violence. From the Commonwealth period onward, there remained a lively association of monarchy with magical, religious, and supernatural essences and practices. Certain sacral rites continued to be associated with the monarch at least through Queen Anne's reign; Anne continued to touch for the king's evil, as had her Stuart predecessors.[56] However, as Sarah Ellenzweig has argued, there is a skeptical strain in English religious thought in this period that discounts the truth of Christianity but values the Anglican Church for its power to regulate and discipline.[57] Similarly, alongside these sacral (we might say "magical") practices, even those writers who discount the divine right of monarchs place some importance on the cultivation of a sublime sovereign mystery.

William Pietz's classic account of the concept of fetishism traces its emergence to Portuguese contacts in Africa well before the eighteenth century. In these ambiguous intercultural contexts, full of difficult translations of value and of mutual misunderstandings of ceremonial practices, the term *fetish* comes to be closely associated with certain ritual objects. As Pietz has ably traced, the term derives linguistically from an earlier word used for more benign forms of idolatry and witchcraft. It comes to describe a variety of ceremonial objects in Africa, generally distinguished from idols because of their portability.[58] They are what Atkins in Africa called "material gods" of "infant reason."[59] Pietz suggests that the European technological object entering this intercultural field becomes legible as a fetish as well. The African savage's rudimentary conceptions of law are frequently organized around unsophisticated belief in the "intelligence" of the material. This naiveté is made use of by other, more sophisticated Africans, able to persuade them that their relationship to fetish objects gives them access to occult knowledges; such performances lead to power—"awe and regard," in Atkins's phrase. As Michael Gaudio puts it, "we owe the very idea of the 'savage' to a strongly felt need in the Christian West to imagine a failure to rise above a base materialism."[60] During the eighteenth century, the practice of this "base materialism" became associated with fetishism.

For several thinkers in the French Enlightenment, fetishism came to describe an attitude toward objects that encodes a conception of politics; the fetish

> represented a principle of social order based on an irrational fear of supernaturally caused death rather than a rational understanding of the impersonally just rule of law. It therefore revealed the true political principle (always supplemented by arbitrary despotic violence) that governed all *unenlightened* societies, since ignorance about the workings of physical causality . . . provided the ground of religious delusion necessary for this system of social obligation to work.[61]

These notions—the tension between the rational and the superstitious, between the gullible and the sophisticated, and between tyrannical violence and sovereignty—are already central to the terms in which political power is being analyzed and articulated in the travel writings and fictions of a century earlier.[62] Though the Enlightenment concept of fetishism is not yet fully developed in these fictions, I adopt this term because of its associations with government and politics; I use it interchangeably with other languages about magical objects, since in these writings there are many affinities between the magical and the fetishistic.

For explorers and colonists, the most readily enchanted devices were those that used gunpowder. Gunpowder, along with a few other technologies, was a crucial marker of modernity in the seventeenth and eighteenth centuries, used to position "modern" learning as superior to that of the ancients as well as to savages. Gunpowder had been known to Europe since the thirteenth century, and armaments underwent several major technical developments over the following five hundred years. Artillery, in particular, grew gradually more powerful and sophisticated, as developments in mathematics and metallurgy made it possible to fire cannonballs farther, with more force, and with greater accuracy. Military architecture shifted in response from the high-walled medieval castle to the modern fortress with its low profile and thick walls.[63] Though these changes were largely incremental, artillery seems to have been a special focus of attention in the years following the English Revolution. What appear to be only minor technological developments from a historical perspective clearly made a large impact on the public consciousness. As Jeremy Black has noted, "new machines of war have often enjoyed an impact on the imagination greater than that on the battlefield, particularly if their use is accompanied by dramatic sounds and sights."[64] This attention may have been cultivated by the crown: large artillery pieces during the Restoration were tested on public grounds with some regularity on the outskirts of London, on Hounslow Heath and elsewhere, giving Londoners ample opportunity to be impressed by their spectacular power. Diarist John Evelyn described in the spring of 1687 a mortar test: "I saw a trial of those devilish, murdering, mischief-doing engines called bombs, shot out of the Mortar-piece on Blackheath: The distance that they are cast, the destruction they make where they fall is prodigious."[65] The display of firepower available to the state undoubtedly had an impact on observers disproportionate to the actual military impact of any additions to the technology. This conspicuous display of state firepower perhaps suggests metonymic links between the period's large artillery and the developing power of the modern state. The link between enormous guns and enormously powerful states would have been explicit for those who pondered the motto that appeared across the English Channel on Charles XIV's artillery: "Ultima Ratio Regum"—"the last argument of kings."[66]

Gunpowder's modernity thus had ambivalent connotations; a signifier of power and ingenuity, it also registered as satanic and rebellious, or tyrannical and destructive of chivalry and virtue.[67] Gunpowder features in Francis Bacon's *Novum Organum* (1620) along with the printing press and the compass as the signal invention of modernity, shaping history on a global scale: "These three have changed the whole face and state of things throughout the world. . . . No empire, no sect, no star seems to have exerted greater power and influence in human affairs than these mechanical discoveries."[68] But gunpowder could also be understood as a scourge; its power to destroy could and did signify atrocity and decline as well as progress. And its status as a marker of the modern is complicated by its own mysteries: its origins were obscure and its operations, like combustion more generally, were not well understood. When the savage witnesses gunpowder for the first time and stands in mystified awe of it, he or she is experiencing gunpowder the way "civilized" Britons also experienced it on some level: as a magical or even divine and inexplicable display of power. This instability of signification makes gunpowder available to represent other complex referents in the political sphere, particularly what we have seen is a particularly unstable term, sovereignty.

Narratives of encounters between savages and the technologically advanced had long represented gunpowder as a highly visible marker of the superiority and authority of the European explorer vis-à-vis the savage. The use of gunpowder to intimidate peoples who do not possess this technology (along with other technological wonders such as metalworking, magnetism, and great ships) dates at least to Cadamosto's expedition up the River Gambia in the fifteenth century.[69] However, the first explicit reference I have found in English to the *self-conscious* use of gunpowder and other technologies as props in intercultural performances dates from the Raleigh expeditions to Virginia in the late sixteenth century; it is here in the New World where narratives of colonialism come to rely on representations of savage materialism and European performative savvy. In narratives collected by Hakluyt and Purchas, we find voyagers displaying their guns, making the local Virginians so frightened that they "would fall flat downe at the report of them."[70] Later, impressing them with a display of magnetism (causing a needle to move without touching it), the record states, "This we did to cause them to imagine some great power in us: and for that to love and feare us."[71] Thomas Harriot famously describes the use of gunpowder, timepieces, and burning glasses to suggest to the Algonquian peoples the superior nature of their European guests. Harriot, an Oxford-trained natural philosopher, visited Virginia as part of Sir Walter Raleigh's exploratory expedition in 1585, returning to England in 1586. Harriot's promotional tract suggests that technological superiority instills awe in the savage Algonquin inhabitants, making them docile and tractable:

> Most thinges they sawe with us . . . as Mathematicall instruments, sea compasses, . . . the loadstone . . . , a perspective glasse whereby was showed manie strange sightes, burning glasses, wildefire workes, gunnes, bookes, writing and reading, spring clocks that seeme to go of themselves, and manie other things that wee had, were so straunge unto them, and so farre exceeded their capacities to comprehend the reason and meanes how they should be made and done, that they thought they were rather the works of gods than of men, or at the leastwise they had bin given and taught us of the gods.[72]

Crucially, these contact narratives repeatedly do two paradoxical things: on the one hand, they are self-consciously deceptive, in that they encourage savages to impute supernatural and even holy qualities to devices and techniques manipulated by modern Westerners. On the other hand, they also use these same technologies to suggest that command of these devices really does make Westerners superior; though they are not really godlike, their command of nature vastly exceeds that of the savage, whose eyes cannot penetrate nature's appearances. This superiority permits them at once to imagine a deceptive technique of colonization and to justify that same technique.[73] This imagined superiority perhaps partly compensates for natural philosophy's inability to account for gunpowder's material operations; gunpowder and other combustible substances were not clearly understood until after Joseph Priestley's experiments with oxygen in the late eighteenth century.[74] It is perhaps for this reason that popular writers continued to ascribe quasi-magical origins to gunpowder, such as the tradition linking its development to an anonymous fourteenth-century alchemist.[75]

Gunpowder is not just magical, however; it is also satanic. In England, while the Chinese invention of gunpowder had been accepted as fact by the early sixteenth century, gunpowder continued to be associated with demonic magic.[76] Ben Jonson comically complains of the "Fryar . . . who from the Divel's-Arse did Guns beget," while in a more serious register John Milton famously credits gunpowder to heaven's rebels: Satan and his followers introduce "A triple-mounted row of pillars laid / On wheels" that stun the angels by "Disgorging foul / Their devilish glut, chained thunderbolts and hail / Of iron globes."[77] Milton's rebellious angels are only vanquished by a still more powerful and astonishing machine—the Son's chariot. Jonathan Sawday notes that Milton for a time lived near to the Royal Ordnance works in Vauxhaul, suggesting that this large industrial site perhaps fueled his imagination with the imagery of explosives and machines. Regardless, *Paradise Lost* uses gunpowder as an index not only of evil but more specifically of the specious attractions of rebellion and republicanism; the charismatic and clever Satan may represent allegorically the rebellious and cynical spirit of Oliver Cromwell—or, as Blair Worden argues, of a younger and more republican Milton.[78] In its ambivalence, then, gunpowder is an apt figure for the magical and the scientific, for enlightenment and satanic darkness. Like sovereignty, it is potentially a civilizing and virtuous power and a dangerous tool for the rebel and the murderous tyrant.

As I have suggested, however, gunpowder can also be used not as a weapon but rather as a prop in a performance that seeks to link technology to sovereign authority. Representing these performances, as I have suggested, requires certain assumptions about the savage attitude toward the material and the supernatural world; in particular, it builds on the common belief that the savage mind cannot comprehend abstractions, such that material objects come to be loci of devotion, worship, and fear. In particular, savages tend to make the material object into a focal point of political and religious practice. This primitive materialism is perhaps most visible in early treatments of Africa, from which the term *fetish* emerges. And, just as savages and commoners are imagined as sharing an analogous relationship to sovereignty, so are they often thought to be alike in their attachment to objects and sensations. This similarity, I suggest, partly determines the use of the savage to figure the problem of governance: if the irrational in the savage persists into the modern subject, then that very irrationality may be harnessed and put to use by sovereign performers. Keith Thomas almost half a century ago suggested that non-Christian religious practices such as witchcraft and sorcery, demonology, and alchemy faded as the seventeenth century waned, becoming virtually extinct in the eighteenth.[79] More recent historians have modified this thesis; John Henry, for example, suggests that much so-called magical thought is better understood as natural magic.[80] Jonathan Swift's mentor, Sir William Temple, defined magic as an "excelling Knowledge of Nature" that "produce[s] Effects very different from what fall under vulgar Observation or Comprehension." What Temple's peers would have understood rationally, the "ignorant" call *Magic* or *Conjuring*."[81] The supernatural's role in magic, in Henry's account, was to summon spirits to interrogate about the hidden mysteries of the material world. By the later seventeenth century, natural magic had begun to be appropriated in the name of science or natural philosophy, leaving a remainder now stigmatized as superstitious.[82]

This notional superstition is not only stigmatized but also imaginatively utilized and integrated into ideas about how a nonviolent sovereignty might be practiced in modern Britain. The superstitious savage in these fictions is metonymically linked to the low-born man and woman whose fear of the unknown and limited powers of abstraction could be put to use. Seventeenth-century playwright William Davenant speculated about the prospects for civilizing the nation through spectacular theatrical performances and imagined a theater that could "move an audience through sensory experience to feel emotions which stimulate the reason to initiate actions."[83] This inability to detach from the material is characteristic of the Protestant critique of the universal human tendency toward idolatry—one from which British Protestants were anything but immune. But though the Protestant critique of this tendency (in the form of idolatry) is quite familiar, less attention has been paid to the use of this impulse in the political imaginary. Joseph Addison, for example, argues in the *Spectator* (no. 419) that previous generations of the English, in their "darkness and superstition," were prone to "pious frauds" designed "to amuse mankind, and *frighten them into a Sense of their Duty*" (my emphasis). He concludes that his ancestors "looked upon Nature with more Reverence and Horrour, before the World was enlightened by Learning and Philosophy, and loved to astonish themselves with the Apprehensions of Witchcraft, Prodigies, Charms and Enchantments."[84] This barbarous British past had not vanished entirely, however, in the eyes of seventeenth- and eighteenth-century writers. Even in England, people living in remote areas or not properly brought to a knowledge of Christian doctrine continued to practice magics that sometimes seemed indistinguishable from those of savages.[85] Criminals, too, were sometimes found to be unconverted and uncivilized: as "ignorant of the Principles of Religion, as if they had been born in *Africk*, and bred up amongst the Savages of *America*."[86] The multitude is easily misled and duped; as radical Whig Thomas Gordon wrote in *Cato's Letters*, "the crowd" is very easily taken in by "amulets" and other superstitions, as well as by the more common recourse to free beer: "This shews how much their senses are stronger than their understandings. They are governed not by judgment, but by sensations."[87] That these writers, themselves associated with doctrines of British liberty, are concerned with magic's power to govern is symptomatic of a deeper sense of a need to reenchant the rabble in order to govern without violence. The British people cannot govern and order themselves—at least not yet. They must be governed, and magical practice is a crucial tactic for governing them.

Seventeenth- and eighteenth-century writers, then, are often open to the idea that superstition can facilitate government and, perhaps, even civilize. This conception helps to explain the regularity with which magic, deceit, and sovereignty are frequently considered in tandem. This conjunction is quite striking in the writings of the seventeenth-century French intellectual Gabriel Naudé, whose major works were translated into English and with whose ideas Aphra Behn and Jonathan Swift, at least, were probably familiar.[88] Naudé was notorious in Britain for his support of violent and extralegal state action in the interest of security and stability; he formulated the idea of the coup d'etat as the fundamental sovereign act. For Naudé, the coup d'etat does not describe a sudden takeover of the state by a faction but is broader in application: it is a sudden blow struck outside the law and without prior legitimacy, serving to sustain political community against existential crisis. Naudé was occasionally praised and more often excoriated in Britain, particularly for his scandalous defense of the Paris Massacre— a ruthless extralegal act that, he argued, was necessary to secure France's political stability and safety, despite its horrors. Acts of this sort he describes in terms reminiscent of gunshots and their magic. The coup d'etat is a sort of human-made miracle: it erupts suddenly, unexpectedly, and almost magically. Like the sovereign decision, the miracle has no grounding in any prior order and is entirely the creation of an ungrounded will. Similarly, the coup d'etat is an act of sovereign justice; "contrary to common right," it does not observe any "prior order": "In these master strokes of State, the Thunderbolt falls before the Noise of it is heard in the Skies, . . . the Execution precedes the Sentence; he receives the Blow that thinks he himself is giving it. . . . All is done in the Night and Obscurity, amongst Storms and Confusion."[89] Also like gunpowder, these acts are Janus-faced; they may heal the state but also unleash incredible destructive force and are potentially tyrannical.

Naudé's coups are not uniformly violent. Indeed, he is a staunch advocate of the sorts of political trickery that are characteristic of colonial narrative. In his catalog of outstanding coups, he cites not only the Paris Massacre but also Christopher Columbus's famous eclipse trick in Jamaica. Columbus, his crew threatened by starvation and with local indigenes unwilling to assist him, reportedly convinced them that the impending lunar eclipse would be the mark of his divine power as he commanded the sun to rise tinged red with blood.[90] Among Naudé's first published writings was a treatise, also available in English translation, underscoring the importance of deceitful performances to power. This essay is extended in his work on coups d'etat, identifying them not only with law-preserving violence but with foundational political trickery. The founding of Rome, for example, required violence but was strongly supplemented by Romulus's and Numa's strategic encouragement of wild subjects to understand their sovereign right as being divine.

Naudé's claims, then, despite their poor reputation among liberty-loving Britons, also resonate with certain tactics advocated by Whig and Tory alike: the governing of the unwise, the superstitious, and the unsophisticated by trickery supplemented by violence. If this use of reverence and fear can produce docile subjects, it may also be able to produce a liberal and self-regulating society. But, as I hope to show, the need for exceptional acts—even acts of atrocious violence—lurks behind much of this theory. The construction of stable political communities is, in these accounts, the responsibility of the sovereign decider, and the sovereign actor alone is responsible for their justice.

Chapters

Perhaps, then, politics is a magical art. If uncivilized subjects are to be free from violent repression, they must be governed and shaped in other ways. They must be brought to obey and to labor and to know their place; they must become self-regulating. That, as suggested earlier, is the role of the sovereign. In the fictions I examine, sovereignty's task is to civilize the wild, to compete with their constituent power by meeting their superstition halfway. The superstitious may be enlightened, governed, and brought to correct forms of worship. But a transitional phase is necessary. This phase is figured in these texts through the political fetishization of gunpowder and other technologies.

The chapters that follow trace these intertwined developments in political thought, in British constructions of cultural difference, and in the transformations of magical belief in the century following the publication of political theorist and natural philosopher Thomas Hobbes's *Leviathan*. Hobbes is a crucial starting point for this project, since his writings condense key problems in each of these areas: though he is commonly thought of as a political thinker, Hobbes's influential conception of sovereignty grows out of an engagement with materialism and with epistemology: one of his sovereign's key functions is to adjudicate the boundaries between the sacred and the ordinary, between the miraculous and the mundane. And his thought experiment about humanity in the state of nature decisively shaped, as I will argue, fictional representations of savages. My first chapter, "Enchanting the Savage: The Politics of Pyrotechnics in the Cavendish Circle," examines the rhetorical conjunction of sovereignty, astonishing performances, and savagery in the writings of three members of the circle of intellectuals surrounding the polymath aristocrat William Cavendish, Duke of Newcastle: Hobbes, playwright William Davenant, and Newcastle's wife, the prominent author Margaret Cavendish. In *De Cive* (1651) and *Leviathan* (1651), Hobbes develops two lines of argument: that individuals in the state of nature are forced to live in a "savage" fashion and that humanity's potential can only be realized if individuals voluntarily submit to the rule of an absolute sovereign power. Yet Hobbes is notoriously unclear about how the transitions from nature to law and from savagery to civility might be brought about. Davenant and Cavendish both imagine solutions to these problems, envisioning savages and commoners who are dazzled by seemingly "magical" technological productions. Davenant's writings on theater as well as his defense of heroic poetry in the "Preface to Gondibert" (1650) explore the possibility of using technology to produce spectacular displays, using extreme sensations to draw rough minds toward civility. Margaret Cavendish, in her prose narratives "Assaulted and Pursued Chastity" (1656) and *The Blazing World* (1666), responds to Hobbes's theorization of sovereignty as external to law as well as to Davenant's writings on the political uses of theater. Each author relies to an underexplored degree on the tactical use of wonder and terror to produce and reproduce the political subject. Hobbes famously sees fear of sovereign violence as crucial to the preservation of the political order; Davenant's writings imagine theatrical technologies that will civilize both theater and nation; and Cavendish's romances stage scenes in which gunpowder and fire are deployed both as weapons and as instruments to prop up political authority through wonderful performances among warlike peoples. Cavendish's fiction is particularly important for its association of women and sovereigns as beings exterior to the law—an exteriority that is also repeatedly figured in fictions of colonialism and contact.

This question of exteriority and sovereignty resurfaces with a vengeance during the Restoration; the question of whether the monarch is beyond the law, or perhaps its source, lay at the heart of debates over divine-right monarchy in this period. The status of the monarch, significantly, is routinely interwoven with the status of supernaturally cathected objects such as the monarch's regalia. The status of objects is also at issue in narratives of contact, for intercultural zones are sites in which technological and sacral objects may be viewed from new perspectives. My second chapter, "Fire and Sword: Aphra Behn and the Materials of Authority," examines the role of these defamiliarized or sacralized objects in the production of sovereignty. The chapter focuses attention on a sequence in *Oroonoko* (1688) in which Behn's narrator, visiting an Indian village in Surinam, approvingly watches her kinsman use a "burning glass"—a lens that starts fires by concentrating the sun's rays—to mystify his Indian observers, who imagine him to be a divine being. Most readings of this passage miss the political nature of this performance; by astonishing the Indians, the lens wielder also subdues them, transforming his fellow English settlers from military enemy to divinely sanctioned authority. The scene explores the mechanisms that construct political authority in the colonial contact zone; it also, I suggest, inquires into the role of force and fraud in producing sovereignty and civility, raising questions about the uncanny sources of political authority. Behn's narrative continues an inquiry inaugurated in her drama, which also explores performative and paramilitary techniques for managing the rabble. The alternative material marker of political authority, I conclude, is the mutilated human corpse; Oroonoko's dismemberment at the tale's climax echoes the English crown's recourse to horrifying violence in the Bloody Assizes (1685), which proclaimed the king's power through the mutilated bodies of hundreds of rebels. Behn's texts mourn the collapse of the world of divine right, chivalric virtue, and enchanted objects, while her props gesture toward techniques for operating in the disenchanted regime of pragmatism and popular sovereignty.

The tension between instilling wonder and doing harm is also at the center of my third chapter, "Talking Guns and Savage Spaces: Daniel Defoe's Civilizing Technologies." Here I use Defoe's fiction to explore the continuing problem of sovereignty in the first decades of limited monarchy. Defoe is typically seen as an enemy of tyranny and an advocate of the mixed government to which Behn and Cavendish were opposed. However, Defoe's novels of travel, exploration, and cultural contact, with their intense focus on the transformation of the wilderness into civilized space, and of "savages" such as Friday into civilized Christians, also investigate the problem of legitimate political authority as one incorporating necessary elements of technologically enhanced violence and deceit. Though writers of the early eighteenth century liked to believe they had left the instability of the Restoration behind them, the specter of civil unrest persisted, particularly around the contentious Act of Union (1707), the Hanoverian Succession (1714), the Sacheverell Riots (1710), and Jacobite disturbances, particularly the 1715 uprising. Defoe sees a continued role for sovereign display in fashioning disciplined subjects and orderly spaces. The unrest of this period was frequently discussed in terms of space and place: how might disorderly sites (ranging from the London street to the Scottish Highlands) be tamed? Defoe's novels of exploration and cultural contact address this question elliptically by transforming wilderness landscapes into civilized space and "savages" such as Friday into civilized Christians. This chapter argues that, contrary to most political readings of Defoe's fiction, his novels *Robinson Crusoe* (1719), *The Farther Adventures of Robinson Crusoe* (1720), and *Captain Singleton* (1720) represent violence as inevitable in establishing ostensibly "free" and civilized spaces in Britain and overseas. Defoe's colonial fictions narrate the progress of gunpowder from lawmaking prop to lawless weapon, transforming savage bodies not into subjects but into corpses. I suggest that this fictional arc is indicative of a growing concern on the part of writers in this period about sovereign power's excesses and its capacity to transform normal states into political emergencies, with potentially catastrophic consequences.

Throughout these earlier chapters, I suggest that the miraculous object conveys its inexplicable and apparently supernatural qualities to its wielder. I explore this metonymic aspect of the performance in more detail in my fourth chapter, "*Doctrines Détestables:* Jonathan Swift, Despotism, and Virtue." Here I compare the enchanted technology with a different sort of wonderful object—the luxury commodity—in the context of Swift's interest in the decline of a politics of exemplary virtue. Swift's satiric treatment of luxury goods in *Gulliver's Travels* (1726) and *The Drapier's Letters* (1724) laments the disappearance of exemplary personal merit in the upper classes in Ireland and Great Britain, attacking its replacement by an excessive attachment to attractive personal luxuries. *Gulliver's Travels* displaces this superficiality into the form of a travel narrative, which allows Swift to question the faith that Cavendish, Behn, and Defoe place in performances of power; Swift's text parodically restages Robinson Crusoe's performance of technological superiority in front of savages to hint that European virtue could no longer distinguish itself clearly from that of Europe's "savage" others. The chapter concludes by suggesting that the collapse of exemplary virtue in Great Britain threatens an apocalyptic breakdown of legitimate authority and a reemergence of civil war and savagery—a prospect explored both in Gulliver's narrative and in late satiric pieces such as "A Modest Proposal" (1729).

Swift's writing explores the corrosive effect, then, of modernity on traditional sources of authority that do not depend on sovereign violence. In doing so, he reminds us that most treatments of this period and its politics have assumed that sovereignty plays a smaller role in Britain as the century progresses, displaced by more distributed forces such as print culture and the public gaze, which cultivate an enlightened and self-monitoring civil society. In my final chapter, "Savage Vision: Violence, Reason, and Surveillance in Eliza Haywood," I examine the persistence of sovereignty and the specter of violence in texts that seem initially to leave it behind. Haywood's fictions *Eovaai* (1736) and *The Invisible Spy* (1755) both feature magical devices that correct behavior by encouraging observation and rationality, not display or force; they have been cited as characteristic of a new politics of surveillance and knowledge.[91] However, these devices appear in narratives that point to the limits of vision, repeatedly underscoring the persistence of extralegal violence in the fashioning of rational subjects. *Eovaai*'s eponymous princess is brought out of a state of anarchy and set back on her throne with the aid of a "sacred telescope" that shows her the ugliness of vice; *The Invisible Spy* comprises a series of vignettes related by an anonymous narrator ("Exploralibus"), armed with a belt of invisibility and an enchanted writing pad, who witnesses and transcribes the hidden foibles of the town. But while both narratives underscore the centrality of astute observation and knowledge in the formation of a rational citizen-subject, both also include scenes of war and torture that highlight reason's continued dependence on sovereign violence. I end with Haywood because her writing points so powerfully to the ways in which the figure of the lawgiving sovereign persists even in the unlikeliest of places.

Some readers might complain that this approach to political fiction removes these texts from the spheres of political action and specificity. And no one can doubt, to be sure, that these writers were interested in shaping political outcomes very specific to their times and places. Cavendish and Behn were committed to the House of Stuart; Swift and Haywood were dedicated enemies of the Walpole administration; Defoe worked as a political operative long before he began writing fiction. I attend to these specific moments in the argument that follows, though I avoid reviewing well-established interpretations from scholars who have already carefully situated these texts in their specific historical moments. Instead I focus on the larger ambitions of these texts, insisting that the political thought of these writers is not limited to the narrowest concerns of their immediate political milieu. These writers of fiction not only took an interest in the political thought of their day; they also sought to use narrative to negotiate and explore its complexities and ambivalencies. They were deeply attuned not only to the specificity of their political moment but also to the complex world of political thought and imperial expansion that surrounded them all. From this world, they developed complex representations of a politics waiting—for good or for ill—to be born.

CHAPTER I

Enchanting the Savage: The Politics of Pyrotechnics in the Cavendish Circle

I n "Assaulted and Pursued Chastity" (1656), Margaret Cavendish introduces a polymorphic heroine who frequently shifts personae, beginning as a victimized refugee from civil war and sexual terrorism and ending as a military commander. In a key moment in this narrative, she borrows a page from the history of cultural encounter and colonialism, reshaping earlier tales of "Indians" surprised by European technology into English fiction's first gunpowder performance. The heroine, Travellia, flees the "inhumane multitude" in her civil-war-beleaguered kingdom.[1] Along with her adoptive father, she is taken captive in preparation for a sacrifice; seeking to preserve themselves, they hatch a plot that will not only free them but also set their captors on the path to civility. Making use of her nation's relative technological sophistication, she and her adoptive father astonish and terrify the cannibals by manufacturing gunpowder and a pair of pistols as props in a performance of divine terror. Addressing her captors, Travellia cries, "Why do you offend the Gods, in destroying their Messengers which come to bring you life, and to make you happy? For this . . . the great Sun . . . will destroy you with one of his small Thunder-bolts, killing first your Priests, and then the rest" (435). This ersatz deity then fires the homemade pistol into the chest of the chief priest, killing him instantly. The cannibal crowd responds with astonishment: "The noise of the Pistol, and the flash of the Fire, which they never saw before, and the effect of it upon the Priest, struck them with such a horror, and did so terrifie them, as they all kneeled down, imploring mercy" (435–36).

This performance strangely blurs power with authority, violence with the assumption of a right that transcends violence; it also envisions the institution of a new truth through a sacrilegious lie. The assassination of the priest is an act of violence but also part of a canny performance—one that amplifies the limited physical abilities of Travellia and her surrogate father by giving them claim to a sacred authority of which this violence is only a sign. In assuming the mantle of divinity, Travellia and her father hope to secure their freedom, but their ambitions go beyond that: they also become adored lawgivers. The nation of cannibals converts to a "civilized" lifestyle, abandoning slavery and cannibalism (436–42). The two former captives remain for a time, continuing to be revered like gods: "their persons were thought divine, [and] their words were laws" (443). As Travellia appears to her captors-cum-subjects as a god, her position is inaugural and exceptional; her performance begins a civilizing process and founds a new legal and ethical order through extralegal violence, an astonishing show of power and a calculated imitation of the supernatural.

It is, I think, crucial to our reading of this scene and of Cavendish's thinking about the political that we examine how this performance generates authority. I want to suggest that this intrusion of a colonial topos into a romance narrative is an imaginative solution to certain conundrums of absolutism with which Cavendish is directly, if imaginatively, engaged. Cavendish borrows topoi from colonial discourse: the "first gunshot," cannibalism, conversion. Cavendish here imagines a key moment in which civility is instilled in cannibals through an act of technological terror, but she simultaneously inserts details more characteristic of the romance genre with which she works: not only the shipwreck (one of several in this tale) but also the centrality of a young woman and her travails.[2] Travellia's technological and cultural superiority—her temporal position as more "advanced" and civilized—allows her to use fear and astonishment to transform an uncivilized people. We might say that this moment of terror allows the captive Travellia to institute herself as a sovereign. But central to my reading of this sequence is that Travellia as lawgiver remains fundamentally outside of the legal order she founds: the order is her creation, but she is not, strictly speaking, part of it. And while this topological distinction is enabled partly by her status as a refugee and castaway, it also depends in part on the strange political and legal status of her femininity. Women, Cavendish playfully notes elsewhere, are not strictly legal subjects; they are also endlessly unlocatable, malleable, transitory, subject to pursuit, perpetual and natural refugees. It is this fundamental exteriority—as, simultaneously, woman and colonist—that makes Travellia able to act the part of the sovereign as she does.

Cavendish's romance, I believe, marks the first fictional use of gunpowder as political magic. That is, this is the earliest instance I know of an explicitly fictional text in English featuring a sophisticated traveler using a technological device to terrify and establish authority over a savage people. As I have been suggesting, this act of enchantment or fetishization is not primarily a commentary on colonialism; it is, rather, a meditation on authority more generally, a thematic that the remainder of Cavendish's text makes clear. Cavendish asks how a sovereign can and ought to remake law, including constitutional or fundamental laws, and how a sovereign might use trickery and superstition to transform "the people" or the rabble from dangerous and unstable forces of chaos into orderly subjects. It is also a study of temporality and gunpowder, of the modern technology that—seen from a new angle—becomes magical and inexplicable in ways that destabilize reason and rationality. Critics have noted that Travellia's virginal virtue—her titular chastity—is a mark of the merit that establishes her authority here and elsewhere in the text; Marina Leslie, for example, notes that "Travellia's body is represented as civilizing rather than civilized, colonizer rather than colonized."[3] What has not been noted is that this virtue's invisibility requires a highly visible, if fraudulent, substitute: a technology for translating virtue into power. As we shall see later, this Promethean power in human hands always threatens to slip its boundaries, escalating from lawgiving power into apocalyptic violence. For now, however, I want to focus on this relationship between technological apotheosis and lawmaking, because Cavendish's fictional representations of these technologically enhanced sovereign performances condense certain key ideas in British political thought in ways that run parallel to later fictional meditations on sovereign authority, technology, and the civilizing power of wonder, astonishment, and fear.

In this chapter, I examine the way we can understand this sequence of "Chastity" alongside other moments from Cavendish's oeuvre as directly engaged in her immediate circle's discussions of the fraught problem of sovereign power and authority and of the need to narrate a passage from savagery into civility. The driving intellectual force in this circle is the controversial work of Thomas Hobbes. Hobbes is well known for his theorization of sovereign authority and primitive contract in his *Elements of Law* (in manuscript, 1640), *De Cive* or *On the Citizen* (1642; English trans. 1651), and, most prominently, *Leviathan* (1651).[4] Certain details differ in each account, but each argues for an absolute sovereignty modeled on an originary contract and leaves the sovereign in a state of nature, legally accountable to no human law—in other words, fundamentally exterior to the legal order it sustains. In the state of nature, Hobbes argues, individuals retain sovereignty in themselves, bearing rights though also subject to certain natural laws; within a state of sovereignty, however, natural law is interpreted and enforced solely by the sovereign. Hobbes and Cavendish were certainly not personally close, but they moved during the 1650s and 1660s in a circle that also included the playwright William Davenant and Cavendish's spouse, William, the first Duke of Newcastle.[5] This circle was, at times, quite tight: Davenant and Hobbes read and commented on each other's work, and Davenant fought alongside Newcastle during the Civil War, taking charge of the Royalist ordnance. Hobbes had served as tutor to Newcastle's cousin and as secretary to his uncle and had become acquainted with Newcastle himself at the time that he and his brother Charles Cavendish were performing chemical experiments on his estate. And while we do not know how often Margaret Cavendish met these men or how seriously they regarded her (Hobbes's sole surviving letter to her indicates no more than polite condescension), we do know that she had an interest in their writings, particularly in Hobbes's materialism and his distinctive absolutism.[6] This nexus of political thinkers is of central importance, I suggest, in understanding a key strain of political thought as well as of political fiction over the century that followed. It contributes to a thinking of specifically modern forms of authority, relying on new modes of manipulating affect through technological displays that verge on the magical or the divine. Each of the writers I consider attempts to answer certain latent questions about the sources of political and legal authority, specifically the origins of the constituting authority that undergirds political arrangements in the Hobbesian account, as well as about the visible forms that sovereignty might take. And each illustrates different modes of thinking about what we might call the topology of the political sphere: each attempts to represent sovereignty's exteriority to the order it founds, and investigates the modes in which such an anomalous sovereign can reshape and create a political sphere that is both obedient and free. Though each of these writers is strongly authoritarian, they nonetheless offer programs that seek to amplify sovereign power through indirect and largely nonviolent means. These writers are not imagining the governmentalized freedom discussed in my introduction, but their ideas offer resources and conundrums for the political writings that followed them.

I begin this chapter with a discussion of Hobbes and the problem of civility, focusing on Hobbes's comments on the practice (rather than the theory) of sovereignty. I then turn to a discussion of Travellia's femininity and her temporal and structural place outside of the cultures she inhabits, as well as the role of technology in manifesting her lawgiving virtue. Her topological position makes her akin to a sovereign from the outset—an identification that the rest of the romance underscores. Though Cavendish's cannibals do have a monarch, a legal system, and a priesthood before Travellia's intervention, her trickery and violence tear a hole in the constitutional order, passing briefly through an anomic space into a new order that, among other things, brings them into alignment with natural law by forbidding cannibalism. The chapter next asks what precedes sovereignty and civility: what "savage" elements persist in the civil and sovereign order, and what lessons might the governing of savages hold for the sovereign? Here the focus is on the works of Hobbes and his interlocutors Newcastle and Davenant. Both these authors draw on Hobbes to investigate the form that sovereign power and authority ought to take, how it ought to manifest itself, and how the sovereign contributes to the formation of the docile political subject. Newcastle and Davenant imagine a sovereign who uses fear directly or who uses stage machinery to create the kinds of civility requisite to a monarchy. Cavendish's ruminations on these questions, however, are far more fluid and complex. While "Chastity" explores techniques for manifesting a virtuous sovereign authority, her late romance *The Blazing World* develops a structurally similar plot with a more ambivalent resolution that underscores the perils of extralegal power, anticipating later writings on states of war and emergency.

Sovereign Visibility

Travellia's conversion of the cannibals does not use the language of constitutionality and constituent power, but she clearly abrogates one constitution and establishes another. Cavendish's narrative focuses attention on the implications of Hobbes's writings for the pragmatics of conquest and rule. Hobbes's major writings spend most of their energy analyzing sovereign right, attending less thoroughly to questions about the practice of rule—that is, how sovereign powers should act in order to sustain themselves. Where these writings do investigate the practice of government, they are often muted and contradictory, torn between a desire for a sovereign legitimacy upheld by rational and educated subjects and a pessimistic assessment of human capacities to live justly without an ever-present threat of violence. Hobbes, like Hugo Grotius before him, develops his model of sovereignty in *Leviathan* (and, more briefly, in *De Cive*) by imagining a primordial state of nature and positing an absolute right of self-preservation for every individual in that state. Yet the right of self-preservation in the absence of civil society is fraught; because the threat from other sovereign individuals is unknowable and potentially limitless, this right becomes incredibly expansive. Rights thus inevitably conflict and clash, leaving natural humanity in a permanent state of fear and war. This situation can only be resolved if each individual in a society agrees with each and every other individual to surrender virtually all rights to a sovereign, which may consist of more than one individual but which is better occupied by a single person. This sovereign entity is, as I have noted, exterior to the legal order it sustains. It is itself not accountable to human law and is beholden to no contract or agreement, for, as it is the only enforcer of contracts, there is no competent earthly authority to judge it. This model of the sovereign created by contract Hobbes calls "sovereignty by institution." Only through sovereignty do individuals escape the predatory and unprofitable state of nature and enter into civil society.[7]

Entry into civil society is difficult, however, for Hobbes's humanity is not naturally suited or "fit" for it. While humankind is naturally social, being social is not the same as being fit to enter alliances and form agreements: "man is made fit for society not by nature, but by training" (DC 25). This training, ultimately, is the responsibility of the sovereign. Yet this leaves us with something of a conundrum: if the legal order is created by a contractual arrangement, how do "natural" individuals come together to make such an agreement to create an entity that will, in turn, civilize them, or train them for civil society? After all, before the origins of the civil order that the sovereign facilitates, Hobbes insists that there can be little in the way of cultural or economic progress: "no culture of the earth; no navigation, nor use of the commodities that may be imported by sea; no commodious building; . . . no arts; no letters; no society" (L 186). If civil life requires sovereign training, from where can that training derive?

To resolve this conundrum, we must understand that Hobbes's model of the political contract—"sovereignty by institution," as he labels it—is both a heuristic device and a utopian myth, not a historical account of sovereignty's origins.[8] Most actually existing sovereignty, Hobbes hints, takes the form of "sovereignty by acquisition," or conquest (L 251–53). Sovereignty by institution provides a logical model from which more general principles of sovereign right can be derived. But conquest provides a perfectly adequate and legitimate form of sovereign power, one that differs only superficially from sovereignty's instituted forms. When a person or persons surrender to a force that holds the power of life and death over them—that is, when they exchange their own individual rights for the gift of life itself—they have entered a state of sovereignty that is functionally identical to the more idealized model of sovereignty Hobbes first outlines. "This Dominion is then acquired to the Victor, when the Vanquished, to avoid the present stroke of death, covenanteth either in expresse words, or by other sufficient signes of the will, that so long as his life, and the liberty of his body, is allowed him, the Victor shall have the use thereof, at his pleasure" (L 254). As we will see later, this condition of being conquered—and thus under a regime of sovereign authority—is conducive to a civilizing process.[9]

Travellia, though a refugee and a captive, uses her mastery of gunpowder to establish herself as a Hobbesian conqueror, who kills to establish her power and garners a voluntary surrender from the cannibal nation. Her assassination of a religious figure is supplemented, however, by her impersonation of a divine being, using technological superiority to deceive the naïve cannibals; she offers them not only violence but also a miraculous display. This mock apotheosis also pointedly echoes Hobbes by focusing on terror as a tool of government—one that can sustain sovereign legitimacy and discourage dissent. A key element in Hobbes's model is that the sovereign power must manifest itself in a terrifying way to its subjects. Hobbes is only intermittently explicit about what this might mean; clearly the sovereign must sometimes make use of terrifying violence, but Hobbes also discusses other, more efficacious tactics that harness the irrational in the human mind. Superstitious minds, he argues, fear the unknown, and this fear leads them to imagine panoplies of gods to control and assuage that fear: "in these foure things, Opinion of Ghosts, Ignorance of second causes, Devotion towards what men fear, and Taking of things Casuall for Prognostiques, consisteth the Naturall seed of Religion" (L 172–73).

Hobbes's later chapters in *Leviathan* discussing the "kingdom of darkness" lament the tendency of superstitious minds to give credit to miracles. Because "admiration and wonder" are relative to knowledge—that is, the ignorant admire more readily than the knowing—"the same thing may be a miracle to one, and not to another." The result is that

> ignorant and superstitious men make great wonders of those works which other men, knowing to proceed from nature (which is not the immediate, but the ordinary work of God), admire not at all; as when eclipses of the sun and moon have been taken for supernatural works by the common people, when nevertheless there were others could, from their natural causes, have foretold the very hour they should arrive. (L 471)

Hobbes here perhaps alludes to Columbus's fourth voyage and his trick with the lunar eclipse, discussed earlier. Indeed, Hobbes's conception of civilizing trickery may derive in part from Gabriel Naudé; the two political thinkers were likely to have been acquainted during Hobbes's exile in Paris.[10] Hobbes here describes a gap that separates the learned from the unlearned, the "common people" from the more sophisticated. This gap is the explanation for all forms of nonmiraculous magic, such as the trickery of the Egyptian magicians who compete with Moses in the biblical accounts. Enchantment, Hobbes emphasizes, is not

> a working of strange effects by spells and words, but imposture and delusion wrought by ordinary means; and so far from supernatural, as the impostors need not the study so much of natural causes, but the ordinary ignorance, stupidity, and superstition of mankind, to do them. So that all the miracle consisteth in this, that the enchanter has deceived a man; which is no miracle, but a very easy matter to do. (L 475)

This tendency toward superstition may be exploited as a governing tactic by canny sovereigns: "So easie are men to be drawn to believe any thing, from such men as have gotten credit with them; and can with gentlenesse, and dexterity, take hold of their fear, and ignorance" (L 177). These primary causes are supplemented by men who seek to make subjects "the more apt to Obedience, Lawes, Peace, Charity, and civill Society" (L 173). Sovereignty by acquisition, then, requires acts of deceit to stabilize its power.

Hobbes identifies these acts of deceit not only as a key to stability but also as part of a civilizing process. "The first Founders, and Legislators of Common-wealths," Hobbes argues, kept their subjects obedient by persuading them of law's divine origins: they had little choice but to

> imprint in their minds a beliefe, that those precepts which they gave concerning Religion, might not be thought to proceed from their own device, but from the dictates of some God, or other Spirit; or else that they themselves were of a higher nature than mere mortals, that their Lawes might the more easily be received. (L 177)

In the ancient states of Rome, Peru, and the Orient, Hobbes contends, this sovereign trickery worked to instill obedience. (Things are different in the actual kingdom of God, to be sure, where there is no separation between the temporal and the spiritual dominions.) The science of politics is not for the uninitiated and ought rather to be "wrapped up in fables"; subjects should imitate the ancient commoners, who did not ponder the nature of justice and right but rather "revered sovereign power . . . as a kind of visible divinity" (DC 9). Hobbes here locates a point of origin for both divine and secular commonwealths in human fears and anxieties. Humanity in the state of nature imagines supernatural beings; the ideas of such beings are shaped and manipulated by early sovereigns, using the terror and awe that such objects inspire to begin to teach subjects about subordination. For Hobbes, this is part of a way to answer the question of how men might become civilized enough to come together to form a contract, as well as that of how to keep from sliding back into the state of nature. Though the subject's submission is a legal act, the violence that precedes it and paves the way for civility is lawless.[11] In "The Force of Law," Jacques Derrida suggests that sovereignty is perpetually belated, always justifying itself in light of a future anterior and always lawlessly invoking itself in a way that can only be read as legal or justified retrospectively. For a conqueror who then posits his rule as the product of divinity or posits herself as a divine or magical figure, the conquest that establishes law also establishes the belief system that justifies that conquest—that, in effect, imagines a prior law that undergirds the violence of the founding moment.[12]

Yet Hobbes does express a wish that the politics of sovereign magic might be replaced with a form of enlightened and voluntary obedience. He portrays his own achievement as a way to protect sovereignty through the enlightenment of political subjects, at least some of whom will become convinced that absolutism is essential to civil society. Hobbes proposes what we might call an ideological project; seditious doctrines may be contained and proper ones promoting order disseminated through the universities, from which thoughts are further circulated through the pulpit and polite conversation. "For seeing the Universities are the Fountains of Civill, and Morall Doctrine, from whence the Preachers, and the gentry, drawing such water as they find, use to sprinkle the same . . . upon the People, there ought certainly to be great care taken, to have it pure. . . . And by that means the most men, knowing their Duties, will be the less subject to serve the Ambition of a few discontented persons, in their purposes against the State" (L 728). But the strength of Hobbes's faith in what we might call an ideological solution to the problem of sovereignty's representation is unclear. Both *Leviathan* and *De Cive* also place considerable weight on the collective power of the political nation, embodied in the sovereign, to manifest a terrifying sublimity, though the precise form that sublimity might take is not made explicit. Though Hobbes does not fully develop an argument for how the astonishing display of sovereign power ought to work, it appears that the image of the state's massive power should operate above and prior to the more rational processes of punishment, reward, and education. In other words, the notion of sovereign power plays a key role in the formation of the civilized political subject—civilized in the sense of desiring to obey authority, even before the processes of education and rational study begin. The sublime spectacle of sovereign power appears to work prior to reason, shaping the will at the moment of its inception.[13] Fear not only drives prepolitical selves from the state of war into the state of subjection; this state of subjection perpetuates itself as the collective power that the sovereign represents shapes the will of its individual components:

> The will itself . . . is not voluntary, but only the starting point of voluntary actions (for we do not will to will but to *act*). . . . Nevertheless a man who subjects his *will* to the *will* of another transfers to that other the *Right to his strength and resources*, so that when others have done the same, the recipient of their submissions may be able to use the fear they inspire to bring the wills of individuals to unity and concord. (DC 73)

The "will" is not a faculty under the control of a subject, but neither is it precisely the essence of the subject. It is, however, precisely that which the terrifying countenance of the sovereign acts on to impel subjects where it wills them to go. But how the sovereign is to represent itself—to make this power manifest, visible, and terrifying—is never made entirely clear. Sovereigns certainly lean heavily on the "right to inflict penalties," which conveys the right to compel anyone to do "anything he wants" (DC 78). In *Leviathan*, Hobbes insists that the sovereign's right to punish is justified so "that the will of men may thereby the better be disposed to obedience" (L 353). Yet it is hardly clear that sovereign power can thrive being made visible only at the moment of punishment.

Hobbes's reflection on magic, civility, and sovereign power form the conceptual backdrop for Travellia's performance. She, like an ancient tyrant, mystifies herself so that her new legal order will pass for one established by divine intervention. Her performance uses violence and technological display to instill the fear and astonishment that "conforms" the will of her subjects to the law she bears within her. But her narrative, to be sure, includes multiple details that distinguish it from Hobbes's more general account. I have already touched on and will return to the question of topology—that is, the exteriority of the sovereign (here Travellia) to the legal order. But Travellia also deceives only because of her own vulnerability and necessity. Her conquest and reordering of these people is not merely a de facto situation that grounds right exclusively in violence. Hobbes himself notes that "there is scarce a common-wealth in the world, whose beginnings can in conscience be justified" (L 722). Travellia provides sovereignty with a conscience. Her status as a blameless, victimized virgin casts her conquest not as an acquisitive act of violence but rather as a desperate moment of self-defense; her violence is justified by necessity. And her use of gunpowder also marks her not as simply another conqueror but also as more rational: possessing a technical knowledge of the material world that is unavailable to her new subjects, she has transcended their naive materialism and placed herself in a position to dictate to them and teach them natural law.

Female Sovereignty and Topological Politics

In "Chastity," Travellia's exile from her home country echoes and reinforces her predetermined exclusion from the law as a woman. Ejected from the legal order, she nevertheless carries a copy of the law within her, ready for export to lawless spaces—a law figured by her inviolate chastity and her refusal to enter an extralegal liaison with her married pursuer, identified only as "the Prince," whom she flees despite her attraction to him. When Travellia's homeland disintegrates into civil war and anarchy, she becomes a refugee in the Kingdom of Sensuality. It is this preliminary accident of war, this removal from her place in society and from her native country, that prepares her to occupy the place of a sovereign in the cannibal's land—a political community that, like a Hobbesian commonwealth, she constitutes and manages but remains separate from. Hobbes insists that the sovereign is exterior to the polity it governs, neither subject to human law nor party to the primordial contract, remaining in a state of nature. Giorgio Agamben revises Hobbes's assessment, locating the sovereign uncannily both outside and at the heart of civil society.[14] Similarly, Travellia among the cannibals is fundamentally isolated from the polity she is reshaping, by race, by ethnicity, by language, by temporal placement, and by technology. While contemporary theories of refugee status have sought to understand the refugee as an exemplar of the category of the *homo sacer*—of life stripped of political protections—Cavendish's early modern refugee is that figure's mirror image, a sovereign-in-waiting who transmits an internalized copy of the law into savage spaces.

The reader is introduced to Travellia as a refugee—a young woman entirely cut off from the protections of the civil order, abandoned to warriors and aristocratic sexual predators alike. Nevertheless, following a standard romance plot, she preserves the corporeal integrity—her virginity—that signifies not only a vaguely defined "virtue" but also her compliance with a higher law. She protects her chastity not only from the Prince who assaults and pursues her but also from her own desire, for she loves the Prince despite his regrettable marriage to an older woman (who will conveniently resolve this problem by dying at the narrative's end). What keeps them apart is not any resentment for the rape attempt but rather the fact of the Prince's (unhappy) marriage. They are barred by law, not by any lack of desire: "it is as impossible to corrupt me, as to corrupt Heaven," she tells the Prince, "but were you free, I should willingly embrace your love, in lawful marriage" (59). Her virginity has been read by Marina Leslie and Victoria Kahn as the key to the restoration that concludes this narrative—a virginity transformed over the course of the narrative from a passive into an active virtue, one that begins by resisting its violation but that progresses toward more active forms that become lawgiving as well as law-preserving.[15] This reading is convincing but becomes more powerful when combined with an awareness of Cavendish's play with Hobbesian topologies of sovereignty. Cavendish, attuned to the structural exteriority of sovereignty in Hobbes's model, is using the isolated virgin awash in a world of sin and violence as a receptacle of a natural law.[16] Cavendish has been read convincingly as an early feminist, but I propose that we also attend closely to the way she manipulated received features of femininity to serve as political metaphors, particularly her reappropriation of patriarchal ideologies and of misogynistic discussions of female malleability. She makes use of these figures not only to contest them (though at times she certainly does) but also to isolate and investigate political categories related to sovereignty and civility.

If Travellia is to protect her virtue—to preserve her own body as well as to defend the law that her body's intactness figures—she must also act strategically. This is a pattern we will see again: even the divinely sanctioned monarch must be canny. Her canniness takes the form of being a skilled dramatist and manipulator of props. Her malleability and skill with falsehood is stereotypically feminine. Cavendish herself suggests elsewhere that "all Women are a kind of Mountebanks; for they would make the World believe they are better than they are."[17] Travellia's career as a mountebank begins with her efforts to free herself both from her captivity by the bawd who imprisons her and from the Prince who desires and pursues her. It is significant that her earliest performance requires her to imaginatively enchant a pistol—a device somewhat out of phase with the romance narrative—as she contemplates suicide to avoid being raped by the Prince. In search of a weapon with which to accomplish her own death, she tricks a servant into smuggling a pistol to her. To persuade the reluctant servant, Travellia enshrouds the pistol's true functions in a haze of references to magic, claiming that a wizard had advised her to fire a pistol each year on her birthday, "for by the shooting thereof (said she), I shall kill a whole Year of Evil from doing me hurt" (401). Travellia understands how to enchant objects: though she knows the darker powers and purposes of this weapon, she downplays these characteristics when talking to her common servant, instead enfolding this technological object in the language of wizardry and ritual. Travellia, that is, is capable of shifting guns from one epistemic level to another, moving easily between the spheres of rationalism and science and of fantasy, magic, and talismans. When the Prince arrives intent on raping her, she turns the pistol on him, declaring, "It is no sin to defend my self against an Obstinate and Cruel Enemy. . . . When I kill or be kill'd, I will kill or dye for security" (403). Travellia's pistol is an unstable object, entangled in multiple epistemologies and genres. The gun moves quickly from talisman to tool. Travellia clearly demonstrates a capacity to treat the gun as a tool rather than an enchanted object, shooting not herself but her pursuer.

The romance's conclusion is characteristic of Cavendish's exploratory mode that does not clearly resolve the questions it raises about the topologies of sovereignty. In the last stage of Travellia's roamings, she is also entangled in a mélange of war, sovereignty, and deceitful performance, though one that ends ambiguously. Landing in the kingdom of Amity, the still-disguised Travellia ends up through a series of improbable events leading an army in a civil war—a war fought against an army commanded by none other than the Prince who pursues her. Travellia, a master-mistress of battle tactics, emerges victorious. But, more importantly, as the war ends, the news comes that the Prince's wife has died, making him free to marry Travellia at last. Travellia is ecstatic. Space prevents a thorough discussion of this sequence, except to note that Travellia commands an army through the force of her ability to simulate masculine military virtue—or, rather, through her intuitive understanding of modern battle tactics, which allows her army of commoners to defeat the nobles they face (475–78). I want, though, to attend to a strange topological knot that concludes the narrative. When the Prince is declared viceroy of this new land, Travellia's soldiers demand that she should be vice regent, "which was granted to pacifie them." The Prince responds thusly: "But the Prince told his Mistress, She should also govern him." To this, she replies "that he should govern her, and she would govern the kingdom" (512). This statement makes the status of vice regent ambiguous at best; who is really governing the kingdom—the Prince? The king and queen? Travellia herself? It is difficult to tell if this confusion is genuine—perhaps Cavendish does not wish us to know who is truly sovereign here, or perhaps Emma Rees is correct to suggest that Travellia's secure control of the military and militia renders her husband's authority over her purely nominal.[18] This blurring hardly seems accidental in a text that has throughout been concerned with sovereignty's topological paradoxes. If Travellia has served as a lawgiver during her period as a refugee, her return to the sphere of law is marked by a more ambiguous status; like a political Klein bottle, she is simultaneously interior and exterior to politics, fundamentally indistinct in ways this narrative cannot coherently represent.

Cavendish's figuration of femininity as extralegal recurs at a salient moment in her 1664 text *Sociable Letters*. Disclaiming women's involvement in the public sphere, this letter simultaneously erases them from accounts of legal subjectivity:

> As for the matter of Governments, we women understand them not; yet if we did, we are excluded from intermeddling therewith, and almost from being subject thereto; we are not tied, nor bound to State or Crown; we are free, not sworn to Allegiance, nor do we take the Oath of Supremacy; we are not made Citizens of the Commonwealth, we hold no Offices, nor bear we any Authority therein; . . . and if we be not Citizens in the Commonwealth, I know no reason we should be Subjects to the Commonwealth.[19]

This passage experiments with the idea that women are written out of the legal order—free from the law because not inscribed within it, neither citizen nor subject. As Sara Mendelson and Patricia Crawford have demonstrated, this idea is not unique to Cavendish; at least one group of women in the seventeenth century used female immunity from the law as a legal defense.[20] In the passage that follows, Cavendish suggests that women, who are subjected in principle to their husbands but in practice capable of dominating them with their beauty and attractions, are in fact able to exert a kind of sovereignty through that attraction. This passage offers an odd, undecidable relationship between female subjection in marriage and, in Cavendish's iconoclastic reading, women's position in the political sphere. Occupying a zone of indistinction between power and abjection, women provide a model for the figure of the sovereign that lives outside the law. But women also inhabit a different zone of indistinction, one brought to light by the role that technology plays in these texts. That zone is the space that separates nature from the artificial and the technological—that which, in other words, distinguishes these female lawgivers from other women. If in the preceding passage women are "natural" in their exception from the legal order, here their exception is marked differently—with a technological supplement that exempts them from subjection. Sovereignty and lawmaking are not "natural" in Cavendish's texts; they are the product of technology, performance, and violence. Her royalism is anything but what it has sometimes been taken to be: a simplistic embrace of her husband's and family's divine-right doctrines. Cavendish's writings are alert to the human and constructed nature of sovereignty, and her responses and revisions to Hobbesian theory underscore the techniques necessary for making sovereignty visible, even as they also underscore its underlying violence.

"To Civilize the People": Political Sensations

Hobbes's writings leave uncertain the question of whether a sovereign can govern by means other than punishment and some form of religious trickery. This problem is taken up by other members of the Cavendish circle. William Davenant and Lord Newcastle both penned treatises and dramatic works that draw on and extend Hobbesian ideas, examining the relationship between military power, political authority, and ceremony and display. Both Davenant and Newcastle explore the power and limitations of raw violence, and both begin to investigate the ways that sovereigns might transform violence through representation into something that might peacefully regulate the bodies of the king's subjects. Davenant, in particular, marshals images from colonial contact zones to support his shifting programs of using astonishing displays to contain the unruly and to instill love for the sovereign in the brutish multitude.

Hobbes was closely associated with Cavendish's husband, Lord Newcastle, who himself made a minor contribution to the political thought of the Restoration with a letter of advice written to Charles II just before the Restoration. This letter incorporates and responds to Hobbesian notions, particularly in its assertion of both military force and what he terms "ceremony" as integral components of practices of rule that reshape the will of the multitude. Newcastle was personally close to the new king, having served as his tutor before the civil wars and continuing to be a trusted adviser. Newcastle's discussion of sovereign power reads as a reductive version of Hobbes; his sovereign is made manifest by brute force. Newcastle's tract repeatedly insists on the centrality of military power to the practice of rule: "I begin with the Militia firste, because it is your Majesties Undouted Prorogative, a so well ordered force, doth Every thing, for without an Army in your owne hands, you are but a king upon a Curtesey of others."[21] It is military power that encloses and forecloses faction, discourse, and debate; without it, the sovereign is vulnerable to "the factious, & faine Disputes of

Sophesterall Devines, & Lawyers, & other Philosophicall Booke men," who will "Raise Rebellions" (5). The image of the army here acts directly on the common rabble as well as on the more educated; it matters less how the university is administered than how fearful university teachers are of incurring sovereign vengeance in the form of the militia. Whereas Hobbes's text is not specific about how this sophistry and divisiveness is to be contained or prevented, Newcastle's argument is straightforward: the display of military force shapes language and will. Newcastle's London, in particular, will be cowed into submission by having "two Royall fortes built on Both sides the River of Thames.... Then the Tower [of London] to bee well fortefeyd, & to bee your Majesties prime Magasen, for greate store of Armes of all sortes.... The Tower thus fortified, will comande both the towne & that parte of the River: Ande thus your Majestie shall tame that Rebellius Citeye, & so consequentlye all Englande" (6).

Yet Newcastle also hopes that these performances and manifestations of force might be supplemented by other, more peaceful displays. The king is also to rely on "show"—a conscious performance that relies heavily on imputing supernatural qualities to the sovereign. This "show," to the degree possible, ought to supplant violence, for "people loves not the Cudgell" (7). Instead, the sovereign ought to appear "Gloryously... Like a God ... & when the people sees you thus, they will Downe of their knees, which is worship, & pray for you with trembling Feare, & Love" (45). To produce this awe may require force, but it also requires certain forms of ceremonial behavior that shape customs. Indeed, ceremony is necessary everywhere—"though it is nothing in itt Selfe, yet it doth Every thing,—for what is a king, more than a subiecte, Butt for seremoney, & order" (44). Newcastle echoes his wife's argument that "ceremony is rather of superstitious shew, then a substance," suggesting that the rituals of sovereignty inculcate habits of deference, making them second nature: "So powerfull sire Is Custome, it is converted into nature, & is Nature, & In the bloud."[22] Ceremony "heightens and glories the power of Kings, and States, it strikes such a reverence and respect in the beholders, as it begets fear and wonder, in so much as it amazes the spirits of men to humiliation, and adoration, and gives such a distance as it deifies humane things." Indeed, ceremony "becomes a kinde of a god," preparing a ground for obedience and order (Newcastle, *Ideology and Politics* 70). For Newcastle, a sovereign must sustain his authority with a violence that paves the way for more ceremonial modes of power: force and display can change human nature, creating a polity that will obey of its own will.

Though Newcastle's treatise does not explicitly refer to colonial settings, an isomorphism between domestic and colonial sovereign performances is nevertheless visible here. Compare Newcastle's program with Samuel Purchas's words of half a century earlier: speaking of the New World Amerindian, Purchas argues,

> A cruell mercy in awing Savages to feare us is better than that mercifull cruelty, which by too much kindenes hath made us fear them, or else by too much confidence to loose our selves. . . . Neither doth it become us to use Savages with savagenesse, nor yet with too humaine usage, but in a middle path . . . to goe and doe so that they may admire and feare us, as those whom God, Religion, Civility, and Art, have made so farre superior.[23]

The techniques vaguely alluded to here—the instilling of fear and admiration in the unruly and the savage—are difficult to distinguish from Newcastle's. What this passage highlights in Newcastle's text, however, is the incapacity of the sovereign monarch to attract admiration from the rabble spontaneously. Any right-thinking subject must, of course, revere the monarch, who for Newcastle is indeed a sacral figure. But Newcastle's own experiences during the Civil War and Interregnum focused his attention as much on the techniques of governance as on the rights of rule. He sought, as would later royalists, to imagine modes of monarchical performance that would overcome the rabble's rejection of right authority. But this is, as in Purchas's colonial setting, a lie that produces a truth: ceremonies appeal to the rabble's baser instincts and seek to use their attachment to ceremony to create a second nature in them. Yet that second nature is also nature itself: the rabble should defer to the monarch, and the savage should fear and love the European colonist.

Newcastle does not make the connection to the colonial zone himself, but his friend Davenant did. Davenant's inquiries into politics draw directly on the savage's susceptibility to sensory impressions and dazzling displays. His critical writings, particularly the "Preface to *Gondibert*" (1650) and *A Proposition for the Advancement of Moralitie* (1653–54), imagine poetry and the dramatic technologies of the stage as crucial conduits of sovereignty, tools to tame and train docile subjects. His ideas emerge as part of an ongoing conversation with Hobbes, who claims intellectual kinship with him and vaguely hints that *Leviathan* is influenced by Davenant's ideas.[24] Davenant's works describe commoners as savages, Indians, or beasts and worry how such feral subjects might be tamed. While the preface primarily envisions virtuous aristocratic example to be the key to their conversion, the later work argues instead that the technologies associated with Stuart performances, particularly the courtly masque, may be redeployed to civilize and discipline the British commoner.[25]

Davenant's preface, written in the shadow of Royalist defeat and of Charles I's execution, takes the form of an open letter to Hobbes, who apparently corresponded with Davenant regarding the poem's composition. The essay draws on the intertwined languages of gender and colonialism to attempt to imagine a sovereignty that manifests itself through opinion and ideology rather than violence. Like Hobbes, Davenant underscores the importance of mental states and opinion to sovereign governance, since mere physical force is an unsteady foundation for authority; the powerful bodies of the laboring multitude give them a menacing strength (45). In pondering the production of docile mental states among the multitude, Davenant uses two analogies: colonial governance and patriarchal authority. Davenant offers one model of government based on a husband's power over his wife: though a male has an absolute authority to compel his wife's obedience (particularly in the arena of sexuality), it is preferable for a woman to conform her will to a man's voluntarily; though rape always remains a possibility, wifely consent offers more security. Similarly, the sovereign may command what he or she likes, but a reign will be most successful if persuasion, not terror, motivates subjects. Thus sovereign authority requires the support of poets, whose job is to create images of virtue and obedience so attractive that "beholders should not be able to look off"—to conquer the subjects' minds "like a willing Bride" (46). He concludes that "to such an easy government, neither the People . . . nor Wives . . . can peacefully yield, unless they are first conquer'd by Vertue; and the Conquests of Vertue be never easy but where her forces are commanded by Poets" (46). The image is one of a masculinized magistrate whose "prerogatives" extend to the right to demand submission—even to rape—but who has no need to exercise this right because his power is attractive and encourages voluntary submission. Davenant hopes that his poetry will make civilizing through force less necessary, but it does not deny—indeed, it relies on—the idea that the prospect of the use of force is an essential component of civilizing aesthetics.

But this marital analogy is imperfect. Men are unlikely to experience any significant threat from their wives, for they are assumed to be physically weaker. Not so for the sovereign, who confronts a multitude that is weak of mind but that wields bodies conditioned and made strong through labor. Nevertheless, modern rulers have generally misunderstood their relationship to their subjects, attempting to act directly on the subjects' bodies, "forgetting that the martiall art of constraining is the best, which assaults the weaker part; and the weakest part of the people is their mindes, for want of that which is the mindes only strength, *Education*" (44–45). Davenant's preface wants the heroic romance to instill virtue in the multitude's weak minds, but, unfortunately, the illiterate multitude cannot understand romance well enough to be directly shaped by it. For though "Poets, . . . with wise diligence study the People, and have in all ages by an insensible influence governd their manners" (38), and though Davenant's argument is in large part an argument for the political utility of the heroic romance, using aesthetics to civilize the multitude is difficult precisely because commoners are uncivilized and cannot recognize merit or virtue. The heroic romance is much like a prince's court, alienated from the interests of common subjects, who "looke upon the outward glory or blaze of Courts, as Wilde beasts in darke nights stare on their Hunters Torches"; incapable of experiencing glory themselves, they see in this "blaze" only a ruinous waste of resources. Davenant despairs of the commoner: "The common Crowd (of whom we are hopelesse) we desert," he writes, leaving them "rather to be corrected by laws (where precept is accompany'd with punishment) then to be taught by Poesy" (14). We appear to be back where we started.

But it is precisely at this, the essay's central fault line, that Davenant turns to the realm of colonial fantasy. Significantly, at the time that Davenant was preparing the preface, his own thinking about North American "savages" was presumably developing, as he prepared to set out on an expedition to the New World. Appointed to the directorship of the colony of Maryland in February by the future Charles II (who had come to doubt Lord Baltimore's loyalty), Davenant set out for the New World in early May 1650. Davenant never reached Virginia, his ship being intercepted; he instead returned in chains to England. But his brief, notional involvement in New World practices of government left its mark on the preface and the *Proposition* alike.[26] The preface appears to reflect his thinking about the space of the New World and its denizens, for his model of human nature is based, more explicitly than Hobbes's, on his own interpretations of ethnographic data. "The mindes of men," Davenant argues, are inherently ambitious; it is indeed this ambition that makes empire necessary, allowing new realms for human ambition, a displacement of aggression abroad: "For God ordain'd not huge Empire as proportionable to the Bodies, but to the Mindes of Men; and the Mindes of Men are more monstrous, and require more space for agitation and the hunting of others, than the Bodies of Whales" (36). The counterexample Davenant draws from the American "savages" he expected to find in Virginia: these men are always at war because their ambition is "contain'd in a narrow Folde"; most Indians do not have an "outside" toward which to direct their aggression, he claims. Most (though not all) Indians are "restraind in narrow dominion," and the result is that "they quarrel like cocks in a Pitt; and the Sun in a days travaile there, sees more battailes . . . then in Europe in a Yeare" (36).

But it is in Davenant's discussion of poetry's relationship to government that he makes the most striking reference to colonialism and even to gunpowder. Stephen Zwicker has argued that "wit" is empty of specific content, a placeholder that opposes the more dangerous aesthetic of inspiration, associated with Puritan evangelicalism and other disorderly religious tendencies.[27] But for Davenant, wit is also the property of the "civilized"; the crowd has no real notion of it. This Davenant illustrates with a colonial analogy: wit is, in his handling, an imperial figure, useful for astonishing savages much as gunpowder does. Wit, Davenant tells us,

> is the Souls *Powder*, which . . . breaks through all about it as far as the utmost it can reach, removes, uncovers, makes way for Light where darkness was inclos'd, till great bodies are more examinable by being scatter'd into parcels, and till all that find its strength (but most of mankind are strangers to Wit, as Indians are to Powder) worship it for the effects as deriv'd from the Deity. (21)

The magic of gunpowder stuns savages just as wit stuns commoners. This complex figure manifests a central paradox of invocations of gunpowder: wit is like gunpowder because it simultaneously destroys and disorders even as it exposes and modernizes. Gunpowder, like wit, breaks entities apart and makes them visible: both the technology and the faculty involve a kind of light that an Indian can only stare at in rapt amazement. Wit for common observers is not enlightening but rather deluding; at best, they will worship it without understanding it. And yet because tenor and vehicle in this metaphor are not stable, the implicit argument about savagery and wonder bleeds over into the account Davenant gives of wit's political utility. Davenant here—contrary to what he argues elsewhere in the essay— begins to imagine a way around the illiterate brutishness that limits romance's power. If gunpowder seems supernatural, almost divine, to the savage Indian, and if wit works like gunpowder, then perhaps wit might also be turned to account with the commoner. But how, since the commoner remains fundamentally exterior to wit, finding it merely dazzling?

Davenant seems to have noted these inconsistencies, for only a few years later he reformulated his conception of how the heroic mode might reach the commoner in a way that substitutes the technological power of the stage for wit, claiming that spectacular drama might overwhelm the senses of commoners as a means for transforming them from unruly crowd to docile body of subjects. *A Proposition for the Advancement of Moralitie* is an effort to justify the civic importance of theatrics in an era notably hostile to theatricality; however, Davenant's attempt to rework the masque form into a different mode of representing sovereignty underscores his investment in the political uses of the aesthetic.[28] Returning to England after his capture by the English Navy, Davenant was eventually released and began his efforts to rehabilitate the theater for the new conditions of the Interregnum. Davenant issued a sort of manifesto advocating for the power of the theater—part of a larger program to persuade the Protectorate that public theater might have a place even in the new order.

Davenant was intimately familiar with the tools of stagecraft and the power of generating attractive illusions, having written and assisted in the production of the Caroline court's masques from 1635 on.[29] While a full discussion of the practice of masquing is far beyond my scope here, I must note that Davenant's essay on theater develops and extends the masque's practices of representing sovereignty and civility, imagining the techniques of the theater as themselves capable of civilizing and disciplining the commoner.[30] His courtly entertainments represented the relationship between sovereignty and the unruly subject, at times imagining the power of kingly magic to dispel the forces of savagery, barbarism, and misrule.[31] Douglas Brooks-Davies has argued that masques often depict the sovereign as a kind of magician or alchemist, a figure he calls the "Mercurian Monarch." This figure harnesses a benign natural magic to dispel the disorderly and demonic sorcery that, in the productions of Davenant and others, subverts sovereignty and, in extreme cases, imperils the entire world. In *Salmacida Spolia*, for example, an emblematic figure named Discord brandishes a flaming globe while bragging of throwing the whole world into disorder. Her disorderly and demonic powers are quickly and handily dispelled by the sovereign's more benign magic.[32] Significantly, the masque repeatedly associates dark magic both with rebellious commoners and with non-Europeans, particularly "savages" or "barbarians." The play, Davenant's prefatory notes explain, is loosely based on a Greek legend of magic civilizing violent barbarians: when the "barbarous" Carie and Lelegi are driven from their land by Greeks, they proceed to harass and harry their civilized enemies until they encounter a magical pool in Salmacis. Drinking from this fountain, the barbarians' "fierce and cruel natures" are transformed "of their own accord to the sweetness of the Grecian customs."[33] The masque refers directly to the king's important role as a peacemaker, one who "seeks by all means to reduce tempestuous and turbulent natures into a sweet calm of civil concord."[34] Similarly, in 1638's *Britannia Triumphans*, the sovereign receives heroic help from the knight Bellerophon to dispel the specters of disorder, including the notorious rebels "Cade, Kett, [and] Jack Straw and their soldiers," whose clothing reveals "their base professions" underneath their military gear.[35] In both productions, Davenant imagines a sovereign power using paranormal methods to civilize or dispel the rebellious, the barbarous, and the violent.

The masque provides a fantasy of a supernatural sovereign power, one whose virtue is manifested through magical assistance of the most spectacular kind. Yet it also implicitly acknowledges its own technique, confessing the need for sovereign authority to draw on artifice to display its natural virtue. Davenant in the *Proposition* translates this manifestation of power into popular form. The *Proposition* draws in significant ways on *Gondibert*'s preface, but no longer is the commoner to be lured toward virtue through the power of example. Rather, he or she will be applied to directly, using the overwhelming sensory technologies of the theater. Davenant's text opens by citing the civilizing role of the sovereign authority—an authority that he models on that of the military leader:

As 'tis the principal Art of Military Chiefs to make their Armies civil, so is it of Statesmen to civilize the people; by which Governours procure much ease to themselves, and benefit to those that are govern'd: For the civilizing of a Nation makes them not effeminate, or too soft for such discipline of war as enables them to affront their Enemies, but takes off that rudeness by which they grow injurious to one another, and impudent towards Authority. (242–43)

The role of the statesman is not merely to protect the realm but to make the uncivilized subject into a useful citizen/soldier, not softened but disciplined.

Davenant underscores the nonverbal and sensory advantages of the theater. More traditional forces for governing the subject are inadequate: religion lacks teeth; the military can govern only by force; and the law is no longer reverenced. To shore up support for the state and for public order, sovereignty requires new and more sophisticated tools. The technological wonders of the theater can fill this gap because they offer opportunities for nonverbal communication, speaking through the senses rather than through language.[36] Noting that "the generality of mankind are solely instructed by their senses, and by immediate impressions of particular objects," Davenant argues in the *Proposition* that the force of the sensory impression generated by theater and theatricalized objects will win over the subjects through instilling "abject admiration" (244). In this respect, Davenant is in sympathy with Cavendish's claim that "the Body hath power over the will, for the appetite of the five senses draws the will forcibly, although reason helps to defend it."[37] Davenant is also responding to Hobbes: the multitude, like the prepolitical savage, is governed by the senses and can respond only to material objects, not to generalizations or abstractions. For Hobbes, American "savages" hold only a few truths that could be called rational or philosophical. Instead, humans in their savage state "lived upon grosse Experience," with no "Method" (L 683). This entrancement by and bondage to sensory input is part of what gives us the genealogy of fetishism and idolatry that was to emerge in the eighteenth century, in which Hobbes plays a small role. As Hobbes describes the primitive religion of the gentiles—a description that would extend to idolaters everywhere—the worship of images stems from a human inability to abstract rationally from the senses: "The same Legislators of the Gentiles have added their Images, both in Picture, and Sculpture; that the more ignorant sort, (that is to say, the most part, or generality of the people,) thinking the Gods for whose representation they were made, were really included" (L 175). Davenant does not ask that the playgoing commoner take the stage's representations for deities. But, since appeals to the commoners' reason are likely to prove hopeless, he hopes to attract their attention and infuse controlled doses of affect. Such a plan would "divert the people from disorder" and also, through representations of heroic military actions, will "enamour them with consideration of the conveniences and protections of Government" (*Proposition* 245). These scenes will need to be military in nature—"those famous Battels at Land and Sea by which this Nation is renown'd" (246).

We have come a long way from the masque that represents sovereignty to itself. Such productions must, Davenant insists, make use of new technical innovations in the theater—the domestic equivalent of technological displays on the colonial frontier. Sense impression (as opposed to reason) is crucial to tame the masses, who are "solely instructed by their senses, and by immediate impressions of particular objects" (244). Davenant's academy will use technology to bypass the reason and act directly on the senses and emotions of the subject, using, in addition to music and scenery, some "ingenious *Mechanicks*, as *Motion* and *Transposition of Lights*, to make a more naturall resemblance of the great and virtuous Actions of such as are eminent in Story" (245). This will in the end make the people shun vice and luxury, preparing them to obey (like good soldiers) and to be brave (when national service is required).

Hobbes presents a powerful model of sovereignty, one which others in his circle found immensely attractive. Newcastle's and Davenant's writings, like Cavendish's, respond directly to Hobbes's arguments, but, also like hers, they help pinpoint certain lacunae in Hobbes's argumentation, particularly in terms of what the sovereign must do to create and re-create civility. Both highlight certain problems regarding violence, display, and the cultivation of forms of political affect that preserve political stability. And Davenant, in particular, sees the political space of the colony as a model for techniques of rule in the metropole as well. We do not know with certainty whether Cavendish read these responses, but close examination of her final major romance suggests that she did indeed engage with these issues. Here, however, her argument takes a more skeptical turn, examining the limits of terrifying display and exploring the results of that display's failure, suggestive of states of emergency and even of apocalyptic violence. It is to these issues and her later writings that I now turn.

Blazing Guns, Blazing World

I have argued that Cavendish's modeling of authority through a quasi-colonial narrative is akin to similar treatments in Hobbes, Davenant, and perhaps Newcastle. Each of these authors asks how a sovereign can civilize the people and make authority visible. I now want to inspect the more ambivalent reading of these questions in Cavendish's later writings, which also circle around the problems of sovereign display, violence, savagery, and war. Hobbes famously argues that the state of nature, prior to and outside of civil society, is inevitably one of war, and Cavendish's explorations of sovereignty now turn from the explicit colonial setting into more pointedly militarized tropes. The plight of Travellia is fundamentally linked to war: it is military conflict and the collapse of effective sovereignty that propels her from her home into the perilous state of nature in which she finds herself and within which she can re-create herself as a sovereign agent capable of acting as lawmaker and commander. Travellia's duplicitous conquest, though, unlike a Hobbesian one, is not self-securing, justified retroactively. Rather, the narrative frame of her virginity secures her virtue, value, and legitimacy. Her later writings, however, explore more ambiguous interpretations of authority's relationship to war. These concerns culminate in the complex and troubled vision of sovereignty found in *The Blazing World*.[38] Before examining that narrative's revisions to her earlier colonial fantasies, I briefly discuss her other political writings to demonstrate the persistence of her interest in the ways that war does and does not produce virtuous forms of political authority. Unlike the more closed form found in the romance plot of "Chastity," these writings are more open-ended and ambiguous; with no virginal virtue to anchor authority, political authority seems to grow directly from the spear's tip or the barrel of a gun in ways that trouble conventional assumptions about both authoritarian and populist regimes.

Cavendish at times disclaimed any interest in the political sphere; in *Philosophical Letters* (1664), she argues that politics is "but a deceiving profession" and claims to have read *Leviathan* only for its natural philosophy, ignoring the rest of the book.[39] Yet Cavendish's other writings from the 1660s are suffused with political commentary, both explicit and indirect. Catherine Gallagher argues in her classic essay "Embracing the Absolute" that Cavendish's politics—particularly her unbridled royalism—were of a piece with her efforts to imagine a sovereign self, a "moi absolu" modeled on an absolute sovereign.[40] But while Gallagher's argument is convincing, it remains true that Cavendish, despite her disclaimers, sees her political writing as entering into a dialogue with her contemporaries—including Hobbes, Davenant, and her husband, Lord Newcastle. And exploring this dialogue is crucial to understanding her major work of fiction, *The Blazing World* (1666), as well as to her importance in the traditions of political fiction that this book excavates. Cavendish's most explicit treatments of political authority are found in 1662's *Orations of Divers Sorts*, which directly addresses the prospects for a sovereign right created through military violence. *Orations* is an unusual text in an orphaned genre—a collection of speeches treating a series of political and social crises, expressing different points of view on a wide variety of issues with no clear voice dominating. Some of the orations voice opinions associated with Oliver Cromwell and factions within the New Model Army. Presenting the work as an exercise in rhetoric, Cavendish attempts to make each oration as persuasive as possible.[41] Although no clear set of theses emerge from this strangely centerless work, the orations return repeatedly to questions about the foundations of sovereign right and its roots in violence.[42]

In one oration, a king speaks to his rebellious subjects in language that draws on Hobbes's notion of the despotic sovereign who governs by right of conquest rather than by contract:

> Proud, Presumptuous Subjects! For so you are, that dare bring your Soveraign's Prerogative in question, and dispute His Power: but, Who gave you that Authority? Not my Ancestors, nor your Own: for, my Ancestors Conquer'd your Ancestors, and made them Slaves; in which Slavery, you ought to have been kept, and not to have such Liberty as now you have, which gives you the boldness to come so near, and so high, in your Demands, as to justle me in my Throne; only you cast a Veil of Pretence over your Wicked Designs; and the Pretence is, your Rights and Priviledges: but, What Rights had you, when you were Conquered? and, What Priviledges have you, but what the Conqueror gave? He gave you not the Priviledg to dispute my Power, or to bring my Prerogative in question: neither have you Priviledg to disobey my Command, to resist my Authority, or to break my Laws. (135)

The model of kingship being proposed here (and running through a number of other orations) is Hobbesian—a commonwealth not by institution but rather by acquisition. Hobbes, like Cavendish's anonymous king, disclaims any real existence of the rights of the conquered other than those granted through sovereign donation. The sovereign in both cases has an absolute power over life and death. And this power, ultimately, derives from conquest—the surrender of the defeated, their exchange of rights for bare life.

Though Cavendish might sympathize with such arguments, this speech is juxtaposed with others that highlight the perilously arbitrary nature of violence, underscoring the availability of force and its language to all comers. A soldier's oration argues for the continuance of the army in cynical terms: once disbanded, he notes, the army will revert to being mere subjects, losing both money and freedom, "subject to their Tyranny ruled by their Laws, and commanded by their Power." He continues,

> In short, we shall be their slaves, that are now their Masters; our Arms being stronger than their Laws. Wherefore, let us keep our Strength, and pull down their Authority: for, it were a shame for Sword-men to yeeld to Gown-men, who only love to talk, but dare not fight: and, Shall their Tongues wrest the Swords out of our Hands? (292–93)

Language and law must remain subject to rule by the sword. His rhetoric depicts a world turned upside down, in which common soldiers have become "Gentlemen by Arms; Noble-men, by Victories; and Kings, by Absolute Conquest, and so have Absolute Power" and ought not "be subject to the common, Cowardly Rout" (292–93). Though the soldier prefers swords to tongues, he has a slippery tongue himself, making the clergy, the nobility, and the lawyers into a "common, Cowardly Rout," while his fellow soldiers become gentlemen, nobles, and kings. Examining this oration alongside that of the monarch, it is difficult to discern why the king's legitimacy is paramount while the military's is abject; both underscore the rights of conquest. Does Cavendish seek to discredit the legitimacy of conquest as a ground for sovereignty? Or is absolute power founded on military might the province of the king because of his intrinsic merit and worth to hold such a position? Are these common soldiers threatening only because they are common? Though we have no reason to doubt Cavendish's commitment to absolutism, the mirroring we see here reflects on the military origins of the sovereign's right in ways that *The Blazing World* will exploit.

I suggest that the tension on display here between two competing claims of right by conquest is symptomatic of a more fundamental crux: the difficulty of clearly establishing sovereign right through reason or rhetoric alone. Right continues to rely heavily on the logic of force for its authority, but violence is perpetually available to anyone. Another way of putting this is to note that there is, in these speeches, no sovereign right that can readily establish itself as exterior to its own political scene. A king or army that claims authority through violence remains encompassed in a sphere of war, a sphere in which its own claims are fundamentally challengeable by any other force. In other words, the military and the king remain in a Hobbesian state of nature, whatever claims to the contrary they might make. There is something missing that might propel them outside this state. In "Chastity," Travellia's gunpowder, her gender, and her ethnic and racial difference mark her as distinct from her subjects. Here there are no such distinctions, and the sphere of rhetoric remains enmeshed in the warlike state of nature from which Cavendish's orators have not escaped. Even more importantly, both forces lack a clear marker of virtue—one that would mimic Travellia's chastity—that would lend legitimacy to their cause.

While the *Orations* openly thematize questions about violence and political power, *The Blazing World* handles them more obliquely. *The Blazing World* homes in on the threat of dissention and civil war; if anything, it is more pessimistic than Hobbes's writings, for while Hobbes generates the illusion that sovereignty, once established, creates a relatively enduring government, Cavendish's fiction seems inclined to read the imposition of sovereignty not as a final solution but rather as part of an unfolding historical cycle of civility and corruption, one almost neo-Machiavellian in its temporality.[43] The threat of civil war is omnipresent but is managed through a variety of devices that emphasize performance's power to tame the rebellious and unify tumultuous spirits. But this fantastic narrative, too, ends on an uncertain note, with the Empress of the Blazing World unleashing a holocaust on the recalcitrant nations of her home world—an apocalypse that functions as a sort of limit case for the capacities of performance and violence to secure a stable political order and to solidify sovereignty. Here Cavendish most directly addresses the strain of political thinking in Hobbes and Davenant that I have been tracing, exploring the role of theatricality in producing absolute monarchical power. Like "Chastity," *The*

Blazing World begins with a woman's body in peril—here a young woman abducted by a lust-besotted merchant. Both texts also transform their persecuted refugees into spectacular sovereigns who bring civility and threaten apocalypse. And in both texts, the woman carries out an act of technologically enhanced performance to amplify her violence. As in "Chastity," this performance borrows key tropes from narratives of cultural and technological contact; it also embodies foundational violence in a female body. But Cavendish declines to enclose these tropes within a conventional marriage plot, opting instead for an asymmetrical and irregular narrative form that concludes not with a wedding but rather with a technologically enhanced global war; this narrative choice points not toward a tidy resolution of the tensions between authority and virtue but rather toward an ambiguous meditation on the potential for sovereign violence to explode into excess.

The Blazing World is a romance that tells of a woman who survives an abduction and is carried beyond the north pole to a strange world of light peopled largely by human-animal hybrids. This new world is joined to hers at the pole and reached only after a perilous voyage through an Arctic region. This Arctic setting, with its refiguration of the idea of a Northwest Passage, is only one of the moments at which this text references the history of European exploration and colonization. Upon the woman's arrival in this New World, after another long journey, she meets the Emperor. Though he is no savage, he nevertheless believes her to be a deity, offering to worship her; when she insists on her own humanity, he weds her and, at the same time, grants her "absolute power to rule and govern all that world as she pleased" (132). With this surprising boon, she uses the resources of this new world—with its throngs of devoted man-animal hybrids and spirit beings—to master various forms of quasi-scientific knowledge. Most notable, for my purposes, is her discovery and excavation of a peculiar mineral—a "fire-stone"—that burns relentlessly when exposed to water. She persuades the Blazing World's race of sentient worm-men to mine a quantity of this stone for her, keeping it secret. Significantly, the first use she finds for this stone is to incorporate it into acts of religious conversion: installing it as part of a complex technological apparatus, she creates a Christian church that appears to be filled with the flames of hell—a spectacular reminder to churchgoers of what happens to heretics and atheists. This "emblem of Hell" keeps the denizens of the Blazing World "in a constant belief, without enforcement or blood-shed" (164).

The Empress here distantly echoes Travellia's performance—fire-stones replacing gunpowder, display replacing violence. And while for a time the Empress permits certain kinds of pluralism and dissent, she finds herself regretting it and is advised by her counselor, the soul of Margaret Cavendish, that she ought to return the government to its original, more authoritarian frame (200–202).[44]

Pivoting from her position of absolute power in the Blazing World, the Empress learns from immaterial spirits that her home nation of EFSI is imperiled by war.[45] In a divine masquerade that directly recalls Travellia's gunpowder performance, the Empress returns to rescue her homeland with a massive display of—quite literally—firepower. Here her sovereignty is displaced from a domestic to an international setting. A shift in tactics appears, and she uses more obviously military means to become, in effect, empress of that world as well. Traveling by submarine back across the pole with a small army of worm-, bird-, and mermen, she appears offshore, using her collection of fire-stones to dazzle her home nation and its attackers: "[The fire-stones] being many thousands, made a terrible show; for it appeared as if all the air and sea had been of a flaming fire; and all that were upon the sea, or near it, did verily believe, the time of judgment, or the last day was come, which made them all fall down, and pray" (208). These stones become part of a performance of divinity—and yet they are entirely explicable in material terms, or at least no more inexplicable than any form of combustion. The performance is thus of a piece with Travellia's gunpowder performance: technological superiority masquerading as divinity.

Cavendish extends this presentation of sovereign trickery in the sequence that follows. Appearing to the counselors of her home nation, she continues to astonish:

> The Empress appeared with garments made of the star-stone, and was borne or supported above the water, upon the fish-men's heads and backs, so that she seemed to walk upon the face of the water, and the bird- and fish-men carried the fire-stone, lighted both in the air, and above the waters.
>
> Which sight, when her countrymen perceived at a distance, their hearts began to tremble; but coming something nearer, she left her torches, and appeared only in her garments of light, like an angel or some deity, and all kneeled down before her. . . . But the Empress would not come nearer than at such a distance where her voice

might be generally heard, by reason she would not have that of her accoutrements anything else should be perceived, but the splendour thereof. (210)

The Empress's performance is masquelike in its stateliness and artificiality, as Sylvia Bowerbank and Sara Mendelson have noted, and in its deployment of novel technological innovations—as well as in its figuration of royal power.[46] But it is also, crucially, duplicitous: the Empress's exotic but material accoutrements must seem supernatural. This is more like a gunpowder performance than a masque: Cavendish emphasizes, as she had done in "Chastity" and as Harriot had done in his narrative, the way that technology becomes part of an elaborate, but civilizing, ruse.

And, also like Travellia, the Empress is more than willing to use spectacular violence to achieve her ends. The same technology—the fire-stones—that helped convert the Blazing World's pagans and illuminated her water-walking talks with her home nation will also serve to destroy EFSI's enemies. While her countrymen and countrywomen are astonished by a nearly sublime visual performance, when she turns her attentions abroad in her effort to make her nation's king the absolute ruler of her home world, a more direct application of violence is necessary. The Empress's subjects—worm-men, bird-men, and mermen—carry the fire-stones throughout the world, using them to put to the torch ships, towns, and cities. Her tactics succeed in making EFSI the "absolute monarchy of all that world," in Cavendish's words. In triumph, she appears once again in all her regal majesty before them, leading the assembled princes to say that no other in that world could "have so great a power as she has, to walk upon the waters, and to destroy whatever she pleases, not only whole nations, but a whole world" (215). This vision of an apocalyptic power—both technological and magical—is hyperbolic, but it is an essential component of the Empress's civilizing of this world, guaranteeing its peace by centralizing power and sovereignty. It serves, we might say, to make more prominent and visible the raw power that undergirds authority—the way violence is necessary to sovereignty. But it also points toward what is arguably a new idea: that technologically augmented violence combined with lawless sovereign power threatens apocalyptic consequences. Claude Rawson has argued in a different context that gunpowder-based technologies help to produce the idea of the mass-casualty event, representing vast swaths of deaths not as an accumulation of individual events but as a singularity.[47] Similarly, Travellia's gunshot is amplified, not multiplied; it is not thousands of individuals that she destroys but rather "a whole world."

This apocalyptic power, significantly, is housed in the figure of a technologically enhanced woman. Like "Chastity," *The Blazing World* brings its heroine full circle. The two heroines' once imperiled bodies served as signs of the vulnerability of the unadorned body under anarchic conditions—the condition of the savage in the state of nature or war. They both institute new political orders with technologies so extraordinary that they appear magical. The femininity of these figures is significant not merely because their absolutism enables their selfhood, as Gallagher suggests. Cavendish's colonizing women give law not only to themselves but to others; in doing so, they also participate in heated debates surrounding the role of violence and deceit in the practice of rule, and the role of the sovereign in producing docile subjects. In Cavendish's rendering, women are figured as ideal extralegal agents—reserves of virtue, capable of wielding violence without being corrupted by sexual desire. Masculine sovereignty is threatened by corruption, violence, and an excess of passion; only feminine bodies, it appears, can show us the kind of disinterested virtue that can be entrusted with sovereignty in this violent form—though even here that violence may yield a terrifying excess.

CHAPTER 2

Fire and Sword: Aphra Behn and the Materials of Authority

> What means this violence?
>
> —King Philip, in Aphra Behn's *Abdelazer* (1676)[1]

Aphra Behn's *Oroonoko, or, The Royal Slave* (1688) draws heavily on the tradition of the heroic tragedy and romantic kingship, and yet the eponymous hero's experience in the New World is marked by only a few fleeting moments of ambiguous heroism. Prominent among these is his destruction of a horrific and startlingly resilient tiger that has terrorized the colonists' sheep flocks.[2] Where bullets have failed, Oroonoko's arrow pierces and slays the tiger, and he claims the heart—which has absorbed the settlers' impotent bullets—as a trophy and a mark of his prowess. The heart simultaneously registers the awesome power of nature to resist technological mastery and the wondrous ability of romantic heroism to perform what technology cannot, marking Oroonoko's chivalric heroism and virtue.[3] It also, however, diverts him from his most pressing interest: the task of freeing himself and his wife, Imoinda, from their captivity, which he has for the moment left to time and the appropriate bureaucratic channels. So the heart at the moment of its fetishization is simultaneously a symbol of Oroonoko's misdirected energies and his obsessions with the obsolete virtues of chivalric romance. Instead of confronting the modern problem presented by his captivity—which we may read either as a bureaucratic glitch or as treacherous commercialism trumping justice—he spins out tales of past glory. In this respect, Oroonoko resembles the tiger he has slain, for that beast, as much as it symbolizes resistance to modernity, also seems to be part of a dying breed. Indeed, the heart itself might be read as a figure of Oroonoko's failure. For though this heart is resistant and durable—indeed, though it could not be vanquished by technology—it also attains its power as a fetish only as it has ceased to beat. By being put on display, it testifies not only to its resilience and strength but also to its vulnerability; its value exists only in its embeddedness in a cycle of romantic tales and deferred action. One is tempted to ask whether this is in fact Oroonoko's heart on display; does this scarred curiosity figure virtue and obsolescence simultaneously? Is Behn, with this fetishized organ, bidding a fond farewell to the world of romance and the stylized violence it represents?

Through Oroonoko's relationship with the heart—this fetishized object, redolent of nobility and obsolescence—Behn's text explores the cathexis of objects in the fashioning of political authority.[4] This chapter argues that Behn's writing distills a cultural interest in this cathexis— what we might call political fetishism—at a key moment in British reconsiderations of political categories and practices of rule. Just as *Oroonoko* stands poised at the moment of fracture between rule by divine right and popular sovereignty, so too does it work simultaneously with two ways of embodying violence in objects: as talismans or fetishes, endowed with intrinsic and nonmaterial power; and as technological objects, tools, or, perhaps most aptly, props in the performance of political rituals. Behn's fetishes are mournful markers of the collapse of the world of divine right, chivalric virtue, and magical objects, while her props gesture toward techniques for operating in the disenchanted regime of pragmatism and popular sovereignty. These fetishes and props continue an inquiry inaugurated in Behn's drama, which also explores performative and paramilitary techniques for managing the rabble. In *Oroonoko*, this exploration finds a resolution of sorts in its meditation on sacral and technological objects. I identify the text's key political fetish as the burning glass—a magnifying lens designed to light fires—that Surinam's English settlers use to instill fear and awe in their savage neighbors during a visit to the South American interior. To the colonists in this sequence, the glass is a tool, useful for starting fires and for intimidating Caribs. But to the Caribs, the glass is a form of magic, and those who wield it are like gods. In this scene, we see European technology transplanted into the colonial zone in such a way that the violence of the colonial occupation is elided in favor of awe. The gentle, yet coded, display of technological mastery intimidates while simultaneously deflecting this aggression away from an overt scene of violence; military force is sublimated into an awe-inspiring display of prowess. In turn, then, this performance makes the burning glass into a magical object for the settlers as well, for it allows them to conquer and govern without bloodshed. This deployment of technological spectacle, political magic, and deferred violence is reminiscent of Margaret

Cavendish's similar inquiry into spectacular politics, and like her heroines Travellia and the Empress, Behn's lens-wielding conqueror also figures certain aspects of sovereignty more generally; again the relationship between the colonizer and the colonized models that between subject and sovereign.

Richard Frohock has claimed that Behn's text contrasts a colonial society's rule by force with the natural and legitimate authority of the monarch and his bloodline.[5] I suggest that quite the opposite is true: Behn's text displays no great faith in "natural" authority, coding it instead as dangerously romantic. This coding operates most clearly with respect to objects—the political fetishes I discuss in this chapter. Behn's fiction and drama suggest that those who would be sovereign must treat cathected objects as props in a performance before the rabble. These props must have an aura of mystery and magic; they must code for special—sovereign—knowledge or ability. They must also be menacing, embodying violence and localizing it as the special preserve of the sovereign. But if those who wield these objects cannot attain a cynical distance from them, then they themselves may become impotent victims of the metastasizing violence of modernity. Oroonoko believes he uses the tiger's heart to amaze his listeners; the heart marks his prowess and therefore his authority and his right to liberty. But that same object and the narratives that surround it are distractions from his quest for freedom, and his tales of chivalric violence are reduced to trivial and archaic stories. Rather than deploying the heart as a prop, he allows it to become a different sort of fetish: a memento, a leftover of a romantic past that is also a warning of things to come.[6] In this, it functions for Oroonoko much as Oroonoko's corpse functions for Behn at the novel's end—as both a vestige of an impossible nobility and a harbinger of the horrors of modernity.

Thus Behn's work develops a new approach to the problems explored by Thomas Hobbes, William Davenant, and Cavendish. Like Cavendish's narratives in particular, Behn's texts waver between positing a natural but obscure ground for authority, on the one hand, and the need for human agency to produce and reproduce that authority, whether by force or by spectacular display, on the other. This chapter begins with a close examination of the role that one political fetish—the burning glass—plays in the excursion that *Oroonoko*'s narrator (often interpreted as a stand-in for Behn herself) makes to the interior of Surinam, where the confrontation between the colonist and the savage is sharpest and the implicit conflation of the savage and the rabble is most acute. The rabble is a central concern in Behn's work, as in much of the day's political culture. To underscore the salience of this concern, the second section of this chapter examines key moments in Behn's drama, particularly her political satire *The Roundheads; or, The Good Old Cause* (1682) and her New World tragicomedy *The Widdow Ranter; or, The History of Bacon in Virginia* (1689). Both plays revisit moments from British political and military history; both do so to explore the complex interplay of violence and awe in the disciplining of the rabble, ultimately suggesting that neither performance nor raw force can, unalloyed, shape the rabble into a citizenry. These plays instead examine the role of objects in disciplining this unruly and yet indispensible component of the polity. Sometimes these objects are weapons such as swords, but Behn's drama also experiments with the way other cathected objects can substitute for weapons, disciplining without overt acts of violence. Even here, however, weapons trump props; political props must be weaponized to be made truly effective, as *The Roundheads* in particular emphasizes.

Failure to weaponize one's props is fatal, be the context colonial or European. Both James II and Oroonoko are unable to master practices of performance, and it is their literal-mindedness that is their undoing—and, indeed, the undoing of obsolete forms of sovereignty as well. Behn's fiction climaxes when Oroonoko's body becomes itself an object, simultaneously a sign of failed kingship and of the dangers of relying on force and terror rather than awe to govern. As many critics have suggested, Oroonoko may be understood as an allegorical figure for either Charles I or James II—kings who also neglected the importance of political affect and relied too much on naive ideas about the nature of authority.[7] But the text points outward from there; it begins with the naive Stuart kings, but the elegiac quality of the fiction suggests that Oroonoko also figures the nature of authority under conditions of modernity, when kings can no longer take the deference and obedience of the common orders as a given.[8] Oroonoko's political failure is a problem of object relations: he cannot politicize his fetishes. The consequences of this failure, Behn suggests, are horrifying, for the opposite of the theatrical practice of sovereignty she describes is not naive kingship but a reign of terror. The proper object of this reentry of war onto the political scene is not a technological prop but a corporeal one: the ruined corpse of Oroonoko.

Fire Power: Obedience and Astonishment

Oroonoko entertains a fantasy about the establishment of authority through political fetishes in a key sequence in which the narrator, along with Oroonoko and a throng of colonists, makes a visit to Surinam's interior. During this visit, the narrator offers some ethnological observations that have, I suggest, a powerful connection to the narrative's meditations on the political sphere. The narrator tells us,

> I soon perceiv'd, by an admiration, that is natural to these People, and by the extream ignorance and Simplicity of 'em, it were not difficult to establish any unknown or extravagant Religion among them; and to impose any Notions or Fictions upon 'em. For seeing a Kinsman of mine set some Paper a Fire, with a Burning-glass, a Trick they had never before seen, they were like to have Ador'd him for a God; and beg'd he wou'd give them the Characters or Figures of his Name, that they might oppose it against Winds and Storms; which he did, and they held it up in those Seasons, and fancy'd it had a Charm to conquer them; and kept it like a Holy Relique. They are very Superstitious, and call'd him the Great *Peeie*, that is, *Prophet*. (122)

In this sequence, a technological object instills awe in a savage people—a scene, as we have seen, that draws on colonial and exploratory writings such as Harriot's. This encounter takes place in the rainforests high above the plantation, where the savagery of the settlers is replaced by the distinct but related savagery of the Caribs, who, I suggest, are aligned with the rabble in Behn's thought. Critics have frequently interpreted this sequence in light of its construction of racialized bodies and subjectivities, reading the Carib in relation to the complex racial and gendered identifications of Oroonoko, Imoinda, the narrator, and other English colonists.[9] These readings have most commonly sought to understand the relationship between African and Indian or the intersections of racial constructions with the femininities represented by Imoinda and the narrator. I supplement these readings by suggesting that racial difference here is also a marker for class difference and its political implications. Though early in Behn's text the Caribs figure prelapsarian savage nobility, they appear here in a different guise. This scene, it is sometimes forgotten, takes place under the cloud of a barely suppressed war between the Caribs and the settlers. This condition recalls the tense political conditions of James II's reign, as the king's miscalculations and overreach became intolerable to all but the most adamant royalists. As I will argue, the colonists' tentative resolution to this war is to use a political fetish to instill awe in the Caribs. Lurking beneath the deployment of this glass is a subtext of violence and militarism that is present in Behn's narrative by allusion, though the indirectness of the allusion defers and obscures this violent subtext.

The scene takes place shortly before Oroonoko's rebellion against his enslavers, in a trip to the more remote Carib villages of the interior. Most critics have accepted the narrator's portrait of this voyage as a pleasure cruise. But this, I think, is to suppress the wartime context of the scene and to miss the visit's fundamentally political purposes. It is also, therefore, to ignore the political meanings of the performance of technological power for the benefit of savages. Although the narrator presents this visit as one of entertainment and amateur ethnography, I suggest here that the purpose is rather different: it is an embassy—perhaps even a covert operation—to transform the settlers' dependence on the Caribs into mastery. Without adopting such an explanation, it is difficult to understand this visit, which we know involves some risk. Anxieties that the Caribs will invade the colony are rife. Though the honesty of the Caribs is not in question, their superior numbers and warlike skills make them a persistent low-level security threat to European settlement, as the narrator notes in the opening pages of the narrative; the Europeans "dare" not treat them unkindly (60). The visit to the towns can only be carried out under Oroonoko's aegis. Even once the trip arrives at its destination, after a weeklong voyage, some settlers are so frightened they will not leave their boats (100). The party's first moments in the village are frightening—the "loud Cry" that the Caribs give upon seeing them initially seems to anticipate a murderous confrontation, though it is soon clear that its source is in fact "wonder and amazement" (100). It soon appears that the production of this wonder is one of the important purposes of the trip; despite the narrator's alibi, the narrative describes not merely a pleasure cruise but also a resolution to the military tensions and an assertion of English hegemony. Their entry is staged precisely to induce surprise and awe, as they leave the darker-skinned and poorly clothed members of the party behind; the narrator, her brother, and their female servant go forth like a courtly procession, deploying their "Glittering" clothing to maximum effect among savages known for their attraction to shiny objects (100–102).

That this encounter is intended to instill wonder—and, through wonder, to transform the defensive and frightened condition of the colony into one of hegemony—is made clear by the sequence's conclusion, in which technological power is used to create the image of an awesomely powerful and superior European in the minds of the Caribs. This key moment of technological display simultaneously acknowledges and disavows the role of violence in the establishment of European sovereignty—or, at least, a protosovereignty. The scene suggests that power may best be wielded by a coded and indirect display of violence—not through the force that we have already learned will be ineffective in the face of the Caribbean horde but through the impression of power and awe. This display, though ostensibly nonviolent, in fact crucially alludes to violence; the burning glass draws not only on technological superiority but also on specifically military associations, particularly the classical and postclassical legends of the great Greek mathematician Archimedes.

To many of Behn's contemporaries, devices that focus the sun's rays to start fires represented one of the decisive technological developments of antiquity. The incendiary powers of lenses and mirrors were well known in the classical world. Particularly familiar are legends associating this technology with military applications, such as the well-known myth of Archimedes in Syracuse burning the Roman fleet. The Byzantine author John Tzetzes, drawing on a lost portion of Dio Cassius's history of Rome, describes it this way:

> When Marcellus withdrew [the ships] a bow-shot thence, [Archimedes] constructed a kind of hexagonal mirror, and at an interval proportionate to the size of the mirror, he set similar small mirrors, with four edges moving by links and by a kind of hinge, and made the glass the center of the sun's beams—its noontide beam, whether in summer or in the dead of winter. So after that, when the beams were reflected into this, a terrible kindling of flame arose upon the ships, and he reduced them to ashes a bow-shot off. Thus by his contrivances did the old man vanquish Marcellus.[10]

The veracity of this story was (and to some degree remains) controversial; Livy, Polybius, and Plutarch do not mention it in their discussions of Archimedes. Though Behn would have been unable to read Tzetzes—I find no translation into a modern tongue in this period—the controversy was well known, discussed in the writings of Johannes Kepler and René Descartes, among others.¹¹ Or perhaps she knew a different version of the story, attributing an identical feat to the mathematician Proclus, who was reported to have burned the Mysian fleet at Constantinople. Both feats are mentioned in Robert Baron's *Mirza*, a play supposedly translated from the Persian and published in London in 1647.[12] John Dunton also discusses Proclus's feat in a pedagogical anthology in 1692; though Behn's death preceded this publication, it seems likely that the image of powerful military technologies channeling the sun's rays were in common circulation, even among those without a classical education.[13]

These classical narratives describe the military application of solar power; they do not, however, describe savages, nor are they interested in instilling awe in the enemy. Archimedes and Proclus do not perform; they act and destroy. Behn's burning glass may have closer affinities to Thomas Harriot's account of Virginia. Harriot's is not the only text in which the burning glass appears in narratives of intercultural contact and diplomacy as a device that could inspire awe. In Adam Olearius's 1647 description of his travels in Persia with Frederick III's ambassador, he describes a "mountebank" who lights fires using ice crystals; he uses this trick to support his claims of descent from Mohammed. Olearius sets out to disenchant the Persian observers, demonstrating the ease of the feat; the observers are astonished, saying that if Olearius "had done as much in Persia," he "should have pass'd there for either a great Saint, or a Sorcerer."[14] Like Behn's sequence, this narrative (available to Behn in an English translation) portrays the management of authority in an intercultural context. To be sure, the purpose of Olearius's performance is distinct from that presented in *Oroonoko*. He does not himself offer to trick the Persians; rather, he depicts the Persians as a race with a proclivity for deceit and for being deceived. His performance might be read as proto-orientalist; he demystifies the devices of the Persian clergy, replacing them with his own performance of technological and explicable mastery of the elements.

Nevertheless, Behn's portrait of savage gullibility seems to owe a debt to Olearius's narrative. The Caribs declare the narrator's kinsman to be a Peeie: not the title of a sovereign, precisely, but more akin to the role of Olearius's "great Saint" or "Sorcerer." Although recent historical and archeological work has demonstrated that Carib, Arawak, and other communities in colonial South America in fact operated within large and tightly networked political collectives, Behn's fictional Caribs have no sovereign—no office that serves as final arbiter of custom and law.[15] As she notes very early, the Caribs have no kings, deferring instead to the eldest among the war captains (102–3). However, the indigenous Peeie is charged with healing his people with treachery as well as true medicine; what is more, his trickery distinguishes him from his lessers:

> He is bred to all the little Arts and cunning they are capable of; to all the Legerdemain Tricks, and Sleight of Hand, whereby he imposes upon *the Rabble*; and is both a Doctor in Physick and Divinity. And by these Tricks makes the Sick believe he sometimes eases their Pains, . . . and though they have besides undoubted good Remedies, for almost all their Diseases, they cure the Patient more by Fancy than by Medicines; and make themselves Fear'd, Lov'd, and Reverenc'd. (102; my emphasis)

The Peeie, in other words, produces affect in his patients and his flock. Though his role is not precisely political in the sense of having authority to govern military and civil affairs, his ability to impose magical "knowledge" on "the Rabble" hints at the potential for a political component to his power; his ability to heal might also allude to the sovereign's power to heal the "King's evil"—a practice that had been revived by Charles II and continued by his brother.[16]

However, the lack of a military component renders the Peeie's power incompletely political. The Caribs appear to divide their authority, for military decisions are handled by the war captains, whose display operates on rather different principles. These captains have attracted much commentary because of their grotesque mode of establishing authority and honor. The narrator finds them monstrous—"Hobgoblins, or Fiends, rather than Men" (102). This reference is to their exterior form, which does not reflect their inner qualities; rather, it seems to figure those qualities through a form of inversion or catachresis, for unlike the Peeie, whose motives and honor are open to question, these men have souls that are "very Humane and Noble" (103). These leaders demonstrate a kind of savage virtue; their willingness to sacrifice their bodies is an index of their visible disdain for their own surfaces. The narrator notes that "'tis by a passive Valour they shew and prove their Activity" (103). We must agree with Oroonoko that this is courage in its most brutal form. Yet the passage, read literally, argues that it is through this disdain of their own suffering and their own monstrosity that the generals earn the authority to lead the Caribs into war.

The technological performance of the narrator's kinsman in producing fire, however, manages to attain a political and military result without brutal display. His performance retains an element of menace, but by encasing that threat in an aestheticized display, he simultaneously intensifies the power of the colonists and disclaims their brutality. His ability to blend the military prowess of the war captains with the magical acts of the priests works, we might say, like a charm; the production of political affect trumps violence as relations with the English settlers improve tremendously. Following the trip, there are no more "Fears, or Heart-burnings," says the narrator, "but we had a perfect, open, and free Trade with 'em" (103). The narrator, with her typical unreliability, ascribes this turn of events to Oroonoko, who "begot so good an understanding between the *Indians* and the *English*" (103). But this ascription is undermined in the very next sentence, in which the narrator confesses that the English are determined "to please . . . *Imoinda*, . . . to make her Chains as easy as" they could, "and to Compliment the Prince in that manner that most oblig'd him" (103). The narrator's presentation is muddled, making it nearly impossible to accept her ascription of the improved relations with the Caribs to Oroonoko's mediation; that suggestion sounds, in this second sentence, like a sop to keep a potentially dangerous slave in line. The narrator here appears complicit in an effort to prevent Oroonoko from reclaiming his liberty.[17] The slave prince also acts as a kind of security force in this embassy to transform the balance of power in the space of the colony. This operation uses astonishing technological displays to render the Caribs subordinate, if not docile, and more open to trade.

This returns us to the important question of the burning glass. The narrator's kinsman has stunned the Caribs with his power, inducing them to treat his name as itself a sacral object, keeping his name inscribed on paper as a "Holy Relique" (102). The use of paper with sacred language on it is common in English magical practices from the seventeenth century and before.[18] In instilling a similar belief in the magical efficacy of sacred materials, the narrator's kinsman has produced a model of the way to manage the rabble. The assumption of the mantle of a high priest—a kind of inauthentic honor—rather than that of a warrior is a crucial gesture. Though it is not precisely true that the English establish sovereignty over the Caribs in this passage, they do draw the Caribs into a trade network using displaced and deferred violence and the performance of technological mastery in a way that anticipates *Robinson Crusoe*. This in turn contributes to the slow transformation of Surinam from a savage and wild space into a commercial polity—or would have, were it not for the unfortunate transfer of the colony to the Dutch, which Behn laments elsewhere. The Dutch, for whom every object is a commodity, understand little of this delicate blend of force and diplomacy; in seeking to establish a more encompassing sovereignty, they are themselves dismembered and slaughtered (100). But the power of the English colonists has taught the Carib to engage in commerce, which is another way of saying that it has taught them to keep their contracts. And the keeping of contracts is, at least for Hobbes, a function of civil society, not the state of nature.

Courting the Rabble: Colonial Virginia, Colonial London

> The Rabble 'tis we Court, those powerful things,
> Whose voices can impose even Laws on Kings.
> —prologue, in Aphra Behn's
> *The Second Part of the Rover* (1681)

England's racial others, then, may serve as representations of the rabble. Behn's interest in the rabble is well known and unsurprising.[19] For Behn, the street mob is part of the more general problem of the lower orders not knowing their place; her suspicion of commoners and usurping cits is closely connected to the more general problem of social ferment in the Restoration.

Though Behn sometimes used the term *rabble* in its older and more traditional sense, simply referring to a large and agitated crowd—a mob, or "mobile"—she more often intends a more politically pointed sense: the large crowd of commoners who threaten the stability of the state. For example, in the prologue to *The Second Part of the Rover*, the London theatergoing crowd is associated, half comically, with the mobs who threaten the stability of the nation, just as they did in the days of the Commonwealth and the Protectorate. And in the dedication of that play to the Prince of Wales—soon to become James II—Behn explicitly complains of the "rabble" that posed as kings to misgovern the nation: the "again gathering Faction" of Whigs and republicans seeks to deceive the nation with fine rhetoric of liberty and prosperity, "that lucky Cant which so few years since so miserably reduc'd all the Noble, Brave, and Honest, to the Obedience *of the ill-gotten Power, and worse-acted Great-*

ness of the Rabble."[20] She concludes that "all England found it self deplorably inslav'd by the Arbitrary Tyranny of many Pageant Kings" (228). The pageant kings here remind us of cits—parading in finery which does not befit their station, assuming authority which is not theirs. But they are also clearly part of the rabble that their own rhetoric attempts to mislead. These associations surface as well in Behn's novella *The Fair Jilt* (1688); there, Tarquin's claims to princely status are never decisively supported, and his life is saved from the "heads-man's" sword not only through the executioner's incompetence but by the swift action of the rabble, acting as "one body," who bear him away from the scaffold and shield him from the authorities.[21] Behn's writing confronts the problem that unruly usurpers pose: they cannot simply be destroyed or killed, for their obedience and labor are essential, much like that of the Caribs vis-à-vis the settlers in Surinam. They must therefore be reshaped and used as a resource; though the sovereign, in theory, might have a lawful right to slaughter a seditious mob, they must as a practical matter be cultivated and reformed. Also, like the Caribs, they have raw force on their side, for the virtuous minority is constantly threatened by the power of the unpredictable forces of the rabble.

Like Davenant, Cavendish, and Hobbes, Behn is concerned with the unruly masses and commoners and with the difficult question of how violence and performance can be used to manage and transform them into more obedient though still autonomous subjects. In her tragicomedy, in particular, she builds on Davenant's thinking about aesthetics and politics, using the techniques of metadrama to explore the tension between violence, legitimacy, and performance. Though examples are not difficult to find, two comedies in particular experiment with these strains of Behn's political thought. In *The Roundheads*, set in the chaotic period preceding the Restoration of Charles II, sovereignty has been usurped by elements of the rabble; the same is essentially true of Behn's New World drama *The Widdow Ranter*, in which the fragility of sovereign authority is figured by an absent governor, and the rabble has assumed an undue sway in the colony. In both plays, a more coherent and stable social and political order is restored, as, indeed, the comic plot demands; neither offers even an approximation of the horror of *Oroonoko*. In *The Roundheads*, the legitimate ruler—Charles II—is restored, or brought to the cusp of Restoration, through a complex of violence and theatricality. *The Widdow Ranter* features the self-dramatizing figure of Nathaniel Bacon, whose romantic performances blend with a savage disciplining of the rabble to restore harmony to a colony threatened by savages without and within.[22] Both explore the ways in which violence and theatricality may be essential to sovereignty's foundational moment; *The Roundheads*, in particular, also meditates on props as political fetishes, adducing a necessary cynicism in a way surprisingly similar to that found in *Oroonoko*.

The Roundheads, set in the unstable period immediately before the restoration of Charles II, makes explicit the wobbly relationship between the rabble and sovereign authority. The years preceding the production of this play in 1682 were a period of heightened political instability and social turmoil. The so-called Popish Plot and the concomitant Exclusion Crisis had shaken the foundations of the nation's constitution and openly raised difficult questions about popular power and the location of sovereignty. By 1682, however, these crises were moving toward a (temporary) resolution, and many theatrical productions of this year feature the aggressive reassertions of royal prerogative and divine-right succession that some critics have termed Tory triumphalism.[23] Behn's play redacts her source text, John Tatham's *The Rump, or the Mirrour of the Late Times* (1659), aligning the tumult that preceded the restoration of the Stuart line with the threat to divine-right sovereignty posed by James II's political enemies; the Exclusion Crisis is figured in Behn's play by the travesties of the English Revolution and the Puritan Parliament. This parody of Whiggism is supplemented by portraits of a number of powerful but problematic female characters; the centrality of women to these plots has been ably handled in the few recent essays on this play.[24] I here supplement these interpretations by analyzing the drama's implicit arguments about the way violence and performance ought to produce political affect—arguments in which the play's women are crucial. *The Roundheads* culminates with the resolution of the crises of 1659 and 1660 in which the threat of military violence blends with aristocratic theatricality to refashion the rabble into political subjects. Political sentiment on its own is repeatedly elaborated as futile. Critical to the play's dénouement is the enlistment of the rabble in the cause of Restoration. In *Oroonoko*, the Caribs are subjected through the display of technological power; here technology is not apparent, but violence, cynical theatricality, and political fetishes of a different sort are. The play's performances convert the rabble into incipient royalists, and the usurpers return to their rightful place among them.

The drama takes place in the confused days preceding the Convention Parliament of April 1660.[25] Between the army's dismissal of the Second Rump Parliament in October 1659 and the entry of George Monck into London in February 1660, the scene of English politics was one of disarray, confusion, and brutal competition between key figures, most prominently general-turned-politician John Lambert and the charismatic Puritan Charles Fleetwood.[26] This period—one of chaos, with no clear locus of sovereignty or even of power—has clear affinities with Behn's New World settings in *Oroonoko* and *The Widdow Ranter*. *The Roundheads* lingers over the resulting scramble for power and strongly thematizes the role of violence and performance in establishing sovereign authority. At the center of the play, the leaders of the Committee of Safety hold a session in order "to establish a government"; Fleetwood expresses a proper idea for his own selfish ends when he argues that "we are ... a Body without a Head" (3.1, 44); and, as the meeting deteriorates into anarchy, his sovereignty is nominally accepted by the still-scheming committee. This much is drawn from Behn's source material, but Behn adds intrigue and narrative drive by including two new characters: the dispossessed Cavaliers, Freeman and Loveless, who involve themselves in complex intrigues of seduction and—importantly—lend a theatrical flair to the royalist cause. The play relies heavily on the audience's knowledge of the role of George Monck's military forces in bringing about the Restoration of Charles II and the role of the London masses, in turn, in supporting Monck's actions. In the play, force is mustered to bring about the return of legitimacy, raising difficult questions about the foundational role of violence; political affect produces legitimacy, but that legitimacy itself derives from force, as the course of the play demonstrates.

Behn's drama places the London street mob at the heart of the Restoration's politics, presenting a paradigm of rabble-shaping through calculated displays of violence. The drama opens with a street scene—an exchange between soldiers and skilled laborers that portrays a politics of violence, underscoring the importance of force in the absence of a legitimate constitutional authority. A troop of soldiers (led by the crypto-royalist Corporal Right) encounter two artisans, a joiner and a felt maker. Both groups are representatives of the usurping demotic classes; the scene, however, emphasizes their inability to come to terms with one another and the fundamental arbitrariness of their allegiances. The soldiers support the charismatic military leader Lambert, while the artisans prefer the religiosity of Fleetwood. Their encounter takes the form of a verbal altercation—one which the soldiers largely have the better of, perhaps because they are armed; the argument is one that might need to be resolved by the "push [of] a Pike" (1.1, 14).[27] The joiner and the felt maker, who (feebly) represent Fleetwood's interest, are able to give voice to a kind of rhetoric of liberty, describing themselves as "Free-born Subjects of *England*" and speaking out for "Liberty and Property" (1.1, 26), one soldier notes. But their protest against the establishment of law through the use of force is quickly undermined; though they suggest that the use of force to declare the leader makes the election of Lambert "illegal, and against the Property of the People," the felt maker appends this comment: "I have a high respect for my honourable Lord Fleetwood, . . . and till I find his party the weaker, I hope my Zeal will be strengthened for him" (1.1, 31–33). This link between "zeal" and the balance of power is crucial for Behn; the military power figured by sword and pike is the primary agent that constructs the political subject from the rabble. As the joiner notes, "we do not act by reason"; yet there is reason of a sort involved in the rabble's analysis of force. They are inconstant, as one of the soldiers notes: "I doubt not but to see 'em chop about, till it come to our great Heroe [Charles II] again"—prophetic words indeed (1.1, 90–91). The rabble's attraction to republican language is tempered by an inexorable tendency to respect power. While the burning glass works as a machine that transforms violence into authority, here political power is managed through a much cruder and more visible calculus of force.

And yet even here Behn's drama makes it clear that raw force alone is limited in its effects; violence must be transmuted in some way through representation or performance. The soldiers are explicit in their relentless focus on the military prowess of their preferred leader, Lambert, but their language oscillates strangely between a reverence for military prowess and a respect for political duplicity and performance: Lambert can "act both the Souldier and the Courtier, at once expose his Breast to dangers for our sakes—and tell the rest of the pretending Slaves a fair Tale, but hang 'em sooner than trust 'em" (1.1, 40–41). These cynical virtues are what make Lambert "our General, our Protector, our King, our Keiser, our—even what he pleases himself" (1.1, 57). These virtues are in tension, however; while these men recognize their own need for someone powerful to direct their violence, they also recognize that such a man must necessarily be a duplicitous performer, able to play military and social roles with equal facility. What they seek, in fact, is one who will play the part of a courtier but will be self-consciously acting—and will be able to undermine and withdraw from his performance at any moment, a pageant king telling "a fair Tale" but quite willing to resort to treachery and violence when needed. He will participate in rituals of power and deference, in other words, but by retaining his prowess with the sword, he will always remain able to use the rule of the strongest to limit and direct that context for his own purposes.

Lambert's status as a possible "keisar" implies an absolute sovereignty—like that of Julius Caesar, one reinforced both by the support of the military and the power of duplicity and pageantry. All these things are, in fact, part of what constitutes kingship in some—nay, many—accounts, and we might well ask why Behn objects to them in Lambert. After all, in her encomiums to James II, Behn is no less purple in praise of his military prowess and his smooth-talking skills; indeed, in her dedication to *The Second Part of the Rover* (1681), she had described his military prowess as itself a transparent form of rhetoric. She fancifully describes how her young cavalier hero Wilmore had seen James in battle "like young Cesar in the Field . . . exchanging Death for Laurels, and wondered at a Bravery so early, which still made double Conquest, not only by Your Sword, but by Your Vertues."[28] The young James manifests, in this image, military prowess and an automatic and uncalculated theatricality, inspiring awe in his virtuous witnesses. James Stuart's innate virtues are transparently visible and unproblematically marked by his military heroism. Lambert, on the other hand, is able to instill a limited form of awe through mere prowess and performance; he exemplifies the cynicism of modernity that appears in *Oroonoko*. At this point in history, with Charles II apparently triumphing over the forces of Whiggish anarchy, Behn seems unwilling to countenance this attitude.

Yet the play's treatment of the relationship of violence to dissimulation and virtue is uneasy; though Behn's dedication to James argues that virtue legitimates violence, *The Roundheads* flirts with the reversal of this equation, making violence the necessary precursor of law. The soldiers in this first scene argue as much when they describe a confrontation with the speaker of Parliament, Sir Arthur Hesilrige (Behn's "Haslerig"). The soldiers' description of this offstage encounter violently disclaims any belief in a legitimate government independent of the military; military force in their boasts is the foundation of law in its primordial form, the command: "Our Will was Reason and Law too, and the Word of Command lodg'd in our Hilts" (1.1, 68–70), claims Corporal Right. A few lines later, the same corporal mocks Haslerig for not being fluent in "Souldiers Dialect": "the Language of the Sword puzzled his Understanding; the Keeneness of which, was too sharp for his Wit" (1.1, 70–73). The politician, then, needs to master the soldier's dialect—brute force—should he hope to govern effectively. But the scene does not, I think, simply suggest that Haslerig needs to learn to defend himself with more able swordplay. For we must notice the soldier's own doubled investment in violence and wit: his own witticisms are part of his presentation of his "dialect," and we should understand him to be reproducing the violence of that encounter through a reperformance that calls attention to his own "wit," one that does not lie in his sword.

Thus, from the first moments, this play seems torn between a conception of a violence that surrounds, constructs, and even contains the law and one in which violence itself is part of a linguistic and performative system that simultaneously defers and amplifies the material fact of violence. Of course, the problem remains that this soldier's violence and rhetoric serves no end, since it is exercised on behalf of an unworthy man. If I read this play and Behn's dedication to James correctly, Behn is suggesting that violence and the performances that surround it must be in the service of a great man, who must risk himself in turn; the endpoint of violence must be organized around the hub of the man of quality, who sanctifies this violence and renders it not merely legitimate but even holy. This sort of violence presents its own hazards, to be sure; the great and the self-sacrificing may not be sound leaders, as Behn's *Widdow Ranter* will underscore. But *The Roundheads* remains more optimistic about the power of wise performance to organize violence and grant it legitimacy.

That legitimacy is visible in the leaders who direct the rabble's action at the play's end. The drama concludes with another street scene which reassembles this same rowdy cast, but this time the rabble is mocking Parliament and building fires for the king while the former members of the committee return to their rightful places as peddlers and street mountebanks, as General Monck prepares to enter the city and, as the reader or playgoer knows, paves the way for the Restoration (5.1, 497–525). The anticipation of military victory stimulates the rabble's acquiescence, as language, persuasion, and fidelity alone could not (also making the loyal Corporal Right able to make actual his instinctual inclination toward the king).[29] But, significantly, Monck's victory is also associated with an element of theatricality that is missing from the performances of the Committee of Safety, as a young apprentice uses slippery oratory to transform the mob from cowardly subjects to aggressive advocates for the Restoration. As Monck approaches and public order falls apart, soldiers and artisans once again contend, this time contending not for sovereign power but for the right to plunder the city (5.1, 1–104). The stage is then taken by the "Captain of the Prentices, and a great Gang with him, arm'd with Staffs, Swords, &c." (5.1, s.d.). This apprentice—the captain—merits attention, for his calculated performance sharply contrasts with more straightforward, expressive models of oratory; he is an adept manipulator of the mob's affect. Initially rallying his improvised militia in the service of Monck and the king, he quickly shifts registers and produces a proclamation from the Committee of Safety that threatens to hang those who support Charles II against the committee. Here he tests the power of his rhetoric against the force of law, appearing here as a printed document. The alarmed mob, terrified by the threat of sovereign punishment, immediately begin planning to return to their homes. The captain then uses their reaction to shame them: flinging the scroll at them, he declares, "I did but try your boasted Courages." His chastened militia returns to him, protesting, "We recant, dear Captain, wee'l dy, one and all" (5.1, 87, 91). The apprentices are then rallied to assault the hypocritical preacher Ananias Goggle and the military man Hewson and shortly lend crucial support to Monck as he prepares to enter London.[30] This odd sequence has garnered little comment, but it argues once more that virtuous performances can undercut illegitimate violence. Rhetoric triumphs over force.

The public plot of *The Roundheads* as adapted by Behn, then, inconclusively explores the role of force, fraud, and performance in the restoration of legitimate sovereignty under anarchic conditions. This leg of the plot relies very heavily on a romantic idealization of men of good heart who, when the calculus of force permits, can bring about a restoration of political order. However, the play also features Behn's wholly original subplot of the seductive Cavaliers cuckolding the Rump Parliament's leadership. And while the main plot line exalts Loveless and Freeman as exemplary and idealistic royalists, the subplot displays them from another angle in a scene that offers an important treatment of political fetishes in the guise of sacred relics rather than technological objects of wonder. Behn's treatment of the crown jewels in that play anticipates *Oroonoko* in important ways, particularly in its emphasis on the relationship between passivity and performance in the handling of political relics. The skepticism hinted at in this drama resonates with Sarah Ellenzweig's discussion of Behn's interest in skepticism and freethinking—intellectual tendencies closely associated with the instrumentalization of religious belief to control the lower orders.[31] In the play's fourth act, the superficial and ambitious Lady Lambert and the virtuous though lascivious Loveless are preparing for a performance of a rather different sort—cuckolding Lambert—when Loveless's prospective mistress reveals that the crown jewels are in the room with them. Loveless and Lady Lambert react quite differently to the presence of the jewels—one with a reverent impotence, the other with a callous display of ambition. Though at first the scene appears to endorse Loveless's reverence, the play also hints that a more playful and performative treatment of the jewels might be necessary, if not necessarily virtuous.

The scene opens with the illicit couple entering Lambert's quarters. Lady Lambert uncovers the jewels—to her, glittering ornaments and mere signs of power—saying, "Behold this Gay, this wondrous Glorious thing" (4.2, 147). The use of "gay" here renders her praise visibly problematic; she sees the outer showiness or prettiness of the jewels, but her admiration ends there. The sense of the term as referring to that which is lightweight and morally dubious, even louche, is certainly present as well. Loveless, however, responds with the reverence appropriate to a believer in divine-right monarchy. To him, they are not merely jewels, nor are they unproblematic signs of sovereignty and power. Rather, they take on the character of religious fetishes, associated as much with the horror of the martyrdom of Charles I: "Have I been all this while/ So near the Sacred Reliques of my King!/ And found no Awful motion in my blood,/ Nothing that mov'd Sacred Devotion in me?" (4.2, 149–52). Loveless's reaction, then, is not simply one of admiration but one of self-reproach; he, and we, are led to suspect that his amorous adventures have lured him away from the path of heroic virtue and dulled his senses to the aura surrounding these objects. His response is to kneel and pray to the crown and scepter, performing a kind of idolatry that could not be better designed to irritate a dissenter: "Hail Sacred Emblem of Great Majesty,/ Thou that hast circled more Divinity / Than the great Zodiack that surrounds the World" (4.2, 153–55).

Viewed from the perspective of chivalric virtue and quasi-feudal divine-right doctrines, Loveless's reaction to the crown appears exemplary. We may be forgiven for initially taking this reaction as normative and entirely apt. Indeed, Behn's later poem on James II's coronation ritual uses similar language; her description of the coronation pageant lingers lovingly over each bearer of a regal relic; the great men who bear the swords, scepter, and crown possess untainted virtues that make them worthy of bearing the "Sacred *Diadem*" and other items from the regalia that will shortly decorate James II, "the *Earthly GOD*."[32] In the logic of the poem and of the coronation ritual itself, these objects, though having no efficacy in and of themselves, become sacred through their metonymic associations with the consecrated body of the king. Here that sacral aura is enhanced by the king's martyrdom.[33]

Yet the crown and scepter also neutralize Loveless; his reaction is one of passivity and retreat, reminiscent of Oroonoko's bondage to his own romanticized honor. This passivity—even an inability to perform—anticipates Oroonoko's failures and suggests the need for a compromise formation that would blend reverence with an ironic performativity. Loveless needs to cover or move away from the regalia to execute his libertine plans; in the presence of these cathected objects, play must cease, and a deeper form of affect takes over:

> Had I been conscious I'd been near the Temple
> Where this bright Relique of the Glorious Martyr
> Had been inshrin'd, 'thad spoil'd my soft Devotion!
> —'tis Sacrilege to dally where it is;
> A rude, a Sawcy Treason to approach it
> With an unbended knee; for Heav's sake, Madam,
> Let us not be profane in our Delights,
> Either withdraw, or hide that Glorious Object.
> (*Roundheads*, 4.2, 159–66)

These relics seem to recall him to a seriousness of purpose which he had been lacking; yet they also, paradoxically, repel him, distancing him from the corporeal satisfactions he seeks with Lady Lambert.

But if Loveless sees the jewels as relics, or as political fetishes, Lady Lambert's relation to them is fetishistic in quite a different register; like Henry Kissinger, she seems to feel that power is the ultimate aphrodisiac. "Thou art a Fool, the very sight of this / Raises my Pleasure higher," she cries (4.2, 167–68). She then deepens her sacrilege by suggesting that Loveless himself might wear the crown, albeit in a flirtatious and playful way: "Wou'd I cou'd set it on thy Head for ever" (4.2, 172). Most critics react to such suggestions with a horror that echoes Loveless's. Derek Hughes, for example, argues that this scene demonstrates the way in which a space for female empowerment has simultaneously opened and closed; the ambiguities of the social and political situation have made an emancipationist politics possible, but the women on display in the play remain inadequate to the task of claiming any secure ground for authority.[34] Robert Markley suggests that Lady Lambert's efforts to crown Loveless are not so much perverse as premature; only when she is redeemed as a royalist will she be able to unite her erotic and political desires.[35] But if Lady Lambert fails to perceive the sacred aura that surrounds these objects, seeing them instead as mere theatrical props in the performance of power, this is not entirely a bad thing. Like so many women in the misogynist traditions of satire, she has a taste for display and superficial pleasure, affectively unreceptive to the more hallowed principles of politics. And yet she preserves here an active power that contrasts sharply with Loveless's impotence. She finds Loveless's reaction both "Lovely, and unambitious," and indeed she is right. Similar words might be used to describe Oroonoko's period of passive waiting in Surinam before his revolt.

Behn may be flirting here with the possibility that Loveless could borrow something from Lady Lambert's playbook; if, as I am suggesting, Behn is advocating a less committed, more theatrical and playful form of kingship, then Lady Lambert's suggestion that Loveless parody the role of the king is the other half of a dialectical position awaiting synthesis: what is needed is the reverence and seriousness of Loveless combined with the willingness to indulge in theatricality, irony, and critical distance represented by Lady Lambert. This might, indeed, have been the synthesis Charles II had achieved at his own coronation, which, as Paula Backscheider has demonstrated, made sophisticated use of sacred and secular iconography to convey a carefully calculated representation of Stuart monarchy.[36] Of course, such play would nevertheless require the threat of force to back it up; Charles's sacred martyrdom inspires reverence but not fear, and thus the Stuart line cannot be restored to its rightful position without a prior act that inculcates a provisional virtue in the rabble and in the debased—an act that, as

Behn suggests, must be grounded in fear and power, not nobility or victimhood.

While this ado in London might seem to have little to do with intercultural contact or savagery, I suggest that the anomic space of the London street is, in fact, not so far removed from the similarly lawless setting of *Oroonoko*. To make this connection clearer, I turn briefly to Behn's last play, *The Widdow Ranter*.[37] This text returns to the convoluted relationship between violence and the savagery of the rabble; here, however, the rabble is more explicitly connected to the savages they resemble in their violence and unreason. It shares several concerns with *The Roundheads*, despite the different historical moment of its writing (the cusp of the Glorious Revolution rather than the Tory triumphalism of five years earlier): here, too, we find a lawless and chaotic space without a legitimate sovereign, where momentary performances of violence are necessary to restore an ambitious rabble to its proper place. The affinities of this play with *Oroonoko* have also often been noted, but I want to emphasize one in particular—the figure of Nathaniel Bacon, who, like Oroonoko, is impaired by his commitment to romantic self-narration. Bacon also, however, resembles *The Roundhead*'s Loveless and General Monck, because he fuses theatricality with violence to reconstruct a social order in which he can play no part. By the drama's end, Bacon is dead—a suicide and a victim of his own self-dramatization—but he leaves in his wake a social order restored by his military heroism and by his disciplining of a rabble that the drama hints is a new incarnation of a cannibal horde. The management of the colony has been left to more adept and nimble performers such as the low-born but charismatic widow.[38]

As is well known, Behn's play is loosely based on Nathaniel Bacon's rebellion in Virginia in 1676. The historical Bacon took up arms against the colonial administration of William Berkeley, whom Bacon and many settlers along the colonial frontier saw as sacrificing their safety in the service of trade and personal enrichment. Bacon and his army of frontiersmen first took up arms against the Doegs (and, not being terribly discriminating, killed many Susquehannocks in the process). Berkeley declared this unauthorized combat a rebellion; this declaration led to armed clashes between Bacon's forces and the weaker arms of the colonial administration. As Kathleen Brown has noted, Bacon's revolt crystallized a new form of colonial masculinity, one that emphasized "racist violence, populist politics, and military coercion" in contrast to

Berkeley's more genteel and patriarchal style.[39] Bacon also was adept at manipulating the passions of the frontier settlers of Virginia with racially based attacks on Indian nations; particularly galling to Bacon was the existence of communities of "friendly Indians," protected by English law but not subject to it—thus, in Bacon's view, resulting in unfair treatment of settler communities on the frontier. Bacon and his rebels made a point of attacking Indians indiscriminately and randomly.

Behn alters the facts of this historical narrative in striking ways that are not limited to the necessary simplifications of the stage.[40] Behn's governor is absent, with no one clearly representing legitimate English legal authority. Behn's Bacon is a deluded heroic-romantic; in this respect, he bears more than a passing resemblance to Oroonoko, whose tale appeared almost simultaneously with this play's composition. He also resembles Charles II's illegitimate son, James Scott, the Duke of Monmouth, who blended a cavalier's charisma with political ambition in ways that Behn clearly found both attractive and reprehensible.[41] The historical Bacon occupied Jamestown and burned it to the ground; Behn's Bacon spares it. The historical Bacon detested Indians; Behn's Bacon respects and honors them as noble enemies and entertains a miscegenous love for their Queen Semernia. The historical Bacon apparently died of dysentery in the Virginia swamps in the fall of 1676; Behn's character commits suicide. But Behn's text does draw on one historical aspect of the rebellion: the disintegration of class hierarchies and ordinary systems of government in the colony, the emergence of the rabble as a political force in need of management, and the need for the reimagining of authority in the New World—which here, as in *Oroonoko*, serves as a microcosm of modernity.[42]

Behn's tragicomedy combines two plots. The first involves the titular widow, a social climber who compensates for her low birth with a flamboyant, almost campy, disdain for formality and tradition. The tragic plot, my main focus here, involves Bacon's negotiations and war with the Indians—here lumped together into a single nation, in a textual echoing of Bacon's policy—and his rivalry with the Indian king, Cavarnio, for the love of Semernia, his queen.[43] It also encompasses Bacon's parallel rivalry with the established authorities of the colony, who are represented as part of the rabble, elevated to positions of authority by happenstance and the chaotic conditions of the colony. As in Surinam, the governor is absent—another key divergence from the historical record, for Bacon's rivalry with William Berkeley was central to the rebellion—and the council is controlled largely by the justices of the peace, Timorous Cornet, Whimsey, Whiff, and Boozer. The deputy governor, Colonel Wellman, and his ally Colonel Downright are a mark above these louts, but their effectiveness in governing without them is minimal; they too are dependent on their inferior minions to enforce a sovereign will. (In this, they share several features with the ineffectual though otherwise admirable Trefry in *Oroonoko*.) Confronted by Bacon's rebellion, Wellman and Downright summon the council to advise what should be done while the "governor and forces" from England are awaited (1.2).

Many critics have noted Bacon's romantic ambition; his desire is to become the founding sovereign of a new (possibly miscegenated) nation. But while his ambitions fail him in the end, the play does offer some usually unacknowledged evidence about his style of governance and his ambivalent relationship to popular power—the rabble that follows him. The usurping council rightly fears that Bacon will usurp the Indian king and found a new and hybrid nation, becoming sovereign in his own right of an honorable if wild frontier kingdom:

> 'Tis most certain that *Bacon* did not demand a Commission out of a design of serving us. . . . He passionately admires the Indian Queen, and under the pretext of a War, intends to kill the King her Husband, Establish himself in her heart, and . . . make himself a more formidable Enemy, than the Indians are. (1.2, 19–24)

Bacon perceives himself (and is perceived by others) as an aspiring sovereign lawmaker, battling to forge a new empire or civilization. However, he faces an important obstacle: his followers in this uprising are themselves a rabble, in most respects little different from the members of the council. Indeed, the play depicts his followers as little better than savages themselves in the rare moment when they appear onstage in a brief but important scene in the middle of the play. In this sequence, Bacon is escaping from the councilmen, who have summoned him under the guise of seeking an accommodation; when they attempt to imprison him instead, his followers—the "rabble with Staves and Clubs," in Behn's words (2.4, s.d.)—help him to escape. Yet the rabble exceeds its proper bounds, threatening the lives of some of the corrupt councilmen, and Bacon must himself hold them back—not with display but with a sword (2.4, s.d.). The rabble is not easily put down, however—acting in a manner reminiscent of the savages that surround them, they threaten a council member with fire, even with cannibalism, crying "Let's Barbicu this Fat Rogue" (2.4, 129). As Todd notes in her edition, this is a very early use of the term *barbicu*, antedating most usages given in the *OED*.[44] The term appears to originate in the Caribbean; its earliest recorded usage (in Edmund Hickeringill's *Jamaica Viewed*) is in a discussion of cannibalism: "some [of their captives] are slain, / And their Flesh forthwith Barbacu'd and eat / by them, their Wives and Children as choice meat. / Thence are they call'd *Caribs*, or *Cannibals*; / The very same that we *Man-eaters* call."[45] The rabble here, then, collapses into the savage, using the vocabulary of cannibalism in the service of revolt. The council is corrupt and acting above its station, to be sure, but it is the baser instinct of the mob that is most closely tied to a more specific form of corruption in the New World— the eruption of savagery into nominally civilized people. And the need for Bacon to alternate between using them and suppressing them reminds us that for Behn the mob is both a necessary prop for power and an ever-present savage force that is difficult to civilize.

The play rather abruptly eliminates the problem of Bacon's romantic heroism with his sudden suicide—itself layered over with unstable allusions to preceding heroic narratives, as Derek Hughes has noted.[46] But Bacon also recalls Oroonoko in his reasoning: as his lieutenant asks him what he has done, he replies that he has "secur'd [himself] from being a publick Spectacle upon the common Theatre of Death" (5.1, 292). This common theater—the scene of capital punishment and the reinscription of the rebellious body into a narrative of sovereign authority and power—is avoided here as Bacon claims control of his own narrative and his own body's capacity to signify, just as (as we shall see) Oroonoko fails to do. His fate, as his lieutenant Daring notes, is a bathetic and an ironic one; "he that could have conquered all *America* finds only here his scanty length of Earth" (5.1, 314). This result essentially erases Bacon's body from history, as anachronistic as the narratives he had attempted to inhabit. Like the tiger's heart, he is not meant to survive in the modern world.

Bacon's lieutenants, heirs to leadership of the rabble, patch things up voluntarily (in accord with Bacon's dying wishes) with the council. Bacon's dying words indicate regret for his rebellion and suggest that he wishes he had never forgotten "Duty—and Allegiance" (5.1, 309). In accord with his wishes as well as with the demands of the genre, the play ends on an artificially optimistic note, with the rabble carefully offstage. The rabble's feelings about the resolution of the conflict are not consulted; they are, presumably, satisfied that the Indians have been routed—in this comic fantasy, presumably never to cause trouble again, for they vanish utterly from the text after Semernia's death. The council is purged of its lesser elements, who return to their place among the rabble, and the rabble itself is returned to a docile state. Timorous, purged from the council, promises to return to a rural quietism: "I never thriv'd since I was a Statesman, left Planting, and fell to promising and Lying; I'le to my old Trade again, bask under the shade of my own Tobacco, and Drink my Punch in Peace" (5.1, 395–97). Thus one archaic genre—the heroic romance—is displaced in favor of another—the pastoral.

This artificial resolution—in which the cannibalistic rabble and the usurping council are transformed into a passive peasantry—raises many questions, particularly in its sharp contrast with the grisly and tragic dénouement of *Oroonoko*, to which I will return. It does, however, accord with the ending of *The Roundheads*, which in its final scenes turns usurpers back to their productive trades and marshals the rabble into support of sovereign power. In Behn's Virginia, things are less clear, but one threat to England's sovereignty—the just but impossible claims of the Indians—has been banished through extralegal action. In this sense, then, Bacon does found a new order and can be seen as a kind of lawmaker in spite of himself; his extralegal action vanquishes the lawless forces that threaten the colony, eliminating Indian trouble and reforging an alliance between sovereign and commoner. That he then must die suggests that the genre of the tragicomedy was not equipped to handle the contradictions this figure presented. The future of the colony belongs to Ranter—an unseemly, improper, and low-born woman who is nevertheless a crafty and deft performer. The fluid and indeterminate genre which *Oroonoko* inhabits—prose romance, protonovel, or memoir—does not suffer from such constraints and allows more difficult questions to be posed and managed, if not resolved. *The Widdow Ranter* and *The Roundheads*, then, both offer a version of sovereign power in which the rabble is managed by heroic and lawless outsiders, through a deft blend of violence and awe-inspiring performance. The burning-glass episode offers us a variation on this idea—the rabble, there figured as a racial other, are managed with a magical display that hints at violence but keeps it at a careful distance.

Objects and Obedience

The burning glass, the cavalier's sword, the crown jewels—each of these can serve as props in civility-making performances. I want now to juxtapose these props with the very different strategies for managing tensions between legality and sovereignty that Oroonoko himself uses, both in his West African home and in the anomic space of the colony. In both locations, the heroic prince faces situations in which tyrannical laws constrain him, and in both locations, he initially seeks to work at least nominally within the constraints of the law. In Surinam, however, he reaches a breaking point and seeks to permanently disclaim the colony's authority over him and his kindred, setting out to establish a new provisional legal order. However, Behn's narrative suggests on both occasions that his romantic idealism, including his faith both in the law and in the power of classical oratorical persuasion, are insufficient to meet the challenge of modern government. While Behn's more successful heroes adopt a more flexible attitude toward romance narratives, objects, and politics, Oroonoko's romantic credulity, exemplified by his unironized relationship to the tiger's heart with which I opened, is dangerously rigid, and his reliance on oratorical performance in moments of crisis is alarmingly naive. His calls to romantic heroism are insufficiently strategic; what is really needed, his tale suggests, is a manipulation of his subjects' fears.

Behn locates Oroonoko's origins in a despotic and oriental Africa; Coramantien is constructed from tropes of Asian tyranny and obedience. Coramantien's king, Oroonoko's grandfather, is a form of the oriental despot, treated as divinity incarnate. However, he attends not in the slightest to any transformation or production of affect in his subjects.[47] Indeed, he is blessed by the fact that his subjects "pay a most absolute Resignation to the Monarch" without any such attention (65). "The obedience the people pay their king was not at all inferior to what they paid their Gods" (66), the narrator adds; their adoration of their sovereign is a given, not the product of performance or labor. Indeed, for these orientalized subjects, their sovereign is himself a fetish, imbued with sacral and unquestionable authority, requiring of him no performance or effort of any kind. The text is not unambiguous about the source of this reverence, but the language strongly suggests that there is a natural—even magical—form of obedience and political affect in the kingdom, one that is static and that does not require constant renewal through displays of power. It is true that the threat of the monarch's absolute power of life and death over his subjects is also a theme in this portion of the text. The king's legal abduction of Imoinda into his seraglio gives us both of these reasons, holding them in tension: the narrator notes that "'tis Death to disobey; besides, held a most impious Disobedience" (66). The move from the fear of death to the fear of impiety sounds like bathos, but the passage hints that the infamy of disobedience is more to be feared than death. This sentiment would be understandable in a Christian context, but in this African Orient it registers a romantic attachment to arbitrary authority. Sovereignty and political subjectivity in Coramantien, then, is static and romantic; even a corrupt and degenerate figure like the king must be obeyed absolutely, without regard to punishment.

This passive obedience recalls the idea that "oriental" societies are composed of a binary model of governance, with the entire kingdom enslaved to the arbitrary will of the monarch. Behn uses this situation, however, to highlight tensions and ambiguities internal to absolutist regimes, particularly the question of whether absolute obedience is owed to a law that is supported by the sovereign or is rather to be paid to the sovereign command itself, which can in exceptional cases override legal conventions. Exceptional and extralegal power is, of course, subject to abuse. The difficulties of James II's own regime stemmed in part from what his critics saw as a misuse of the royal prerogative to override statute and convention.

Oroonoko confronts a similar situation when his betrothal to Imoinda is superseded by the king's legal kidnapping of her through the symbology of the veil, which secures her for the king's "use" (66). This situation poses for Oroonoko a legal problem rarely noted in the critical literature, for Oroonoko has a good legal argument against his grandfather; his own betrothal is binding and should not be voided by the king's extralegal action. Yet the king's word is also law, and there is apparently no mechanism for holding the king accountable. It is quite telling that Oroonoko's counselors suggest that rather than confront his grandfather directly, he ought to evade the strict performance of the law and regain his betrothed through trickery: "it was objected to him, that ... Imoinda being his lawful Wife, by solemn Contract, 'twas he was the injur'd Man, and might, if he so pleased, take Imoinda back, the Breach of the Law being on his Grand-father's side; and that if he could circumvent him, and redeem her from the *Otan* . . . it was both just and lawful for him so to do" (68). This little-noticed argument is peculiar. That Oroonoko might violate a royal edict in the service of a higher or more natural law—that he, in other words, evade the law in the service of justice—is a form of action usually considered using the language of equity, as Elliott Visconsi has noted.[48] So, while it is possible to look at this sequence as a defense of passivity, as Corrinne Harol has recently argued, Oroonoko's proximity to the throne suggests an alternative reading.[49] His father's actions have created an exceptional situation, and Oroonoko's resistance is not that of an ordinary subject but rather that of a shadow sovereign, taking extralegal action in defense of the law.

But further reflection suggests that if Oroonoko acts in accord with a higher law—that of honor—his actions in the service of those principles are dangerously deficient in cynicism. Oroonoko's efforts to circumvent his grandfather are only partially successful; though he does consummate his betrothal and blocks his grandfather's sexual access to Imoinda, his actions are discovered, and Imoinda is sold into slavery as punishment. The ancient king dissembles about this punishment, since he fears a rebellion on Oroonoko's part, believing with Imoinda that the army will side with the prince in any civil conflict (77)—a belief that sits strangely with the kingdom's strong traditions of obedience. In fact, it is here that we see what trumps the king's absolute cultural authority: love and honor, the twin virtues of romance and heroic tragedy. Oroonoko rebels against the king's authority but is true to a higher law: the principles of honor, which encompass those of love. If his officers and soldiers are loyal to him, it is because for them the laws of honor trump even those of their king.

Behn's portrait of Coramantien, then, is fashioned from two overlapping and competing discursive traditions: the fantasy of oriental despotism and the traditions of chivalric romance. This intrusion of the romance narrative into the imagined stasis of her despotic oriental kingdom is crucial to our reading of Oroonoko's actions in Surinam, where Oroonoko holds true to the narratives of romance and honor despite the fundamental difference of the setting and narrative mode. For Hobbes, romance narrative threatened the stability of kingdoms, encouraging dreams of vainglory that served as the aristocrat's counterpart to religious enthusiasm.[50] Behn's critique of romance works differently: while in Coramantien, romance attitudes are part of efforts to outdo tyranny by sleight of hand, strict adherence to chivalric convention in the New World by characters like Oroonoko and Bacon reveals a hazardous rigidity, a mark of a premodern sclerosis of thought. When Oroonoko grows to find his captivity intolerable, he urges his fellow slaves to rise and throw off their chains, appealing to honor in an effort to transform the slaves from victims of violence into virtuous subjects in a new social order. But his appeal to honor is a crucial error; he relies on the power of oratory as such to motivate the slave rabble in the service of a noble cause but cannot muster the actual violence that his plan requires. He thus crucially underestimates the degree to which violence, implicit or explicit, is an essential element in civilizing the modern rabble.

Legally, Oroonoko's problems in Surinam are similar to what he suffered in Coramantien. As was the case there, he is subjected to laws that operate unjustly, or at least against his interests; yet he prefers, for a time, to allow the legal order to remain intact, preferring to wait for the arrival of a higher authority to make him free in law, rather than attempting to take matters into his own hands and free himself. In choosing this passivity, he is encouraged, perhaps cynically, by the narrator and Trefry. To restore himself, Imoinda, and his heir (still in utero) to their proper places, he must either clear up this legal mess from within the legal order or—as he eventually opts to do—make a radical political move by nullifying the authority of his captors, establishing for himself a new and separate polity. This, I think—and not, as Harol suggests, a departure from the sphere of politics—is why he joins hands with his fellow slaves and leads them into the forest and out of captivity; this is also why in his rhetoric he treats them as though they are savages to be brought out of the state of nature.[51] The deprivations they suffer, he argues, are "fitter for Beasts than Men; Senseless Brutes, than Humane Souls. . . . They had lost the Divine Quality of Men, and were become insensible Asses" (105). Oroonoko proposes a flight through the forest and looks forward to a new legal order: "They would Travel towards the Sea; Plant a New Colony, and Defend it by their Valour; and when they could find a Ship . . . they wou'd Seize it, and make it a Prize, till it had transported them to their own Countries" (106). This heavily gendered language of valor and liberty blurs the line between civic humanism's borrowings from Roman political rhetoric and the lushness of romance. Full of the language of masculine honor, it also carries echoes of the Ciceronian version of the civilizing process, in which rhetoric brings wild folk from the state of savagery into a civil order. The violence and valor that the escaped slaves will exhibit will make them human again and may allow them to found a new city, but it is through the foundational power of Oroonoko's rhetoric that they can be persuaded to make the effort to pursue this restoration, with Oroonoko himself serving as his leader and their sovereign.

Behn prominently features Oroonoko's efforts to civilize through oratory in ways that recall the writings of Roman rhetoricians, particularly Cicero, for whom oratory, not violence, is the crucial element in bringing men from savagery into civility and founding the civil order. In an influential passage from the beginning of *De Inventione*, he writes,

> There was a time when men wandered at large in the fields like animals and lived on wild fare; they did nothing by the guidance of reason, but relied chiefly on physical strength. . . . At this juncture a man—great and wise I am sure—became aware of the power latent in man and the wide field offered by his mind for great achievements if one could develop this power and improve it by instruction. Men were scattered in the fields and hidden in sylvan retreats when he assembled and gathered them in accordance with a plan; he introduced them to every useful and honourable occupation. . . . He transformed them from wild savages [*feris et immanibus*] into a kind and gentle folk.[52]

To Cicero, this kind of foundational rhetoric is also essential to the preservation of justice and equity: "Certainly only a speech at the same time powerful and entrancing could have induced one who had great physical strength to submit to justice without violence, so that he suffered himself to be put on a par with those among whom he could excel." Language and performance come together to overcome mere strength and violence.[53] Behn was familiar with this Ciceronian story of origins; she references it in her early verse tribute to Thomas Creech, in which she compares women to savages and the translation of classical literature into the vernacular as a civilizing moment.[54]

Behn's Surinam crushes Ciceronian idealism. While Ciceronian and chivalric modes of leadership and sovereignty are hardly identical, Behn brings the two together in the person of Oroonoko, whose admiration for heroes and for Romans blinds him to the practical problems of modern sovereignty. In this microcosm of modernity, violence is an essential supplement to performance. The failure of Oroonoko's rhetoric shows this clearly; it can inspire momentary action but is unable to fundamentally change political relationships. The slaves are unable to be roused by mere words; blinded by English whips and disheartened by the cries of their women and children, they abandon and betray Oroonoko to the ragtag army of commoners they face. Oroonoko excoriates his turncoat minions because they are ready to "be whipped into the knowledge of the *Christian Gods*" (109). Even as he laments the failure of his rhetoric, Oroonoko offers a backhanded compliment to the violence inherent in the civilizing process.

The Caribs are not "whipped into knowledge," as we have seen. Rather than experiencing enslavement, they are drawn onto a path of greater civility and subordination—docility in the face of overweening technological power—a trope that will be repeated with a vengeance in Daniel Defoe's writings. As I have noted, the colonial subjection of the Caribs offers a model for the management of the rabble. This management is also taken up in Behn's drama of the 1680s in her treatments of the unruly underclass and the pretentious cits who are their alter egos. The drama, like *Oroonoko*, positions these classes as ineradicable features of modernity; it also hints, as *Oroonoko* does, that they are best managed with a performance of deferred violence.[55] The final section of this chapter argues that Oroonoko's execution and dismemberment offer nightmarish visions of what happens when the rabble cannot be managed and when anarchic violence is unleashed to pose as sovereignty. Oroonoko's failure to found an independent colony leaves his fellow slaves in a savage condition; the absence of the governor also leaves the rabble as the sovereigns of the colony, with disastrous consequences.

Mangled Kings

Oroonoko, like *The Widdow Ranter*, might also be said to feature a barbecue; the colonial rabble's desecration of Oroonoko's corpse can be understood as a distant relative of Caribbean cannibalism. More persuasive, perhaps, are some critics' efforts to see Oroonoko's body as a figure for the tobacco trade.[56] If these readings are correct, then we might suggest that the burning glass makes a covert return here as well; such devices were commonly used as a way to light tobacco, and it is in fact likely that the narrator's kinsman carried the device to Surinam for just such a purpose. Hobbes himself refers to this practice in his *Philosophical Problems*: "You have seen men light their Tobacco at the Sun with a burning glass, or with a ball of Cristal, held which way they will indifferently."[57] Burning glasses were commonly used in some contact zones in the Americas; though I have no direct evidence linking the two in Surinam, it certainly seems likely, given the role that the substance and the device play in this text. By the early eighteenth century, tobacco boxes were being built with burning glasses encased in their lids. If the burning glass in the Carib village defers the violence it refers to, translating it into political affect and fantasizing a subordinate and disciplined role for the savage and the rabble, then the violence it embodies resurfaces here, in Oroonoko's devastated body.

Such a resurfacing seems less peculiar when we realize that Oroonoko's punishment serves, in part, as an emblem of the hazards of practicing a sovereignty whose authority relies entirely on violence—a kind of governance that is not categorically illegitimate in Behn's worldview but one that is alarmingly subject to reappropriation by the very savages and commoners it is meant to control. If Oroonoko is read as a version of James II (and, by extension, the tendencies of his style of governance), then this scene may reflect a concern about James's reputation for brutality. Critics have not taken sufficient note of the way the specific manner of Oroonoko's execution replicates the traditional English (and European) punishments for treason—a punishment used throughout English history from medieval times into the nineteenth century but rarely used with such extravagance as during James II's reign, especially during the terrible period following the suppression of Monmouth's uprising.[58] Behn's narrative ought not be read as a straightforward allegory of these events, certainly, but it is quite possible to see Oroonoko's fate as simultaneously representing the excesses of James II's political violence and a warning that this violence might return to haunt him. In fact, I suggest, the confusion and collapse of any easy analogy here may be precisely the point: the excessive violence of James's response to the uprising has created conditions in which the line between sovereign and anarchic violence has become indistinct, and hence Oroonoko simultaneously figures James II's victims and the sovereign himself. And when the colonists seek to transform Oroonoko's maimed body into a fetish of their own power, they find that the raw violence objectified in Oroonoko's limbs signifies in ways that they cannot control. The placement of his quarters in prominent locations throughout the colony is a performance of a sovereign power: it fails to establish legitimacy, however, because what it signifies is mere terror bereft of reverence or mystery.

Oroonoko faces a traitor's traditional fate: he is first forced to witness his own mutilation and partial immolation and then posthumously quartered and displayed. Behn's narrative here calls to mind the wave of executions in England—the aftermath of the Bloody Assizes—that followed the Monmouth uprising. Hanging, drawing, and quartering had been the law of the land to punish treason since 1351, when it was enshrined in the Statute of Treasons:

> That you be drawn on a hurdle to the place of execution where you shall be hanged by the neck and being alive cut down, your privy members shall be cut off and your bowels taken out and burned before you, your head severed from your body and your body divided into four quarters to be disposed of at the King's pleasure.[59]

This sentence had been carried out against the regicides in the wake of Charles II's restoration and against suspected Jesuit plotters during the period of the Popish Plot.

But the Bloody Assizes in 1685 made use of this sentence on an unprecedented scale. Following the Duke of Monmouth's uprising, at least a hundred of his supporters were subjected to this punishment, their dismembered corpses decorating crossroads and town gates throughout western England.[60] Peter Earle informs us that

> if anyone should miss the sight of the actual executions they could hardly avoid the two hundred and fifty pickled heads and the thousand quarters of corpses which were even more widely distributed than the executions themselves, being stuck on spears and poles at cross-roads, bridges, and other prominent places throughout the area. Here they were to stay till the summer of 1686 when the King made his tour of inspection of the West Country. Now he was to see what his subjects had had to see for nearly a whole year and, sick at the sight, he ordered the rotting heads and quarters to be taken down and buried.[61]

Like Oroonoko's corpse, the corpses of the Monmouth rebels—and most others subjected to this sentence—would be preserved and memorialized in a way that reinscribes them in a narrative of state power, then into material markers of sovereign supremacy and the fate of rebellion. (They would also, perhaps not incidentally, be coated with tar, making them as glistening and black as Oroonoko's fine skin.) But these corpses did not signify in an unambiguous way, and they lent strength to the Whig opposition by creating a new catalog of martyrs, useful for rallying Protestants against James II's succession.[62] Behn's text plays on this ambiguity.

By seeking to replicate sovereign power, the colonial administration in Surinam attempts to cathect Oroonoko's corpse, transforming it from a body into a sign of their power, an icon of their authority. In so doing, they seek to make the body speak in their own words, rather than giving voice to its own authority. Oroonoko, we notice, tries to reverse the grammar of this ritual in a very specific way, when he disembowels himself. Having failed to hold off the crowd that seeks to bring him to justice, "he ripped up his own belly, and took his bowels and pulled them out" (116). Though we might join Charlotte Sussman in seeing this gesture as an allusion to Imoinda's pregnant womb—which Oroonoko has also destroyed, securing his offspring from slavery—it is also suggestive of the longstanding punishments for treason.[63] In tearing out his own intestine, he attempts to preempt the scene of punishment; by attempting to make himself his own executioner, he suggests that he now recognizes himself as the only legitimate sovereign in the scene, with authority over his own body. In this, Oroonoko echoes the Caribbean war captains; abandoning the claim to sovereignty over others, he chooses instead the stoic path of a radical self-sovereignty. But the gesture's inflection with the language of treason underlines a more specifically political significance.[64]

Indeed, the events leading up to this garbled execution are specifically staged to highlight questions about how law and sovereign authority work with or against one another. After Oroonoko's rebellion, he is sheltered at Parham, the estate of the absent governor Willoughby, currently managed by Trefry, Willoughby's agent and Oroonoko's master. Oroonoko is sought for punishment, however, by the representatives of the colony, in the form of the deputy governor's council. Byam, the deputy governor, is a character drawn from history and one who probably knew Behn in Surinam; though a royalist, Behn makes him here stand in for the worst tendencies in the growing hegemony of the rabble over their social betters. He appears first in the narrative agitating against Oroonoko after the slaves have fled the plantation; Behn notes that he seems to be motivated by personal pique and ambition, for he holds no property in the colony: "he had nothing, and so need fear nothing" from the rebellion (107). Though Byam governs the plantations at large by virtue of his appointment, his authority does not extend to the estate of Willoughby—that authority has been left to Trefry. Thus Behn, once more revising the historical record, stages a conflict between two systems of law when Byam and his council prepare to move against Oroonoko. The council administers the law; Trefry, acting on behalf of the monarch, represents principles of justice, honor, and equity that exceed and surpass positive law.

The council, like Byam, are largely propertyless and low of birth; a tragic counterpart to Virginia's comic counselors, they are "such notorious Villains as *Newgate* never transported; and possibly originally were such, who understood neither the Laws of *God* or *Man*," hardly better than savages themselves (112). These "special Rulers of the Nation," as the narrator calls them (112), are summoned by Byam to discuss Oroonoko's fate. They resolve to hang him as an example to other rebels. But Trefry calls on the higher law of sovereign equity to overrule the council; representing "the King's Person" (112), Trefry has the right to offer sanctuary to his servants and slaves. Byam, historically a royalist, is here aligned with low-born modernity, exercising a tyrannical authority that may only be resisted by the exceptional sovereign prerogative. His response to Trefry's claim of sovereign immunity is to use deceit, decoying Trefry while his agents kidnap Oroonoko. In using his cleverness this way—to apply the positive law of the council even in the face of a sovereign decision—unexpectedly repeats Oroonoko's own end run around the law in resisting his grandfather's seizure of Imoinda. Positive law grants Imoinda to Oroonoko and grants Oroonoko to the governor's council for punishment. Oroonoko resists the exceptional sovereign decree; so does Byam when, leading Trefry away from the colony, he delegates his henchman Bannister to remove Oroonoko from the sanctuary and return him to the space of colonial law.

If the text manifests, in part, a warning to James II that his role as sacred king is jeopardized by his own violent excesses, we might find evidence to support that view in the way that *Oroonoko*'s climax blends the anarchic violence of the savage rabble with the horrifying spectacle of sovereign terror. Mingling colonial anomie with James's heavy-handed response to treason, Behn's narrative warns that violence is a fragile basis for sovereign authority. In the narrative's catastrophe, the anarchic violence inflicted on Oroonoko mimics and parodies the violence of sovereign power; Oroonoko is butchered in a way that approximates the prescribed techniques for drawing and quartering but also garbles them. His genitals are severed and burned, though he is not hung; he is quartered but not disemboweled. The garbled syntax of his execution blurs the lines between sovereign punishment and lawless violence.[65] The fact that Behn continued to insist on James's legitimacy does nothing to undermine this interpretation. She here merely recommends a policy that would deploy a different kind of sovereign theatricality, instilling a kind of respect, civility, and awe, not fear, in his subjects.

In the end, Oroonoko's body is as much a romantic memento as that of the tiger's heart with which this chapter opened. Behn mourns its obsolescence even as she argues, reluctantly, for a revived and strengthened monarchy more aware of the artificial and performative quality of cathected objects. The sovereign in her work must not only stand outside the civil polity and above the law; he must also stand outside and above the objects that symbolize that authority, using them as tools rather than deferring to them as imbued with nonmaterial value. To immerse oneself in the chivalric ideology of kingship was a luxury no longer available to modern sovereigns. Albert Rivero has suggested that we read *Oroonoko* as a work of mourning for a passing world of fixed aristocratic values and virtues.[66] And if Richard Kroll's argument that Oroonoko serves as a warning to James II is founded on more precise and compelling scholarship than Rivero's, it is nevertheless the case that Rivero's attitude stands out as more perceptive, positioning James II's failure not as a defect that could still be corrected but as a crucial flaw that has already sown destruction. But Rivero's reading can be supplemented by a recognition that Behn saw an alternate model of leadership and of a discipline I have called rabble management. Disciplining the rabble, much like civilizing the savage, requires practices that delicately blend violence and performance. By superimposing the rabble and the savage in the burning-glass episode, *Oroonoko* emphasizes the role of trickery and deceit in the civilizing process. Instead of blending oratory or persuasion with violence, which the drama offers us, the burning-glass episode emphasizes the essential element of mystery that must shroud the threat of violence. In so doing, it suggests a temporal dislocation between sovereign and subject not found in the drama. And it demonstrates clearly the attitude that a modern sovereign must, regrettably, have: cynical, distant, and unromantic—all the things that Oroonoko and his tiger's heart are not.

If, in Behn's drama, violence is an integral part of performance, then the burning-glass episode suggests that the logical endpoint of this performance is the strategic deployment of mysterious objects—or props, depending on your point of view. We might say that the narrative argues for a calculated fetishism that explores how sacral objects might be employed to tame the savage or the rabble. And yet Behn's critique is hardly that of the Enlightenment. I do believe that she saw the role of fetishes in establishing authority as in some ways transitional; there might be hope for a sort of neofeudal subjectivity that would depend less on fear and more on genuine love for one's superiors. But Behn's corpus leaves us with the sense that this dream of natural affection is at best obsolete, at worst a dangerous fantasy. This is no less true for the domestic savage than it is for the unenlightened Other of colonialism. The English rabble also finds itself incapable of a nonfetishistic relationship to political power, requiring concrete objects to instill it with the reverential affect appropriate to the political subject. The tiger's heart is one such object, transformed from body into the kernel of a sequence of romantic narratives. But because Oroonoko is himself entwined in the tales he tells—and cannot affectively stand outside the romantic narratives suggested by the oft-wounded heart—he is ultimately a failure. Had he acted more like the narrator's brother—a cynical manipulator of objects—he might have found a way to use the quasi-magical status of the heart to further his bid for freedom. His failure instead allows his corpse to become a sign of the dangers of the opposite pole—raw force—in the practice of government.

CHAPTER 3

Talking Guns and Savage Spaces: Daniel Defoe's Civilizing Technologies

> As for the gun it self, he would not so much as touch it for several days after; but would speak to it, and talk to it, as if it had answer'd him, when he was by himself; which, as I afterwards learn'd of him, was to desire it not to kill him.
>
> —Daniel Defoe, *Robinson Crusoe*[1]

Friday may understand guns better than Crusoe does. Although Friday is innocent of the gun's inner workings, he sees something that Crusoe has missed: it is Crusoe's power to dispense violence, rather than cultural authority or friendship, that has started Friday down the path toward civility and virtue. Conversely, Crusoe's disavowal of his own violence reverberates throughout the novel, from his escape from the Barbary captivity to his trip across the Pyrenees at the novel's end. But his disavowal is particularly pronounced in the novel's precolonial settings: Africa and Crusoe's Caribbean island. In these scenes of colonial encounter and technological power, Daniel Defoe uses Crusoe and his gun to explore the role of violence in creating civil subjects, as well as the ways in which the ideology of British liberty veils that violence. Crusoe's weapons serve as a figure for sovereignty's violent underpinnings as well as of the ideology of liberty that makes sovereignty's violence tolerable.

Gunpowder plays a key role in Defoe's complex ruminations on authority and violence. *Robinson Crusoe* (1719) tempts readers to see the gun as a straightforward index of Britain's temporal advancement and fitness to civilize the savage, but Defoe's other colonial fictions point toward a more complex reading in which gunpowder figures more disturbing aspects of modernity. In *The Farther Adventures of Robinson Crusoe* (1719) and *Captain Singleton* (1720), gunpowder appears most prominently in scenes of atavistic violence and massacres—particularly massacres perpetrated by men untied from traditional forms of social organization and authority. Like Aphra Behn's, Defoe's writings show an extraordinary interest in the loci of political power and the dangers that mob rule poses to political legitimacy; his fictions of encounter extend and complicate his poetic ruminations of the late Stuart and early Hanoverian eras discussed in the introduction. Defoe criticism has often noted his interest in what we might call the modern individual unloosed from traditional authority—both that individual as posited by variations on liberal theories of government and as experienced historically in the erosion of social hierarchy. However, these texts reflect a number of serious reservations about this new political individual and display concern with the question of how that individual might best be governed.[2] Defoe's politics are what we might call modern not primarily because of any individualist or protodemocratic impulses; rather, facing new forms of social and political organization, he struggles to understand how the undisciplined body and chaotic political spaces might be made civilized and thus capable of self-government. The prescriptions for improving self and government in Defoe's late writings are well known, and scholars such as Mary Poovey have closely examined the tensions in Defoe's writings between impulses toward improved self-government and an ongoing interest in the role of the state in managing the liberal individual.[3] Crusoe's island initially seems to provide a model for a new indirect form of government, one that recalls Behn's tactical displays of magic: Crusoe's gun civilizes Friday by amazing and enchanting him. However, when Crusoe leaves his islands for more open, less well-defined spaces—what Everett Zimmerman has called "no-man's lands"—gunpowder unleashes rather than restrains human passions and unruly bodies.[4] In tracing the trajectory of gunpowder from civilizing agent to enabler of mobocratic massacre, I am also tracing one of the possible histories of modernity as Defoe understood it: the desacralizing of sovereignty which I take these texts to narrate.[5]

The objective counterpart to the ideology of liberal individualism is the transformation of the British state and the monarchy in the decades following the Glorious Revolution. The events that Behn had warned of and abhorred had, by 1719, simultaneously reduced the power of the monarch and begun a tremendous expansion in the size of the state, enlarging both its civic institutions and its military capacity. Defoe as a poet, polemicist, and propagandist had been intimately involved in the practicalities of this expansion since the late seventeenth century. Speaking broadly, Defoe generally championed the doctrine of a people's right to rule, but his definition of "the people" is sharply limited to property owners, excluding the majority of male Britons and virtually all women. In this respect, of course, Defoe follows the dominant strain of liberal and republican thought, which was in general not egalitarian, as I have already discussed. Throughout these decades, the rapid development of new state institutions (the permanent army, the National Bank) progressed alongside new challenges to the precise boundaries of the political community of Britain, as the Act of Union fused the previously distinct parliaments of Scotland and England and as public debate swirled around the question of how much authority popular power ought to have over the crown as well as the Houses of Parliament. The legitimacy of state institutions and of new political arrangements were repeatedly called into question, both in print and, during the Jacobite rising of 1715, on the battlefield. Questions of resistance and conquest continued to exert pressure on notions of an English liberty that guaranteed the rights of all Englishmen, or Britons, against the powers of the sovereign. A number of events in the decade preceding the publication of *Robinson Crusoe* highlighted issues of force and liberty; the highly visible Sacheverell trial of 1709–10, for example, engaged the question of whether William III gained the English crown by conquest. This question of the role of force in the revolutionary events of 1688 had purportedly been laid to rest in 1693, when the radical Whig Charles Blount's tract *King William and Queen Mary Conquerors* had been publicly burned by the hangman. The Sacheverell trial reawakened the issue, however, and it continued to make appearances in political writings of the period.[6] The Jacobite risings of 1715 undoubtedly reinforced these questions and reignited interest in the role of force in establishing political legitimacy.[7] If, as I have argued, Defoe's writing is troubled by the question of how property and political right develop, his fictions of cultural difference and political origin are very much invested in renarrating founding political moments with an eye to the question of how a liberal subject might be governed.

This question of the conquest—one which concerns not just the events of 1688 but those of 1066 as well—is intimately connected with the ideology of English (or British) liberty and the development of modern liberalism. Ascendant Whigs in the early eighteenth century sought an ideological framework and governmental practices suited both to the demands of a more powerful and centralized state and to the complexities of a modern commercial society. While emphasizing the limited role of the British monarch, the Whig regime also presided over significant challenges to the traditional rights of British subjects. This period of its reign coincided with emergency legislation that closely monitored and suppressed Tory and Jacobite dissent, sometimes violently, in what Kathleen Wilson describes (perhaps hyperbolically) as "state-sponsored terrorism."[8] The Whiggish relocation of sovereignty from the monarch into Parliament had not, many political writers argued, fundamentally liberalized the nation; a sovereign parliament could be just as tyrannical as a monarch.[9] Hence the relationship of state power, violence, and consent could hardly have been more visible during the years leading up to the appearance of Defoe's novels of contact. I suggest that these problems are at the heart of Defoe's texts and undergird their use of guns as a form of sovereign magic and as emblems of modernity's unleashed passions.

How to Say Things with Guns

Defoe's *Robinson Crusoe* has long been subject to political readings; its presentation of Crusoe in isolation from society and political institutions has often been read as a watershed in literary studies of "natural man," while more recent criticism has explored constructions of race and empire through the relationship between Friday and Crusoe.[10] By approaching Defoe's most famous novel through a singular intercultural object—Crusoe's guns—I seek to reframe this discussion to read the novel as symptomatic of an unstable, labile attitude toward shifting theories and practices of sovereignty in Defoe's day. *Robinson Crusoe* uses gunpowder in part to underscore the way that British liberty emerges from and depends on civility-making violence. Military technology is portrayed as a simultaneous display of and mystification of power, using the flagrant display of violence—"the unrestrained presence of the sovereign," in Foucault's words—while also mystifying Crusoe's relationships as voluntary, friendly, and benevolent.[11] Crusoe's muskets and pistols are the key figures in this exploration of the violent origins of British political order, for gunpowder's workings are both spectacular and mysterious. The novel's precolonial settings are crucial to its politics not only because they elaborate and develop fictions of a state of nature but also because they use martial technology as a figure for the mysterious and yet flamboyant violence of sovereign power. Crusoe's gun speaks powerfully and yet, in its inscrutable operations, cloaks the violence that it represents. This enchanted technology, which simultaneously conceals and reveals, allows Defoe to speculate about the efficacy of violence and ideology, suggesting that political order is sustained by a veneer of freedom laid over a foundation of overpowering force. As Crusoe encounters various savages, he is very much conscious of the puzzle that his gun poses to them; nevertheless, he consistently disavows the shadow that his technological power casts over his relationships with Africans and Caribs, preferring instead to characterize his relationships as free, open, and founded on benevolence and loyalty. However, the novel does not unambiguously affirm Crusoe's violence or his Machiavellian practices; discomfort with the logic of sovereign violence is visible at several points in the text. In particular, the figure of Friday interrupts and interrogates Crusoe's violence and his blindness. Friday's relationship with Crusoe's gun suggests that he recognizes the limits of Crusoe's benignity; his knowledge facilitates his later appropriation of that technology's power for his own ends.

The rhetoric of liberation and concealed violence is prominent in Friday's first appearance in the novel—which is simultaneously his entry into Western political relationships and the beginning of his conversion to Christianity. The novel presents this moment both as a military encounter and as an ambiguous rescue mission. In this scene, Friday is about to be devoured by his political and military enemies; Crusoe's firearm slays an attacker and leaves Friday at liberty to make a choice—whether to align himself with an alien wielding a weapon of startling power or to run for his life:

> The poor savage [Friday] who fled, but had stopped; though he saw both his enemies fallen, and kill'd, as he thought; yet was so frighted with the fire, and noise of my piece; that he stood stock still, and neither came forward or went backward, tho' he seem'd rather enclin'd to fly still, than to come on; I hollow'd again to him, and made signs to come forward, which he easily understood, and came a little way, then stopp'd again. . . . I cou'd then perceive that he stood trembling, as if he had been taken prisoner, and had just been to be kill'd, as his two enemies were. (203)

Crusoe, gun in hand, is an ambiguous savior. Friday is forced to make a decision that is more difficult than it first appears: to approach the mystery of technological power or to trust in the nontechnological but tried-and-true recourse of his own body.[12] Crusoe himself has dreamed of this moment in advance and imagined it as a way in which he, too, could be delivered from his island captivity.[13] In Crusoe's reading of the event, the scene is an unambiguous instance of his own benevolence. Friday, on the other hand, makes visible the ambiguity of his rescue and conversion. Though Friday opts to take shelter behind Crusoe's gun, his relationship with that weapon remains unsteady. While he appears to place his trust in Crusoe, he suspects that real power does not lie with the man but with his mysterious weapon. Imbuing that weapon with subjectivity as well as power, Friday petitions it with prayer, as we have seen: "As for the gun it self, he would . . . speak to it, and talk to it . . . which, as I afterwards learn'd of him, was to desire it not to kill him" (212). Still in fear of his life, Friday trusts only tenuously in Crusoe; he remains visibly aware of Crusoe's sovereign power of life and death over him. But his mistrust is displaced from the agent of violence to its tool; he fetishizes the weapon, imbuing it with a fictional, and potentially hostile, subjectivity.

We might, with apologies to Henry Louis Gates, Jr., say this sequence inaugurates the "trope of the talking gun." In Gates's classic reading of early slave narratives, he identifies the Talking Book as a crucial trope in early Anglo-African writing, recurring in early slave narratives by James Gronniosaw, Quobna Cugoano, Olaudah Equiano, and others. The trope seeks to engage with the "paradox of representing, of containing somehow, the oral within the written, precisely when oral black culture was transforming itself into a written culture."[14] The trope, in its purest form, represents an unlettered African or Amerindian who listens to a book, expecting or hoping to hear it speak. In Equiano's *Interesting Narrative*, for example, the youthful Equiano expresses "a great curiosity to talk to the books": "for that purpose I have often taken up a book, and have talked to it, and then put my ears to it, when alone, in hopes it would answer me."[15] Equiano also extends this trope to other Western technologies. Trying to sleep while traveling from the Caribbean to North America, he is disturbed by devices that appear to observe his every move:

> The first object that engaged my attention was a watch which hung on the chimney. . . . I was quite surprised at the noise it made, and was afraid it would tell the gentleman any thing I might do amiss: and when I immediately after observed a picture hanging in the room which appeared constantly to look at me, I was still more affrighted, having never seen such things as these before. At one time

I thought it was something relative to magic; and not seeing it move I thought it might be some way the whites had to keep their great men when they died, and offer them libation as we used to do to our friendly spirits.[16]

Gates points out that Equiano's performance of naiveté suggests a high degree of sophistication, a critical relationship to the power of technology in European culture. Equiano's belief that a clock or a book speaks to his master is accurate, in a sense:

> Under the guise of the representation of his naive self, he is naming or reading Western culture closely, underlining relationships between subjects and objects that are implicit in commodity cultures. Watches do speak to their masters, in a language that has no other counterpart in this culture, and their language frequently proves to be the determining factor in the master's daily existence.[17]

However, Gates emphasizes that Equiano's reading of European culture calls attention to his own status as a commodity. Gates argues that the commodity status of the slave makes it impossible for him to enter into a discursive relationship with other commodities; the commodity requires a subject to endow it with life: "Of course the book does not speak to him. Only subjects can endow an object with subjectivity; objects, such as a slave, possess no inherent subjectivity of their own."[18] Friday's reading and performance, however, unveil a different moment in the history of violence and servitude: the way that military technology facilitates and complicates scenes of commerce, contract, and friendship.

The parallels between Equiano and Friday are surprising and important. Like Equiano, Friday begins his relationship with European "civility" as a slave, albeit in a way less clearly defined by structures of law and economics than in Equiano's world. Seeing Friday as a slave, it is possible to understand his efforts to fetishize Crusoe's gun and thus to communicate with it as an independent agent. Friday observes the operations of power in his relationship with Crusoe, much as the "naive" voice of Equiano registers something true about technology's power to signify. But powerful as watch, portrait, and book are in Equiano's narrative, they do not manifest the naked force of the firearm. When Friday prays to Crusoe's flintlock, he displays an awareness that sovereign power grows from the barrel of a gun. That Crusoe himself does not appear to recognize this connection suggests that Defoe is investigating a problem of ideology: the benign sovereign and exemplar of civilization is not able to acknowledge the extent to which the social field in which he exists is constituted by violence. Friday's encounter with Crusoe's weapon, and his perception of its determinative role in establishing the discursive relationship between Crusoe and himself, offers a different reading of that process. We see, in Friday's relationship with Crusoe's technologies of violence, a kind of Caribbean signifying, in Gates's terms. Friday's "mistake" correctly identifies the locus of authority on the island and calls attention to the violent conditions in which civilization and liberty emerge.

Crusoe's political relationship with Friday is foreshadowed long before Crusoe is cast away in the Caribbean. In this section of the novel, Crusoe escapes from captivity in Salé ("Salee") and flees down the coast of West Africa. In Crusoe's encounters with Xury, the Moor, and with the African peoples he meets during his escape, his gun signifies the violence that is a key component in the establishment of "free" association and trade. But the role of violence is obscured—cloaked, in Xury's case, only by the misreading of his submission to power as "loyalty" but, in the encounter with the savage, figured by the cryptic and invisible power of gunpowder. Crusoe's bid for freedom from slavery in North Africa is strangely framed in order to deflect its implicit violence. After spending several years in captivity, Crusoe escapes by means of trickery and a captured fowling piece. At sea with an adult Moor and a "boy," Xury, Crusoe throws the former overboard and threatens him with a gun; Xury is also threatened, but Crusoe agrees to make him "a great man" in exchange for his undying loyalty (23). Xury professes loyalty to Crusoe, although this loyalty is obtained under duress; the same fate of being tossed overboard awaits him if he does not agree. The boy chooses a submissive friendship with Crusoe over a likely death. In Xury's case—notoriously—this choice ends badly, with the boy sold into slavery. Yet Crusoe here manifests a remarkable ability to commit acts of violence and disguise them in the rhetoric of liberty, accepting Xury's statement that he is "willing" to be sold (34).[19]

The configuration of violence and acquiescence is repeated and elaborated when Crusoe and Xury encounter savages on the coast of West Africa; this elaboration in its turn offers a paradigm for later episodes with Friday and other Caribs by describing a meeting filled with latent violence in terms of a successful, and peaceful, parley. Crusoe's deployment of his gun in this scene simultaneously displays and mystifies power. The Africans, in their reaction to Crusoe's gun, anticipate the amazement of Friday and of other Caribs who view the technology of force with shock and awe. In this instance, the gun's violence is unleashed on wild beasts rather than in mortal combat with other men, as Crusoe's initial parley is interrupted by an explosion of animal savagery—an eruption that is quickly ended when Crusoe flaunts his prowess by striking down a leopard:

> We made signs of thanks to them, for we had nothing to make them amends; but an opportunity offer'd that very Instant to oblige them wonderfully, for while we were lying by the shore, came two mighty creatures one pursuing the other, . . . with great fury. . . . We found the people terribly frighted, especially the women. The man that had the lance or dart did not fly from them, but the rest did; however as the two creatures ran directly into the water, they did not seem to offer to fall upon any of the negroes but plung'd themselves into the sea. . . . I had loaded my gun with all possible expedition, and bad Xury load the other; as soon as he [the leopard] came fairly within my reach, I fir'd, and shot him directly into the head. (30)

The response of the Africans is one of astonishment and mystification: "the negroes held up their hands with admiration to think what it was I had kill'd [the leopard] with" (31). What perplexes the Africans is not so much the ability of Crusoe to kill at a distance; they can, after all, kill from a distance with a spear or an arrow. Rather, their mystification derives from the invisible operation of the gun's mechanism. Since the shot from Crusoe's weapons flies too fast to be seen, it cannot be tied directly to his agency or to the gun that he carries; it appears to strike magically, like lightning. The gun itself attracts attention as an object of fear and "astonishment," because of "the noise and the fire" it produces (203), but the display cannot be clearly connected to the event that it precipitates (the death of the leopard).

Crusoe's intervention is, then, a mysterious performance of prowess. This performance overshadows his commerce with the Africans, despite his apparently nonhostile intentions. Crusoe's journey down the coast has been haunted by his fears of violence at the hands of Africans: "whole nations of Negroes were sure to surround us with their canoes and destroy us; where we could ne'er once go on shoar but we should be devour'd by savage beasts, or more merciless savages of humane kind" (23). Crusoe fears more than his new slave Xury does; the boy's solution is simply to frighten the Africans with the gun: "then we give them the shoot gun, says Xury laughing, make them run wey" (24). Crusoe effectively adapts Xury's suggestion; in an early feat of gunboat diplomacy, he frightens the Africans without scaring them away. What his weapon does instead is create the conditions for nominally peaceful negotiations. The Africans appear initially to be in control, since Crusoe displays no arms, while the Africans have one visible armed man, whose abilities with the lance keep Crusoe and Xury waiting some distance offshore. The Africans offer food before learning about the power of Crusoe's firearms; it is unclear to the reader (and to Crusoe) whether they are offering a gift or attempting to open a rudimentary trade relationship. More importantly, after the gunshot goes off—after the moment that the relationship of power has changed—Crusoe views every transaction as an exchange of "gifts" rather than as commerce:

> I found quickly the negroes were for eating the flesh of this creature, so I was willing to have them take it as a favour from me, which when I made signs to them that they might take him, they were very thankful for, immediately they fell to work with him. . . . They offer'd me some of the flesh, which I declined, making as if I would give it them, but made signs for the skin, which they gave me very freely, and brought me a great deal more of their provision, which tho' I did not understand, yet I accepted. (31)

These are signs, of course, that the Africans are "friendly," in Crusoe's terms, and their gifts are "free." But as this is a representation of an archetypal colonial encounter, we are entitled to read it skeptically, particularly given the text's other instances of "free" or voluntaristic arrangements that seem, on inspection, to operate in the shadow of physical force.

This force is linked to the introduction of regimes of commerce into uncivilized spaces. The man holding the lance is not particularly afraid of the unusual eruption of nature on the scene in the form of two battling beasts, but neither does he appear to be able to intervene in their contest; his stance is a passive one of self-defense. Crusoe, on the other hand, takes the problem as an entrepreneurial opportunity, killing the leopard, offering it up as a goodwill gift to the Africans, and accepting the gift of its skin in return—said skin soon entering the sphere of commodity exchange when he sells it to the captain who rescues him, from which it doubtless enters the larger sphere of imperial circulation as a luxury good (34). The gift of the leopard is significant: Crusoe leaves behind himself a sign of his technological power and his capacity for violence, figured in the mutilated body of the animal. Simultaneously, the transformation of the animal's pelt from natural object into commodity is linked crucially to the military technologies that Crusoe uses. The gun permits the transformation of nature into commodity and luxury; earlier and less powerful forms of technology do not permit this sort of entrepreneurship. Hence violence in this scene is metonymically linked to peace and imperial trade by the figure of the gun. The savages here are not civilized in the way that Friday will be, but they are, for a moment, "liberated" from nature by virtue of Crusoe's "gifts" to them. If we are suspicious of the act of amity, then so, too, will we want to consider carefully the relevance of violent coercion to Crusoe's "civilizing" of Friday.

Once Crusoe is shipwrecked on his island, he repeats the process of violent display and disavowal. As his efforts on the island gradually move from mere survival toward Christian virtue and the civilizing mission, we are meant to see that violence remains at the core of his civilizing project, despite his own protests to the contrary. His other virtues—such as his evangelical work—are themselves dependent on the power of military technology, which simultaneously amplifies and mystifies violence as a source of authority; his ostensibly consensual relationship with Friday begins with and remains troubled by the power of his gun. Crusoe thinks that his power over Friday and other savages flows from his position as a civilized Christian. But as Friday understands, it depends on firepower; this knowledge, which is portrayed in his early attempts to converse with the gun, appears later as he learns to make his own language and traditions speak even as he pillories Crusoe's self-representation as a man of peace and commerce.

Crusoe most clearly rejects the violence of imperial conquest when he recognizes the madness of his panicked genocidal fantasies of slaughtering Caribs. Having discovered that the island that has sheltered him for many years is also the site of frequent cannibal feasts, he is driven briefly mad, cowering in his miniature fortress and fantasizing about slaughtering "these monsters." However, he gradually comes to adopt a stance of rationalized indifference toward them and disavows his genocidal fantasies, instead embracing a philosophy of noninterventionism and moral superiority:

> My opinion of the action it self began to alter, and I began with cooler and calmer thoughts to consider what it was I was going to engage in. What authority, or call I had, to pretend to be judge and executioner upon these men as criminals, whom heaven had thought fit for so many ages to suffer unpunish'd, to go on, and to be as it were, the executioners of his judgments upon one another. How far these people were offenders against me, and what right I had to engage in the quarrel of that blood, which they shed promiscuously one upon another. (170–71)

Crusoe's rationalizations would seem, from one perspective, to be sincere and admirable. He has begun to master his passions—to come to terms with his anger at the horrid otherness of the Caribs and to dispassionately consider what his ethical duties might be in this situation. He continues, asking, "How do I know what God himself judges in this particular case? . . . They think it no more a crime to kill a captive taken in war, than we do to kill an ox; nor to eat humane flesh, than we do to eat mutton" (171). The categories of violence that Crusoe has been working with are here breaking down. Without any legible divine sanction for his judgment, he must content himself with a more legalistic approach:

> Albeit the usage they thus gave one another, was thus brutish and inhuman; yet it was really nothing to me: these people had done me no injury. That if they attempted me, or I saw it necessary for my immediate preservation to fall upon them, something might be said for it; but that as I was yet out of their power, and they had really no knowledge of me. . . . It could not be just for me to fall upon them. (171)

To do so would be to imitate the Spanish "in all their barbarities" during the conquest—"where they destroy'd millions of these people, who . . . were yet, as to the Spaniards, very innocent people" (171–72). Crusoe here, significantly, rejects the doctrine of Hugo Grotius that holds that sovereign entities have the right to punish obvious violations of natural law such as cannibalism.[20] But this self-denying pacifism is a part of Crusoe's self-representation, as is his distaste for the brutalities of the Spanish conquest. His decision in favor of peace matches his protestations of peaceful intent that we find elsewhere in the novel—which, as we have already seen, are not entirely trustworthy.

Crusoe's passionate urge to massacre Caribs is sublimated into a desire to convert and civilize the savage; this desire eventually finds its object in Friday. Crusoe's rhetoric suggests that his relationship with Friday is founded on gratitude and voluntarism and that these, in turn, prepare the way for Friday's conversion and Crusoe's own spiritual growth. Friday's status as a slave, albeit a "voluntary" one, clouds the relationship. Friday in many ways resembles Xury, since Defoe presents Friday as a happy and willing slave, a servant who need never be whipped or punished because his obedience and loyalty are beyond question. But as with Xury, the portrayal is hardly without problems. Though Friday appears to offer voluntary submission, his conformity to Western norms develops in the shadow of the threat of violence and death. The threat appears most clearly in the sequence when Friday is persuaded to abandon cannibalism. At this time, we learn, he still longs to eat human flesh, but Crusoe's threats keep him in line: "Friday had still a hankering stomach after some of the flesh, and was still a cannibal in his nature but . . . he durst not discover it; for I had by some means let him know, that I would kill him if he offer'd it" (208). Friday's process of civilizing and conversion, in other words, begins with a death threat. The threat seems somewhat excessive, since Friday has already sworn to be Crusoe's slave and servant forever; one might think that such an oath would be sufficient to command his obedience. If that service is voluntary, surely Crusoe's threat goes beyond what is required to produce obedience. What the text appears to suggest is that there remains a gap in Friday's loyalty—a gap brutally mended by Crusoe's gun. Friday understands that the gun is the determining element of his life, the author both of his rescue from death and of his forcible conversion to Western civility; it frames his rescue and his submission. No wonder he prays to it.

Friday's submission to Crusoe, then, echoes the scenes in Africa; he submits to Crusoe's violence, despite Crusoe's preference for a more benign interpretation of these events. Friday submits to Crusoe's power; he is also, at first, in awe of the mystery of Crusoe's gun. Defoe's narrative underscores the steps Crusoe takes to keep Friday mystified. Loading his guns only out of Friday's field of vision, Crusoe's shooting becomes self-consciously theatrical, a conjurer's trick that takes advantage of the savage's attraction to magical and fetishized objects. Crusoe notes of his servant, "he was the more amaz'd because he did not see me put any thing into the gun; but thought that there must be some wonderful fund of death and destruction in that thing, able to kill man, beast, bird, or any thing near, or far off" (211–12). This performance enhances Crusoe's power, but it also emphasizes that power's tenuous nature; the secrets of gunpowder must remain secret and seemingly magical for them to work psychologically and indirectly, turning Friday into a slave rather than a corpse. We might be surprised, given Crusoe's hostility to idolatry, that he here seems to countenance exactly that. But for Crusoe, the gun is not so much an idol as a prop in a performance of authority. Defoe's other writings are not strangers to this practice of magic. In his *Political History of the Devil* (1726), for example, Defoe's narrator attempts to improve the character of an attractive young woman by convincing her that her vanity is devilish—and using a doctored mirror to prove it. Defoe there and elsewhere is interested in the tendency of the unwise to attribute satanic or magical power to technological complexity.[21]

However, if technology and violence are the source of Crusoe's authority—and Friday's prayers to the gun suggest that they are—then those same forces may be reappropriated and redeployed by others, civil or otherwise. Friday does indeed begin to master Crusoe's technology and his tactics as well. Defoe's Friday, in fact, offers us an alternate perspective on Crusoe's violence, particularly late in the novel when Friday shifts from slave to mimic, parodying the veneer of benevolence that conceals the role of violence in constructing the social order. Friday is eventually trusted with firearms, though only after he has testified to his growing civility in other ways (wearing clothes and converting to Christianity). When Friday joins Crusoe to rescue his father and a Spaniard, Friday carries a pistol and muskets, though Crusoe has already loaded them; it is not clear whether the workings of gunpowder remain a mystery to Friday, but he is at least no longer terrified of it. Indeed, during the assault, Friday demonstrates a superior command of the weapons, if Crusoe is to be believed. He instructs Friday to imitate him, as they carry out what might be Friday's first fire-armed assault. Friday's imitation is exact:

> I set down one of the muskets, and the fowling-piece, upon the ground, and Friday did the like by his; and with the other musket, I took my aim at the savages, bidding him do the like. . . . Friday kept

his eyes close upon me, that as I had bid him, he might observe what I did; so as soon as the first shot was made, I threw down the piece, and took up the fowling-piece, and Friday did the like; he see me cock, and present, he did the same again. (234)

Friday's imitation is effective, however; he is an excellent marksman, for one thing. Perhaps more important, he is now in a position to use the firearm to terrify other Caribs, who are themselves baffled by its invisible prowess: "[The Caribs] were, you may be sure, in a dreadful consternation; and all of them, who were not hurt, jump'd up upon their feet, but did not immediately know which way to run, or which way to look; for they knew not from whence their destruction came" (234). Friday now stands on the other side of the technological divide, able to inflict psychic wounds with invisible bullets.

Crusoe's work of civilizing Friday might be complete at this point; Friday has learned his language, his lifeways, and his religion as well as his war-making tactics. Indeed, Friday replicates and even parodies Crusoe's tactics by extending them into the animal kingdom in the notoriously odd bear episode, in which Friday toys with and eventually kills an ursine antagonist. In doing so, Friday blends Western military technology with savage hunting techniques simultaneously to rid the travelers of a threat and to offer a parody of colonial domination. Friday's courage as a hunter has already saved members of his traveling party from a wolf attack—an attack that Crusoe suggests would have paralyzed a European with fear (292). His hunting prowess takes a more puzzling form in his encounter with the bear, however. Friday uses the opportunity, I suggest, to stage an intercultural performance—a display of power and mastery that strangely echoes and even parodies Crusoe's use of his guns to awe pretechnological Africans and Caribs. Friday prepares to commit an act of violence against an animal and thus aligns himself firmly on the human side of the human/animal divide, in an uncanny inversion of Crusoe's killing of the African leopard. Friday's language of friendly greeting—"Me shakee te hand with him"—echoes Crusoe's putative friendships with African and Carib alike. The same might be said for Friday's efforts to communicate with the bear—like Crusoe's signs to the Africans and to Friday, it is difficult to believe that they are understood in any but the most general way: "Friday coming pretty near, calls to him, as if the bear could understand him; Hark ye, hark ye, ... me speakee wit you" (294). He then abandons the pretense of amity, exposing the violence that the performance had thus far concealed. Luring the bear onto a tree limb, he briefly teases the bear before shooting him at point-blank range, leaving him "dead as a stone" (296). Friday then awaits the applause of his spectators, saying, "so we kill bear in my country," though noting that his countrymen would have used "great much long arrow" (296–97).

Friday's performance may be seen as a kind of gift offered to the travelers—a minstrel-like piece of slapstick that Friday proffers for their amusement. But, like Crusoe's gifts to the Africans, the gift of an animal's body signifies here in unexpected ways. The act can be fruitfully read as a parody of Crusoe's commerce with Africans and Caribs. It literalizes and exposes Crusoe's self-presentation as a bringer of liberty and civilization. Friday's rhetorical performance positions the bear as both animal (subject to being slaughtered for the benefit of others, as a sign of goodwill) and as a savage man (who may receive a handshake and whom one may talk to, however uncomprehending he may be). The rhetoric collapses with the gunshot—the bear becomes both ritual gift and a parodic sign of the violent consequences of colonial sovereignty. To be sure, the performance is unsettling; drawing on both Friday's traditions and the technologies of Europe, it reveals a Friday whose grasp of the power of the gun has expanded from his attempts to communicate with it like a deity. Perhaps Friday has now come to understand that the power of violence depends as much on display as on raw force, that the performance of technological superiority is, after all, a performance.[22]

If, as Homi Bhabha argues, the English book is an "ambivalent text of authority," then Friday's parodic performance of colonial violence reveals a similar ambivalence in the violent technologies that undergird Crusoe's politics.[23] Friday in this scene is not so much a naturalistic character or a symbol of resistance as he is an ideological escape valve. Stating it more formally, we might say that Friday is at this point in the narrative a symptom of the tension in the text between the ideology of English liberty and the inherent violence of sovereignty and the creation of civil communities. The Whig regime of the early Hanoverian period, with all its rhetoric of liberty, sought to impose its authority through violence direct and indirect. The novel seems to resolve these tensions through the figure of Crusoe; yet the resolution is incomplete and uncomfortable. Friday offers a cryptic and surprising way to give voice to and acknowledge those aporiai. In so doing, the subaltern Friday appears to have found a way to speak, in the most unexpected of places. What he has to say is not merely a complaint against the horrors of colonial sovereignty, though it is that. He also warns and admonishes the political subjects of Britain. For if the shadow of violence hangs over voluntary associations of commerce, contract, and gratitude, it is no longer clear that Great Britain itself is "free." The Revolution of 1688—officially anything but a conquest but visibly maintaining itself by violently suppressing dissent—may not be so readily distinguished from Crusoe's ambiguous absolutism. Colonial sovereignty, perhaps, has followed Friday to the British Isles.

Technologies of Anarchy: The Desacralization of Gunpowder

Crusoe's fetishized gun plays a crucial role in transforming Friday's wildness into a capacity to be governed—and, eventually, to govern himself. That Friday figures not only the racial other but also the category of the political subject more generally, I believe, becomes clear when this novel is examined in the wider context of Defoe's other fictions of exploration and colonization. These fictions, I suggest, recast the figure of the civility-bringing colonizer in a more ambiguous light and change the valence of gunpowder's significations. *The Farther Adventures of Robinson Crusoe* and *Captain Singleton* offer a more skeptical version of civility-making violence. If Crusoe's gun begins as the key fetish of sovereignty—one that works simultaneously as a tool of destruction and a prop in a performance of power—these later texts highlight the raw violence enabled by gunpowder, no longer cloaked by a rhetoric of civility and cultural superiority. At the same time, the confrontation between the civilized male and the savage begins to lose its coherence, as the civilizing sovereign migrates from a singular figure into a dispersed multitude, individual bodies that figure not constitutional law but rather anarchy. Gunpowder no longer operates as a mysterious sign of divinity or even a tool for carving out a civilized space in the wilderness; it now becomes more closely associated with ungoverned human passions detached from sovereign authority. In other words, gunpowder increasingly blurs the line between savage and civilized people and between legitimate sovereignty and mob rule. Jonathan Elmer has argued that in the New World, sovereignty undergoes a Deleuzian deterritorialization: "a process of fragmentation" in which its "codes" are loosened, disorganized, and reconfigured.[24] In Madagascar, too, the linkages between the sovereign individual and the lawgiver become blurred in ways that also comment on a similar process at work in Britain; the ambivalent significations of gunpowder allow it to symbolize this blurring. This process of fragmentation is most salient in two massacres, in both of which gunpowder plays a key role in unleashing the dangerous passions of a newly sovereign multitude.

Defoe's first massacre is staged in Madagascar at a transitional point in *The Farther Adventures*. Crusoe has left his Caribbean island behind and set off on a mercantile adventure that Robert Markley has described as a revision of the first novel's emphasis on autonomy and selfhood.[25] Defoe's *Farther Adventures* spends its first half wrapping up loose ends as Crusoe returns to his island and learns of the trials and successes of the mutineers and Spaniards he left behind. That done, Crusoe leaves them with a formal constitution. Disclaiming any further interest in his island, he departs with his nephew on a voyage to the trade routes of the East. Bound for Asia, Crusoe pauses for one last island encounter en route to the trade routes of Asia; it is here, in Madagascar, where Defoe's text uses gunpowder as an index of a rather different version of modernity, one characterized by unbridled passion and unrestrained violence. Madagascar occupied an unusual place in the early eighteenth-century imagination as a site of colonial failure. The island had been of interest for over a century as a potential stopover and port for voyages to the East—indeed, for the East India Company, a nearly essential one until a regular stopover was established in the nearby Comoros Islands. But disease and indigenous resistance had made the island inhospitable as a European outpost. In the eyes of many people in England, it remained a savage land, inhabited only by brutish Africans and (more brutish yet) pirates.[26] I underscore the historical fact of colonization's failure here because it appears that historical Madagascans were quite adept at maintaining political and military control over the boundaries of their island in a way that varies sharply from Defoe's presentation.

Crusoe's Madagascans differ somewhat from the savages encountered on his Caribbean island. Their savagery is primarily economic and technological; they are not cannibals, and they practice a form of civility and a particular understanding of political space—one based on custom and tradition rather than on technologically enhanced fortifications and enclosures. The villagers are characterized by a striking ethnographic detail that sharply distinguishes them from other "savages" that

Crusoe has encountered. They have developed a formalized ritual for occasions of contact—a spatial configuration that defines the practices to be followed when encountering groups alien to their polity. When two potentially hostile groups approach one another, they create a provisional architecture of poles that demarcates two militarized spaces— one for the Madagascans, one for their visitors or intruders. Between these two spaces, the poles mark out a neutral, agora-like space: "you are perfectly secure within the three Poles, and all the Space between your Poles and theirs, is allo'd like a Market, for free Converse, Traffick, and Commerce."[27] This ceremonial architecture defines the space of cultural contact, creating three zones—"ours," the enemies', and a neutral no-man's-land in which various types of nonviolent commerce can take place. But this space is fragile, and its status as a zone of peace depends on both parties recognizing it as such. It is a deployment, that is, of customary signs and expresses a faith in the ability of custom to restrain violence.[28] The Madagascans' system incorporates nonviolent commerce, banishing weaponry to a militarized zone behind a protected space of commerce. Their technologies for demarcating political space, we might say, are purely symbolic.

This attractive and civilized system for managing the space of encounter is unfortunately shattered by the aggression of Crusoe's companions, in a narrative turn that underscores the vulnerability of purely symbolic technologies to violence. The pole-defined truce is breached when a sailor kidnaps and rapes a young woman (224–25). The Madagascans respond by attacking the ship's crew and driving them offshore. The rapist, Thomas Jeffry, is left behind and, as we soon discover, captured and killed by the outraged Madagascans. A few nights after the escape, a party reenters Madagascan space, hoping to locate and rescue Jeffry. This fresh intrusion into the Madagascans' political space, importantly, is supplemented by gunpowder, which allows the Britons to remap the space of the island with little fear of reprisal. Their technological superiority combines with Madagascar's anomic political space—that is to say, with the absence of any effective law or authority to restrain their behavior—to give free reign to their passionate rage when they discover that their shipmate has been executed for his crime. Defoe's text strongly highlights the dark synergy created by two distinctly modern phenomena: the technological (gunpowder) and the political (the modern individual, not beholden to any divinely instituted or traditional authority). Upon arriving at the village, the Britons discover the maimed corpse of their shipmate, "hang'd up naked by one Arm, and his Throat cut" (230). Outraged, the sailors destroy several houses in the town with guns and grenades. The marauding Britons pay special attention to the compound next to Jeffry's corpse, since it houses many of the men who had led the earlier attack on the crew, as well as the local ruler (their "prince, or king, or whatever he was," as Crusoe says). This house is destroyed with a grenade—a gunpowder-based technology against which the Madagascans are utterly defenseless (231). As the entire town begins to blaze, the crew turns its guns on the defenseless and terrified villagers, "still calling and hallowing to one another to remember *Thom. Jeffrys*" (232). Though the architecture and layout of this village are not carefully described, the sequence nevertheless suggests that the transition from sleepy hamlet to free-fire zone is, among other things, a spatial one. The text is clear that Jeffry's desecrated corpse hangs next to the local ruler's residence—the political center of power in the village. Much as the mutilated bodies of criminals and traitors signified sovereign power in Europe, so too does Jeffry's body remind readers of the proximity of the village sovereign to violent and absolute power. The eviscerated and displayed body here localizes violence and power around the sovereign's abode. But this village leader lacks the cultural and material technology to transform this semiotics of violence into a practical defense. From the sailors' standpoint, of course, Jeffry's body signifies quite differently.

Crusoe's description of the scene explicitly links this destruction to the collapse of political space in Europe as well, alluding to the infamous aftermaths of the sieges of Drogheda and of Magdeburg. For Crusoe, civilized political communities are dependent on the technologies of architecture and gunpowder to keep states of war and nature beyond their walls. When those technologies are not adequate to the task, security vanishes to be replaced by anarchical violence:

> I had heard of Oliver Cromwell taking Drogheda, in Ireland, and killing man, woman, and child; and I had read of Count Tilly sacking the city of Magdeburg and cutting the throats of twenty-two thousand of all sexes; but I never had an idea of the thing itself before, nor is it possible to describe it, or the horror that was upon our minds at hearing it. (234)

Crusoe's emphasis is on the horror of the scene, but this horror is one that follows the collapse of walls and the overrunning of civilized spaces by barbarism.

All this begins in Crusoe's absence. As he approaches the village with his nephew, he comes upon ruined houses and a mingled pile of corpses of men and women alike. Appalled, Crusoe reads these signs of violence as markers of a "Rage altogether barbarous and of a Fury, something beyond what was human" (234). Crusoe's reaction emphasizes precisely the inhuman quality of his shipmates' violence as he describes the flight of men and women in "Terror and Consternation" from "three of our *English* Butchers . . . in their Rear, who, when they could not overtake them, fir'd in among them, and one that was kill'd by their Shot fell down in our sight" (235). The "English Butchers" have gone beyond their initial task of killing the local rulers; they now, in their rage, seem to aim at a universal destruction. Their gunpowder-fueled weapons enable this task: their pogrom could not succeed were their weapons not so powerful and the village's defenses so weak. The primordial passion of revenge is augmented, the scene suggests, by a fully modern technological potency that extends the range and power of their violence to an apocalyptic degree; the structural openness of the village is no match for their amplified passions. These sailors are literally beyond the pale—unwalled and unleashed—as they go "roving over the Heaps of Bodies they had killed, all cover'd with Blood and Dust, as if they wanted more People to massacre" (236). Challenged by Crusoe, the ship's boatswain shows no remorse, saying, "we have not half done yet. . . . I'll kill as many of them as poor *Tom.* has Hairs upon his Head. We have sworn to spare none of them, we'll root out the very Nation of 'em from the Earth" (237).[29] Crusoe's own nephew, when he is shown the torn body of Jeffrys, shares the sentiment: "As to the People, he thought not one of 'em ought to live" (237); he later notes that the sight of Tom's body had left him bereft of self-control: "he was not Master of himself, neither could he govern his passion" (239).

This massacre, then, presents the reader with a group of Englishmen who, having no masters, cannot master themselves. And the village and its people inhabit a political space organized around a symbolic architecture (a system of poles, the village chief's unfortified compound) without military effect or technological embodiment. Custom's haplessness in the face of modernity is its undoing; equally striking, however, is that it is also the undoing of the civility of the men who have annihilated it. Unrestrained by law or master, their anger spirals out of control, augmented to an apocalyptic degree by modern weaponry. This sequence's treatment of space inverts the problem Crusoe first faces on his island, where so much of the narrative is driven by Crusoe's terror of cannibals until he develops the ability to control some elements of the island's space through his fortified compound and its environs. On the very different island of Madagascar, space is similarly undefended. What is new is the presence of customs that symbolically inhibit violence but that in fact fail to discipline the violent passions and bodies of this band of marauders. This, I suggest, stages a confrontation between tradition and modernity that has implications and applications for Britain's own painful political and social transformations during this period. The consequences of the marauders' lack of restraint are devastating in part because they are explicitly associated with modern technologies, which form a pointed contrast with the less modern technological forms in the village. These sailors, like Crusoe, are among other things figures for human selfhood unharnessed from authority.

As the *Farther Adventures* draws to a close, another violent encounter underscores the complexity of the relationship between civility-making violence and anarchical passion. In Central Asia, Crusoe himself is unveiled not simply as a sovereign bringer of civility but as a more self-righteous version of the marauding sailors he had condemned. After trading in Asia for a number of years, Crusoe begins making his way back to Europe across the plains of Tartary—a "no-man's land" full, once more, of a savage and ungoverned multitude. Crusoe's caravan encounters a village off Tartars worshiping a wooden idol. This idol, known as Cham Chi-Thaungu, is a revolting and misshapen thing, in Crusoe's eyes. He is repelled not only by its associations with devil worship and irrational idolatry; its very shapelessness offends him. Its filthiness derives from its mixture of disparate animal qualities, the exaggerated size of its organs, and its lack of proper bodily integrity; Crusoe is revolted that it has no "Proportion of Parts" (329). This idol, this "frightful Nothing," is an index of human depravity; Crusoe's horror is at the way that nominally rational savages debase themselves to worship such a "sordid and brutish" object (329). The intensity of Crusoe's rage is striking; perhaps he is envious of this powerful rival, an irrational inversion of his technological fetishes.

If so, it is appropriate that when Crusoe resolves to destroy this idol, he makes use of the same technologies that converted and civilized Friday. With the support of two Scottish fellow travelers, Crusoe resolves to destroy Cham Chi-Thaungu with fire. Forcing several hapless Tartars to watch, he packs the idol full of gunpowder and destroys it. As one of Crusoe's Scottish acquaintances points out, this whole enterprise is unlikely to prove edifying to the Tartars, since they have no writing and barely any human language at all. Neither do they show any of that astonishment and admiration that Defoe elsewhere associates with gunpowder. Indeed, the only obvious result of Crusoe's iconoclastic raid is to trouble relations between the Russian state and the Tartar villages nominally under its jurisdiction. The text insists that this is an irrational outburst on Crusoe's part; no longer speaking with gunpowder, he now uses it merely to destroy. Yet, in its form, this is recognizably a gesture toward civility-making violence; it is inspired by a passion to bring reason to the savage, to enlighten, and to destroy the barbarous materials that hold them down. Civility-making violence and passionate outburst are difficult to distinguish here.[30]

Gunpowder, in this sequence, figures a collapse of conventional or traditional notions of civility in the face of two uncontrolled forces: the unleashed passions of the modern individual and the enhancement of that individual's power through gunpowder. Technological power is still controlled by European hands, but it is no longer the strict possession of a virtuous civilizing sovereign; and the rampant passions of this broader strata of warriors remakes the moment of colonial contact from one of civilizing awe into one of passionate and uncontrollable violence. That this disintegration is represented spatially is no coincidence, for there is a very close relationship between the production of civilized subjects and the governing of the spaces those subjects inhabit. Defoe's interest in the violent synergies created by undefended spaces and unleashed human passions is not limited to the imperial periphery; Defoe's *Augusta Triumphans* (1728), for example, suggests regulating the crime-infested streets of London by creating network of armed watchmen.[31] The absence of effective fortifications in Madagascar in this case represents another instance of sovereignty's dependence on technology for the production of civility.

Nations of Horses: Fortification and Ungoverned Spaces

The Madagascan village errs in trusting symbolic architectures to enforce a truce. This sequence's absence of walls and fortification, and the reliance on symbols to preserve the peace, draws on a discourse on colonialism and fortification that links politics, space, and violence and that in turn informs British political thought. The fortress functions in much of Defoe's writing as a metonym for the modernization of political space through rationalization and force. The fortress in the early eighteenth century represented a manufactured political space: a civility created by founders not of cities but of military outposts. The space of civility that a fortress can create is marked out from the space of savagery—open, undefined, unwalled, and full of the potential for chaotic violence. If, as Henri Lefebvre suggests, the idea of sovereignty implies a space against which violence is directed, then in the seventeenth and eighteenth centuries a corollary idea forms—the idea of savage space where violence remains random, dispersed, and unimpeded rather than focalized.[32]

Defoe's mode of imaging the modern space of civility, figured by the fortress and the gun, however, explores the ways in which modernity unleashes savages of its own. In order for civility to emerge—and, indeed, for commerce to take place—sovereignty must control and discipline space, assuming and directing its violence. In the history of seventeenth- and eighteenth-century colonial enterprises, fortifications were essential to this disciplining of space. The fortress—capable of defending civilization within as well as promoting it beyond its walls—becomes an offensive rather than a strictly defensive force. The fortress establishes toeholds in savage spaces, transforming them directly by building fortified and civilized enclosures; it also projects a civilizing violence outward, creating spaces of sovereignty. Crusoe famously does this with his island compound, which is defensive and offensive at once.[33] This compound, which he repeatedly refers to as his "fort," his "fortifications," and, in a moment of xenophobic panic, his "castle," reshapes the island, giving it for the first time zones of interiority and exteriority, inside and outside, safety and vulnerability (*Robinson Crusoe*, 154). When, later in his stay on the island, Crusoe learns of the presence of cannibals on the island, he retreats in panic to his fortress, only slowly daring to venture out once more with his other primary tool for controlling space—his musket. As John Bender has observed, Crusoe's fortifications enable not only self-defense but also a projection of power—becoming a "walled city that can contain and subjugate as well as defend"—a projection aided immeasurably by his modern weaponry. Together, gun and fort transform the island into a space of civility.[34]

Defoe's earlier nonfiction had anticipated this linkage of civility to military architecture. Several critics have noted Defoe's careful attention to fortresses in his *Tour through the Whole Island of Great Britain*.[35] Defoe's critique of Parliamentary debates about the Royal African Company's West African fortifications also cite the importance of fortifications to the construction of civilized spaces. Over the course of the seventeenth and early eighteenth centuries, the Royal African Company established fortresses along the west coast of Africa, seeking to create well-defined spaces where the trade in minerals and slaves could take place with relative security. These forts were part of an intercultural zone that gradually became familiar to European and British traders, in contrast to the African interior, trade with which was controlled by African-born intermediaries.[36] The forts varied widely in size and technological sophistication. The largest, Cape Coast Castle, had been captured from the Dutch in the Second Anglo-Dutch War in 1664; in Defoe's day, it was a fortification in the most current modern style, complete with outworks and bastions, though a few other "fortresses" were little more than factories protected by dirt mounds.

Though these forts were primarily, in practice, used to defend British traders from European navies, it was also possible to imagine them as structures that would eventually herald a project of conquest and settlement. If Africa was typically seen as a place of lawlessness, violence, and unpredictability, the fortress is a means of creating a zone of civility and stability, not only inside but also for some distance beyond its walls. The British colonial fortress looked outward, seeking not only to enclose but also to project civilization. For some European writers, in fact, it was possible even at this early stage to see some African nations as subject to European authority. The Dutch writer Willem Bosman—whose account of West Africa was available in a popular English translation (1721)—claims that the Dutch, at least, used their fortress at Elmina to establish sovereignty over Africans living near their compounds, claiming tolls from fishermen operating out of their villages. "This sort of Toll we yet reserve at three places besides, *viz.* at *Axim, Chama* and *Elmina*, by reason we have conquered these places," Bosman notes. The Dutch alone have established "this peculiar Prerogative, nor do any of them exercise such a Sovereign Authority over their *Negroe* Subjects as we; which is indeed chiefly their own fault," Bosman concludes.[37] Here Bosman (or his translator) explicitly links the fortress, the conquest of African nations, and the political condition of sovereignty. If Britain itself cannot be said to hold sovereign sway over any African nations, Bosman suggests, that may be because it is not trying hard enough.

Bosman's comments usefully illuminate Defoe's journalistic writings on British fortifications in Africa.[38] In the 1710s, Parliament and the press debated the supply and maintenance of these African outposts; separate traders suggested that the crown or Parliament should offer financial support, while the Royal African Company preferred to reestablish a monopoly and return to self-funding the forts.[39] Defoe's writings are an interesting footnote to the history of the British slave trade, but they also underline the important role of fortification in his vision of Britain's civilizing mission. Describing the origins of European outposts in Africa, he writes that early Portuguese traders in Africa "found the Natives, Wild, Barbarous, Treacherous, and perfectly untractable as to Commerce"; to establish a regular trade, "they made little Settlements there; but finding the Natives frequently insulted, plunder'd, and sometimes Murther'd the Agents and People they left there: They found it at last necessary to fortify themselves, and maintain their Possession by force, and so keeping the Natives at a Distance, preserv'd both themselves and their Trade" (*Defoe's Review*, V, 2, 560). This passage is fascinating for the nakedness with which it displaces violence from colonizer to colonized. The unwillingness of Africans to trade on Portuguese terms is itself a hostile act that may legitimately be countered with violence—a trope that recurs in Defoe's fiction. It also links British trading enterprises in the region to a history of European intervention: rather than seeing other European nations as competitors, it rhetorically aligns them with Britain.

But what is most important is its representation of technology's transformation of African space. Specifically, Defoe here imagines African space as savage, inhabited by treacherous, bestial, and dangerous people. The space in which Africans live is a place of violence, in which plunder and murder are to be expected. And the construction of civilized zones of commerce requires that Africans be kept at a distance by force:

> All the other Nations who have settl'd there since the *Portugueze*, have found this the only Method to carry on that Trade, and the several Persons whom they have ventur'd among the Natives, on attempts of meer Trade, presuming upon the most Civiliz'd Part of them, have yet been so generally Murthered and lost, that those Dear Experiments have taught us, *if we please to learn* this Maxim in the African Trade, that it is no way to be carried on by but Force; for a mere Correspondence with the Natives as Merchants, is as impracticable, as it would be if they were a Nation of Horses. (V, 2, 560)

The "nation" of West Africa is aligned with the animal kingdom here—bestial and intractable.[40] Thus the open spaces of West Africa were for Defoe spaces of violence in more senses than one. Europeans intruding into them found themselves in an anarchic space where violence might be directed from any side and where no security was to be found. As we have seen, however, unfortified spaces do not merely leave settlers and traders vulnerable to violent assault. In ungoverned, anomic spaces such as this fantastic Africa, Defoe suggests, traders and voyagers put their own personalities at risk, freeing their passions and unleashing the savage within.

The association of civility with fortified spaces extends to European military architecture as well. In Defoe's 1720 novel *Memoirs of a Cavalier*, the protagonist witnesses the notorious slaughter that followed the siege of Magdeburg—a massacre that is one of Crusoe's touchstones in describing the slaughter in Madagascar.

> This Calamity sure was the dreadfullest Sight that every I saw; the Rage of the *Imperial* Soldiers was most intolerable, and not to be expressed; of 25000, some said 30000 People, there was not a Soul to be seen alive, till the Flames drove those that were hid in Vaults and secret Places to seek Death in the streets, rather than perish in the Fire: of these Miserable Creatures some were killed too by the furious Soldiers, but at last they saved the Lives of such as came out of their Cellars and Holes, and so about 2000 poor desperate Creatures were left; the exact Number of those that perished in this City could never be known, because those the Soldiers had first butcher'd, the Flames afterwards devour'd.[41]

The "rage" of these soldiers—a kind of passion that exceeds the laws of the human as well as the laws of war—is in this presentation closely connected with the fall of the fortified city and thus restages the collapse of civility into savagery. Here we find a connection between the forces of civilization—historically represented by the city and its walls—and the forces that threaten to tear this settled and fortified place down. Here the forces that threaten are the forces of war, juxtaposed to the polite and civilized interior of the city. When the walls collapse, so does civility, and the imperial soldiers, like Crusoe's shipmates, lapse into an archaic savagery.

Indian Engineering

Fortresses not only preserve civility; they also create it, or at least prepare the ground for it. They can be seen as the emblematic tools of a civilizing sovereignty, providing an institutional and technological foundation for the transformation of savage subjects and their political spaces into proper subjects. Even in the British Isles themselves, fortresses were explicitly conceived as tools for the eradication of the last vestiges of savagery. One version of this impulse appears in Newcastle's proposal to civilize the London commoners with royal garrisons, noted earlier. North of the Tweed, similar ideas were entertained, and with more immediately bloody results. Southern Scotland had a great deal in common with England, despite its political independence and differences in politics and religion. And as the Lowlanders looked to the northern Highlands, many saw a savage space in need of taming. This civilizing process took various forms, but the Lowlanders clearly saw the establishment of fortified outposts as a critical component of their political strategy. In 1689, the Scottish Convention Parliament, considering the varied political and military problems presented by the Highlands, declared,

> It is believed that it will the sooner be effectuate, by reason of some Remains of fortification that yet continue there, since the time the English were in those Parts and made Inverlochy [at the southern end of the Great Glen] the chief garrison and had quarters in all those Highlands, which kept all the savage inhabitants of those countries in great awe, and forced them to live regularly, as their Lowland neighbors used to do.[42]

In other words, the work of the English to civilize the Highlands through terror and violence must be continued by the Lowland Scots if the Scottish nation is to have a functioning political order where subjects "live regularly." The policies actually carried out during the Restoration and the reign of William and Mary followed this program.

Yet Defoe's fictional rendering of the relationship between fortifications and civility is no more straightforward than is his treatment of gunpowder's civilizing effects. The Madagascan massacre in *Farther Adventures* reverses the polarity of savage and civilized, imagining a polity governed by custom but which cannot contain the technologically amplified violence of modern individuals. Defoe's next novel, *Captain Singleton*, contains a bizarre and horrifying sequence that similarly depicts indigenous people who are vanquished by ungoverned passions, while also continuing to desacralize gunpowder. In this sequence, savages are blasted from their natural fortress—the inside of a hollow tree—with gunpowder. The sometimes-reluctant pirate Singleton and his crew, having nearly completed a tour of the known islands of the Pacific and Indian Oceans (including stops in the Philippines, New Guinea, and Ceylon), stumble on an uncharted island where they perpetrate a massacre of their own. Critics have wrestled to understand this disturbing encounter.[43] I suggest that it becomes easier to interpret once we understand this precolonial zone—once again—as a simulacrum of British political space and as a site that peculiarly conjoins individual and sovereign violence to highlight the fine line between sovereignty and anarchy in the strange new world of the modern. The island, though wildly different from modern Britain, nevertheless serves as a figure for a common fantasy about Britain's political space: the idea that Britain's integrity and sovereignty depend on nature rather than on artifice. But as in Madagascar—and, perhaps, as in Britain as well—natural political and military institutions are incapable of resisting modern sovereignty's power, here figured again through gunpowder.

The rhetoric of Britain's political space as a product of nature rather than human artifice has its roots in a commonplace about England: that the sea, rather than human architectures, gives England its identity. William Shakespeare famously puts the following speech into the mouth of John of Gaunt, who describes England as

> This fortress built by Nature for herself
> Against infection and the hand of war,

> This happy breed of men, this little world,
> This precious stone set in the silver sea,
> Which serves it in the office of a wall
> Or as a moat defensive to a house
> Against the envy of less happier lands.[44]

Shakespeare's rhetoric reconciles nature and fortification. Walled off from foreign entanglements, England was able to enjoy a free and peaceful political space.[45] This conception of political space as an organic product is challenged but also renewed by the incorporation of England and Scotland into a new political entity, Great Britain, following the 1707 Act of Union. Pro-union rhetoric, including Defoe's, underscores the new identity of nature and nation. Britain's "natural" boundaries, that is, allowed it to do without the extensive fortifications which might force the British to acknowledge an earthly master. The Act of Union of 1707 could be read as simply ratifying a national border that already existed incipiently—that the division between Scotland and England was unnatural. At last, one Anglican minister commented, there would be a perfect congruence between the state and the natural world, resulting in a naturally fortified island that would be safe from dissention at home and from foreign invasion:

> For us . . . GOD hath reserved the Glory to become perfect *Britains*, and to have Hearts as large as our Island, and to guard it effectually from the Breakings-out of our own Passions and Fury; even as GOD hath signally guarded it from the Fury and Passion of all other Nations, by the Sea which surrounds it.[46]

Defoe, the union's semiofficial propagandist, expressed this geographic determinism most powerfully:

> And as these two people inhabit one island, neither separated by dangerous Seas or unpassable Mountains, neither bounded with vast Deserts or great Rivers, by which either the Communications of Peace and Trade, or the Access of War might be rendered difficult, the on-looking World has beheld with no less Wonder than Pleasure, that they have not to this Day been able to unite in one Body.[47]

Defoe's passage preserves the idea that the Scots and the English constitute "two people[s]"—a construction that participates in a significant erasure of the role of fortifications in constructing the British nation.

Captain Singleton's encounter in the Indian Ocean reconfigures this island imagery, reimagining Britain as an island whose political space is defended not by the ocean but rather by a paradoxically natural fortification: a cleverly adapted hollow tree. This scene, like the sequence in Madagascar, figures the unstable boundary between a customary political and spatial organization and a very different space, remapped by modern forces that I have described as grounded in the passions and in modern technologies of violence. Natural space and natural sovereignty come off the worse in this confrontation. If the *Crusoe* series showed us the importance of technology in constructing spaces to tame the passions and civilize the savage, here Defoe meditates on the contradictions this construction entails. Or, perhaps, he extends and intensifies the concerns of the Madagascan massacre. The inhabitants of this uncharted island are devastated not only by the transformation of their own space through technology but also by the ungoverned passions of the pirates who assail their island, seeking to make its space their own. Here again, modern technology intensifies modern passions.

Elsewhere in this novel, fortification signifies the very boundary of the human; open spaces are the space of the subhuman or the animal, and the very definition of humanity is to be walled. When Singleton and his companions had paused in their transit of Africa to collect gold, they had built a fortification from stakes to defend themselves from the wild animals outside—animals who on one occasion laid siege to their compound, nearly overrunning them.[48] In that sequence, the exterior of the fortress is the space of the inhuman, while the people inside are confirmed in their humanity and their civility. But in the novel's second half, Singleton's crew of pirates find a different form of political space: a space of savagery that is not quite so permeable as that in Madagascar and where natural fortifications force a reconsideration of the boundary between the human and the inhuman. Here the crew encounters a group of savages who have adapted a natural feature—an ancient oaklike tree—into a fortress. In this sequence, the savages—inhabiting a naturally fortified island space—figure a form of sovereignty and political space that is premodern and yet impermeable; in other words, they offer a portrait of a set of natural defenses not unlike those attributed to Britain. The ersatz oak tree, I suggest, indicates that these savage islanders represent a savage simulacrum of British sovereignty. In particular, they seem to be associated with that strain of thought that associates a natural form of kingship and sovereignty with the Stuart line. Defoe's protagonist and his minions display the abhorrent and dark side of technological mastery, reappropriating the space of native fortification into the form of an offensive weapon. The text thus juxtaposes "natural" and "technological" forms of sovereign and political space; I argue that the cataclysmic outcome of this scene suggests the inevitability of modern technological power and a horror at its effects, which seem here to transcend any individual desire. Technology here seems to take over, offering its own logic of penetration, unveiling, and control of political space, intensifying the Hobbesian beast in the human.

Singleton and his crew have sailed from supply stops at Mindanao (in the Philippines) and "new Guiney." Leaving behind the more-or-less charted regions of the ocean, they head southward. Here, in the uncharted and "nameless" regions of the "vast unknown *Indian* Ocean," they encounter an island peopled by unsociable and truculent natives: "When we landed, they fled up the Country, nor would they hold any Correspondence with us, or come near us, but shot at us several Times with arrows as long as Launces.... They shot our Flag of Truce tho' several times with their Arrows" (205). These savages embody an extreme but not unknown type; they prefer to isolate themselves on their island, not wishing to engage in truce or commerce, and are unwilling to allow themselves to be plundered. They are, we might say, an antitype of the English—an impolite and uncommercial people.[49]

In lieu of any friendly response on the part of the natives, the pirates (without comment or special justification) decide to take any cattle or foodstuffs they might find (206). This marauding is typical of European encounters with "unclaimed" spaces; the island is imagined to be fully penetrable and available to British use, an idea that finds support in natural-law theory from Grotius to Locke.[50] But when their marauding is interrupted by a surprise attack, Singleton's crew finds that the savage islanders propose to close this space. Singleton describes the encounter this way:

> They soon found, to their Cost, that they were to use more Caution ... and that they were to discover perfectly every Bush and every Tree, before they ventured abroad in the Country; for about fourteen of our Men going further than the rest, into a Part of the Country which seemed to be planted, as they thought, for it did but seem so, only I think it was overgrown with Canes.... Venturing too far, they were suddenly attack'd with a Shower of Arrows from almost every Side of them, as they thought, out of the Tops of the Trees. (206)

The men run away, but not before trying that old expedient—frightening the savages with gunfire: "tho' they could not see the Enemy, so as to shoot at them, yet perhaps the Noise of their Shot might terrify them, and that they should rather fire at a Venture" (206). They indeed succeed in frightening the enemy, but the fear does not lead to paralysis; rather, the savages respond with a salvo of arrows and an eerie and bestial sound, "more like the Howling and Barking of Wild Creatures in the Woods, than like the Voice of Men, only that sometimes they seemed to speak Words" (207). This strange sound echoes the sounds of the predatory animals in Africa—threatening death and madness. It also offers an uncanny counterpoint to the failure of gunpowder to inspire awe; its earsplitting sound is no match for the disturbing noises of the savage. Yet this sound is simultaneously linguistic, or quasi-linguistic—if the sounds are mostly uncouth, there are what sound like words scattered within them. There is a horrible mixture here—the human with the inhuman—that resonates with the savages' monstrous ability to fortify their own spaces.

Thus far we have seen some of Defoe's earlier tropes repeated with unsettling differences. These savages appear to be uncivilizable through the display of firepower; unlike Friday, the shock of gunfire spurs them to further acts of violence. The events that follow reconfigure our understanding of political space on the island. Unlike Africa, it is not a mere chaos of violence; rather, the savages are capable of deploying the natural world as a kind of fortification—a natural version of the British ideology of political space, with a politics based in geography and natural features rather than on technological interventions.

The natives' defensive capacities become visible as Singleton's men hastily withdraw, having learned that the space they had approached as permeable and open to exploitation is, in fact, as full of danger as any African wilderness. But the encounter has only just begun. As they are returning to the ship, the party passes an ancient and gigantic tree which "stood like an old decay'd Oak in a Park, where the Keepers in England take a Stand, as they call it, to shoot a Deer" (207). Just as the savage headdress resembles a grenadier's cap, so does this tree resemble the great English oak. It is perhaps too much to associate this oak with the Boscabel Oak of Jacobite mythology, in which Charles II hid to evade Cromwell's forces in 1651. And yet the tree's associations with sovereignty and political space, I suggest, make such an association possible, if not inevitable.[51] The savages' concealment inside this tree reads like a perverse version of the Jacobite image of Charles II concealing himself from Cromwell's New Model Army—a "natural" king using the natural world to thwart the forces of the modern. And the savages' position inside the tree can be taken as a form of sovereignty, albeit an imperiled form. But in the end, the crew demonstrates a greater mastery of technology and of nature by redeploying the tree for its own purposes and reconfiguring the interior space of the fortress into a quite different place—that of a gun barrel. The fetishized arboreal icon of Jacobitism is transformed into a demystified and demystifying tool.

For the savages have adapted this tree into a fortress, enabling them to retain, if not mastery over the island, at least a protected and impermeable zone within it. They ambush Singleton's men as they pass beneath it, killing two. The men do not attempt to flee but rather "run close to the tree, and stand, as it were under it; so that those above could not come at, or see them, to throw their Launces at them" (207). Hiding in this position, they succeed in shooting down one of the "enemies and Murtherers" who lurk above. In response, the savages once again produce sounds of wildness: "our Men heard a strange Clutter of them in the Body of the Tree, from whence they concluded they had made the Tree hollow, and were got to hide themselves there" (208). This natural fortress, however, is about to do battle with the modern technologies of siege craft and gunpowder. The enterprising pirates believe that they have victory in their hands; using the language of siege craft, they project their mastery of the people inside it and anticipate removing them from concealment to make their bodies vulnerable and more subject to their power:

> They made no Doubt however, but that they had their Enemies in a Trap, and that a small Siege would either bring them down Tree and all, or starve them out: So they resolved to keep their Post, and send to us for Help. Accordingly two of them came away to us for more Hands, and particularly desired, that some of our Carpenters might come with Tools, to help cut down the Tree, or at least to cut down other wood, and set Fire to it; and That they concluded would not fail to bring them out. (208)

The resulting confrontation is a siege in miniature. Singleton distances himself somewhat from the proceeding; his reading of it as a military operation contains a hint of irony: "Accordingly our Men went like a little Army, and with mighty Preparations for an Enterprize, the like of which has scarce been ever heard, to form the Siege of a great Tree" (208).

But the task is more difficult than they had anticipated, for the tree is very thick indeed. The natural world, properly adapted, is quite capable of trumping the technological, or so it appears at first. The siege proceeds in several stages over several days. Singleton's crew at first plans to smoke out the savages, but this plan is abandoned following a sudden attack by the savages: "for when it was done, who would venture up among such a Troop of bold Creatures as were there?" (209). They opt instead to dash quickly to the top of the tree, throw in some firebombs, and dash back down again; this, however, produces no results. A stink bomb is then lobbed in, after which they hear nothing from the tree for a whole day. "We concluded the Men within were all smother'd: When, on a sudden, the next Night, we heard them upon the Top of the Tree again, shouting and hallooing like Madmen" (210).

At this point, the crew has spent almost a week on the island. They have found no provisions or goods to take with them on their trip; there is nothing particularly worth plundering. They nevertheless remain. Initially, their motives appear to have been an impulse to avenge the deaths of their crewmates; however, at this point something even less reasonable has taken over: "We were all enraged to see our selves so baulk'd by a few wild People whom we thought we had safe in our Clutches; and indeed never was there so many concurring Circumstances to delude Men, in any Case we had met with" (210). This sense of being baulked, frustrated in their will, is significant. The natives challenge the power of modern individuals and their military technology over the colonized subject and the natural world. The crew's actions are disconnected from any pragmatic goal. Instead, they are driven as though automatons themselves to demonstrate the power of technology over that of the natural world. At first, the men's principle had been to avenge their crewmates; now it appears that they must avenge the insult the natives have committed by successfully resisting the crew's technological power and preserving a space that is impermeable to their will and their violence. It is as if the technology is now using them rather than the other way around; the rationality of modernity here threatens to slide into madness, not unleashing terrifying passions but rather erasing agency from acts of violence that are done, as it were, by gunpowder itself.

After yet another plan to set the tree ablaze fails when the savages dump water from the treetop onto the fire, Singleton's first mate realizes the savages' secret: they are confronting not merely an opportunistic use of nature but rather an adapted fortress, consisting of a hollow tree and a subterranean tunnel. Having penetrated these defenses mentally, Singleton's nominally pacifist adviser William Walters will next seek to open them to more direct exploration:

> Says *William*, this is certainly the cunningest Piece of *Indian* Engineering that ever was heard of. . . . This is an artificial Tree, or a natural Tree artificially made hollow down into the Earth, thro' Root and all; and . . . these Creatures have an artificial Cavity underneath it, quite into the Hill, or a Way to go thro', and under the Hill, to some other Place, and where that other Place is, we know not; but if it be not our own Fault, I'll find the Place, and follow them into it, before I am two Days older. (211)

To discover the hollow, the party under William's direction uses gunpowder to blast open holes in the tree trunk (212). This practice succeeding, Singleton's crew discovers a "Cave or Hole" dug from the interior of the tree to a larger cave farther back, from which they can hear "the Voices of several of the wild Folks" (212). William and three other men enter the opening, grenades in hand, but are repelled by wily savages wielding stinkpots (212). Singleton says admiringly, "Never was a Fortification so well defended, or Assailants so many ways defeated" (212).

Singleton, finally, begins to urge his crew to abandon their futile siege: "I could not but laugh to see us spinning out our Time here for nothing; that I could not imagine what we were doing. . . . It would vex any Body to be so baulked by a few naked ignorant Fellows; but still it was not worth our while to push it any further" (213). Singleton here is attempting to back away from the point of pride that appears to be driving the assault. William essentially agrees but suggests one remaining motive for being persistent: curiosity. But this need to satisfy curiosity once again loops back into a desire for revenge: the ship's gunner asks to take "Satisfaction of the Rogues" by "mak[ing] a Mine of" the tree to "see which way it had Vent."

> Upon this he fetches two Barrels of Powder out of the Ships, and placed them in the Inside of the hollow Cave, as far in as he durst go to carry them, and then filling up the Mouth of the Cave where the

Tree stood, and ramming it sufficiently hard, leaving only a Pipe or Touch-hole, he gave Fire to it, and stood at a Distance to see which way it would operate, when, on the sudden, he found the Force of the Powder burst its way out among some Bushes on the other Side of the little Hill I mentioned, and that it came roaring out there as out of the Mouth of a Cannon. (213)

Here we see revealed the slippery nature of William's curiosity—a curiosity that seems to sit adjacent to technological violence. Indeed, the violence that the pirates commit here—transforming a native defensive fortification into a "cannon"—is itself a kind of figure for the relationship between imperial science and discovery, on the one hand, and the politics of conquest, on the other.[52] But it also figures the role of technology in mastering protocolonial spaces. The crew has been confronted by a savage nation that is nevertheless able to claim its space as its own. The crew's technological mastery, however, is able to turn even that protected interior into an offensive weapon, transforming the fortress into a firing chamber. The results of the "experiment" may be found on the other side of the hill:

First, We saw that *there* was the other Mouth of the Cave. . . . There we saw what was become of the Garrison of *Indians too*, who had given us all this Trouble; for some of them had no Arms, some no Legs, some no Head, some lay half buried in the Rubbish of the Mine, that is to say, in the loose Earth that fell in; and, in short, there was a miserable Havock made of them all, for we had good Reason to believe, not one of them that were in the Inside could escape, but rather were shot out of the Mouth of the Cave like a Bullet out of a Gun. (213–14)

Here again is the figure of the gun: if the cave is transformed into a cannon's firing chamber, then, by extension, the bodies inside the cave have become bullets. Their status as victims is elided by this catachrestic substitution; rather than being pierced by invisible bullets, they have become bullets themselves—and bullets can hardly be the objects of empathy or pity. In becoming bullets, propelled by gunpowder, their bodies have also become products of technology; in death, the distinction between bullet and body vanishes. Most significant of all, however, is the text's representation of the British oak of sovereignty as a contested arena of struggle. Initially held by the "traditional" local inhabitants, the tree can be transformed handily into a weapon for other, more anarchic forces. This horrific gunshot figures sovereignty in its most violent, least mediated form.

The selections from the Crusonian novels that I have selected point toward Defoe's interest in civilizing wild subjects and modernizing and containing wild spaces through technology. But this process in the end appears an ambivalent one, as Crusoe's early faith in the civilizing power of the firearm is gradually unmasked as uncontainable: the power of display by a civilizing sovereign rapidly deteriorates in later writings into a sign of merest anarchy. If, as I have argued, precolonial spaces offer the reader an opportunity to examine and reconfigure more general problems of political modernity, then these massacres—these pessimistic readings of politics, passion, and technology—are also examinations of Britain itself, with its masterless servants and highwaymen. I see in the Madagascans' failure to exert military control over their territory an implicit comment on the forms that state power ought to take to assert control over individual bodies. If in *Robinson Crusoe* the gun is a civilizing agent, here the gun's figural power shifts, becoming an argument not for more strategic use of guns but for the need for formal state structures to exert force and to control the means of violence within its borders. Defoe's *Robinson Crusoe* points toward an ongoing interest in sovereignty's power to civilize without violence; his scenes of massacre, however, point in a more complex way both toward the need for sovereign violence to govern passion and toward the terrifying violence that may lie at the heart of modern sovereignty.

CHAPTER 4

Doctrines Détestables: Jonathan Swift, Despotism, and Virtue

> The next Thing he demanded was one of the hollow Iron Pillars, by which he meant my Pocket-Pistols. I drew it out, and at his Desire, as well as I could, expressed to him the Use of it, and charging it only with Powder. . . . I first cautioned the Emperor not to be afraid; and then I let it off in the Air. . . . Hundreds fell down as if they had been struck dead; and even the Emperor, although stood his Ground, could not recover himself in some time.
>
> —Jonathan Swift, *Travels into Several Remote Nations in the World* (1726)[1]

The Lilliputians are no savages; they are a settled and commercial nation. So it is somewhat surprising to find them replicating these tropes from the colonial archive and to find that they, like most of the peoples that Gulliver encounters on his travels, are strangers to gunpowder. Like Defoe's Caribs, they stand awestruck, falling down as if dead. This sequence illuminates Swift's plundering of the colonial archive for contact tropes that illustrate political affect. But unlike Friday, the Lilliputians are not civilized by this technological display. Rather, Gulliver immediately surrenders his weaponry and begins his process of assimilating to Lilliputian values—values which of course mimic the superficial obsessions of Swift's own Britain and Ireland. The scene, then, may be read as a parody of Defoe's narrative of the civility-making violence.

Jonathan Swift's *Travels into Several Remote Nations in the World* (1726) holds a vital place in the tradition of colonial and imperial fiction alongside the work of Margaret Cavendish, Aphra Behn, and Daniel Defoe. Gulliver is an explorer and a proponent of British civilization; he is also, at times, a self-appointed agent of the British civilizing mission, hoping to improve, for example, the Brobdingnagian system of government with a liberal application of gunpowder. And if most of Gulliver's encounters are not with savages, the narrative nevertheless uses the settings of Lilliput, Brobdingnag, Balnibarbi, and Houyhnhnmland to invoke (sometimes explicitly, sometimes implicitly) the familiar topoi of colonial encounter and military technology.[2] Swift's fiction also comments directly on British (and Irish) political philosophy and practice. Critics have read the *Travels* for its sources in the imperial archive as well as for its satire of English and Irish politics, but few have linked the two. This chapter investigates exactly this connection, arguing that the colonial world and its contact zones are for Swift key sites for investigating the place of violence and political subjectivity in modernity more generally. For Swift, the civilizing mission of the empire is metonymically linked to the responsibility of the sovereign and the aristocrat to exemplify a virtuous citizenship and thereby inspire civility in others. When they fail, the *civitas* returns to savagery and the rule of the strongest: a violent state of nature from which a civilizing despotism will reemerge.

In making this suggestion, I am challenging some cherished ideas about Swift's politics and his contempt for tyrants. Swift's political thought is often described in terms of his adherence to the political parties and ideologies of his day—variously Whig, "Old Whig," Tory, or Jacobite—and his putative anti-imperialism.[3] More recent critics have emphasized Swift's own distaste for political labels and the lability of his political alliances and allegiances, seeing him as an operative within constraining political rhetorics or as a pragmatic defender of the established church with otherwise flexible political principles.[4] My approach here breaks to some degree from readings that assume a clarity and intentionality of principle on Swift's part; the political commitments of his literary efforts are too complex and ambivalent to associate clearly with political factions or alliances. It is more productive, I argue, to understand Swift's manipulation of and recurring investment in specific rhetorical positions, particularly with the concepts and languages of virtue, political affect, and violence. Warren Montag has suggested that Swift's literary treatment of concepts might be understood not as themes but rather as "nodal points," rhetorical positions "where diverse and conflicting meanings condense and combine." This chapter presents a similar approach to violence and political affect as problems that Swift's writing engages and even thematizes but does not master.[5] Swift always publicly professed himself to be a sort of high-church Whig, from his early association with William Temple, through his heyday as a propagandist for Queen Anne's last ministry, and into his final years in quasi-exile in Ireland.[6] This political writing emphasizes commonplace themes of British liberty and a contempt for tyrants; its key mediator is not the violence of the sovereign but the power of virtuous example. But his texts betray a lack of faith in this delicate balance of virtue and display, instead fretting over the prospects of inspiring virtue without violence and the threat of violence without virtue.

Swift's preferred manner of governing and civilizing was exemplarity and imitation: the best men ought to inspire patriotism and public spiritedness through example.[7] But the corruption of virtue in contemporary Britain and Ireland made Swift fear—but also, I think, ambivalently desire—the reintroduction of savage violence to restart a dialectic of tyranny and resistance that would rebalance the constitution. The dilemma of political modernity left Swift positioned between two extremes: a willingness to entertain civilizing violence and even absolutism, on the one hand, and a sense that the violence of modernity is already a return to barbarism, on the other. If civility can only be produced by a transition through absolutism—if even civility remains a state of war—then it follows that modernity can be seen as a new kind of barbarism.

The idea that violence or virtuous example are the options for preserving civic order has close analogues in colonial narratives, as Swift certainly recognized. The tools used to discipline unruly subjects—virtuous example and the sword—are the very same tools that, ideally, bring civil life and Christianity to the world's savages. However, whereas Defoe and others see technological objects or fetishes mediating between the categories of exemplarity and violence, for Swift these functions divide into luxury consumer goods (which produce mere admiration) and apocalyptic technologies (threatening universal violence without mediation). Swift suggests that Britons may have lost the ability to admire and imitate virtue; whereas admiration of one's betters had once seemed potentially transformative, it appears under conditions of modernity to be a politically neutralized and superficial form of the aesthetic or of mere fashion. Or perhaps it is more accurate to say that Swift's attitude toward awe is held in suspension, potentially transformative but also full of frippery and display. Swift's texts hold out hope for a kind of virtue remaining in civilization and the idea of the civilizing mission and long for a civilization that could bring absolutism to the savage in order to bring the whole world to civility. Yet they also withdraw from this resolution; modernity has rendered the hope for this form of virtue untenable, and thus *Gulliver's Travels* is a text of a disappointed imperialist posing as a liberator.

Empire is, to be sure, not far removed from tyranny. And tyranny is precisely what Swift claimed to have spent his career opposing. Yet the intensity of Swift's writings against tyranny and absolutism suggest a more complex attitude than is sometimes acknowledged. The hatred is real, but the hatred is conjoined with a fascination that I argue is related to his fear that tyranny, though abhorrent, was nevertheless inevitable as a civilizing influence. The importance of these ideas to Swift is made clear in his marginal notes in Jean Bodin's *Six livres de la republique*. Bodin is the early modern period's most well-known theorist of indivisible sovereignty and exercised a potent influence on Thomas Hobbes's writing. Swift's response to this theory in his marginal note—written in 1725, during the composition of both the later letters as the Drapier and *Gulliver's Travels*—is to label it a *"doctrine détestable."*[8] While Bodin was content to place trust in an absolute monarch who would act as a benign father to his subjects, Swift asks, "and who will put trust in such a king?"[9]

These comments, written by Swift for no eyes but his own, are on one level remarkable glimpses of his private reading practices and his authentic political attitudes. But they also serve to complicate the very idea of an "authentic" political attitude. For although Swift damns absolutism and tyrants, his writing cannot seem to leave behind the problems to which tyranny appears as a partial solution. And Swift's own writing suggests that tyranny is, if never desirable, at least inevitable at a certain stage of social and political development. The ambivalence I find here echoes in some degree—and indeed is closely intertwined with—a similar ambivalence that many critics have located in his attitudes toward violence and the body. If Swift's writings on the grotesque body exhibit, simultaneously, revulsion and fascination, then we might suggest that Swift's political writing has a similar relationship with sovereignty.[10] If the female body is the object of the greatest revulsion and hatred in Swift's writing, then the figure of the tyrant runs a close second; yet the very obsession Swift's writing displays with this figure suggests that it is an imago from which he could not completely disentangle himself.

Gulliver's Travels is among other things an explicit engagement with these political problems and with the way that lawless violence and tyranny intersect with foundational and transitional moments in politics and civic life. This engagement appears in each section of the *Travels*: sequences in Lilliput and Brobdingnag replay the scene of colonial encounter and the awe-inspiring gunshot, investigating the problem of political affect as it is inflected through the aestheticization of violence; the presentation of Gulliver's obsession with objects of display and extravagance connects the power of awe to the rhetoric of luxury consumption; and Laputa offers us the image of a superiority that is merely technological, devoid of the power to civilize except through violence. Gulliver's coda to his experiences in the land of the Houyhnhnms engages directly with the issues raised by colonialism and conquest, satirizing the civilizing mission while at the same time remaining unable to resist the idea of violence as a civilizing agent. It is this figure of the colony, and of the savage in need of sovereignty to pull him out of anarchy into the political order, that offers us access to this place in Swift's thought, that allows us to see the ambivalence of his attitude toward tyranny. It is in the colony that Swift sees violence and tyranny as both necessary and not, as inescapable stages of political growth as well as detestable doctrines.

The tyrant, as we shall see, is simultaneously the most dangerous enemy of the *civitas* and the foundational moment of the political order. This chapter turns first to two early Swiftian tracts: *A Discourse of the Contests and Dissensions between the Nobles and the Commons in Athens and Rome* (1701) and *Sentiments of a Church-of-England Man* (1711). Reading them in light of Gulliver's comments on war, I argue that that Swift's early thinking, despite its Whiggish allegiances and its defense of "liberty," nevertheless presumes that civility can only emerge from either foundational moments of lawmaking or civility-making violence or from the dialectical struggle of the rebellious savage against the tyrant. These considered, the chapter then turns to the split in the political fetish between the consumer good and the apocalyptic weapon.

State Failure and the Origins of Civility

Gulliver famously concludes book 4 of his *Travels* with a caustic denunciation of empire and its failures. The story of colonialism, in Gulliver's reading, is nothing more than this:

> A crew of pirates are driven by a storm they know not whither; at length a boy discovers land from the topmast; they go on shore to rob and plunder, they see a harmless people, are entertained with

kindness; they give the country a new name; they take formal possession of it for their king; they set up a rotten plank, or a stone, for a memorial; they murder two or three dozen of the natives, bring away a couple more, by force, for a sample; return home, and get their pardon. Here commences a new Dominion acquired with a Title by *Divine Right*. (294)

Though this passage is frequently taken as a denunciation of imperialism more generally, I suggest that it registers something more complex. These passages do not deny the intrinsic merit of empire and its civilizing mission; the problem is rather one of, as we would now say, implementation. Imperial conquests, in Gulliver's famous treatment, are nothing more than manifestations of ad hoc plunder, carried out by rogues in the name of the state; recorded in history as part of the progress of civilization, they are in fact mere manifestations of lawlessness and violent anarchy. The passage, conjoining piracy and divine right, uses imperialism to excavate the close but uneasy kinship between anarchy and tyranny. This indictment of colonialism is a caustic burlesque of every aspect of the colonial enterprise; where there ought to be reason and purpose, there is arbitrariness and accident; where we should find benevolence, there is violence and rapine. It is notable that Gulliver invokes the language of the divine right of kings, for this usage links the colonial project to the questions of domestic sovereignty and the parliamentary and royal prerogatives. The passage shows us pirates who gain the title of divine right through conquest, in a close analogue of tyranny more generally. This form of sovereignty, however, breeds only cruelty and violence:

> Ships are sent with the first opportunity; the natives driven out or destroyed; their princes tortured to discover their gold; a free license given to all acts of inhumanity and lust, the earth reeking with the blood of its inhabitants: and this execrable Crew of Butchers, employed in so pious an Expedition, is a *modern Colony*, sent to convert and civilize an idolatrous and barbarous People. (294)

Gulliver's imperialists perpetrate massacre, extermination, and ethnic cleansing. They are agents of law, though in name only; in fact, they see themselves as sovereigns freed from law, raping, murdering, pillaging, and doing as they will, like beasts. The end result of this tyrannical lawlessness is massacre and a devastated political space populated only by steaming corpses.

Importantly, however, Gulliver's next words make clear that he, at least—and I would argue, Swift as well—has a normative vision of empire's role in spreading civilization. Gulliver, ironically seeking to exempt England from his catalog of horrors, tells us that his critique must not be taken to apply to Britain, whose representatives

> may be an example to the whole world for their wisdom, care, and justice in planting colonies; their liberal endowments for the advancement of religion and learning; their choice of devout and able pastors to propagate Christianity; their caution in stocking their provinces with people of sober lives and conversations from this the mother kingdom; their strict regard to the distribution of justice, in supplying the civil administration through all their colonies with officers of the greatest abilities, utter strangers to corruption; and, to crown all, by sending the most vigilant and virtuous governors, who have no other views than the happiness of the people over whom they preside, and the honour of the king their master. (294–95)

Swift uses Gulliver to offer an inverted litany of the tasks that most need to be carried out in the colonies: support for propagation of the Gospel; the foundation of virtuous communities with profound respect for the rule of law; and, in particular, the governing of these colonies by disinterested and public-spirited men. In fact, England's colonies—and Swift is surely including Ireland here—are quite different from this portrait; they are instead governed by self-interest, greed, and vice, failing their duty to propagate civility. Yet the duty itself is not here satirized—quite the opposite. The problem is that the agents of the imperial mission are not exemplars of virtue; rather than spreading the Gospel and considering the public interest, they are instead debased figures, typical of the modern, incapable of civilizing with anything other than an imperial and tyrannical violence and a modern corruption.

This moment in Swift's text is much noted, but no one to my knowledge has perceived the way that this backhanded endorsement of empire is linked to the larger corpus of Swift's political writing. In what follows, I attempt to use Swift's political tracts to reconstruct an incomplete and contradictory political theory that envisions the dependence of the political on violence. Swift constructs a fantasy of an empire that is necessarily predicated on conquest and violence. Civility having been established, there is a hope that the virtue of the "best men"—the natural leaders of the civil order—will infuse others with sentiments and forms of affect that will support self-sacrifice and public virtue. But when exemplarity fails, as Ireland's leaders will fail in the 1720s, the result is a horrifying, if necessary, return to the political state of the savage and the tyrant, in a dialectical struggle to remake society and re-create liberty.

Two of Swift's early political tracts, *A Discourse of the Contests and Dissentions between the Nobles and the Commons in Athens and Rome* and *Sentiments of a Church-of-England Man*, are entangled in this paradox of civility and violence. Critics have read these texts in their local rhetorical contexts as well as for signs of an embedded Whig or Tory perspective. I supplement these readings by suggesting that these texts, like Swift's later writings, are engaged with the political paradoxes of constituent power and violence that I have been examining. Among other things, they probe the role of violence in the foundation of the civil order and the construction of political communities. The *Discourse*, in the course of criticizing excesses in popular power and praising mixed forms of government, also relies on the figure of a unitary sovereign who fashions law and preserves balance; *Sentiments*, alongside its advocacy of British liberty, also imagines that liberty as the product of a dialectical struggle between the insurgent savage and the tyrannical sovereign. Both texts understand political communities as fluid and dynamic, evolving in ways that can only be stabilized by a blend of violence and virtue. And both, though not explicitly engaging with the imperial project that Gulliver criticizes and promotes, nevertheless investigate a closely related set of problems: the role of violence in the construction of civility and the relative importance of virtue and awe in creating a political affect that can contribute to that stability.

The *Discourse* is political polemic posing as history.[11] Ostensibly a Polybian examination of the balance of power in the Athenian and Roman states, its most immediate purpose is to attack the new Tory leadership in the Commons. Tensions between Whig and Tory factions were high in the wake of the Nine Years' War and the Treaty of Ryswick (1697) that ended it. Many Britons feared that France's power and ambitions would provoke another war and possibly an invasion of England in support of the Stuart claim to the throne. This context gave parliamentary battles the character not of reasoned discourse over policy but of an existential struggle over the fate of the nation. The new Tory ministry's political maneuvers included the impeachment of several Whig lords, known as the Junto, who had been closely aligned with William III during the war. The impeachment charges related, among other things, to secret partition treaties negotiated with France in 1699 and 1700. This impeachment followed close on the heels of the imprisonment of a group of petitioners from Kent, charged with sedition for their strong appeal to the Commons to take stronger measures to defend the English coastline from a possible French invasion.[12] These petitioners were most likely acting at the instigation of Whig agitators, probably including Daniel Defoe.[13]

By the time Swift's treatise appeared, the immediate crisis had passed—the impeachment effort had already failed and the petitioners had been released with the prorogation of Parliament. The *Discourse* nevertheless attracted attention because of its examination of persistent questions about the nature and location of sovereignty in England. The tract argues not for unitary sovereignty but for a dynamic balance between the three estates (monarch, lords, and commons). Its final pages are a despairing jeremiad, hyperbolically suggesting that England's constitution was collapsing just at the moment that the nation was most threatened by French aspirations to universal monarchy. Significantly, however, for all that the essay decries tyranny and doctrines of unitary sovereignty, it also repeatedly relies on forces exterior to the balancing act of politics; the three estates do not balance themselves automatically but require an external agent to restore and maintain balance and to stave off emergencies. This obscure agent, I think, must be read as a unitary sovereign, Swift's protests to the contrary notwithstanding.

Swift's tract begins by arguing that constitutions emerge not from contract but from moments of existential political or military crisis. At these crucial junctures, great men appear to vanquish the enemies of the community. These men are founding sovereigns, civilizing warriors who expel illegitimate violence from the political community. Such a leader, after violently expelling hostile and disorderly people from the realm, is able to transform his prowess into charisma, which in turn transforms the undifferentiated multitude into political subjects. These heroic lawgivers are exemplified for Swift by Theseus and Romulus, the mythical founders of Athens and Rome. Theseus is credited in the classical tradition with creating the possibility of civic life by taming the countryside and settling the nomad; Theseus "brought the Grecians from a barbarous manner of life among scattered villages, into cities" and then founded the Athenian state, "assigning to himself the guardianship of the laws, and chief command in war" (204). Slaying master criminals and encouraging families to adopt a settled way of life, Theseus and Romulus are warrior-sovereigns whose violence creates the possibility of civil order. Versions of these lawmaking heroes may also emerge during later periods of political or military crisis; at these junctures, that founding moment is repeated, as "one eminent spirit," Swift argues, "having signalized his Valour and Fortune in Defence of his Country, or by the Practice of popular Arts at Home, comes to have great Influence on the People, to grow their Leader in warlike Expeditions, and to preside, after a sort, in their Civil Assemblies" (196). The esteem he inspires "is grounded upon the principles of Nature and common Reason, which, in all Difficulties and Dangers, where Prudence or Courage is required, do rather incite us to fly for Counsel or Assistance to a single Person, than a Multitude" (196).

The props of monarchy in this account are terror and admiration, a product of military emergency. The monarch and the people form an alliance that tends toward tyranny; in response, the landowning aristocracy must band together to preserve its property interests. The *Discourse*, channeling Polybius, envisions the domestic balance that results as an internalized and institutionalized form of warfare, with peace a condition established tenuously through fear.[14] The free state, then, is one where civil war is not eliminated but merely suppressed. War cannot break out as long as each side fears to break the balance; fear becomes institutionalized, and competition sustains a dynamic equilibrium.

However, for all Swift's arguments on behalf of balance, the *Discourse* nevertheless finds itself unable to offer an image of a stable polity that does not ultimately rely on a version of the sovereign exception. Each estate internal to the balance longs to expand its power, breaking the balance and engrossing more power to itself. In Swift's tract, it is the multitude, figured by England's House of Commons, that is most often guilty of this ambition. At the conclusion of the essay, Swift explicitly connects these classical disputations to contemporary events, attacking the Tory ministers who were directly assailing the power of the nobility by impeaching the Whig Lords. This assault hints at claims of limitless powers to come. Swift describes the Tory Commons as a geometer's compass that will center itself "wherever they think fit" while expanding its other leg as wide as it wishes, "without describing any Circumference at all" (231). This paradoxical compass, with its arbitrary center and its limitless circumference, aptly describes the lawlessness of an absolutely sovereign political institution.

If the Commons will not limit its own powers, what can? The answer ultimately lies in Swift's obscure figure of "the hand that holds the balance." Swift translates the somewhat abstract notion of balance offered by Polybius into the more concrete image of a scale. But a scale, Swift points out, has two balancing pans, not three; the scale also needs a fulcrum and a hand, to hold it. Though Swift's "hand" is a position that might, in theory, be occupied by any one of the estates, in a contest between the many and the few it is the monarch who must sustain the balance and "deal the remaining Power with the utmost Exactness into each Scale" (197). As F. P. Lock notes, this gives the monarch "the really decisive role, for he is not . . . a king with fixed and limited powers" but rather a source of decision-making in the last instance.[15] While the monarch holds the scale's fulcrum, however, there is another possible external agent that might rebalance the system: the *vox populi*, or constituent power. In the final paragraphs, the essay implicitly threatens that the people's love for their monarch and their fear of French power will cause them to turn against their representatives in Parliament, which, it speculates, might place "the Balance of Power a little more upon an Equality" (235). Swift has here, somewhat ambiguously, located sovereignty—the responsibility for preserving the balance in the constitution—both in the monarch and in the people at large.

It would be hazardous to use this text as exemplifying Swift's "true" political beliefs, since it is first and foremost a rhetorical performance with partisan intent. Yet the political language he adopts and its ambiguous stance on popular and monarchical power resonate not only with the political paradoxes noted by writers of colonial fictions but also with his own later essays and satiric writings. Though the *Discourse* does not specifically invoke the language of colonialism and savagery, Swift would use that language in another political performance a decade later. His *Sentiments of a Church of England Man* (1711) suppresses the explicit question of political violence but simultaneously deflects the conception of foundational violence into the language of colonialism and savagery, suggesting that tyranny and imperialism are the predecessors of the "balanced" state described in the *Discourse*.[16] In his comments on politics in this tract, Swift stakes out the territory of pragmatism and moderation, claiming no intrinsic merit for any of the three Aristotelian systems of government (monarchy, oligarchy, and democracy), instead proffering the republican commonplace that the virtue of the citizenry is in fact far more important to the survival of civil society than are the external forms or technicalities of governance: "Few States are ruined by any Defect in their Institution, but generally by the Corruption of Manners; against which, the best Institution is no long security, and without which, a very ill one may subsist and flourish" (14). This depiction of the relationship between politics and virtue—which is, I argue, closely related to the language of sovereignty and civility— here seems to lack a civilizing agent. That is, the character of the people must preserve political institutions, but there is, at this juncture, no acknowledgment that political institutions might influence the character of the citizenry. As we shall see later, however, Swift's tract does imagine that political institutions exist in a dialectical relationship to the virtue of the citizenry: if sovereigns cannot directly civilize, the struggle against them can. It is this dialectical relationship, similar in structure to Swift's earlier redaction of Polybius, that links this discussion of contemporary British politics to the discourses of colonization, conquest, and savagery.

The argument of *Sentiments* relies at crucial moments on the rhetoric of civilization and savagery. Indeed, it is not too much to say that the references imagine limit cases or moments of exception—exceptions that serve, arguably, to redefine the limits and the context of the moderate political stance it presents, opening a back door for absolutism and sovereign power even as it explicitly excoriates them. Swift suggests that "whoever argues in Defence of absolute Power in a single Person, although he offers the plausible Plea, that *it is his opinion*, . . . ought, in all free States, to be treated as the Common Enemy of Mankind" (15–16). This is strong language indeed. Borrowing Cicero's formulation regarding piracy, Swift suggests not that an absolute sovereign is to be regarded as the equivalent of a pirate but rather that anyone who argues on behalf of such power (such as Hobbes) should be seen as an intellectual pirate, not to be tolerated within the parameters of civil speech.[17] This rhetoric anticipates Gulliver's equation of the tyrant and his pirates in the making of the colonial world, discussed earlier. But the text remains indebted to Hobbes and others who wrote on the question of savagery, the state of nature, and the emergence of sovereignty. On the one hand, *Sentiments* uses this sort of language in its overarching treatment of authoritarianism and absolutism, noting that "Arbitrary Power . . . [is] a greater Evil than *Anarchy* itself; as much as a *Savage* is in a happier State of Life, than a *Slave* at the *Oar*" (15) This is the champion of liberty that we generally expect to find in Swift. And yet just a few pages later, Swift offers an important concession, seeming to contemplate an exception—but an exception that also has universal implications. He notes that "Arbitrary Power is but the first natural step from *Anarchy* or the *Savage Life*; the adjusting *Power* and *Freedom* being an Effect and Consequence of maturer Thinking" (19). For Swift, then, slavery and arbitrary government are both deplorable, but both are also necessary "steps" for a full flowering of civility. As we have seen, this suggestion that a form of tyrannical sovereignty is an essential precursor of civil liberty is familiar from a variety of republican accounts; it is not Swift's invention. But Swift's linkage of this tyranny to the savage in this passage illuminates once more the ways that colonialism and liberty are complexly intertwined.

This is an important qualification of Swift's position, one that his essay does not develop. But as in the *Discourse*, it reminds us of the interpenetration of the savage and the civil; the civil threatens to return to the savage and thus perpetually invites the prospect of the return to lawlessness and, in turn, the emergence of a lawmaking warrior-sovereign. Since, as we have seen, arbitrary power is difficult in practice to separate from the powers associated with conquest, then is Swift suggesting that both political power and civilization emerge from acts of conquest—a dialectical struggle between the anarchic impulses of the multitude and the depredations of the conqueror? If so, then colonialism may be not only permissible but even necessary to the savage's advance toward civility. Swift's text leaves open—or perhaps suppresses—the question of how force and awe come into play in this dialectic of violence and governance, however. For a treatment of these issues, we must look to first to *Gulliver's Travels* and then to Swift's Irish writings.

The Force of Fashion: Gulliver, Gunpowder, and Awe

Like Lilliput, Brobdingnag, Swift's land of giants, is a land without gunpowder. Gulliver's stay in this land includes a stint in the court of the Brobdingnagian sovereign. In an effort to ingratiate himself, Gulliver offers to the king the gift of gunpowder:

> I knew the Ingredients very well, which were Cheap, and common; I understood the Manner of compounding them, and could direct his Workmen how to make those Tubes of a Size proportionable to all

other Things in his Majesty's Kingdom; and the largest need not be above two hundred foot long; twenty or thirty of which Tubes, charged with the proper Quantity of Powder and Balls, would batter down the Walls of the strongest Town in his Dominions in a few Hours; or destroy the whole Metropolis, if ever it should pretend to dispute his absolute commands. (110)

Claude Rawson has highlighted the implicit temporality of this sequence: Gulliver's modern knowledge enables a brutal satire of technological modernity.[18] However, I want to underscore more directly than Rawson that this is a deployment of a colonial trope—the introduction of gunpowder to a community that inhabits a different temporality, one preceding the invention of black powder. In books 1 and 2, Gulliver borrows tropes from colonial discourse to investigate the relationship between military technology, awe, and civil polity. As we will see in Swift's Irish tracts, the political failures that haunted Swift at this time were those of virtue and political affect—the failure, especially, of the socially superior to instill awe and virtue through example. In *Gulliver's Travels*, we see Swift specifically translating this problem into the language of colonialism, where awesome virtue gives way to awe-inspiring violence. Gulliver's captivity in Lilliput serves to make the firearm an icon of the poverty of modern European civilization, which remains pompously proud of its superiority but is easily lured from its own foundation and ensnared in the values of the Other. This problem is figured through technological devices; what appear as political fetish objects in other works, however, here divide into luxury goods and apocalyptic weapons. The Lilliputians and, indeed, Gulliver himself are obsessed with fashionable objects of display and extravagance, including Gulliver's gallantish watch as well as his weapons. In book 1, colonial astonishment, admiration, and conversion are parodically reduced to economies of fashion and luxury consumption.

Gulliver's first contact with Lilliput echoes the moment of colonial encounter, but it does not follow Robinson Crusoe's method of civilizing through intimidation. Instead, Gulliver appears impotent in the face of the Lilliputian horde that surrounds him, and his weapons offer him not the power of civilizing absolutism but its polar opposite—a servile and disgraceful captivity in which his admittedly great powers serve the foolish whims of the emperor. Lilliput, like Brobdingnag, is unacquainted with gunpowder. Indeed, although not a "savage" society by any means, the Lilliputians do not appear to possess much in the way of mechanical or chemical expertise. Like savages, they are unfamiliar with timekeeping devices. Investigating the watch, they have this to say: it is a "wonderful kind of engine":

> [It] appeared to be a Globe, half Silver, and half of some transparent Metal: For on the transparent Side we saw certain strange Figures circularly drawn, and thought we could touch them, until we found our Fingers stopped with that lucid Substance. . . . We conjecture it is either some unknown Animal, or the God that he worships: But we are more inclined to the latter Opinion, because he assured us . . . that he seldom did any Thing without consulting it. He called it his Oracle, and said it pointed out the Time for every Action of his Life. (18)

This description anticipates Olaudah Equiano's encounter with his master's watch and also echoes Friday's encounter with Crusoe's gun. The Lilliputians fetishize the watch, imbuing it with imaginary life; they also present it as a deity, though they themselves do not join in Gulliver's worship. It is worth noting that the language of wonder is here applied to an object that had, from its origins, been associated with a style of display closely linked to luxury consumption and superficiality. That Gulliver is represented as seldom doing anything without consulting his watch suggests already that the language of awe and technological superiority is being conjoined with the criticism of the culture of consumption; that this display is associated with the weapons that follow is indicative of Swift's critique of modern European culture as enfeebled and unable to play the role of exemplary civilizing agent.[19]

Swift then offers a pointed parody of the narrative of technological contact that we have been discussing. Just as the watch here signifies not technological superiority and awe but superficiality and display, so too do the weapons signify pleasurable display more than power. The language first imitates that of awe in Defoe and elsewhere, as Gulliver displays his weaponry. The sword comes first, and it indeed has the power to dazzle. The sword catches the light of the sun and offers a blinding display of power: "all the Troops gave a Shout between Terror and Surprize; for the Sun shone clear, and the Reflexion dazzled their Eyes" (19). This moment will be echoed in Brobdingnag in a different register, when Gulliver experiences the awesome display of the militia. But here, the sword invokes colonial discourses of awe and submission more directly and offers a more straightforward parody of those discourses. Like the gunshot that follows, Gulliver's performance dazzles.

This threat intensifies as Gulliver introduces a new technological innovation to the Lilliputians: the firearm. We have already seen how Gulliver's firing of the weapon imitates colonial discourse, especially in its detailed description of the Lilliputians' astonishment (19). But in doing so, he is also a politically destabilizing force. Gulliver, upon surrendering his weapons, warns against the misuse of the black powder, for "the smallest Spark" might "blow up [the Emperor's] imperial Palace into the Air" (20). Again, the text continues its relentless connection of powder to political authority; the misuse of powder by the ignorant poses a literal challenge to regal architecture, but more profoundly, the idea that the misuse of gunpowder can threaten the power of the sovereign—perhaps inaugurate a new, volatile form of sovereignty—is one that runs throughout this text. We might here be reminded of 1605's Gunpowder Plot, which famously threatened to decapitate England's political system.[20] Swift's allusion to this apocalyptic scenario here is casual, but it anticipates a more significant reference to the plot in book 3, discussed later.

But Gulliver's experience in Lilliput from this point forward downplays his power, shifting the parody into a different register. It now emphasizes Gulliver's own malleability; instead of acting as a civilizing agent, he becomes a transculturated subject, too oriented toward consumption and pride to transform the island on which he finds himself.[21] Gulliver immediately surrenders his implements of destruction—and, indeed, the powers of his body and his very political allegiance—to the Emperor. Gulliver's gesture here is undoubtedly a self-serving one; when he voluntarily hands over the gunpowder to the legal authorities that hold him captive, he enters a different sort of economy, one that seeks a role in a locally defined system of values and transactions. Gulliver does not seem particularly interested in translating the Lilliputians' awe into anything grander than himself; there is no hint that there is anything at work in his display other than mere self-aggrandizement. He appears to be more impressed with his powers of display than with his power to effect civilizing change or inculcate virtue; rather than an improving agent, Gulliver is malleable and consumption oriented. In Lilliput, we remain in the register of the parodic: Swift's presentation of this scene of contact is merely deflationary of awe as yet another form of display, part of a reduced and superficial aesthetics of the commodity rather than of the transformatively political.

Gulliver's presentation of gunpowder's virtues in Brobdingnag is much less ambiguous. Gulliver in book 2, despite his admiration for Brobdingnagian culture, advocates a lawless and indeed savage absolutism that depends on raw force, particularly the unanswerable technologies of gunpowder. But Swift also uses Gulliver to hint that virtuous display could be effective as a civilizing agent, as the gunpowder satire is juxtaposed with the virtuous display of the Brobdingnagian militia, which briefly appears to civilize even Gulliver himself. Gulliver's discussion of gunpowder with the king shares the quality of colonial narratives, as we have seen. Among other things, the technological limitations of Brobdingnag force Gulliver to use the defamiliarizing language common to narratives of colonial encounter. But this scene also offers us something else—a strong connection between this modern technology and the regressive political effects it might cause, producing, simultaneously, savagery and civility. Gulliver describes gunpowder's potency in language now familiar to us as:

> A certain Powder; into an heap of which the smallest Spark of Fire falling, would kindle the whole in a Moment, although it were as big as a Mountain; and make it all fly up in the Air together, with a Noise and Agitation greater than Thunder. That, a proper Quantity of the Powder rammed into an hollow Tube of Brass or Iron, according to its Bigness, would drive a Ball of Iron or Lead with such Violence and Speed, as nothing was able to sustain its Force. That, the largest Balls thus discharged, would not only Destroy whole Ranks of an Army at once; but batter the strongest Walls to the Ground; sink down Ships with a thousand Men in each, to the Bottom of the Sea; and when linked together by a Chain, would cut through Masts and Rigging; divide Hundreds of Bodies in the Middle, and lay all Waste before them. That we often put this Powder into large hollow Balls of Iron, and discharged them by an Engine into some City we were besieging; which would rip up the Pavement, tear the Houses to Pieces, burst and throw Splinters on every Side, dashing out the Brains of all who came near. (109–10)

Gulliver continues, offering this Promethean technology to the king in a passage quoted in full earlier, seducing the king with promises of the power to "batter down the Walls of the strongest Town in his Dominions in a few Hours; or destroy the whole Metropolis, if ever it should pretend to dispute his absolute commands" (110). No reader of this passage, alert to Swift's engagements with political theory, could miss this linkage of absolutism to military technology. More obscure is the fact that Gulliver sees in Brobdingnag a political system which is potentially decentralized and in need of a technological supplement to render it more "absolute." He is also, we must note, using his knowledge of this technology to tie himself more closely to the king; he seeks to mitigate the sufferings of his captivity, and his diminutive stature, by aggrandizing himself through a closer connection to political power.

Much to Gulliver's disapproval, the Brobdingnagian king declines this opportunity to establish absolute sovereignty over the "Lives, the Liberties, and the Fortunes of his People" (111). Gulliver, on the other hand, is momentarily exposed to an astonishing military display that might, the text hints, have begun to civilize him in turn. When Gulliver observes the Brobdingnagian militia, he experiences an awe that was missing in his conversation with the king:

> I have seen this Whole Body of Horse upon the Word of Command draw their Swords at once, and brandish them in the Air. Imagination can Figure nothing so Grand, so surprising and so astonishing. It looked as if ten thousand Flashes of lightning were darting at the same time from every quarter of the Sky. (113)

The lightning flashes here recall not only Gulliver's scimitar in Lilliput but also the commonplace comparison of the display of gunpowder to thunder and lightning. The quality of the spectacle that awes Gulliver is similarly celestial. Gulliver responds to the militia in a way that also echoes colonial narrative, as well as his own earlier deployment of gigantic scimitar and pistol. He stands astonished before a spectacle of implicit violence—a form of violence that in Swift's political rhetoric is normative. For his awe is immediately connected to the particular organization of political violence in accordance with virtue and political balance—institutions that reinforce hierarchy and stabilize institutions. What Gulliver is converted to, however temporarily, is the admiration of civic virtue; the admiration of this virtue is not mediated through technology, since this is a gunpowder-free military, bearing archaic arms. A thorough review of the role that the militia plays in the imagining of virtue in Swift's day is beyond the scope of what I propose here, but it is worth noting that Swift, through Gulliver, codes this militia as conducive to both virtue and public stability. We learn that Brobdingnag's militia system was set up in response to a long history of civil wars, the three estates contending for their various interests, including the crown's quest for "absolute Dominion" (114). The militia is "made up of Tradesmen in the several Cities, and Farmers in the Country, whose Commanders are only the Nobility and Gentry, without Pay or Reward." As in the English militia ideal, praised by civic humanists, "every Farmer is under command of his own Landlord, and every Citizen under that of the principal Men in his own City."[22]

Regrettably, however, Gulliver shows no lasting benefit from his affective response to this display. Were he himself more savage, its effects might be more profound. Under conditions of modernity, his emotional and political response to this aesthetic display is no different from the pleasure provided by any other commodity. The awe that Gulliver feels hints at how virtue might find an adequate signifier, a display or a performance that could closely align exemplary value systems with attractive and instinctively appealing outward shows. The prospect of political violence is refracted here through a strategically distorted imperial discourse that is meant to offer a normative response to the display of civic virtue in the moment of its most forceful expression. That Gulliver cannot respond to it suggests once more that he is enmeshed in a modernity that does not know how to read beyond the surface of things.

Thus, what began as a parody of the power of technology as an awe-inspiring agent of civility and empire has ended in a meditation on tyranny and modernity in which the militia is a vital agent. Gulliver here figures modern Britain and Ireland at once, both of which, following the civic humanist critique, come to prefer luxury to virtue and the standing army and absolutism to the militia and a balanced polity. Gulliver, like Swift's own nations, is impervious to awe and perhaps is governable only by force. Swift's text here offers little hope that England, Ireland, or any modern nation will return to civic virtue, balanced government, and self-reliance; and if the display of gunpowder to savages in the colonies is hardly likely to set them on the path toward virtue, then neither is an aesthetic response to civic virtue likely to inspire the English citizenry to take up the reins and preserve their liberty.

Exemplarity and Cannibalism: Ireland on the Brink of Ruin

Gulliver's Travels is written from exile; following the cataclysmic political events of 1714, Swift had permanently lost his close ties to the seat of sovereignty, spending the rest of his life as Dean of St. Patrick's Cathedral in Dublin. With his erstwhile political patrons imprisoned or in exile, he transformed himself from spokesman for the state into radical critic. His writings from this period famously exhibit a complex attitude toward Ireland and its political communities.[23] I add to other studies by arguing that Ireland, for Swift, highlights the paradoxes of liberty and sovereignty. This is particularly true of the series of pamphlets now collected under the heading of *The Drapier's Letters*, which suggest that the Irish "nation" needs to respond to the threat of British military power—which is ultimately, in Swift's rendering, the source of British authority in Ireland—by developing a self-reliant virtue, a collective affect and courage that could resist the lure of imported luxury items. These pamphlets, predating the writing of *Gulliver's Travels*, read the salvation of Ireland in the virtuous habits of the better classes; a virtuous aristocracy will, following William Davenant's model, inspire and lead a revival among commoners.[24] In later writings on Ireland, however, Swift's exhortations turn to a bitter satire; apparently despairing of the power of virtuous example, these tracts seem to anticipate a nigh-inevitable collapse back into the dialectic of tyranny and savage violence.

In one thing, at least, Swift might agree with his contemporaries in England: Ireland was to a large degree an uncivil and savage island. The reasons for his dissatisfaction with his home country are legion, but among these was a prominent unhappiness with the state of Protestant Irish culture: there was little politeness to be found, and the language was full of localisms.[25] Worse, Ireland's Catholic majority was in a condition little better than savagery in Swift's eyes; as Sean Moore has recently underscored, his public writings sought to clearly distinguish the Anglo-Irish elite from the "*savage Irish*" conquered by that elite's ancestry.[26] Swift could and did attribute some of the remaining savagery in the population to Britain's failure to carry the full weight of its responsibilities as an imperial power. Writing to Dean John Brandreth of Tipperary in 1732, Swift describes the Irish countryside and its inhabitants as victims of imperial neglect: Ireland presents a bare face of nature, without house or plantations; filthy cabins, miserable, tattered, half-starved creatures, scarce in human shape. . . . There is not an acre of land in Ireland turned to half its advantage; yet it is better improved than the people; and all these evils are the effects of English tyranny.[27]

The oppressed Irish are barely human, and the British state that ought to remove them from this condition instead only exploits them rather than improving them. For the English, and for at least some Anglo-Irish, this population presented a military problem rather than a part of the political community. Over a third of the British army's peacetime establishment was deployed to Ireland during Swift's lifetime; Ireland served as a convenient place to quarter the controversial standing army but also had a highly visible role in the maintenance of political order.[28] Swift's location in this militarized zone powerfully contributed to his thought on the intractable relationship between violence and civility, posing the question of whether it was possible to make Ireland into a place where civility, balanced government, and Protestantism could thrive, and, if so, what role military violence should play in this process. Swift's writings suggest that the Irish should ideally be civilized through virtuous Anglo-Irish example, but the language of tyrannical military force and of anarchical or savage violence permeates these writings.

"Is there virtue enough left in this deluded people to save them from the brink of ruin?" Swift asked in 1720's *Proposal for the Universal Use of Irish Manufacture*.[29] The answer, for most of Swift's life, appeared to be no. Swift's texts direct ire at George I, but they also turn a wrathful eye to Ireland's national failure. The fundamental corruption of the nobility and the affluent, in part, made it difficult for them to act as awe-inspiring nation builders. The exception to this general rule would be the response to the Wood controversy. In this Irish crisis of political authority and economics, Swift's *Drapier's Letters* played a central role, serving as a model whereby textual exhortation might replace violence as a force for instilling virtue and civility. These letters famously oppose the British crown's grant to William Wood of the right to mint copper coinage for Ireland. This coinage, not redeemable for gold or silver, was at the center of a firestorm of controversy about the power of England to legislate for Ireland and the extent of the royal prerogative. The value of this coin would be merely by the king's fiat; nothing material would back it up. In this respect, it was comparable to the empty paper promissory notes of the South Sea Bubble and the stock-jobbers that Swift famously despised. Currency becomes a lens through which the power and violence of the sovereign becomes visible, as this currency was quite literally to be forced on Ireland.[30]

Swift's intervention in this controversy brings the relationship of sovereignty and violence into the foreground. Sovereign power is intimately connected with the power to coin currency, which is, at a fundamental level, to decide what will constitute value. But the sovereign's subjects, Swift asserts, retain a veto over this power, and to override that veto is to treat one's subjects as colonized savages. "His MAJESTY's *patent*," Swift writes, "does not oblige you to take this *money*, so the *laws* have not given the *crown* a power of forcing the *subjects* to take what *money* the KING pleases: for then by the same reason we might be bound to take PEBBLE-STONES or *cockle-shells* or *stamped leather* for *current coin*, if ever we should happen to live under an ill PRINCE" (8). Here, the authority of the absolute sovereign threatens a return to savagery; the linkage of base currency to the sorts of signs of value used in colonial encounters, particularly shells, is clear. Shells were also an integral form of currency in the European slave trade, imported by the East India Company to London and reexported to West Africa.[31] The letter suggests that savage currency will be inflicted on Britons by violence and tyrannical colonial power. In asserting a right of the people to refuse to accept such currency, Swift is ascribing a constituent power to the people of Ireland. Their collective decision would override the sovereign fiat and manifest itself in the form of currency exchange.

To force this currency on Ireland, Swift suggests, would be an act of war—a declaration of enmity between Britain and Ireland. Swift exploits Robert Walpole's veiled threats of military action against Ireland in a dense extended metaphor that describes Wood's coinage as cannon fire in disguise. In an edition of Dublin's *Flying Post* discussing the controversy, Walpole was reported to have said that he would make the Irish "swallow his coin in fire-balls."[32] The Drapier pretends to take Walpole's statement literally, unfolding a play on words that imagines how a currency might be backed not with gold but with military power. If the entirety of the metal to be used in the coins were to be melted down and molded into throat-sized balls filled with gunpowder, the

Drapier calculates, this would amount to "about seventeen balls of wild-fire a-piece to be swallowed by every person in this kingdom." To "administer this dose" is impractical, since "there cannot be conveniently fewer than fifty-thousand operators" required (68). Making the figural literal is one of Swift's favorite satirical techniques, of course, and he uses it here to brilliant effect. More significant, however, is the estimate of fifty thousand operators: this is a barely veiled reference to the military force that would be required to thoroughly subjugate Ireland. The statement he makes is tantamount to threatening an Irish rebellion against England. It is little wonder that Swift's tract was seen as verging on sedition.[33]

But Swift's tracts are, in fact, very far from advocating for open rebellion against Britain; such allusions serve to highlight the role of colonial force in Ireland's relationship with Britain, not to declare independence. Even if Swift were prepared to countenance such a step, there would, in fact, be no "people" to rebel; as Carole Fabricant and Sean Moore have suggested in different ways, Swift was very conscious of the lack of unity in the Irish population and the challenges associated with thinking of them as a people or as a public. As a partial remedy for these difficulties, the Drapier's letters urge Swift's readers to firm up the Irish people's virtue. This rhetoric concentrates on the problem of luxury consumption, particularly by women and "the young fops who admire them."[34] As Swift correctly notes, the oppression which Ireland endured at Britain's hands had a great deal to do with colonial objects—fetishized commodities rather than weapons. British policy severely restricted Ireland's mercantile trade; unable to export commodities and completely dependent on goods imported from Britain, Ireland's economy simply could not expand. Swift accurately blamed Britain for acting in a tyrannical and imperial fashion, but he also found room to blame the Protestant Ascendancy for its failure to respond virtuously to the economic crisis: "I never have discoursed any reasonable man upon this subject, who did not allow that there was no remedy left us, but to lessen the importation of all unnecessary commodities" (126). But these solutions failed because of the "fops" and the "vanity and pride, and luxury of the women" (126). The consumption of luxury fabrics, chocolate, and tea in effect made Ireland a collaborator with its imperial oppressor. Swift exhorts women to prefer their "country shifts" and "native linen" to imported "diamonds and brocade" (127). Swift's tract concludes by hoping that the masculine leadership of the nation will reassume the mantle of authority and ensure that their families refuse all imported goods:

> A thorough, hearty, unanimous vote, in both Houses of Parliament, might perhaps answer. . . . Every senator, noble or plebeian, giving his honour, that neither himself, nor any of his family, would, in their dress or furniture of their houses, make use of any thing except what was of the growth and manufacture of this kingdom; and that they would use the utmost of their power, influence and credit, to prevail on their tenants, dependents, and friends, to follow their example. (127)

The plight of Ireland in this figure becomes a failure of backbone of the male leadership as well as feminine vanity. Women may be the primary consumers, but it is the job of the nation's male leadership to bring them back into line.[35] Swift's rhetoric elides the brute facts of economics and politics by relying heavily on a politics of exemplarity that concentrates as much on the failures of the Irish ascendency as on British imperialism.

Swift's rhetoric rallied the Irish, and Wood's patent was rescinded. But this moment of crisis and success did not result in the development of an awe-inspiring virtue in a unified nation, and Swift's writings increasingly seem to return to the rhetoric of the *Sentiments*, envisioning a future not of a virtuous nation civilized by example but rather of cycles of savage struggle against arbitrary power. His Polybian thinking on the temporal dialectic of political history resurfaces: the failure of political rhetoric to create a virtuous and civil nation may force Ireland into a military contest akin to that described in his early pamphlets. Swift's most pessimistic assessment of Ireland's political situation is of course *A Modest Proposal for Preventing the Children of Poor People from Being a Burden to Their Parents or the Country, and for Making Them Beneficial to the Public* (1729). This tract has attracted ample attention, and I will not dwell on it in great detail, except to note two things. First, its satire is, as suggested by Rawson and others, an attack on the Irish as well as on the English—indeed, perhaps more so.[36] Second, it offers us a perverse but important figure of the savage returning to the metropole in a way that has important implications for Swift's political thought in

Gulliver's Travels in particular. The Modest Proposer suggests on the one hand a peculiarly modern form of capitalist rationality: a "project" to reduce human bodies to objects of pure utility. But on the other, he takes his idea quite literally from the "savage" world of the American Indian: it is none other than a "very knowing American" who suggests that children make an excellent and marketable meat.[37] The savagery in the Proposer's eyes is not limited to the British and to the landlords; the only people called "savage" in the tract are the poor, predominantly the Catholic poor. And while Swift could hardly be identified with his proposer, his cornucopia of anger and scorn certainly is ample for the native Irish to take their share; there is a level on which their savagery and sexual promiscuity are the causes of their (admittedly excessive) punishment. Swift would also more than half agree with this statement:

> [The native Catholics are] our most dangerous enemies, . . . who stay at home on purpose with a design to *deliver the kingdom to the Pretender*; hoping to take their advantage by the absence of so many good Protestants, who have chosen rather to leave their country than stay at home and pay tithes against their conscience to an *Episcopal curate*. (114)

This passage strikes primarily at dissenters and absentees, certainly. But the threat of the breeding Catholic multitudes overcoming the island of Ireland in the absence of any real leadership is also present.

Without the nonviolent and virtuous leadership of the Protestant ascendancy, the Proposer sees the violence of the savage as the only apt solution. That Swift was horrified by this vision I have no doubt. But his language also suggests that a horrifying and savage violence against Irish Catholics was inevitable in the absence of any leadership for the Protestant nation. The Proposer is a target of the satire, to be sure, but the violence he proposes is a hyperbolic but not unreal consequence of the failure of exemplarity and virtue. This point is driven home ruthlessly in the tract's climax:

> I can think of no one objection, that will possibly be raised against this proposal, unless it should be urged, that the number of people will be thereby much lessened in the Kingdom. This I freely own, and 'twas indeed one principal design in offering it to the world. I desire the reader will observe, that I calculate my remedy *for this*

one individual kingdom of Ireland, and for no other that ever was, is, or I think, ever can be upon Earth. Therefore let no man talk to me of other expedients: *Of taxing our absentees at five shillings a pound: of using neither clothes, nor household furniture, except what is of our own growth and manufacture: of utterly rejecting the materials and instruments that promote foreign luxury: of curing the expensiveness of pride, vanity, idleness, and gaming in our women: of introducing a vein of parsimony, prudence and temperance: of learning to love our country, wherein we differ even from Laplanders, and the inhabitants of Topinamboo: of quitting our animosities, and factions, nor act any longer like the Jews, who were murdering one another at the very moment their city was taken: of being a little cautious not to sell our country and consciences for nothing: of teaching our landlords to have at least one degree of mercy towards their tenants.* Lastly, *of putting a spirit of honesty, industry, and skill into our shop-keepers, who, if a resolution could now be taken to buy only our native goods, would immediately unite to cheat and exact upon us in the price, the measure and the goodness, nor could ever yet be brought to make one fair proposal of just dealing, though often and earnestly invited to it.* (116–17)

Swift's Proposer mask cracks here a little, and the heavy sarcasm of Swift himself may be heard behind these words. The familiar proposals that Ireland free itself from dependency, unite to face a common enemy, and curtail its addiction to luxury are all here disavowed as impossible objectives. Since the proper leaders of the nation (who might have served as virtuous examples to their lessers and propagated virtue through their own awe-inspiring examples) have failed to rise above the level of foppery, then there is only one logical solution: unremitting violence to cull the herd and to transform flesh into profit. The savagery of the proposal is not in fact so savage as the lack of patriotism in the breasts of the Irish leadership; they themselves have debased themselves to the level of the savage, lacking the spirit of patriotism of which even Lapps and South American cannibals are capable of. We are, sadly, left with Swift's vision of the failure of virtue and balanced government to produce liberty. But what the hyperbole figures is not merely cruelty or poverty or the ruthlessness of the mercantile capitalist, though it is those things, too. It is first and foremost a concession that Ireland's problems could not be resolved through civility but only through a bloodbath.

Universal Destruction:
Laputa and the Prehistory of Aerial Warfare

But if they still continue obstinate, or offer to raise Insurrections, he proceeds to the last Remedy, by letting the Island drop directly upon their Heads, which makes a universal Destruction both of Houses and Men. —Jonathan Swift, *Travels*, 171

In book 2 of *Gulliver's Travels*, Gulliver offers the Brobdingnagian sovereign the power to establish absolute power not merely over his entire nation but specifically over the metropolis: the cannons he proposes to construct "would batter down the Walls of the strongest Town ... or destroy the whole Metropolis, if ever it should pretend to dispute his absolute commands" (110). To my knowledge, no critic has noted this invocation of a specific kind of political space; what Gulliver proposes is to turn an archaic system with distinct centers of power into an open field of violence, with no walls to protect citizens from the violent whims of the sovereign. Gulliver's is a modernizing project; this collapse of localized authority in the face of a concentrated and centralized sovereignty closely approximates the transition of feudal forms of kingship to the more centralized forms characteristic of the modern state. The logical conclusion of this transformation of space through technology and violence is massacre: the ultimate penalty for disobedience. This open space where walls are rendered meaningless is, among other things, a portrait of savagery. In the *Discourse*, we recall, the settling of nomads in cities is a crucial element of Theseus's lawmaking violence. In Brobdingnag, the erasure of the city's boundaries returns the political nation to a new barbarism, paradoxically made possible by modern military technology.

Earlier I noted that Swift feared that a people who could not be awed into virtue by example would be led like lambs to the slaughter. The excesses of *A Modest Proposal* are satiric, but only by virtue of hyperbole; the violence that Swift projects in that volume only exaggerates the violence he saw all around him as his ideal of the virtuous Irish nation collapsed. In book 3 of *Gulliver's Travels*, this image returns in a way that emphasizes spatial politics. Recalling Defoe's figures of fortification and atrocity, it uses them differently, emphasizing the collapse of the civil order into revolts as a collapse of civic space. Reversing tropes of colonialism, it figures sovereign violence as a destabilizing of space and a return to barbarism. Swift, describing the history of the city of Laputa, describes the violence that occasionally erupts in the cities below:

> If any Town should engage in Rebellion or Mutiny, fall into violent Factions, or refuse to pay the usual Tribute; the King hath two Methods of reducing them to Obedience. The first and the mildest Course is by keeping the Island hovering over such a Town, and the Lands about it; whereby he can deprive them of the Benefit of the Sun and the Rain, and consequently afflict the Inhabitants with Dearth and Diseases. And if the Crime deserve it, they are at the same time pelted from above with great Stones, against which they have no Defence, but by creeping into Cellars or Caves, while the Roofs of their Houses are beaten to Pieces. (171)

The flying fortress of Laputa here replicates the power that the cannon offered to the Brobdingnagian sovereign. The primary site of opposition to absolute sovereign power is the walled city, and it is precisely these political strongholds that the superior technology of gunpowder and the flying fortress are able to subvert. The power that is described here is not, in fact, limitless, as we shall see later. But in the imagination of the Laputan sovereign, at least, the logical response to the resistance of the fortified town is the same as what Gulliver proposes in Brobdingnag: massacre and the "universal Destruction both of Houses and Men."

This literal and figurative leveling of the political space of sovereignty through superior technological power is the focus of this section. Swift here raises the specter of an ultramodern military force capable of flattening the distinctions among distinct centers of power in the nation, creating an open field for the operation of absolute power and extreme violence. This specter has a colonial valence for two reasons: first, because the superiority of technology remains a key trope of colonialism; and second, because Swift's position in Ireland—figured by the relationship between Laputa and Lindalino, though this is not the only tenor of the metaphor—forced him to consider the nature of colonialism and spatiality in his representation of political authority and its relationship to violence.

I will return to Laputa later, but first I wish to discuss two alternate readings of the power of flight of which Swift may well have been aware and on which he may have drawn. In one, Swift's onetime collaborator and friend Joseph Addison meditates on the relationship between flight, commerce, and virtue; in the other, the noted Jesuit scientist Fr. Francesco Lana-Terzi contemplates the dreadful military applications of his proposed flying machine. I discuss these two moments in the speculative history of flight because of the way that Swift's vision of Laputa draws together these intertwined conceptions of virtue, commerce, and military power to demonstrate the power of technology simultaneously to establish new forms of national space and to import barbarism back into Europe.[38] Flight for Swift carried meanings different from those discussed by Srinivas Aravamudan, whose deft reading of the trope of flight emphasizes the superior power of surveillance and vision, particularly the "omnivoyance exercised by the oriental despot."[39] Swift's treatment draws from an alternate genealogy of flight that is more directly linked to conquest and colonialism than to the orientalism that is Aravamudan's focus. In this genealogy, flight is militarized, linked closely to schemes of conquest and colonialism. But the power of flight—a fantastic technology that echoes the power of the technological colonizer over the savage, transplanting that relationship into the military situation of Europe—becomes a perverse form of reverse colonialism as well. Critics of the power of flight in Europe and England suggested that introducing this power might enable an absolute sovereignty based on military power while simultaneously reintroducing barbarism and destroying civility. Lana-Terzi imagines that his invention's military applications might return Europe to barbarism. Addison's essay takes us back to the superficial in modernity, linking flight to a consumer culture devoid of virtue and to a social space drained of particularity.

Lana-Terzi, a Jesuit and professor of mathematics in Brescia, Italy, published a proposal for an airship in 1670: the *Prodromo overo saggio di alcune inventioni*. Lana-Terzi's proposal for what would now be called a vacuum balloon was theoretically sound, though impracticable; it met with interest and skepticism in England. His work caught the attention of Robert Hooke, who published it in his *Philosophical Collections* in 1679.[40] The invention Lana-Terzi proposes is to parallel ocean navigation: "a Ship which should pass through the Air, as if it were sustained by the Water" (18). But Lana-Terzi's proposal contains an unusual coda in which he reflects on the political and theological consequences of his invention. His fear is that the device would destroy civilized life in Europe:

God will never suffer this Invention to take effect, because of the many consequences which may disturb the Civil Government of men. For who sees not, that no City can be secure against attack, since our ship may at any time be placed directly over it, and descending down may discharge Souldiers; the same would happen to private Houses, and Ships on the Sea. . . . And this they may do not only to Ships but to great Buildings, Castles, Cities, with such security that they which cast [artificial Fire works and Fire-balls] down from a height out of Gunshot, cannot on the other side be offended by those from below. (27)

In Lana-Terzi's rendering, the spatial organization of the city and its politics are erased; the city is transformed from a political unit with a politicized spatial organization protected by walls into a field ready for flattening. To the aerial bomber, all spaces in the city are equally open and equally vulnerable. The same is true of the fortress; the walls of the fortress only protect it in two dimensions, so the addition of this third perspective again essentially makes the fortress into a flattened target. Walls are erased by this addition of the third dimension, and the political space that is constructed thereby is also transformed into an empty grid. That creating such a space would be a temporal leap backward into barbarism is underscored in an amused addendum by Hooke. Hooke dismissed the balloon scheme as impractical, but added,

> A man that hears all these things, and should believe the terrible and mischievous consequences, would possibly be of the Authors mind, and think also that he very much deserved to be punisht himself who had thus unluckily discovered so Diabolical an Engine, that should at once subvert the Government, peace and security of mankind, and bring in swarms of *Barbarians* to disturb the quiet and civilized world. (28)

This remapping of military space by the power of flight has a clear and likely direct relationship to Swift's portrait of Laputa.[41]

This return of barbarian to the civil spaces of Europe is echoed in a comic register in Joseph Addison's 1713 essay on flight. The July 20 number of the *Guardian* (no. 112) discusses, with a droll sarcasm, proposals for flying machines and the decline of virtue and civility to which such a technology would lead.[42] Addison's comments use flight as a hyperbolic figure for all the technologies that facilitate commerce, trade, and luxury and thus also link this technology to the British empire. His opening informs us that

> the philosophers of King Charles his reign were busy in finding out the Art of FLYING. . . . The humor so prevailed among the virtuosos of this reign, that they were actually making parties to go up to the moon together, and were more put to it in their thoughts how to meet with accommodations by the way, than how to get thither. (383)

This rhetoric connects the practice of flying with the tradition of exploration and empire. Addison then publishes a mock letter from one inventor of a flying machine; the writer, "Daedalus," plans to garner a government monopoly on the design of functional wings—thus connecting himself to the crown and court faction—and to run a monopoly in the style, perhaps, of an imperial trading company. This secured, he says, "I shall appear at the next masquerade, dressed up in my feathers and plumage like an Indian prince, that the quality may see how they will look in their traveling habits" (384) This rhetoric of masquerade and cultural otherness further connects flight and imperialism. The rhetoric of appropriating the almost-magical powers of the animal in some ways parallels the processes of colonialism's exploitation of Amerindians. But the rhetoric also suggests an ironic reversal of colonialism, for it is the "Indian" sovereign, in feathered regalia, who intrudes on the British court, not the other way around.[43]

Daedalus's arguments about the utility of flight go further, however, suggesting that the loosening of the restraints on commerce and trade have their counterpart in the loosening of moral standards and the concomitant encouragement of luxury and loosening of virtue. In describing the public benefits of his invention, Daedalus tells Addison that "the roads of England will be saved" when they are supplanted by flight.

> I need not mention posts and packet-boats, with many other conveniences of life, which will be supplied this way. In short, Sir, when mankind are in possession of this art, they will be able to do more business in threescore and ten years, than they could do in a thousand by the methods now in use. (384)

The *Guardian*'s response to this letter is dryly skeptical. It is also pointed in its condemnation of the technology of flight as promoting illicit liaisons and a general decline of virtue. The expansion of commercial space into multiple dimensions breaks down the ordinary constraints of civility, here described in erotic terms:

> It would fill the world with innumerable immoralities, and give such occasions for intrigues, as people cannot meet with who have nothing but legs to carry them. You shall have a couple of lovers make a midnight-assignation upon the top of the monument; and see the cupola of St. Paul's covered with both sexes, like the outside of a pigeon-house. . . . The poor husband could not dream what was doing over his head. If he were jealous indeed, he might clip his wife's wings; but what would this avail, when there were flocks of whoremasters perpetually hovering over his house? (384)

The focus here on sexual immorality and the freeing of desire is suggestive, considering the arguments of, for example, Laura Brown on the linkage between the figure of the sexualized woman and the demand for commodities under conditions of an increasingly imperial form of capitalism in this period.[44] Wings here unleash sexual desire, particularly female desire, though gallants and whoremasters are also suspect. They permit the redeployment of the city's political and religious nodes as sites of pleasure and decadence, transforming the city not into a killing field but rather into an undifferentiated space of erotic pleasure.

Swift was, I suspect, acquainted with both Addison's and Lana-Terzi's work (in Hooke's translation). And his treatment of Laputa draws together strands from each vision of flight, recognizing the common thread that unites them: modern technology's paradoxical introduction of barbarism into the civilized world in a specific reversal of the narratives of colonial encounter. Recognizing this buried trope helps us redefine our understanding of Laputa's political significance. More traditional readings of Laputa's political meanings emphasize the allegorization of Anglo-Irish relations in the conflicts between Laputa and Balnibarbi. Others have focused more on Laputa's literal disconnection from land on which it depends, linking this figure to Swift's stated belief that political authority should reside in land owners; the Laputans seem connected, in this reading, to the "moneyed interest" and hence the Walpole administration.[45] Both of these readings, I would suggest, are accurate; the floating city is a heavily condensed figure that can encompass both interpretations. But such readings fail to account for the elements of colonial discourse in book 3; neither do they succeed in accounting for the conjunction of massacre and tyrannicide in the noteworthy canceled passage, discussed later.

Laputa embodies an extremely powerful technology with obvious military applications. In this respect, it resembles gunpowder, and its (literal) superiority over the nation which lies below also positions it as a specifically imperial technology. Also like gunpowder, Laputa begins with the ability to astonish—an overwhelming sight as it glistens and glides through the clouds—and ends with the power to massacre those who are unwise enough to rebel. Much like gunpowder in Brobdingnag, it attempts to render the fortified city obsolete, embodying something that gunpowder sometimes promised but could rarely deliver except in fantastic form: absolute power of the sovereign over the subject. But its reliance on force to discipline its subjects simultaneously reveals its dependence on them. Even setting aside for the moment the interpolated description of the Lindalino crisis, the sky-city is already paradoxically dependent on the island it hovers above. It cannot aspire to universal empire, for it is materially linked to a geographically defined national space—an island, no less. This connects its purported independence to its actual dependence on the subject. It is a figure of a sovereignty that imagines itself to be detached and all-powerful but is in fact limited by the will of its subjects. It is, in other words, a figure for the failures of colonial and sovereign violence.

This dependence appears only gradually, however. Gulliver's first encounter with Laputa does not emphasize the extreme violence of the form of sovereignty it represents, instead alluding to colonial tropologies of awe. Gulliver, having been set ashore on a deserted island by the mutineers who have stolen his ship, has returned to the state of nature, as Warren Montag points out.[46] He is rescued by a technologically advanced power that is at once a source of terror and of hope:

> The natural Love of Life gave me some inward Motions of Joy; and I was ready to entertain a Hope, that this Adventure might some Way or other help to deliver me from the desolate Place and Condition I was in. But, at the same time, the Reader can hardly conceive my Astonishment, to behold an Island in the Air, inhabited by Men, who were able . . . to raise, or sink, or put it into a progressive Motion, as they pleased. (157)

Astonishment and awe, as we have seen, are not merely tropes of the aesthetic; they are often tropes of political affect as well. And they are elsewhere in the *Travels* closely linked with such scenes of encounter as we have here. One might expect some process of the civilizing of

Gulliver to ensue, with his awe at the sight of this technological wonder translating over time into some form of political virtue or assimilation. The analogue is imperfect but suggestive. Gulliver experiences awe that reminds us of Lilliput and is about to be rescued from nature into what might be a superior civilization.

We rapidly learn that the superiority of this civilization is, to say the least, highly questionable. The men of Laputa, as consummate moderns devoid of merit or even the vestiges of common sense, offer a suggestive reversal and parody of the trope of civilizing awe. Their conception of civilization, like Gulliver's in Brobdingnag, is fueled and supported by modern sciences.[47] Here as elsewhere, presumptions of superiority are based on technological innovation, including but not limited to its military manifestations. But as the narrative proceeds to suggest, this superiority is decidedly lacking in virtue. In theory, the Laputans can imagine themselves as a civilizing influence on the people below. But as Gulliver's later travels in Balnibarbi demonstrate emphatically, the lower beings' efforts to imitate their airborne counterparts can hardly be described as civilized.[48]

When Laputa's awe-inspiring display fails to civilize, it has another recourse: massacre and atrocity. Yet while the flying city threatens massacre, it is also vulnerable to it. If in Defoe, fortresses stabilize political space and sovereignty—and the massacre is a sign of the failure of civilizing sovereignty—so, too, do fortresses, space, and sovereignty interact in the relationship between Laputa and the island it dominates. For the fortress and the besieged city hold each other off with mutually threatened massacres. On the one hand, the fortress threatens, in the last instance, to literally crush rebellions. On the other hand, however, this moment of contact is also a moment of vulnerability, since the crushing of rebellion may also lead to a literal "fall" of this airborne fortress, and what might ensure would be a massacre of a different sort and a triumph of anarchy.

This point is driven home in a passage that appears to have been canceled, not appearing during Swift's lifetime. This passage describes the rebellion of Balnibarbi's second city, Lindalino, against the king. Rebels locate lodestones of their own and place them on pointed spires at the corners of their city. The king follows his usual procedure, letting his island hover over the city, cutting it off from sun and rain. The Lindalinians skillfully manipulate the lodestones to attract the city downward, alarming the Laputan navigators and forcing the king to acquiesce to their demands. This sequence has generally been interpreted as an allegorization of Swift's role in the Wood controversy, discussed earlier. There is indeed compelling evidence to suggest a link of this nature, notably the pun on the name of the city (a stand-in for Dublin: "Lindalino" being the city of two "lins").[49] Also significant is that this passage never appeared in any edition of the *Travels* in Swift's lifetime or indeed until the dawn of the twentieth century. (It is included in the Davis edition only in the textual notes.) The passage is found in the interleaved copy of Swift's friend Charles Ford with instructions for it to be added. Critics have generally assumed that its close linkage to the Wood controversy—as well as the explicit reference to regicide at the end of the interpolation—made it too dangerous to print.[50]

Nevertheless, the significance of the passage is not limited to the Wood controversy or even to the Irish context. Indeed, it is its very connection to the larger question of regicide and rebellion that may have made the passage too dangerous for inclusion. The danger it threatens is the unmasking of sovereign authority as a sham—and the way that the failure of awe and the political affect it can inculcate is the first step on the road to open violence and civil war. We should recall that the Lindalinian rebellion occurs while the king is "in his Progress over his Dominions," in the midst of displaying his power and authority to his subjects in a (presumably) highly ritualized form. After the king departs,

> the Inhabitants, who had often complained of great Oppressions, shut the Town Gates, seized on the Governor, and with incredible Speed and Labour erected four large Towers, one at every Corner of the City (which is an exact Square) equal in Height to a strong pointed Rock that stands directly in the Center of the City. Upon the Top of each Tower, as well as upon the Rock, they fixed a great Loadstone, and in case their Design should fail, they had provided a vast Quantity of the most combustible Fewel, hoping to burst therewith the adamantine Bottom of the Island, if the Loadstone Project should miscarry. (309)

The king follows the procedures he has already described: Laputa hovers over the city, cutting its citizens off from the sky and awaiting their surrender. Instead, he receives only "very bold Demands, the Redress of all their Grievances, great Immunitys, the Choice of their own

Governor, and other like Exorbitances." The king then escalates the conflict to the next stage, tossing rocks and beginning a descent to threaten the city with massacre and oblivion. However, the crafty Lindalinians use the technology of the Laputans against them:

> The King being now determined to reduce this proud People, ordered that the Island should descend gently within fourty [*sic*] Yards of the Top of the Towers and Rock. This was accordingly done; but the Officers employed in that Work found the Descent much speedier than usual, and by turning the Loadstone could not without great Difficulty keep it in a firm Position, but found the Island inclining to fall. They sent the King immediate Intelligence of this astonishing Event and begged his Majesty's Permission to raise the Island higher; the King consented, a general Council was called, and the Officers of the Loadstone ordered to attend. (309–10)

This unexpected descent is the result of the Lindalinian's crafty redeployment of the Laputans' technology, supplemented by this unspecified "combustible Fewel."

The reader might interpret this passage as Swift's gloating triumphalism, but the extremity of the image and the reference weighs strongly against that view. The event of the island's destruction and the massacre of the king and lords is no happier an occurrence than the universal destruction of the metropolis would be. If the "combustible Fewel" is indeed gunpowder, then the destruction of the sovereign power from underneath it is surely an allusion to the Gunpowder Plot—an event that Swift could never have seen with anything other than horror. The passage, I suggest, blends Swift's own writings with the memory of the Gunpowder Plot, and his resistance to sovereign power with that of Guy Fawkes and his co-conspirators. Though this blend seems wildly improbable at first glance, it is actually only an extreme instance of Swift's ambivalent presentation of sovereign power and authority. The suggestion here is, I believe, that Laputan sovereign has brought a catastrophe on himself and on the nation by his reliance on a (partially) military technology to keep his people in awe. Instead of using his powers of display to inspire civility or to preserve a balanced government, he has lost himself in abstract and self-indulgent speculations, depending on the awe-inspiring technology of the island to preserve him and his state. But this slackness and corruption lead toward a crisis in which his life and his government are imperiled:

Gulliver is "assured by a great Minister, that if the Island had descended so near the Town, as not to be able to raise it self, the Citizens were determined to fix it for ever, to kill the King and all his Servants, and entirely change the Government" (310). This is not the only place in *Gulliver's Travels* where regicide appears. Most notably, Gulliver offers high praise for the tyrannicide Marcus Brutus (196). Gulliver is not representing Swift's views in any uncomplicated way in that passage. There might be a violent velleity at work. But it seems more likely that this canceled passage is a darkly ironic and miniaturized form of tragedy; the sovereign and those with the responsibility to set examples for the nation have instead settled for a quasi-colonial and violent form of intimidation. The price they pay, potentially, is not only their own deaths; it is the death of the political order and civility itself. Their sovereignty threatens to unleash a new savagery on their civilized island.

Swift saw his career as one of devotion to liberty. But this devotion was troubled, not so much by his sympathy for policies that we today find painfully authoritarian as by a crucial paradox in his thought. Liberty depends on virtue and civility, and these depend on civil society and its origins in civility-making violence. From the opening of his career as a political writer in England to its conclusion in the subjugated space of Ireland, Swift found himself radically opposed to the ideas of indivisible sovereignty, arbitrary power, and the atrocious violence with which they are inextricably linked. And yet his writings all retain a trace of the problem of war and conquest. It is therefore not surprising that *Gulliver's Travels* returns to this theme throughout. Indeed, the meditation on colonialism with which the work ends fantasizes briefly about the power of violence and conquest to subdue the unruly passions of the European world. In considering the imagined conquest of Houyhnhnmland, Gulliver writes,

> The HOUYHNHNMS indeed appear not to be so well prepared for war, a science to which they are perfect strangers, and especially against missive weapons. However, supposing myself to be a minister of state, I could never give my advice for invading them. Their prudence, unanimity, unacquaintedness with fear, and their love of their country, would amply supply all defects in the military art. (293)

The Houyhnhnms are unprepared for European gunfire and, in fact, even for slings and arrows. Yet these "defects"—if they may be said to be such—are compensated for by their character traits. These traits are those of a Toryish patriot and stoic, as well as a militiaman: they are courageous and pragmatic, of course, but just as important, they are united, undivided by faction; and they are true patriots, loving their country. Their very bodies, too, are capable of reducing the (wasted and atrophied, in Gulliver's view) bodies of Europeans to mush: "Imagine twenty thousand of them breaking into the midst of an European army, confounding the ranks, overturning the carriages, battering the warriors' faces into mummy by terrible Yerks from their hinder Hoofs" (293). This disordering echoes the figurative disordering that European bodies undergo in Gulliver's mind as he compares their disease and degeneracy to the health and power of the horse's body. The violence of the comparison is made literal and visceral here. These defects of the European body are supplemented and compensated for by modern medical and military technologies, which run parallel to the commercial and military technologies that enable the global trade and consequent degeneracy that make such supplements necessary, feeding a vicious cycle. Gulliver's denigration of the European vis-à-vis the Houyhnhnm culminates here, with this sequence that brings together European degeneracy, military technology, conquest, and violence. This passage connects guns and the modern decline of virtue, contrasting them with the unaugmented virtue of the Houyhnhnms. Though the virtue of the Houyhnhnms is surely intended to be excessive—and certainly Gulliver's reaction to them is absurd and exaggerated—in this respect at least, they are held up as paragons in their use of virtuous violence to defend their homeland.[51]

Gulliver fantasizes that the Houyhnhnms' prowess might enable them to civilize modern Europe: "I rather wish they were in a capacity, or disposition, to send a sufficient number of their inhabitants for civilizing Europe, by teaching us the first principles of honour, justice, truth, temperance, public spirit, fortitude, chastity, friendship, benevolence, and fidelity" (293–94). The passage does not openly imagine a military invasion of Europe by the Houyhnhnm nation, but it does hint at it, playfully suggesting not only that the gunpowder-wielding European might be bested by a more honorable (and gunfree) force but that such a conquest might be truly civilizing. We are left, then, with a choice: submit to the virtue and force of a superior nation, and become civil, though colonized; or reenter the dialectic of savagery and tyranny, figured obliquely in *A Modest Proposal*. The choice is not meant seriously, of course. But the pessimism that undergirds the irony is deadly earnest.

CHAPTER 5

Savage Vision: Violence, Reason, and Surveillance in Eliza Haywood

> They not only seem to think there is an Intelligence in those material Things that are of immediate Good or Hurt to them, but also the *Fetish-Men* to have Conversation, and by it to be acquainted with their most private Affairs at any distance, which preserves Awe and Regard.
>
> —John Atkins, *A Voyage to Guinea, Brasil, and the West-Indies* (1735)[1]

John Atkins, who reported on affairs in West Africa following his travels there as a naval surgeon, aligns in a familiar way the savage with superstition—in this case a belief in the uncanny power of "fetishmen" to use objects to spy on and intimidate common folk. Just as in contact narratives, objects are enchanted and ensnared in schemes of power—though of course here the deceit is indigenous, much as it was among Aphra Behn's Caribbean priests. This power to spy—to gain knowledge of "private affairs"—works as a sort of savage panopticon; you never know when the eye of the fetish-man might be upon you. Atkins's description of the fetish-man, intriguingly, is contemporary with the emergence in Britain of another technology for inducing self-consciousness: the explosion of writings (periodical and otherwise) that seem intended to create a self-conscious and self-monitoring population. In popular periodical literature, in particular, we frequently encounter barely visible protagonists who see into the private spaces of the British middle classes and elites; periodicals modeled on Joseph Addison and Richard Steele's *Spectator* circulate the idea of self-monitoring subjects who will turn a normalizing gaze on themselves, producing civil subjects far more efficiently than sovereign violence ever could.[2] In Britain, this apparent shift away from sovereignty and legal violence, it has sometimes been assumed, correlates closely with political events; as Britain's government increasingly takes on the form of a bureaucratic state rather than a sovereign monarchy and as memories of the civil wars fade, the true problem of British politics becomes not the suppression of criminality or revolt but the normalizing of a new and more inclusive class of gentlefolk to provide a broader foundation for civil order and government. Britain's literary politics, in this reading, are part of a national shift toward something like Foucault's disciplinary society.

To be sure, this is a somewhat potted version of the Foucauldian model; Foucault himself did not in fact imagine a straightforward succession of power regimes.[3] Perhaps more importantly, several critics have noted that the project of self-monitoring is not without a violence of its own and that its efforts to normalize readers could spark resistance.[4] Eliza Haywood's writing is an important site for the investigation of these limitations because it is highly attuned to this violence and this resistance—and to the sharp limits to that resistance in a world still governed in many ways by violence. Her early writings such as *Love in Excess* (1719–20) and *Fantomina* (1725) show little interest in depicting "normal" and decorous men and women; her later periodical and novelistic writings (such as *The Female Spectator* [1744–46]) are sometimes taken to be signs of Haywood's reform but are in fact more complicated and reveal skepticism about emerging norms, as numerous critics have suggested.[5] I wish in this chapter to focus my attention on a slightly different set of issues raised by two of Haywood's later works, *Eovaai* (1736) and *The Invisible Spy* (1759), both of which specifically attend to questions of self-monitoring, autonomy, and sovereign violence. Both are interested in the ways that law and civility are, or are not, guaranteed by various forms of surveillance and violence. In examining these texts, I build on the recent critical boom in Haywood studies. Paula Backscheider, Catherine Ingrassia, Katherine King, and numerous others have offered us a Haywood radically different from the once-current image of a writer of erotica who later reformed and turned her attention to moralistic and didactic writing. It is now a critical commonplace that Haywood was interested in and invested throughout much of her career in public politics as well as private reform and that her apparently conservative publications on women's conduct are not as straightforward as they once appeared.[6] I build on this tradition, encouraging critics to see Haywood as a savvy and sophisticated political thinker as well as a popular writer.

My focus on Haywood might seem to turn this book's attention away from the figure of the savage and of the peripheries of the British empire. While *Eovaai* has been read for its role in developing the oriental tale as a viable genre that competes with novelistic realism, none of her most well-known narratives explicitly feature sequences of colonial exploration or contact between civilized and savage peoples.[7] But while the peripheries of the British empire appear only occasionally in Haywood's work, it is nevertheless true that her writings recycle tropes of savagery, contact, and technology in ways surprisingly similar to more explicit treatments of empire. Recurring in Haywood's texts we find the figure of the uneducated woman, obedient (or not) only to commands, rather than following the dictates of her own reason; this figure, I suggest, has striking affinities with representations of savagery and of empire's civilizing aims. Haywood's texts almost obsessively return again and again to women who are innocent because naive and the father figures who seek for varying reasons to preserve their innocence—preserving them, we might say, through sovereign command. This ignorant innocence, however, proves dangerous because it leaves women vulnerable to seduction; it also, finally, fails to make women rational and civil. The weapons that can rectify this are reason and education, which are represented in these texts by magical objects, associated with the colonial archive, that transform mere sensation into reason and a deeper access to truth.

Eovaai and *The Invisible Spy* both, in different ways, exemplify a revised understanding of citizenship—here, as with Margaret Cavendish, figured through female subjectivity. This understanding relies not on the terrified, docile, and admiring savage but rather on the rational, thinking, autonomous subject of the modern polity. In other words, both of these texts appear at first to imagine the world after sovereignty: the world in which subjects are to internalize rational moral and ethical precepts, without a heteronomous fear driving them. The two Haywood narratives I discuss here, then, allow us to observe a more highly developed model for how sovereignty might leave its violence behind—but ultimately cannot. *Eovaai* remains powerfully interested in the location of sovereign power and with the problematics of sovereign display; *The Invisible Spy* follows models of exemplarity and satire, drawing in part on the British periodical tradition which Haywood had already done so much to shape. *The Invisible Spy* offers a fantasy of an invisible observer who might be present anywhere at any time and whose anonymous critiques of private behavior seek not merely to scandalize the hypocrite but also to improve the morals and manners of the nation. But though the spy is easily read as a figure for new modes of power that supplant sovereignty, Haywood's text reattaches elements of sovereign violence—particularly violence against women—to this character, leaving him dependent on magical objects that, in turn, derive their force from covert acts of violence. Though both texts understand the projects of civility to involve the construction of new citizens or subjects civilized because rational (especially women), both find it difficult to leave behind the violence intrinsic to this exertion of power and of subject formation. In particular, by continuing to localize power in individual and inevitably desiring and ambitious bodies, Haywood's texts exhibit a fundamental pessimism that leavens their efforts to imagine a self-monitoring society and a rational citizenship for men and women alike. While Haywood's use of technology in her writing marks a moment in the transition from the awe-inspiring display of sovereign power toward a more dispersed surveillance enabled by technologies of observation and transcription, it also reveals ways in which this power still leans on violence and on a father/sovereign as the ultimate guarantor of polite and virtuous behavior.

Exceptional Women: Extralegality in Eovaai

At a crucial moment in *Eovaai*, the narrative unexpectedly incorporates a version of the first gunshot topos. The eponymous princess, forced to flee her kingdom after its disintegration into civil war, has accepted comfort in the arms of the vile tyrant Ochihatou. She is on the verge of surrendering her virtue to him when she receives from a divine being a gift that is simultaneously technological and magical: a "sacred Telescope" that dispels illusions, revealing more authentic truths.[8] This narrative move has affinities with descriptions of intercultural contact, as well as with the fictional reworkings of those encounters that this book has been examining. In the case of the eponymous heroine of *Eovaai*, however, this gift is not a prelude to conquest and settlement; rather than rendering her passive with astonishment, the magical telescope allows her to penetrate superficial appearances and to see virtue and vice clearly. Though the gift of the telescope is frequently associated with oriental tales, particularly with Ali's telescope in the *Thousand and One Nights*, I want to examine here different interpretive possibilities made available by attention to another textual prehistory. This quasi-colonial conjunction of the magical and the technological condenses underexplored elements of Haywood's political thought, especially her interest in reason, constitutionalism, and gender. When Eovaai is displaced from her throne and kingdom, she, like Thomas Harriot's Algonquians, is estranged from virtue, reason, and law. Her reentry into the sphere of legality and constitutionalism is mediated by a technological fetish that significantly shapes that reentry. Eovaai's magical telescope, with its associations with cultural contact in zones beyond the law, figures the possibility of a new relationship of women to the legal order and, in particular, to rational citizenship.

The gift of the "magical" telescope, then, invokes European conceptions of temporality and cultural progress, as a talismanic technology associated with modern reason dispels the lies, illusions, and irrational desires of archaic magics deployed by demagogues. This sacred telescope figures the bringing of persons excluded from law and reason—savages or women—out of their extralegal condition. For a colonizing power, this movement brings racial Others closer to a state of civility but also subjects them to an alien sovereign authority. Haywood borrows but revises this trope: the gift of the telescope enlightens Eovaai, making her worthy of rational citizenship. Borrowing from other writers such as Margaret Cavendish who had emphasized women's exclusion from the legal order, Haywood rhetorically yokes savages and women to explore their common exclusion from the law.[9] Savages, however, are unlike women in that their lawlessness is not merely extralegal but also prelegal, since a savage people may eventually develop a social contract or be incorporated into another's. By linking women with savages, Haywood experiments with the idea that women must be dislocated temporally, passing through a state of nature in order to clear the ground for a renewed and more just constitution.[10] This emphasis on temporality is reinforced by Haywood's manipulation of genre, as she juxtaposes the "timeless" conventions of pastoral and romance with other, more dynamic and complex settings and characters.

Eovaai's portrait is notably different from the romantic conventions used to depict most of the text's characters. The princess, initially embedded in a pastoral landscape, develops into a character more akin to the lusty and desiring women of Haywood's scandalous tales and amatory fictions; cast out from her pastoral setting, her body and her desires roam freely. In Haywood's portrayal, women's desire and women's virtue outgrow the confines of romance narrative, leaving pastoral innocence behind in ways that parallel the passage of passively virtuous savages into a more complex and tempting modern world.

Eovaai, however, wavers between optimistic and pessimistic assessments of that passage, for the exceptional state of war and the return to savagery offer both opportunities to reestablish the constitution on more equitable ground and a perilous dependence on a masculinized military power for that reestablishment. Eovaai's ambiguous passage from dependent daughter-sovereign to imperiled body in the state of nature is, Haywood suggests, a necessary step on the path to rational citizenship, but it is also a perilous movement through a dangerous, Hobbesian world which, in this narrative, can be tamed only by masculine violence.

In this section, I demonstrate these theses in three phases. First, I argue that *Eovaai* uses a flattened version of romance to underscore limitations in the conception of constitutional monarchy; the princess Eovaai encodes a dynamic feminine personality not capable of containment within the political structures of patriarchy or the conventions of romance narrative, both of which are figured as static and archaic and are challenged by Eovaai's characterization.[11] Haywood's text conflates constitutional monarchy and romance narrative to point to the exclusion of both women and desire from the contractual model that undergirds the former. In particular, the text highlights the contradictions inherent in a constitutional monarchy that is subject to law and that yet subjects women to a kind of absolutism that does not allow them to act as desiring yet rational citizen-subjects. While much of *Eovaai*'s political rhetoric is deeply engaged in its historical moment, giving voice to Patriot Whig and Tory criticisms of the reign of George II and the Walpolian Parliamentary regime, its experiments with genre and its revision of conventional political rhetoric also point to these less obvious thematic undercurrents. I then turn to look at Haywood's identification of women with savages in an essay on female education in her later periodical *The Parrot* (1746)—an essay that explicitly links imperial reason to the idea of the rational self-directed woman. While savages in other fictions are stunned into submission by European technologies, the savage woman in Haywood's tale is instead freed from the constraints of nature but is, tragically, not educated to use her freedom rationally. Lastly, I examine the crux that results when Haywood attempts to imagine a new constitutionalism arising out of a state of lawlessness. Eovaai's disobedience has created a "real state of emergency," to borrow Walter Benjamin's language; that is, she has taken actions that shatter the constitution and the normal order of the law and now takes part in the fashioning of a new, remade constitution.[12] However, my reading suggests that the narrative ultimately reverts to romance tropes to obscure the problem posed by the military power that undergirds this new constitution. The restoration that concludes the narrative is often read as a triumph of a Patriot opposition ideology, figured by the noble prince Adelhu, probably a figure for George II's estranged son, Prince Frederick. But this emphasis on military power, rendered as romance heroism, underscores the patriarchal content of pastoral tropes and acknowledges the alarming dependence of the new rational woman on masculine violence.

Eovaai has frequently been understood as a hybrid of two paranovelistic traditions in the eighteenth century: the scandal chronicle or secret history, and the oriental tale. Eovaai is the princess and heir apparent of the "pre-Adamic" kingdom of Ijaveo; her tale is recorded by (fictional) Chinese scholars and translated by an (equally fictional) Chinese expatriate in England. The tale's inaugural crisis is the collapse of Eovaai's kingdom after she fails to respect her father's commands: his dying wish is that she preserve intact a talismanic necklace he has bequeathed her, and when she comes to doubt its magical efficacy, her sovereignty collapses, leaving her vulnerable to multiple captors. After a period of imprisonment and near seduction by the neighboring nation's corrupt minister Ochihatou, a figure for Robert Walpole, her kingdom is finally restored to her through the intervention of the exiled prince Adelhu. While earlier critics have been correct to emphasize the novel's most salient generic affiliations, I wish to complicate our sense of *Eovaai*'s genres by shifting attention to its refigurations of contact narratives, as well as its conscious manipulation of the emerging distinction between "probable" fictions and "romance." The text conflates constitutional monarchy and the temporally frozen improbabilities of pastoral romance. The princess Eovaai differs from her ancestors and from most of the texts' characters because she is torn between impulses toward virtue and her illicit sexual and political desire, while most of *Eovaai*'s characters are simply virtuous or vile without duality or dynamism.[13] Her desires spark the novel's political crises and point to the limitations of constitutional monarchy as a framework for liberty for women. My claim is not that female desire is typically excluded from romance narrative but rather that the dynamism and instability of Eovaai's desires mark her as distinct from the more static characters found in the narrative. In particular, Haywood herself strongly marks

Eovaai as a countertype of the romantic masculine characters she encounters, who hew especially closely toward the poles of virtue and vice, as we shall see. Haywood's characterizations not only comment on the status of women but also explore the intertwined questions of political and social constitutionality: what power or authority founds the legal order that preserves limited monarchy and excludes women from citizenship? Haywood's complex narrative, in the end, suggests that gender inequality, enforced by masculine power and feminine subservience, is both the source and result of that order. However, it also suggests that Eovaai's disobedience, though it terrifyingly pops the bubble of the law and opens the kingdom to a lawless chaos, may be a necessary step toward the revision and reconstruction of a new constitutional order.[14]

Eovaai's character—particularly the growth and eventual taming of her desire—is the axis around which the plot revolves. While much of the story centers on the temptation of Eovaai and her ultimate victory over Ochihatou, I want first to attend to the narrative's opening: the pastoral setting that precedes the civil war triggered by Eovaai's skepticism and desire. Haywood offers a familiar pastoral fantasy, to which she adds references to theories of constitutional monarchy and elements of Patriot Whig rhetoric. Under the reign of Eovaai's father and his benign predecessors, the kingdom had remained in a happy condition of pastoral innocence, where "the Earth produced all kinds of Fruits and Flowers: the Rivers abounded with the most delicious Fish: the Air afforded a vast Variety of the feather'd Race, no less beautiful to the Eye, than exquisite to the Taste; and to crown all, the Climate was so perfectly wholesome, that the Inhabitants lived to an extreme old Age, without being afflicted with any Pain or Disease" (53). This portrait of an Arcadian kingdom protected by a benign (and limited) monarchy is decidedly conventional, romantic, and timeless; however, in a move that parallels Eovaai's shift from stasis to dynamism and desire, this kingdom is shortly to topple headlong into history. Haywood's deployment of romance and pastoral topoi is not, however, typical of the pastoral romance. Rather, her simplified, reduced form of that genre functions as a foil and as a tool of her satire of politics and patriarchy, not as a serious treatment of romance as a genre in its own right.

This pastoral land is governed by the virtuous Eojaeu, who rules as a hereditary but constitutionally limited monarch. He emphasizes that he is "bound by *Laws*" and that his subjects "have a *Right* to call [him] to account for any Violation of them" (53; Haywood's emphasis).[15] His family is long serving, having governed without war or insurrection for fifteen hundred years. By forcibly conjoining the pastoral to modern political theory, Haywood inscribes limited sovereignty in a nearly timeless genre, reimagining Britain's recent political arrangement as one so traditional and stable as to have no visible point of origin. In doing so, she invokes a common anti-Walpolian discursive construct: the Patriot King, theorized most famously by Lord Bolingbroke but appearing frequently in other writings from the period.[16] This blend of the traditional and the contemporary, however, apparently can accommodate neither female desire nor skepticism. Eojaeu's magic has told him that his reign will be the last peaceful one in Ijaveo; his daughter's will instead be characterized by a "long and terrible Interruption" of the kingdom's peace and prosperity (52)—an interlude of state failure and civil war. To mitigate the effects of this interruption, he attends carefully to his daughter's education, training her in the paths of both political and sexual virtue; instead of cultivating feminine attractions, she is well instructed in Ijaveo's political theory and practice. Eojaeu underscores the limitations of Ijaveian sovereignty in terms recalling Britain's 1689 settlement and Patriot Whig invocations of patriot princes, noting that the king's "glory" is "the Liberty of the People" and warning Eovaai of the "false Lustre of *Arbitrary Power*." He continues,

> Remember, you are no less bound by *Laws*, than the meanest of your Subjects; and that even *they* have a Right to call you to account for any Violation of them:—You must not imagine, that it is meerly for your own Ease you are seated on a Throne; no, it is for the Good of the Multitudes beneath you; and when you cease to study *that*, you cease to have any *Claim* to their *Obedience*. (53)

Here we find Whiggish political theory distilled into a few pedagogical phrases, authorized by the voice of a virtuous king and father: the monarch exists to serve the people, to govern their bodies and goods for their own enrichment, pleasure, and delight, not to transform limited sovereignty into the perverse, even libertine, authority of the oriental despot or the Hobbesian sovereign. The sovereign is inscribed within the circle of human law and must, primarily, give order to civil society so that it may live in harmony with natural law and bring wealth and peace. But our understanding of Ijaveo's politics shifts as Eojaeu nears death and the accession of his young daughter looms. Indeed, the collapse of this magical pastoral harmony into war and conflict is simultaneous with the intrusion of new impulses and desires into Eovaai's character—impulses alien, apparently, to the generations of royals that preceded her.[17] Unlike her predecessors, Eovaai develops into a passionate, ambitious, and lusty woman.

The romantic king fits readily into the constitutional monarchy model the text praises; borrowing from the Patriot emphasis on the accountability of monarchs, Ijaveo's polity is explicitly opposed to both divine right and Hobbesian absolutism. Despite important distinctions between these two forms of absolutism, both exclude the sovereign from the legal order, since the sovereign sits outside of law, bound by it but not to be judged by any human authority.[18] On the other hand, Haywood populates Ijaveo with sovereigns who are bound by and accountable to human law, whose implicitly contractual status gives their citizens the right to judge their actions. The tropes and conventions of romance allow Haywood and the reader to imagine this king as perfect and desireless; though accountable in theory, his perfect character means this accountability will never need to be exercised. Ijaveo, much like Lord Bolingbroke's romantic vision of a Patriot King, synthesizes "seemingly incompatible monarchical languages," in Christine Gerrard's phrase, but while Bolingbroke's king is an effort to bring together Tory and Court Whig, Haywood's portrait is more ambiguous.[19] This ambiguity can be seen in the way that Eovaai parts from romance tropes and represents a more modern form of selfhood, troubled by desires and, as the narrative unfolds, unconstrained by conventional authority. Unlike preceding monarchs, which the narrative imagines in relatively generic, stable terms as patriarchs subject to law but apparently not inclined to abrogate or violate it, Eovaai's desires (erotic and political) threaten the established order. Her desires underscore some of the difficulties in conceptualizing constitutional monarchy, tensions concealed by the fantastic qualities of archaic pastoralism. Eovaai's desire forces questions about the stability of this political norm, as well as about the possibility of imagining a virtuous yet liberated female subject. Constitutional monarchy, perhaps, relies on a static and pointedly romantic understanding of kingship.

Haywood's gendered critique of constitutional monarchy becomes more visible when we examine Eovaai's accession to the throne. Haywood uses this transitional moment to suggest that this romantic frame of limited monarchy conceals an absolutism as regards women—that the constitutional monarch and his romantic kingdom are inimical to women's independent reasoning. Though earlier sequences emphasize Eovaai's careful indoctrination into a feminized version of patriotic virtue (shunning luxury and disclaiming private interest), Eovaai's father on his deathbed gives her an implicit command to limit the sphere of her inquiry regarding an unusual magical object: a jewel set into a necklace. Eovaai's father admonishes her not to lose or damage this talisman, though he does not offer any explanation of its importance; implicitly, his command is also to avoid probing the mystery of the jewel and to accept its magical efficacy unquestioningly:

> Receive from me a Jewel of more Worth than ten thousand Empires.—A Jewel made by the Hands of the divine *Aiou*, the Patron of our Family, and most powerful and beneficent of all the *Genii*. This, if you preserve entire, and in its present Purity and Brightness, will avert the most malevolent Aspect of the Stars, and even the inveterate and incessant Attempts of the fiery *Ypres* themselves; and defend you, and the Nations under you, in all the Dangers with which you are threatened. In speaking these Words, he took off a Carcanet, which he had constantly worn upon his Breast, and put it upon her's. Let neither Force nor Fraud, resumed he, deprive you of this sacred Treasure: Remember that what ought to be infinitely dearer to you than your Life, your eternal Fame, and the happiness of all the Millions you are born to rule, depend on the Conservation of it. (55–56)

Most commentators on this passage have noted the figuration of Eovaai's chastity and feminine virtue in the form of this "jewel." But while such an analysis is correct so far as it goes, it misses the peculiar way in which the implicit command of a sovereign father works here—a command that Eovaai, plagued by desire, will not be able to obey. Eovaai has been well educated, but this education's outer boundary is her father's command; she is not invited to inquire as to the reasons behind this order, and when her curiosity disobeys this command, her fall (fortunate or not) begins.[20] From the moment Eovaai takes the throne, her rule is governed and limited by this fatherly command—Eojaeu requires blind, unquestioning obedience, not thoughtful collaborative governance or inquiry. The good king is not only a pastoral figure and an emblem of patriarchy: he is also, crucially, a believer that the father's command and the magical objects associated with it must not be questioned or investigated. This command makes explicit what is implied in Harriot's presentation of similarly "magical" objects to the Algonquians; their political efficacy requires that their power not be scrutinized. Eovaai is not invited to understand the mystic object she wears any more than Harriot's Algonquians are asked to understand the inner workings of clocks or telescopes. Another way of saying this is that the father's command and his talismanic necklace figure a kind of constitutional law: he positions himself as a representative of the fundamental authority that undergirds and authorizes all other laws. With regard to his people, the king is subject to law, but when facing his daughter at the crucial moment of accession, his will is akin to the "emptiness and standstill of the law" that Giorgio Agamben associates with dictatorial power.[21] We could, in other words, read Eovaai's father not only as the guardian of his people—a constitutional monarch—but also as the primordial sovereign that underlies and preserves the constitution and its day-to-day operations.

Interpreting Eovaai's father this way opens up new possibilities for understanding the politics of this text, which can now be read as bringing together the public political order of sovereignty and the constitution with the question of women's legal status. It is all the more significant, then, that Eovaai goes on to question his command, shattering her nation's constitution. The gendered command of the father is equated not only with patriarchal authority but also with a constitutional law that subjected women, rendering them unable to act as citizens or to make use of their rational faculties inside the legal order. If the father represents the authority of the constitution as an authority that women, in particular, must not question, then Eovaai's disobedience figures not her lost virtue but rather her first step toward changing the legal order; the political collapse of her kingdom may be a necessary passage through an extralegal state in which the previous constitution is abrogated and can be rewritten. Eovaai's counterpastoral personality—her desiring, curious selfhood—cannot abide this injunction for long, and her desire gets the better of her, sending her through a series of misadventures that will only be overcome by the outside intervention of the technology-bearing genii.[22] After having reigned happily for some months, the instructions her father gave her fade, as she begins to experience "Emotions, to which hitherto she had been a Stranger" (57). These feelings lead her to question her father's instructions regarding the jewel; though it is beautiful, she "cou'd not conceive how it shou'd be of so much consequence to her Happiness as she had been told; and perceiving some mystic Characters engraven on the Inside, which yet were seen through the Clearness of the Stone, she resolv'd to consult all the learned Men of her Kingdom, for the Interpretation" (57). Interpretation: the first step on the road to perdition. For rather than merely accepting her father's word, she hopes to make this secret matter visible and legible: to render the magical and the paternal knowable in rational terms. In examining the necklace, she also seeks a rational explanation for her authority and its underpinnings.

The results of her investigation are cataclysmic. The jewel falls out, leaving only the "exterior Ornament" that had held it, and is carried off by a bird, apparently vanishing forever (57). Eovaai's political apparatus quickly collapses, and the peaceable kingdom descends into civil war. In the thick of this tumult, Eovaai finds herself captive rather than sovereign, as rebel groups "ambitious of the sovereign Sway" keep her alive only to lay claim to her throne (60). This sequence, I suggest, asks us to take note of what happens to a peaceful limited monarchy when that monarch questions the singular, seemingly irrational command of her father—or, in other words, what happens when rational inquiry looks closely at the constitution and the settled forms of authority encoded therein. In doing so, it also makes a gendered argument: inscrutable magics and unquestionable commands will only be accepted by the women of pastoral fantasy.[23] A reasonable assessment of the female personality must grapple with the problem of female desire rather than wishing or commanding it away. In Eovaai's attempt to analyze and make legible the object that condenses and preserves her father's final and most important command, she returns her kingdom to a war of all against all.

This is her condition, and that of her kingdom, when she is "rescued" or perhaps captured by the corrupt Ochihatou. Carrying her away in a bizarre vehicle that resembles an amalgam of fish and bird, which Haywood calls a "Leviathan," he dazzles her by cloaking his hideous visage in a magical disguise and by stunning her senses with the wealth of his corrupt court (68).[24] Ochihatou is plainly a figure for a corrupted Robert Walpole, and by associating him with Hobbes's *Leviathan*, Haywood points to the Patriot opposition's critique of an absolutism based not in divine-right sovereignty but in a corrupting ministerial power. Ochihatou's corruption overwhelms and tempts

Eovaai with new kinds of sensory pleasure, however illusory, and she succumbs to the temptation of "Rich Viands, delicious Wines, Musick, Dancing, Dalliance, and, above all, the ardent Pressures of a Man whom . . . she infinitely liked" (78), almost surrendering that other "jewel," her virginity. This seduction of her political and personal virtue leads her to the verge of sexual experience even as it cultivates in her a sympathy for lawless quasi-Walpolian absolutism. But while her passage into lawlessness places her in tremendous danger, it may also be necessary for her eventual return to a new constitutional order that operates on reason and clearness of vision and, significantly, that offers those powers to women as well as men.

For that to happen, however, Haywood needs to introduce a different mode of narrating lawlessness and lawgiving: to negotiate Eovaai's passage back into law, Haywood draws on the colonial archive and its narratives of cultural contact. To overcome the temptations that beset her—the irresponsible desire for political power and sexual pleasure, both readily available in Ochihatou's court—Eovaai must cultivate the urge toward rational inquiry that led her to this pass in the first place. However, Haywood's presentation of Eovaai's development suggests that left to herself, she is unlikely to abandon libertinism for rational and virtuous citizenship; she needs an external force to encourage or compel her to resume the mantle of virtue and her throne. The narrative's opening gives us her fortunate fall; her redemption comes through a narrative move that, as I have suggested, draws on narratives of imperial exchange and cultural contact: the genii's gift of the magical telescope.[25] This "sacred Telescope" will dispel the illusions encircling Ochihatou's obscene power and allow Eovaai to see the vile usurper in all his repellent glory. Thanks to this magical object, Eovaai finds that this seemingly handsome man is in fact deformed, his skin coated with demons "which sat upon his Shoulders, clung round his Hands, his Legs, and seem'd to dictate all his Words and Gestures"; it is at their "Instigation [that] Rapes, Murders, Massacres, Treasons, all Acts which tend to universal Ruin are committed by him" (94). Ochihatou's illicit sovereignty—which, hidden by magical illusions, had so tempted Eovaai—is here shown to be undergirded with ruthless ambition and violence.[26] Only through the intervention of a power simultaneously technological and divine is she able to return, gradually, to the correct path. Most readings of *Eovaai* attend to its participation in the eighteenth-century vogue for oriental tales, but no critics to my knowledge have noted this other aspect of cultural difference that surfaces at moments when magic and science overlap to highlight the archaism of libertinism and the paradoxes of female education. This alignment of education with the imperial surfaces, significantly, in another moment in Haywood's literary corpus in a way that points toward the analogue of woman and savage. This analogue works for Haywood's purposes because savages and women are both rhetorically excluded from the law—women because contractual notions of monarchy are based on masculine citizenship, and savages because they have not left "nature" to enter civil society. Savages, like women, live outside the constitution.

Haywood's interest in and use of this comparison is visible in a late periodical essay from *The Parrot* (1746). In a brief tale that is broadly homologous to *Eovaai*, Haywood uses the figure of the savage woman to underscore the importance of female education and rationality, critiquing the idea that mere commands can preserve the "native" virtue of women.[27] In the process of arguing for a woman's education, Haywood's eidolon—an Asian parrot—tells of an Indonesian "Indian" whose virtue is briefly preserved by an English gentleman but who is eventually corrupted by London's erotic temptations. It is a cautionary tale, which the parrot uses to illustrate the moral that innate goodness cannot preserve virtue alone; what is required is the inculcation of reason through proper instruction. This female savage is innocently virtuous as long as she remains in her own quasi-pastoral permanent pastness. But once she is drawn forcibly into the modern world and its temptations and desires, virtue will depend on education, not on nature. That education, in this sequence, is decidedly imperial, for it is contact with emissaries from the "civilized" world that contaminates her timeless pastoral savagery, and it is only an explicitly imperial education that might have saved her. The parrot intends in this essay to treat "Woman," who is "the last, and most finished Work of the omnipotent and all-wise Creator." He describes women of his own country as simple but virtuous, "wild and untaught" yet with a "native Simplicity" among those who have not been corrupted by European contact. The savage woman he introduces is rescued from a rape attempt by an English merchant. Won over by her displays of gratitude, he takes her on as a servant and eventually his "Housekeeper" with "Command over all his other Slaves" (269–70).[28] But when the woman accompanies her master to England, her naive virtue is contaminated, and she finds the city's temptations irresistible. Seduced by another servant, she degenerates into harlotry and vice, becoming "the perfect reverse of what she had been:—That Chastity she once had set so high a Value upon, as to chuse Death rather than be deprived of, was now prostituted, not only to him who had first betrayed her, but to as many as attempted it." She becomes a "vain, pert, and arrogant" harlot and thief, and her master deports her (271).

This savage woman's tale approximates the structure of Eovaai's: naive innocence contaminated by contact with a new world of desire. What is most striking about her story, however, is the conclusion that the parrot draws—not that her innocence should have been preserved but that her European master should have taught her to use reason to restrain desire. The parrot writes that he has only transcribed this tale

> to shew how very necessary a good Education is; for though an innate Modesty may render a Woman Proof against all Temptations for a long Time, (it is possible for Life,) yet without she is able to give a Reason for what she does, and maintains her Virtue from Principle, as well as Inclination, all the Dependence on her is but precarious; and if she once falls, she falls forever, incapable for want of the Power of comparing her past with her present State, ever to return into the Paths of Honour. (271)

Education and reason are the guarantors that feminine bodies will remain within bounds. Women can be proper possessors of the right of self-determination, assuming they are governed by education and reason rather than by mere naiveté and good nature. Here Haywood echoes Mary Astell, who also insisted that masculine expectations of "blind obedience" from women are misguided and that women should be trained to regulate their own behavior using reason.[29] Haywood's parrot insists that female virtue—chastity—must become rational and principled, not merely habitual.[30] Natural virtue may be adequate to the challenges of pastoral romance or noble savagery, but it is no match for the temptations of modernity and no foundation for female citizenship. Had the Indian woman been morally educated, the parrot suggests, she would not have fallen.

As we have seen, Eovaai's fall is (just barely) prevented not by education but by a fantastic gift of a technological object: an eruption into the narrative of a paradoxically magic-dispelling magic. The narrative has already highlighted one object: the cryptic necklace that embodies the unquestionable command of a father. But the sacred telescope instead teaches Eovaai to observe and perceive correctly for herself, not commanding but rather imparting judgment, thus offering a fantasy of noncoercive education producing self-commanding female citizens.[31] These technologies speak to the way that Eovaai's character, in order to become autonomous and not merely obedient, must first be shaped by outside forces, here distantly figured through the tropes of colonialism. The genii is a dreamlike displacement of the colonizer, her telescope a metonym for the civilizing mission.

Eovaai also rhetorically links women and savages in the digressive tale of Atamadoul, whose corruption suggests the dangers of unreasoning desire and irrational spectatorship, while her species-shifting links her to savagery. Eovaai meets Atamadoul while being held captive by Ochihatou. Atamadoul, though human, is trapped in the form of a monkey; she, too, is a captive of Ochihatou, but unlike Eovaai, she has no magical telescope to dispel her desire. Her unreasoning lust for Ochihatou had, years earlier, led her to trick him into a tryst with her, for which offense Ochihatou has transformed her into a brute animal and keeps her chained up in his bedchamber, an unwilling witness to his further seductions. Eovaai returns her to human form and assists her in a bed trick; Ochihatou copulates with Atamadoul, mistaking her for Eovaai. Their erotic passion, however, stirs Eovaai's own desire, sending "unusual thrillings thro' every Vein" (135). Inspired by voyeuristic urges, she peers through her magic telescope, but what it reveals gives her no pleasure, for she sees that the true source of their "polluted Joys" is a crowd of vile spirits dousing them with "sulphurous Fire." Repelled, she pauses to reflect on the "Meanness of suffering Passions of any kind to get the Mastery of Reason" (135). Though the scene encourages some sympathy for Atamadoul's plight, it also offers an emphatic contrast between her bestial—even savage—desire and Eovaai's technologically enhanced rationality. Like the parrot's uneducated savage, Atamadoul cannot restrain her untutored desire and lapses into amorality.

Haywood's return to the savage here, I think, is a way to imagine a point of origin for female citizenship. Excluded from the political order, women need a foundational or exceptional moment to bring them into being as citizens or even legal subjects. Eovaai is not "uncivilized" as the eighteenth century usually understood that term, but Haywood does present her as *ungoverned* and in need of some force to bring her into being as a rational, civilized, autonomous citizen. The genii's gift represents that return to civility and citizenship. But this passage is not a simple one, and *Eovaai* acknowledges the difficulty of imagining this benign and nonviolent reshaping of subjectivity in its conclusion's return to romance tropes and its attention to the role of force in establishing constitutional order.

The Parrot's turn to a colonial setting has an analogue in *Eovaai*'s frequent references to political emergencies such as civil wars and tyrannical usurpations; these representations of failed states lie, like the natural savage, outside of sovereignty and law. These exceptional states have, Haywood suggests, the potential to liberate, for a self-commanding woman must free herself from blind dependence on her father's orders and, analogously, from a political constitution that excludes women from rational citizenship. However, despite the potential of these extralegal conditions to liberate, they are dangerous, for they are vulnerable to capture by other forces, particularly masculine ones. In the end, Haywood's text worries, masculine military violence lies at the heart of constitutionality. This danger is signaled not only by allusions to military violence in the text's political rhetoric but also by the peculiar return to romantic characterization (in particular, romantic heroism) at the narrative's conclusion. For Haywood's text does not resolve the paradoxes of gender and power; its concluding deus ex machina relies on another conventional and static character—a romance hero—as a way of acknowledging the contradictions inherent in the wish for political transformation.[32] For *Eovaai*, extralegal states of nature, of war, and of emergency open spaces for revised constitutions and new places for women. However, the passage out of that state of lawlessness is not a simple result of female education, or even the quasi-magical enlightenment enabled by the gift of superior technology. Eovaai is not returned to the throne by a powerful rhetoric or by her newfound political wisdom but by military violence: it is the warrior prince Adelhu who, embodying perfect, selfless virtue and carrying with him Eovaai's lost jewel, restores order to the kingdom by force. Eovaai takes the throne, but that throne is reestablished under the terms of a new constitution enshrined by the violence of her hero and husband-to-be.

Haywood has hinted well before the narrative's denouement that masculine violence is at the heart of lawmaking. In an important sequence following Eovaai's first escape from Ochihatou, she temporarily shelters in the neighboring republic of Oozoff (108). Having escaped temptation by the charms of despotic power in Ochihatou's kingdom, she finds herself debating her political principles with a republican who emphasizes the threat that temptation and desire pose to constitutional monarchy; though he does not frame it so, his critique is essentially that a realistic assessment of human nature will not tolerate even limited monarchy. Eovaai does not defend absolute monarchy, emphasizing that she is advocating only "Monarchies, where *Power* is limited by *Laws*, where the *Tenure*, by which the *Prince* holds his Crown, is the *Observance* of those Laws" (114)—in other words, constitutional monarchies like Ijaveo's and like Britain's, where a constitutional settlement divides sovereignty and power among multiple parties. In such systems, Eovaai emphasizes, the king cannot wage war, form treaties, or spend public funds without duly consulting "his People" (114). Under such constitutions, the position of the sovereign cannot be corrupted by the mere desires of the embodied monarch; Eovaai, indeed, takes a romantic view of kingship, noting that "such a King surely cannot be said to act by the Instigations of his *own Will*. . . . He is indeed the Head of a large Family; for whose Happiness he is perpetually contriving, who *watches* for *their Repose*, *labours* for their Ease, exposes himself for *their Safety*" (114). Eovaai here gives voice to Patriot rhetoric: Bolingbroke's *The Idea of a Patriot King* speaks of a king who will "espouse no party, but . . . govern like the common father of his people."[33] For Eovaai, as for a Patriot Whig, an ideal sovereign's own desires vanish inside a selfless public personality.

These fine sentiments certainly accord with the rhetoric of Britain's own constitutional settlement, particularly as it was understood by the Patriot opposition. But Eovaai's confidence in these principles is shaken over the course of the argument, as Haywood's text gives voice to a radical antimonarchical republicanism.[34] Her republican interlocutor rejects constitutional monarchy as an illusion, suggesting that there is in fact an absolutism latent within every supposedly limited monarchical constitution. His antimonarchical stance is extreme, pointing to the way that the monarch's power to grant titles and honors, and thus to use state employment to corrupt, renders legal restraints moot. Where such power inheres in the sovereign, de facto absolutism replaces de jure constitutional monarchy, and the distinction between tyrant and limited monarch evaporates. Some of these criticisms are identical to satires on George II, Walpole, and the British state penned by Toryish Scriblerians and Patriot Whigs.³⁵ But Eovaai's interlocutor goes further than all but the most radical of Whigs, arguing that even in a kingdom where the law is strictly observed, the delicate balance between limited monarch and the people is untenable, since "the Balance of Power cou'd never be so equally pois'd, but that one Side or other wou'd have some little reason for Complaint. . . . Misinterpretations wou'd be put on every thing: Heart-burnings wou'd rise to Animosities, and these break forth at length into open Ruptures" (116). In short, the republican suggests that limited monarchy is either absolutism in disguise or a state of civil war held briefly in abeyance; there is, from his perspective, no formula for a workable limited monarchy. This rhetoric draws heavily from an antique republican tradition, but it is striking that this republican echoes Hobbes in suggesting that a mixed government is in fact not a fully constituted state at all but rather something more akin to a balance of terror.³⁶

But interestingly, the republican does not offer an affirmative defense of his commonwealth's political practices, and the manner in which this commonwealth is made stable is never articulated. The republican and the other inhabitants of this land are, unlike Eovaai but like her father, apparently free of "heart-burnings" themselves, not afflicted by the desires associated with Eovaai and with the genres of the scandal narrative and the novel. Though Oozoff is hardly pastoral, the virtue spoken of by the republican nevertheless invokes a functionally similar set of narrative conventions—the founding and stabilizing factors in this polity remain invisible and unimagined; their constitution's origins date from their throwing off the yoke of a neighboring power, but it is not clear how their exact equality originated or how it is maintained. In other words, Oozoff's spokesman offers a cogent and perhaps unanswerable critique of constitutional monarchy—one that exposes its limited capacity to respond to the new world of desire, passion, and interest—but is himself oddly silent on the nature of his own constitution, in ways that suggest that his citizenry's characters are intelligible and credible only in the codes of a quasi-romance narrative that erases those modern passions and interests. I would again suggest that Haywood's mixing of genres is strategic. The critique of limited or mixed forms of sovereignty is nowhere answered, least of all by Eovaai, who finds herself "little able to confute" these arguments (118). This is not to say that Haywood's text endorses republicanism; the text presents these doctrines in an ambiguous and multivoiced fashion and may, as Ros Ballaster has noted, associate them with the misogyny of the text's fictional translator.[37] Yet it is also important to scrutinize other ambiguities in this sequence, particularly the way the narrative presents republicanism as an apparently unanswerable critique of limited monarchy and Patriot conceptions of the 1689 settlement, even as it reveals that same republicanism to require a fantastic and romantic erasure of unvirtuous human desires.[38] Using the figures of Eovaai, Ochihatou, and others, the text has repeatedly emphasized that human desire is an intractable problem for individuals and sovereign alike and that republicanism, like constitutional monarchy, requires a magical and romantic underpinning.

Haywood's republican is particularly suspicious of military power, which is inimical to republican institutions. His narrative of the rise of civil society is grounded in the sense of war's tendency to strengthen the oppressive institutions of monarchy. Once, at the beginning of time, "there was no Precedency, no Subordination," he notes, but when the demonic *Ypres* break loose, "Self-love, Discord, Avarice, the Lust of Power, and every kind of Vice, corrupted the native Simplicity of our Manners." Then

> we . . . grew arrogant and assuming . . . seizing by *force* what *Fraud* cou'd not obtain. Then, dividing ourselves into Parties, Wars ensued; various Instruments were every day invented, to destroy the Workmanship of Heaven; and Death triumph'd in those Plains where Love, and Peace, and sweet Society before had reign'd. In these Skirmishes, he who had shewed himself the boldest, or most cunning in the fatal Science, was look'd upon with the greatest Respect: Here began *Distinction*; and such a Man, in a future Engagement, was put at the head of the others, by their joint assent. (111–12)

This warrior slowly transforms himself into a king, bribing the majority to support him. Thus kingship comes into being through the corruption of military heroism.

Yet in a gesture that anticipates *Eovaai*'s conclusion, the republican leaves a Trojan horse embedded in his argument: the state of emergency that requires a moment of absolute decision. Though hostile not only to Ochihatou's tyranny but to kingship in any form, he confesses that one-person rule can be justified under exceptional circumstances—states of emergency, or "extraordinary Exigencies." And while contending that emergencies are temporally circumscribed, since "all Men have in them the Seeds of Tyranny," he has little to say on how republicanism can cope with or return from these periods of dictatorial power (112). Yet any republican thinker must be aware of the hazards of this line of thinking; these exceptional conditions are, after all, what paved the way for various tyrants that threatened the Roman republic, from the second decemvirate to Julius Caesar himself. The republican's logic exposes an aporia in his commonwealth's constitution. I would suggest that this passage cannot escape the paradox; the inclusion here of the state of emergency—of the necessary exception—seems purposeful, as does Haywood's own refusal to assign a clear rhetorical triumph to one party or the other in this debate.

Haywood's narrative closure, too, ultimately depends on military force, albeit in a romanticized form, since her military backing comes not from an army but from Eovaai's idealized husband-to-be, the prince Adelhu. This figure embodies much of what the republican had left permissible in his brief allusion to emergencies. Adelhu comes to the kingdom of Ijaveo following his exile from his own kingdom of Hypotosa under Ochihatou's tyranny; believed dead, he wanders for a time before arriving in Ijaveo and rescuing it from civil war and from a vaguely described "monster" that has threatened it. Eovaai's servant describes the state of the kingdom on his arrival:

> The Nobility, the Populace strove to outvye each other in laying waste this unhappy Land—all things were in Confusion, and to make perfect our Undoing, the offended Gods sent among us a dreadful Monster, who in a short space of time devour'd thousands of your wretched Subjects. . . . [Then] a gallant Stranger arrived, and with his single Arm laid dead this Terror of the Earth, as did his Wisdom afterward reconcile the jarring factions, and what before was Discord converted into Harmony. (156)

This "stranger" now reigns in Eovaai's stead, duly elected and reigning, like Oliver Cromwell, as "Protector," rather than king. The way in which he attains this position is reminiscent of the state of emergency alluded to briefly by Eovaai's republican acquaintance. But more important than his title is the fact that this hero has paved the way for Eovaai's return through military heroism. It is the realm's good fortune that he is an inherently virtuous prince of romance rather than a tyrannical figure of satire or of the despotic East, but they nevertheless depend absolutely on his military prowess.

In other words, Adelhu—son of the sedated and subordinate king Oeros, who is in thrall to the minister Ochihatou—is a lawmaking sovereign, stabilizing the political order or, rather, crystallizing it from the state of nature and restoring law. His role as lawmaker is made apparent in a moment of narrative crisis, as Adelhu prepares to leave Eovaai. The narrative drive underscores the irony of his failure to recognize Eovaai as the rightful owner of the gem which he has found and continues to bear and thus as the person for whom he is destined. But a political reading encourages us to recognize the fact that Adelhu spends his last day in the kingdom attempting to set a constitution in order that can survive his absence—"to fix the Government of this Kingdom, if possible, in such a manner, as shall prevent it from falling again into the Confusions I relieved it from" (157).[39]

Adelhu's significance as a restorer of stability and monarchy goes beyond this, however. While Eovaai's virtue must be secured and produced by outside forces—particularly by quasi-magical technological fetishes—Adelhu seems to require no such education. He is a stereotypical romance hero, devoted to his lady and entirely devoid of the complex desires and temptations that have driven Eovaai's adventures. The narrative seems unable to imagine a language in which an enlightened Eovaai can claim the throne for herself, and it must fall back onto romance conventions. Much as she could not be brought into reason by herself or by blindly following her father's commands, neither can she bring herself back to the throne, instead requiring the military support of an exceptionally virtuous lawgiver who stands outside and guarantees the legal and political orders—a founder figure who is also a military man. Having passed through the state of emergency and been granted reason through a divine infusion of technology, Eovaai is still dependent on masculine military heroism. Here, perhaps, Haywood's narrative bumps up against the limits of the imaginable. Women may become rational citizens, and perhaps only through extralegal means. But the constitution of state power will remain dependent on the military power that this text, at least, cannot imagine in female hands; the final law is still the rule of the stronger.

Invisible Politics: Magic and Violence in The Invisible Spy

If *Eovaai* presents itself as a satire on Walpole and public affairs, *The Invisible Spy* reads like a return to the older tradition of the scandal narrative. Consisting of a series of vignettes related by a Spectator-like narrator (the eponymous spy known only as Exploralibus), it relates tales both dark and titillating of what happens behind the closed doors in London's ostensibly polite society. *The Invisible Spy* proposes to civilize the nation by making its private habits public. Subjecting the nominally private—particularly sexuality and upper-class domesticity—to public scrutiny, Exploralibus claims to use the power of the public sphere and print to make visible and to regulate and correct hidden vices, bringing them closer to socially defined norms. Focusing in particular on the "morality" of prominent young women—"celebrated toasts"—he uses magical devices that allow him to sneak into their drawing rooms and bedchambers to report on what he finds there, though assuring us that he never looks into the bed itself.[40] Given the setting of this work in the 1750s, it is tempting to cite it as a straightforward exemplar of power's multiplying tools, in which sovereignty does not disappear but is instead supplemented by other modes of transmission, panoptical, institutional, and biopolitical. Exploralibus declares in his opening manifesto that he will use his powers of invisibility to seek out private spaces that are, as he puts it, "above the law": gaming houses, the collections of virtuosos, or, particularly, the bed chambers of the great and powerful. The putative author claims to blend curiosity with a social purpose: he will "expose vice and folly, . . . strip a bad action of all the specious pretences made to conceal or palliate it, and shew it in its native ugliness" (1:23). Exploralibus seeks to distinguish his exposés from romans à clef or secret histories by avoiding malice and particularity; he will not name names, for, he says, "my aim in this work is not to ridicule, but reform. . . . I inscribe no real name to the picture" (1:23–24). His intertwined projects of observation and publication bring private life into public view, making all aspects of human behavior open to political criticism and correction in the public sphere, while simultaneously inculcating a self-monitoring habit in gentlefolk.[41]

Exploralibus does at one point intrude specifically into public politics; significantly, this political moment concerns the problems of political community and of constituent power. Addressing the Marriage Act and the Jewish Naturalization Act (both 1753), this interlude links constituent power to concerns about collapsing public virtue; or, in other words, it links Exploralibus's putative project of reform to debates about citizenship and popular power. The acts of 1753 are examples of a new attention in political economy to the biological makeup of the nation and population dynamics; the Marriage Act was framed in part as a tactic for fostering a healthy and productive English population, while the Naturalization Act focalized concerns about the nature of the British nation as a racially and religiously homogeneous community.[42] Exploralibus overhears a coffeehouse debate over these bills, but the coffee-swilling citizens soon turn their conversation to yet more fundamental questions about the nature of political power, particularly the authority of Parliament to pass laws to prevent its recall or new elections. The coffee drinkers correctly note that such a power could, in principle, make Parliament an absolutely sovereign body, capable of altering the constitution without being challenged. The next question is whether there is a constituent or popular power that might challenge such a move: one of them argues that "the people" would not tolerate "a perpetual dictatorship," while another disagrees: "Indeed they would bear that and every thing else; . . . your fellow subjects . . . are not what they were in former days." Another gentleman agrees: "The ancient stubbornness of the people of England has been worn off. . . . The luxuries of life have taken off all their fierceness" (1:117–18). Haywood here offers not so much a serious rumination on electoral law as a passing reflection on the chicken-egg problem of constituting and constituent power and the troubling problem of public virtue and political authority. As we have seen, sovereign authorities are frequently charged with the responsibility for civilizing the commoner, with making a kind of modern liberty distinct from anarchy possible for a polite and commercial people. Yet here it is the degeneracy of the people—their inability to exert influence in the political sphere because of their enervation, their excessive selfishness and refinement—that enables parliamentary tyranny. Thus even this text's apparent turn away from direct engagements with institutional politics and sovereign authority is part of a larger critique of the public and its limited capacity to govern itself. The technique for preserving a publicly engaged citizenry is the subject of *The Invisible Spy*'s narrative; combating the institutionalization of an absolutist despotism requires the construction of a worthy and engaged public. This is precisely what Exploralibus claims that he sets out to do.

However, Haywood's text is ultimately less a replication of the espionage periodical than it is a critique. The spy's project of correction and normalization is dependent on violence and arbitrary male power; it makes visible the masculine sovereign command that lies behind the corrective project. The critique is visible in particular in Exploralibus's magical devices, which, though very precisely distinguished from sovereignty's tools, are nevertheless implicated in and dependent on atrocious acts of violence. Exploralibus's belt of invisibility is supplemented by a magical writing tablet that transcribes conversations precisely so that they may later be published. With these two items at his command, Exploralibus transforms himself into a one-man panopticon, capable of observing, recording, and reporting any behavior, public or private. The collector from whom he receives these items as gifts notes that these two devices are "concomitant; and the satisfaction that either of them would be able to procure, would be incompleat without the assistance of the other" (1:13). The trick of observing is incomplete without a parallel power to record, preserve, and circulate. These two tools envision power as observation rather than display. Significantly, the narrator rejects another magical concoction—an "Illusive Powder" that is more than slightly reminiscent of gunpowder: "A Small quantity of this powder, blown thro' the quill of a porcupine when the Moon is in Aries, raises splendid visions in the people's eyes; and, if apply'd when the same planet is in Cancer, spreads universal terror and dismay" (1:5). This item is redolent of alchemy, astrology, and archaic forms of knowledge. It is also, not coincidentally, appropriate to an increasingly archaic form of political power. This item, Exploralibus notes, is best wielded by the powerful who seek to attract and control the vision of the crowd. The author leaves it behind, having "judged it fitter for the possession of some one or other of the mighty rulers of the earth" (1:5). Lies, dissimulation, and deceit are here left behind as the tools of sovereignty; Exploralibus seeks a different form of power.

Significantly, however, the tools Exploralibus chooses are also implicated in a different kind of violence. The magic tablet has a peculiarity: though it can transcribe at will, it can only be erased by the breath of a young girl who knows no desire—an absolute innocent, preserved by highly artificial means in a state of absolute naiveté. It is not sufficient, Exploralibus finds, that this girl be merely innocent; she must be so "ignorant" as to never "have once thought on the difference of sexes" (1:14). To create such absolute ignorance is the labor of years; the narrator purchases a child from a poor widow and has her raised by an elderly woman who keeps her prisoner in a windowless room, depriving her of rich foods and adequate sleep (1:15). This connection of female innocence and violent confinement is repeated in multiple forms throughout the narrative in ways that, I argue, invoke the overlapping categories of woman and savage, magic and technology.

Though this text does largely turn away from the specific problematics of constituent power and sovereignty that *Eovaai* engages, it does so in ways that call attention to the limitations of print culture and observation, which both depend on and are powerless to change the violence that women, in particular, are subject to. It is not trivial that this text imagines what we might call a very modern form of government—distributed and invisible rather than spectacular—with the same sort of antique, mystical knowledges and powers that are so evocative of savagery and the primitive in other texts. If *Eovaai* uses the tropes of sovereignty to investigate the prospects for women in the public sphere of law and legality, *The Invisible Spy* investigates the limitations of other forms of political power, extralegal in a very different way from what I have been considering so far. Haywood here offers a superficially optimistic take on the power of surveillance and observation to replace other forms of power; but the narrative pointedly undercuts this logic by founding it on an act that suppresses female desire through captivity. I argue that for Haywood, regimes of observation are not intrinsically less violent than the sovereignties they replace. Or perhaps it would be more accurate to say that biopower and surveillance are also contaminated by the same excesses that attend sovereignty: Exploralibus's violence and corrupt curiosity are in no way distinct from the temptations toward tyrannical power that have beset so many other sovereigns.

Exploralibus's invisibility, in fact, immediately links him to this very indistinction between sovereignty and other forms of power; there is a lengthy literary heritage associating invisibility with both sovereignty and lawlessness. Haywood's immediate sources are to be found in the scandal fictions which her text simultaneously invokes and critiques. In Delarivier Manley's *The New Atlantis* (1709), the divine Astrea invisibly moves among the aristocracy, witnessing repeated instances of atrocious behavior; Haywood had herself borrowed this formula in her earlier anti-Walpolian satire *Memoirs of a Certain Island* (1725).[43] Invisibility had been a convenient plot device for these scandalous writings, facilitating a fantasy of easy observation and secrets revealed. However, *The Invisible Spy* uses this device quite differently, particularly in its lingering and detailed treatment of these magical objects themselves. The scandal chronicles, including Haywood's *Certain*

Island, do not use such devices, relying instead on vaguely outlined godlike powers or misty spells. The use of a talisman to create invisibility, interestingly, makes the device portable and transferable: it imagines powers of observation that are available to anyone holding them rather than to the divinely ordained or the magically gifted.

This more portable invisibility is more like that conferred by Plato's well-known myth of the ring of Gyges, which in Plato's telling is found by chance by a mere shepherd.[44] In this myth, invisibility, as opposed to spectacular visibility, is simultaneously an extraordinary threat to sovereignty and law and a powerful tool in the hands of a sovereign. Plato's dialogist Glaucon relates this tale in the second book of *The Republic*, describing the Lydian shepherd Gyges who discovers the ring following a storm. Learning accidentally of the ring's powers, he uses it to seduce the Lydian queen, slay the king, and install himself as tyrant.[45] Glaucon's tale makes invisibility a valuable tool to the usurper of sovereign power. But Plato's text also closely associates invisibility with an invulnerable libertinism. Invisibility figures impunity: to be seen is to be accountable, and to be unseen is to be able to act without check, without answering for one's actions to any higher authority, any sovereign. Glaucon continues,

> Suppose now that there were two such magic rings, and the just put on one of them and the unjust the other; no man can be imagined to be of such an iron nature that he would stand fast in justice. No man would keep his hands off what was not his own when he could safely take what he liked out of the market, or go into houses and lie with any one at his pleasure, or kill or release from prison whom he would, and in all respects be like a God among men.[46]

As is common with matters related to sovereignty, there is slippage between the absolute power of the immune individual and sovereign power: Gyges the invisible not only takes what he likes; he also, in this version of the tale, attains the throne himself. Lawmaker and libertine become partly indistinguishable in this account.[47] Gyges's ring and the belt of invisibility suggest something about the partibility of modern sovereignty, perhaps, as well as about the hazards of being an observer with no outside, no sovereign, no government. Invisibility, in effect, returns one to the state of nature.

Exploralibus's lack of accountability is undercut to some degree, however, by the salience Haywood gives to his acts of violence against women—violence reminiscent of that directed against Eovaai and the female savage. The magic writing pad is, as we have seen, an essential complement to Exploralibus's belt. And this tablet, I have noted in passing, crucially depends on violence: its functioning depends on the maiming of female desire. Though the pad may be written on freely, it is difficult to erase: the only eraser is the breath of a virginal woman who has no knowledge of men:

> [The tablet] can no way be expunged, but by the breath of a virgin, of so pure an innocence as not to have even thought on the difference of sexes;—after such a one, if such a one is to be found, has blown pretty hard upon it for the space of seven seconds and three quarters, she must wipe it gently with the first down under the left wing of an unfledg'd swan, pluck'd when the moon is in three degrees of Virgo. (1:10–11)

Such a purity is hard to obtain, Exploralibus finds; even his virginal acquaintances have too much knowledge and cannot perform the erasure. He is forced, therefore, to manufacture a suitably "pure" virgin. As I have noted, this virginal girl must be forcefully sequestered from anything that might infuse her with knowledge or desire. She repeats, that is to say, something of what I have called Eovaai's savagery: she must remain fully enclosed, unseeing, unknowing, and, in a sense, irrational, her chastity enforced heteronomously rather than founded on an internalized law. Exploralibus contracts with a poor widow to let him "have a girl, of about three years old, to bring up and educate" as he "judged proper"; he then leaves this girl with an older woman whom he directs as follows:

> The little creature was kept in an upper-room, which had no window in it but a sky-light in the roof of the house, so she could be witness of nothing that pass'd below;—her diet was thin and very sparing;—she was not permitted to sleep above half the time generally allow'd for repose, and saw no living thing but the old woman who lay with her, gave her food, and did all that was necessary about her. (1:15)

Exploralibus often visits this strange domicile while invisible to ensure that his instructions are followed and, presumably, to allow the old woman to have the child erase the tablets. (The difficulty of this proceeding is elided in the text.) Significantly, we must assume that the child remains illiterate, for otherwise she would surely be corrupted by the very text she must erase.

A few commentators on *The Invisible Spy* have noted the ways in which this dependence on an imprisoned young female compromises Exploralibus's ethical status, participating as he does in a traffic in women. Panoptical surveillance, then—this new and nonviolent form of power—is founded at the outset on a strange act of violence, an imprisonment that though not physically brutal is designed to shape and enforce a profoundly damaged and unnatural female subjectivity. This innocence—enforced, as with Eovaai, by an unquestioning command—is the essential component of the textuality of the tablet. What at first appears to be a replacement for sovereign violence instead is linked both textually and conceptually to foundational commands and violences of its own.[48] Anthony Pollock has argued that Exploralibus represents a masculine power that is "unable to reflect upon or to avow the repressive conditions of its own activity."[49] Just as Eovaai's obedience rather than her rational virtue is the key to her father's vision of the preservation of the kingdom and just as the Indian's chastity fails her because her earlier virtue is naive and habitual rather than a product of education, so too does this young girl seem to be an even less natural version of this problem, isolated from the temptations of sexual difference by an allegedly benign higher power, Exploralibus. This innocent girl is another iteration of the deformed subjectivity produced by a model of virtue that takes thoughtless obedience as its starting and ending point.

This inaugural fact underlying these powers—the maimed subjectivity of the girl—is repeated in many of Exploralibus's vignettes, strongly suggesting that Haywood, rather than reflexively endorsing her narrator's blurring of voyeurism and biopower, is in fact skeptical of him—and, by extension, of the project of regulating sexualities and protecting innocence that he represents.[50] Though Exploralibus observes much misbehavior of many different sorts, he lingers in particular on several sequences in which women are imprisoned either to preserve their "innocence" for nefarious purposes or, conversely, as punishment for erotic transgressions. He catalogs the travails of these unfortunate young women at first in an effort to fight injustice, seemingly unaware that these captivities and delusions are structurally identical to his own sacrifice of a young girl to his mission. For example, in his first lengthy secret history, he relates the distresses of Alinda, whose lack of education and obedience to her father's commands leaves her vulnerable to other men. Alinda's story exposes masculine malfeasance and offers a plea for female education as preferable to blind obedience. Alinda is, much like Eovaai and the ignorant savage that is her analogue, made artificially innocent, sheltered to her detriment by an absolute command. Fearing for her virtue, Alinda's father ensures that she receives only a minimal education. As she grows older, he entrusts her to a tutor in the figure of a failed member of the clergy, who makes use of her innocence for sexual gratification and material gain. Taking advantage of her simplicity, he persuades her that their physical relationship is merely affectionate; she says, "I conceived the most tender affection for him;—alas I was then too young—too innocent, to know what was meant by the word love, any farther than that love which we naturally bear to a father, brother, or some other near relation, and thought not that what I felt for him was any more" (1:104). He also dupes her into signing a contract giving him veto power over any other potential suitors. She, uneducated and unreasoning, sees no harm in the situation; following her father's perverse injunction, she loves her tutor and trusts his statements that their sexual relationship is not, in fact, sexual. Her innocence thus becomes the primary tool for her exploitation.

It is not until after the death of Alinda's father that she is forced into grappling with the realities of her situation. Simultaneously virginal and nonvirginal, still partly under the control of her lover or obscene father, she is secretly sexually active, though her innocence is intact. She remains unaware of the perverse quality of her physical relationship with her tutor until he himself confronts her, hoping to become her husband—noting that it is remarkable that she would think of another man after the tokens of affection that have passed between them. It is at this point that she first manifests "shame" alongside a newfound "rage" at him (1:121). In the end, Exploralibus believes that while her behavior cannot be defended entirely, her indiscretions are largely due to a poor education and upbringing: it is lack of "reason—example—precept—authority, and the rudiments of a good education" that condemn her in the end, but these must be laid at the feet of her foolish father (1:137). There is something of an act of restoration, however, in the publishing of her tale. Her privacy did not protect her body, her estate, or her reputation; but the last of these can be restored through print, which, in turn, is enabled through invisibility. And yet Exploralibus, pointedly, does not recognize the rather obvious similarities between Alinda's miseducation and that of his own young captive; both are kept "innocent" because deprived of knowledge and the capacity to exercise judgment.

Alinda's perverse innocence is revisited in the homologous closing tale of Aglaura and Cleanthes, which more forcibly raises the question of the narrator's complicity in violence against women. In this sequence, Cleanthes snaps under the pressure of his wife's notional infidelities and tortures her at sword-point, threatening to disfigure her and then subjecting her to simulated drowning in the Serpentine. Initially a doting husband, Cleanthes gradually becomes aware that his wife continues to play the coquette about town; her behavior is the subject of comment by several other figures. (The text does not give us any reason to believe that Aglaura is not guilty of these infractions.) The town is surprised by a change in Cleanthes's behavior; the once-doting husband imprisons Aglaura in a room and, like a tyrannical inquisitor, feeds her only bread and water. Only the narrator knows that this imprisonment follows an even more brutal encounter. After forcing her to strip, Cleanthes forces her head underwater, bringing her to the verge of drowning before releasing her and beginning again:

> The vindictive husband then snatch'd her rudely from the earth, and taking fast hold of both her shoulders plung'd her into the river, keeping her under water 'till she was almost strangled, then suffer'd her to raise her head; but it was only in order to renew her torments, for the moment he found she had recovered breath he press'd her down again,—so that without being drown'd she felt all the agonies which that kind of death inflicts. (4:283)

The torture finished, he tosses her on the grass and shortly allows her to reclothe herself and return home with him, where he imprisons her before finally sending her to live with a relative in Yorkshire.

This record of torture could be read as a straightforward exposé of the violence that women were often subjected to in marriage—a subject familiar to us from historical sources, though not often appearing in such horrifying form in realistic fiction from this period.[51] Kathryn King argues that *The Invisible Spy* and Haywood's earlier scandal writings are interested in "bringing to light grievances that cannot be redressed by law or remedied through established legal channels."[52] Certainly Haywood seems interested in deploying the public sphere as a way to regulate privatized behavior, including violence against women.

But Exploralibus's conflicted reaction to this scene suggests that his spectatorship is almost as troubling as the scene he describes. As Pollock notes, Exploralibus does nothing to aid the poor Aglaura or indeed any other woman subjected to male violence in the text.[53] Yet in this final explosion of violence, Exploralibus records that he is seriously shaken. However, his emotional distress does not prevent him from reveling in his own secret knowledge when he hears the town discussing the strange imprisonment of Aglaura: "I laugh'd in my sleeve, believing,—I dare say with a good deal of reason,—that no one person in the whole world, excepting the Invisible Spy, was at the bottom of this secret" (4:278). What are we to make of this conflicted, peculiar contradiction in his reaction?

The reader here is intended to see an unconscious recognition on Exploralibus's part of his complicity in violence against women. I draw this conclusion for two reasons. First, the narrative abruptly—even startlingly—terminates just after this account. The only material following this final episode is an explanation for the end of the spy's adventures: the desireless girl who erases the tablet has, unfortunately, seen an image of a man and has come to understand sexual difference and sexual desire. The tablet can no longer be erased and reused by the breath of ignorant innocence: "the dialogue last repeated remains still unexpung'd, and leaves no room for any future impression" (4:288). The only dialogue that remains, sopping up all the available space, is the terrifying torture of Aglaura; this violent attempt to punish female vanity or sexual desire blocks all future transcriptions. The failure of this magical device is closely linked to the trauma of seeing this unfettered male violence. On the other hand, might not this scene of violence recall the narrator to the knowledge that his imprisonment of an innocent girl has uncomfortable parallels with the terrifying torture and captivity he witnesses here?[54] Exploralibus is exercising a form of power: surveillance. This power depends entirely on the observer being removed from, distanced from, uninvolved in, the scene of the action. Yet this apparently nonviolent power depends on a primary act of violence—an imprisonment and suppression of a female body and its desires. The young girl's plight very closely follows that of Eovaai— both forbidden certain forms of knowledge, both rendering magical objects useless as they are demystified. Exploralibus's captive girl is subject, in a way, to a sovereign command no less absolute and no less problematic than Eojaeu's.

The publication history of *The Invisible Spy* uncannily inverts the finality of this tale, erasing its most horrifying elements. Perhaps this sequence was found to be too extreme; perhaps the literary marketplace could not countenance narratives that so starkly depicted the violence that troubled marriage. Only two editions of this work were printed in Haywood's lifetime, a four-volume version in London and an almost simultaneous two-volume issue in Dublin. The second London edition, printed by Haywood's longtime associate Thomas Gardner in 1759, cuts almost the entirety of the torture sequence. This redacted version retains Exploralibus's chance encounter with the couple by the Serpentine, but in this censored version, he sees nothing of import, only hearing their heated conversation about her infidelities. This conversation still leaves him shocked, but the reader not familiar with the original edition will have little idea why such an argument would have so much as surprised him. This edition serves as the basis for several later editions, including the version included in the serialized anthology *The Novelist's Magazine* in 1788.[55] This redaction was not made to the 1768 Dublin edition—presumably based on the earlier Irish printing—which retains the original sequence in all its violence. Hence the edit presumably comes from Gardner. I have not located any hostile reviews that cite this passage, but in any case, it seems possible that the sequence proved shocking not only to Exploralibus but also to at least some readers.

Exploralibus is a kind of private sovereign, a secret agent of virtue, painting invisible vices and cruelties to make them public. And yet there is an important relationship between Haywood's imagining of a new role and a new sort of power for an author and the magical tools that Exploralibus uses. His reliance on magical objects rather than on mere stealth is a way of linking this new figure of the author to figures of sovereignty. Exploralibus's detachment allows him to present himself as a modern, leaving sovereignty behind. But there is a kind of exceptional, extralegal violence that he, too, participates in—the psychic maiming of a child's desire. And it is witnessing a kindred act of violence that appears to force him to retreat into silence, having recognized his own eroticizing of his fantastic, unobservable, and untouchable sovereign position. One of Haywood's key contributions to the invisibility genre, perhaps, is that invisibility ceases to become a trope simply of narrative convenience but rather calls attention to aspects of the narrator—an unseemly side he would prefer to discount. Even the invisible, untouchable observer, who simply transcribes the venality to which he is a witness, remains tainted by sovereignty's violence. Kathryn King argues that we ought to read Haywood's politics not simply in light of her public political affiliations but also with regard to her concern with the privatized patriarchal power of marriage.[56] With the tortured body of Aglaura, Haywood suggests how terrifying this overlapping of sovereign and patriarchal right can be, as Cleanthes and Exploralibus conspire to transform the women in their power into *homines sacri*.

Coda: Enemies

> The specific political distinction to which political actions and motives can be reduced is that between friend and enemy.
> —Carl Schmitt, *The Concept of the Political*[1]
>
> *American Citizens Split on DOJ Memo Authorizing Government to Kill Them*
> —*The Onion*, February 2013[2]

Eliza Haywood reminds us in the eighteenth century, as Margaret Cavendish did in the seventeenth, of the peculiar political status of women. Haywood's Aglaura and Exploralibus's imprisoned innocent point toward continuity in an era of shifting modes of power. As legal norms and print culture work together to produce liberal and obedient subjects without overt violence, authorities both public and private continue to claim legal and extralegal powers to punish, imprison, and kill. While Haywood's texts attempt to imagine the political subject as a rational and self-mastering female citizen, they also offer grounds to suggest that the problem of sovereignty has not been left behind. Sovereignty is a phenomenon characterized by both law and violence that perpetually threatens to spill over the boundaries of the legitimate and to injure those whom it was instituted to protect. Haywood's suggestion is that this violence forms part of modes of power that at first glance appear to operate quite differently, such as the normalizing strategies of print culture. If Cavendish shows how women from outside the legal order (refugees or wives) are mirror images of lawgivers, Haywood demonstrates the limitations of envisioning women as reasoning citizens, since those citizens remain vulnerable to the patriarchal and militaristic institutions of the state as well as to the privatized tyranny of domesticity. Women are like savages, targets of a civilizing process without end, permanently inhabiting an unending state of exception.

This characterization may seem hyperbolic. Perhaps it is. But it is truthful to the tone of more radical critiques of patriarchy circulating in Haywood's time. Consider, for example, the essay *Beauty's Triumph*, in which we read the following comment from "Sophia":

> If we have been subjected to [men's] authority, it has been by no other law than that of the stronger: And that we have not been excluded from a share in the power and privileges which lift their sex above ours, for want of natural capacity, or merit, but for want of an equal spirit of violence, shameless injustice, and lawless oppression, with theirs.[3]

This passage appeared in 1751, reprinting an earlier translation of writings from the seventeenth-century Cartesian feminist François Poullain de la Barre. Sophia's language refers directly to debates about violence and law: subject to the "rule of the stronger," women must submit to "lawless oppression" and tyranny. Patriarchy is not, Sophia tells us, a law of nature; it is rather a holdover from a Hobbesian state of nature, a kernel of lawlessness preserved within and immune to the law. The husband-wife dyad in this rendering is another version of the lawlessness that colonist and savage, that sovereign and *homo sacer*, share.

The tortured Aglaura and the pitiable wife link the plight of women to this book's other concerns with the problem of violence, political community, and those who may be said to live outside or beyond the law. I have argued that a range of writers have used colonial encounter to imagine the political, especially the way that the political community might be created, sustained, and regulated through acts of sovereign performance and violence. These fictions supplement and sometimes challenge other accounts of the political, particularly fictions of a state of nature that derive from natural law theory. Whether generally royalist, like Cavendish and Aphra Behn, or more politically ambiguous, like Daniel Defoe, Jonathan Swift, and Haywood, each of these writers is participating in broader efforts to imagine a politics that results not in a Hobbesian absolutism but rather in a self-sustaining political and socioeconomic community, one that will not need excessive or regular violence. These fictional narratives respond to and critique theories of political origins and obligation; they are also part of the prehistory of Enlightenment theories of savagery, society, and government that transform fictional tropes into speculative histories of political evolution and the language of modern fact.[4] It is valuable to consider these earlier narratives in part because of their pessimism and interest in the tendency of sovereignty to overrun the law and make subjects into enemies. This tendency is particularly relevant in the present historical moment, when the state of exception has, some observers argue, become the norm and sovereign rule over unruly subjects operates tactically inside liberal governmentality.[5]

I want briefly in this coda to broaden my critical lens to consider the role of enmity and violence in the imagining of political community, taking in not just the liberalized governmental forms of the eighteenth century but also the more democratic impulses that have emerged to compete with them. Specifically, I suggest that boundary figures such as savages—and, for that matter, women—trouble political efforts to distinguish clearly between friends and enemies, yielding narrative alternatives that point either toward universalism or toward atrocity. In Carl Schmitt's influential formulation, political community is distinct from other forms of association because it requires recognition of the difference between friends and enemies. The friend is a member of the community, with whom one may experience conflict but who is inside a sphere in which violence is excluded. The enemy, on the other hand, is always a potential threat to political community: one is not always at war with the enemy, but the defining characteristic of enmity is the possibility of a battle to the death: "To the enemy concept belongs the ever-present possibility of combat."[6]

Significantly, however, enmity is a political, not a moral, category; the sovereign designates an outsider as a legitimate enemy against whom a member of the political community may be required to fight, but this is not an ethical judgment on the enemy's virtues or faults. The enemy is targeted by the sovereign and the political community because he or she may threaten that community's existence, but this enemy remains fully human and legitimate and operates inside a structure of legality that for Schmitt defines modern warfare. This figure, though he or she may be killed in war, does not lose the status of a human being; by being engaged in a conflict legitimated by sovereign decision and designation, and because operating legitimately as part of a political grouping, the enemy does not fall in status to the bestial or the inhuman. On the other hand, Schmitt claimed, liberalism, universalism, and pluralism, in replacing the enemy with a universal rights-bearing subject, inadvertently produce another category of enmity: the inhuman enemy of all humankind who is thus exposed to violence without limit. This is because for Schmitt liberalism and universalism can only understand the enemy as evil, not simply as a pragmatic threat: "The adversary is thus no longer called an enemy but a disturber of peace and is thereby designated to be an outlaw of humanity." For Schmitt, when enmity is no longer stabilized by national borders and battlefields, it goes underground. Universalism and liberalism cannot recognize the legitimacy of an enemy combatant, who becomes a mere disturber of the peace, an outlaw, and an inhuman agent of violence.[7]

Schmitt writes from the context of the Weimar Republic, complaining of what he understood to be the dangerous softness of that regime, but his concept of friendship and enmity has inspired much discussion, particularly in the wake of the 9/11 attacks, the Bush administration's classification of military enemies as "unlawful combatants," and the Obama administration's assertion of a right to use lethal force against U.S. citizens.[8] Thinking about the figure of the savage, and the way that figure could blur eighteenth-century lines between friend and enemy, may contribute to this discussion. The savage, I suggest, figures the point of indistinction between friends and enemies and is thus in these contact narratives linked to sovereign decisions about them. Literary savages exist outside of the law and without modern sovereignty; they also, importantly, exist in relation to the colonist that comes before a sovereign decision on enmity. That is, when the explorer or the colonist encounters a savage in these fictions, the savage remains suspended between friendship and hostility—as, for that matter, does the colonist. The performances I have been considering here do the work of transforming the savage into a friend, or at least a potential friend. Sovereign excess, on the other hand, transforms the friendly or subjected savage into an enemy. Indeed, to exert the power of killing—the right to kill—is for many thinkers the very definition of sovereignty.[9] In establishing sovereignty, the colonist—much like the king or parliament—is arguably establishing a state of enmity (or remaining in such a state) relative to his or her subjects.

Ian Baucom has recently sought to revise Schmitt's conception of the enemy by way of posing a challenge to Giorgio Agamben's discussion of the *homo sacer*. Suggesting that we conceive of the form of life produced by sovereignty not as "bare" but as "inimical," Baucom traces the genealogy of the killable life back through figures such as the brigand, the pirate, the traitor, and the Hottentot, all representing a form of enemy who is not proper or legitimate because not acting as part of a recognizable state structure, continuing to exist in a wild, disorganized, undirected life that refuses sovereignty's claims.[10] As Baucom notes, the figures I have been calling savages play a leading role in the trajectory of this inimical enemy. Occupying an anomic zone outside European law, their lack of (or refusal of) sovereignty and civility make them potentially universal enemies. Travel accounts often portray them as violators of the laws of nature, committing acts of cannibalism and other depravities. Following the standards laid down by Hugo Grotius in the early seventeenth century, they may be punished by any sovereign—anyone not in subjection to another—as enemies of nature and of humankind: "War may be justly undertaken against those who are inhuman to their Parents, . . . against those who eat human Flesh, . . . and against those who practice Piracy," Grotius argues, for each of these is a manifest and egregious violation of the fundamental laws of nature.[11] For Grotius, the right to punish these transgressions is inextricably linked to sovereignty and to the masterless sovereign's remaining partly in a state of nature. The right to punish is a natural right; it is surrendered by those who enter civil society as subjects, but it is retained by sovereigns, who are subject to no one: their right to punish comes "not as they have an Authority over others, but as they are in Subjection to none" (2:1021). By killing, the sovereign makes the world a better place for the properly human. Quoting Seneca, Grotius defines the inimical enemy as the person for whom *"so great a Depravity of Mind has cut him off from human Society, and makes him to me, and all the World, a Foe"* (2:1024) "War against such is natural," Grotius concludes; "the justest War is that which is undertaken against wild rapacious Beasts, and next to it is that against Men who are like Beasts" (2:1024). In this reading, the cannibal is an enemy of all humankind; this savage would always be inimical, killable, having stripped himself or herself of even natural law. Abjected not only from the political but from the human community, the bestial savage as universal enemy provides a way to define the civil; civility is grounded in and defined by that savagery it rejects, and its stability is confirmed by imagining acts of sovereign punishment. This figure, Baucom argues, lingers or recurs in the contemporary figure of the terrorist or the unlawful combatant.

However, savages also represent the potential for friendship; their presence in eighteenth-century fiction is often a gesture toward a version of universalism. If guided toward states of civility, they have the capacity to become Christians, partners in trade, or both. They may lack education, the trappings of civility, and religious practice, but they could be transformed into civilized persons with whom one might have a peaceful relationship. Cavendish, Behn, and Defoe all offer accounts of savages who can be reformed and brought into line with natural or Christian law, or at least made sufficiently docile for commerce. Swift's savages learn civility through struggle; Haywood's savages parallel women in their lack of education, which can be remedied.

If, as I have been suggesting, there is a synecdochical relationship between savages and subjects and between colonists and sovereigns, then the ambivalent status of the savage suggests that fictions of colonialism are in part meditations on the instability of sovereign decision on the status of the subject. This instability is the engine that drives these narratives of conversion or of extermination. This instability is perhaps itself driven by the ambiguous status of the institution of sovereignty, which remains itself outside the law. The sovereign, in the formulation of Grotius, Hobbes, and Agamben, remains in the state of nature; subject to no external government, it remains savage in a legal sense.

Even John Locke, as David Bates has recognized, implicitly imagines a sovereign who remains partly in an anomic state of nature; since the entity responsible for foreign relations and the executive must occupy the same position, this institutional fusion offers a pathway for political decisions to reenter and trouble the domestic sphere.[12] Political decisions are for Locke driven fundamentally by the confrontation with inimical forms of life, not subject to the peaceful rationality that governs both his state of nature and modern governmentalized societies. The intrusion of the enemy requires more extreme responses. Here Locke describes the character of the criminal, who becomes a figure of the domestic and savage enemy, obeying passion rather than reason:

> Every man, in the state of nature, has a power to kill a murderer, both *to deter* others from doing the like injury, which no reparation can compensate, by the example of the punishment that attends it from every body, and also to secure men from the attempts of a criminal, who having renounced reason, the common rule and measure God hath given to mankind, hath, by the unjust violence and slaughter he hath committed upon one, declared war against all mankind, and therefore may be destroyed as a *lion* or a *tyger*, one of those wild savage beasts, with whom men can have no society nor security.[13]

Locke's murderers and instigators of wars lose any claim to membership in civil society. William Rasch has noted that this model of criminal-as-enemy is akin to Schmitt's critique of liberalism.[14] For Schmitt, Locke's model does not allow a sovereign to declare that there might be a sort of legitimacy to conflict or to hostility. The enemy for Locke cannot really be the lawful combatant but remains an inimical and savage outsider. The magistrate, having had the right of punishment delegated to him, here takes on the role of the sovereign who decides on the exception—in this case, on the exceptional case of humans who have removed themselves from the realm of the human and thus exposed themselves to sovereign violence. Against such an enemy, there can be little occasion for mercy.

Considerations such as these were not abstractions but practical problems in the seventeenth and eighteenth centuries. During the serial crises that followed the Restoration, the traitor figures as an enemy who tested the boundaries of political community and the rights of the sovereign. Treason trials were conducted under different rules from standard criminal cases, reflecting their exceptional nature; defendants were prohibited benefit of council, among other things. Other extraordinary measures were sometimes taken, including parliamentary bills of attainder that could impose penalties against traitors without trial.[15] The traitor could not be handled entirely within the sphere of law because traitors posed an existential threat to the existence of the state; trying a treason case required treating the traitor as a political enemy rather than as an ordinary criminal. Defending bills of attainder, future Lord Chancellor of Ireland Richard West anticipated twenty-first-century defenses of extralegal security measures when he asked in 1716, "Is it possible, that a Society of many Millions should not have that Right, which no single private Man can ever be supposed to be without? Can a Nation be ever reduced to such Circumstances, as to be deprived of the Use of such Means, as are absolutely necessary to its preservation?"[16] Treason trials and bills of attainder played significant roles in defending the political community from alleged Catholic plots during the 1670s and against real and notional Jacobites following the Glorious Revolution.[17]

Distinguishing between friend and enemy was also a pressing practical question after 1707's Act of Union brought thousands of Highland Scots—some quite "savage" by London standards and many sympathetic to the Jacobite cause—into the nominal political community of Great Britain. Much has been written about the problems of nationalism and identity that complicated this merger, but I am interested in something narrower: the definition of the political community and the question of whether Highland Scots could be made into friends. During the last Jacobite rebellion in 1745, the Highlanders were frequently described as enemies and savages both, not yet the noble remnants of a virtuous and bold people they were later to become. Midcentury tracts often describe them as savages, "Hottentots," and cannibals.[18] Portraits of them echo some contact narratives, including even references to technological disparities between the warring parties:

> Down rush'd the Foe with direful Clamour rude
> Like Cannibals that gorge on human Food
> But mindful of their Gen'ral's great Commands
> Firm as a solid Rock the Soldier stands
> ....
> In vain is brandish'd high the threatening Blade
> In vain oppos'd the Target's idle Aid
> As the grim Savage with a thund'ring Pace
> Comes furious on full in his horrid Face
> The Bullet flies deep in his riven Breast
> With deathful Stroke the pointed Steel is prest
> Groaning he falls he bites the bloody Sand
> The Sword the Shield drop from each nerveless Hand.[19]

In this passage from a poem of tribute to William Augustus, the Duke of Cumberland, Highland warriors occupy a temporality akin to that of the cannibal facing modern military technology for the first time. Unlike later romanticized images of an admirable nobility attributable to the Highlander, he is here a grimly passionate berserker; valor is due to the well-armed Lowland Scot or Englishman, whose musket renders these barbarous tools irrelevant.

These literary representations had their analogues in the political, military, and legal decisions made during and immediately after the rebellion. Jacobite rebels, in the eyes of Phillip Stanhope, 4th Earl of Chesterfield, could not be treated as a proper enemy: "We cannot be at war with them," he wrote. But because the Highlands were a military zone, they could not be considered as entitled to due process rights under the law, either. Calls for the sterilization and extermination of the entire population of the Highlands were floated in the press.[20] Yet the Highlander was, in the end, transformed into a full-fledged member of the British political community. The construction of new fortresses, widespread killing of recalcitrant Jacobites, radical revisions to land-tenure arrangements, strict restrictions on attire—all of these played a role in the state's reconfiguration of Scotland into a region that could be integrated into the modern British nation. The Scottish Highlands were over the next half century transformed from the home of enemies to the motherland of friends; Highlanders became domesticated and were crucial to the populating and management of the British empire for the century to come—a project, of course, that directed violence against enemies across the globe.[21]

Chantal Mouffe is among the critics who have found in Carl Schmitt's notion of a necessary enmity a powerful resource for rethinking the political. Specifically, she has described contemporary liberal democracy as an irresolvable tension between the universalism of liberalism and the specific requirements of democracy, which require a definition of "the people" that by its nature cannot be universalized. Mouffe, however, sees this tension as productive:

> The democratic logic of constituting the people, and inscribing rights and equality into practices, is necessary to subvert the tendency towards abstract universalism inherent in liberal discourse. But the articulation with liberal logic allows us constantly to challenge—through reference to "humanity" and the polemical use of "human rights"—the forms of exclusion that are necessarily inscribed in the political practice of installing those rights and defining "the people," which is going to rule.[22]

Mouffe's starting point in this critique is Schmitt's commentary on the pitfalls of parliamentary democracy. Mouffe accepts the broad outlines of this critique while refusing Schmitt's solution—the necessity of a preexisting social formation that can serve as the basis for a political "self" consisting of "friends," to be juxtaposed with "enemies" across the border. For Mouffe, the enemy is always a contingent enemy, who might, as the field of the political shifts, become a friend—much like the savage. But in that troubled interim, we might ask how the boundaries of that community are to be understood and sustained. Schmitt is very clear on the question: the enemy is always subject to violence. Those who would revise Schmitt for left-leaning ends might ask what takes the place of the enemy in his formulation of the political. Is it possible to imagine a community that does not constitute itself by enmity or in which something else takes the place of the enemy?

Barry Unsworth's historical novel *Sacred Hunger* (1992) returns to the eighteenth century to explore these very questions.[23] Set in the mid-eighteenth century, Unsworth's novel tells the story of a mutiny on a slave ship—a mutiny involving both white crew and enslaved Africans. The mutineers establish a culturally and racially mixed commune in the deep woods of South America. Unsworth's tale does not tell us precisely what governs the politics of this miniature republic, but he does insist on its dependence on enmity and violence. Its origins lie in a violent mutiny; its precarious situation within the jurisdiction of the empire but outside its authority makes it vulnerable. Yet that originary violence and that vulnerability fuse its citizens into a political community. Unsworth's mutineers re-create that violence by mythologizing it: the heroic tales the mutineers tell their children sustain the community through references to acts of primordial illegality (510–12, 518–20). Similarly, when the commune faces a threat from a mixed-race band of slavers working in the area, the group decides it is essential to kill them. They do this for pragmatic reasons—the enemy might give away their location, making them vulnerable to sanction by the British empire—but these killings also play a symbolic political role. The group's visionary leader, Delblanc, sees these men as an opportunity to transform the nascent polity from a vulnerable assemblage of onetime enemies into a cohesive group of friends; the violence he proposes is essential, in particular, to erase the racial divide within the polity: "We must kill them. . . . It is providential—they are mixed white and black, just as we are. By killing them we cancel the distinction. . . . It is the only thing that will keep us together" (518). And indeed, for a time, it does: "It was on this blood [that] their small republic had been founded" (520). The community's informal leadership attempts to ensure ideological and social cohesion (and an erasure of the colony's fractious prehistory) by creating new narratives of foundational violence; their myths reproduce the community and secure its boundaries. Those who have themselves lived through and perpetrated that violence carry a legendary—indeed, a wondrous—status in the village. One of the novel's protagonists, Matthew Paris, describes these figures as living fetishes, "so charged with a particular event that they carried an evocative aura about them" (519).

This aura of wonder—this cathexis of individuals—is here decoupled from the images of technology that this book has trafficked in. The novel is, to be sure, inspired in some degree by the technological artifacts that supported empire and the slave trade. In the wake of the commune's first military expedition, Paris notices that the forest has been silenced by his gunshot (520). Unsworth's novel returns to this trope again in describing the execution of a murderer—the only such act in the history of the commune. When the men had discharged their muskets on the criminal, "at that sudden explosion of sound great flocks of birds had risen from the marshes" (548–49). These passages indirectly quote Defoe's description of Crusoe's first gunshot on his island: "I had no sooner fir'd but from all the Parts of the Wood there arose an innumerable Number of Fowls of many Sorts, making a confus'd Screaming, and crying every one according to his usual note."[24] But unlike Crusoe's performances, the gunshots of Paris and his fellows require more active shaping and mediation to transform their colony into a political and social whole; the technologies that preserve their community are not those of iron and sulfur but of rhetoric and memory.

Unsworth's novel intervenes quite intentionally, I think, in the political paradoxes associated with law, narratives of origin, and political community. "The people" in Unsworth's rendering are created through violence and the shaping of that violence through calculated performances. They also inhabit a political space that is fragile and, the novel suggests, unsustainable. But while it is sustained, it is sustained by a Schmittian friend/enemy distinction, made flesh in acts of violence and in their replication and enchantment through narrative and performance.

I close with Unsworth's mediation on the politics of violence and wonder. The novel ultimately disavows the more extraordinary dreams of Delblanc, whose colony is being pulled apart by internal developments before it is destroyed by the force of official law. But the novel does seem to endorse the idea that a more democratic politics requires the deployment of both force and wonder, albeit in a different formation than in the eighteenth-century texts I have discussed. It also suggests that Mouffe's politics elide the question of violence and of the specific mechanics that are needed to form a polity. Unsworth's utopia is held together not by reasoned discourse but by violence and affect. His meditations on spectacular and foundational violence remind us that the problems raised by these eighteenth-century texts remain to be resolved. The question of violence, in particular, is one that a democratic politics must continue to consider. Perhaps a democracy requires myths and violence to sustain a political culture that can undergird the public sphere of reason and deliberation.

But there is another possibility. Unsworth's small utopia was not meant to last. It begins to fragment as time distances its citizens from the moments of its founding; performance can prolong memory and wonder, but not indefinitely. Yet it is decisively ended not from within but by enemies from without—agents of the British empire. The fictions of civilizing violence I have discussed are working toward peace—a peace that encloses both the savage and the civil, seeking to transform enmity into friendship. Yet they remain entranced by apocalypse. Unsworth's colony might offer an alternative if we consider not the community's figures of enmity, which are not, in the end, adequate to the task of preservation. We might rather attend to that community's constitutive fragility and vulnerability. We might imagine a utopian politics that understands peace and political community as perpetually and constitutively threatened, not by enemies but by the very impossibility of any absolute security. Marc Redfield has recently described peace as "an impossible figure . . . constitutively exposed to a failure it cannot accept, and in hock to images of failure by which it cannot help being entranced."[25] If my study has suggested anything, then, it is that for readers and writers in this crucial period of modernity, sovereign violence and political community are paradoxes from which it is difficult to imagine an emergence. Perhaps they might have followed a different course, however: seeing in the bodies of non-Europeans not lives that must be constrained in order to become truly free or antagonists in cycles of violence without end but figures for the universal precariousness of life that it could be the task of politics to redress.[26] To recognize the savage as the point where friendship and enmity converge might be to perceive a responsibility for life itself, a universal mutuality grounded in a vulnerability that both precedes and permeates political and social life.

Notes

INTRODUCTION: MAGICAL GOVERNMENT

1. Exemplary studies include Srinivas Aravamudan, *Tropicopolitans: Colonialism and Agency, 1688–1804* (Durham: Duke University Press, 1999); Roxann Wheeler, *The Complexion of Race: Categories of Difference in Eighteenth-Century British Culture* (Philadelphia: University of Pennsylvania Press, 2000); Richard Nash, *Wild Enlightenment: The Borders of Human Identity in the Eighteenth Century* (Charlottesville: University of Virginia Press, 2003); Felicity Nussbaum, *Torrid Zones: Maternity, Sexuality, and Empire in Eighteenth-Century English Narratives* (Baltimore: Johns Hopkins University Press, 1995); Laura Brown, *Ends of Empire: Women and Ideology in Early Eighteenth-Century English Literature* (Ithaca: Cornell University Press, 1993); Harriet Guest, *Empire, Barbarism, and Civilisation: James Cook, William Hodges, and the Return to the Pacific* (Cambridge: Cambridge University Press, 2007); Suvir Kaul, *Poems of Nation, Anthems of Empire: English Verse in the Long Eighteenth Century* (Charlottesville: University of Virginia Press, 2000); Lynn Festa, *Sentimental Figures of Empire in Eighteenth-Century Britain and France* (Baltimore: Johns Hopkins University Press, 2006). See also the essays collected in Daniel Carey and Lynn Festa, eds., *The Postcolonial Enlightenment: Eighteenth-Century Colonialism and Postcolonial Theory* (Oxford: Oxford University Press, 2009).

2. Jean Bodin is arguably the first political thinker to define this term in this sense, though his definition draws on older humanist traditions. Jean Bodin, *On Sovereignty: Four Chapters from Six Books on the Commonwealth*, ed. and trans. Julian H. Franklin (Cambridge: Cambridge University Press, 1992); Quentin Skinner, *The Foundations of Modern Political Thought*, vol. 2, *The Age of Reformation* (Cambridge: Cambridge University Press, 1978), 284–301.

3. *Constituent power* is a contested term and not one explicitly used during the earlier eighteenth century. Originating with Abbé Sieyès's essay "What Is the Third Estate?" (1789), the term has commonly been used to describe the power that fashions the constitution or fundamental law; by contrast, constituted powers derive their authority from that constitution and cannot change it. As Martin Loughlin notes, however, the concept though not the term is a crucial component of political contestation in seventeenth-century Britain. Martin Loughlin, "Constituent Power Subverted: From English Constitutional Argument to British Constitutional Practice," in *The Paradox of Constitutionalism: Constituent Power and Constitutional Form*, ed. Martin Loughlin and Neil Walker, 27–48 (Oxford: Oxford University Press, 2007). The term is generally associated with the notion of popular power or popular sovereignty. For Antonio Negri, the term embraces not so much an entity but the creative process of the multitude; Giorgio Agamben, on the other hand, sees it as an aspect of sovereignty, or enclosed within the act of sovereignty. Despite these ambiguities, I invoke the term here instead of its alternative conception of "popular sovereignty" for several reasons. Most significantly, as Negri points out, constituent power is best understood as transformative and fluid, while sovereignty is a force that attempts to regulate and to instill order. Fundamental or constitutional law is or may be challenged by popular forms of action; while a sovereign may overrule and suspend law, it is generally in the service of regularity and order. Antonio Negri, *Insurgencies: Constituent Power and the Modern State*, trans. Maurizia Boscagli, 2nd rev. ed. (Minneapolis: University of Minnesota Press, 2009), 1–35; Giorgio Agamben, *Homo Sacer: Sovereign Power and Bare Life*, trans. Daniel Heller-Roazin (Stanford: Stanford University Press, 1998), 39–47. See also Srinivas Aravamudan, "'The Unity of the Representer': Reading Leviathan against the Grain," *South Atlantic Quarterly* 104, no. 4 (2005): 631–53.

4. J. G. A. Pocock, *The Machiavellian Moment: Florentine Political Thought and the Atlantic Republican Tradition* (Princeton: Princeton University Press, 1975), 340. See also Pocock, *The Ancient Constitution and the Feudal Law: A Study of English Historical Thought in the Seventeenth Century* (New York: Norton, 1957).

5. In two recent books, Paul Kahn analyzes the consequences of the relocation of sovereignty from the person of the king into the body of the people: *Sacred Violence: Torture, Terror, and Sovereignty* (Ann Arbor: University of Michigan Press, 2008); *Political Theology: Four New Chapters on the Concept of Sovereignty* (New York: Columbia University Press, 2011). For an important recent discussion of the radical, though not democratic, nature of the Glorious Revolution, see Steve Pincus,

1688: The First Modern Revolution (New Haven: Yale University Press, 2009). There is a considerable literature on the theory and practice of politics in this period; among the most helpful for my research have been the following: Victoria Kahn, *Wayward Contracts: The Crisis of Political Obligation in England, 1640–1674* (Princeton: Princeton University Press, 2004); David William Bates, *States of War: Enlightenment Origins of the Political* (New York: Columbia University Press, 2012); Elliott Visconsi, *Lines of Equity: Literature and the Origins of Law in Later Stuart England* (Ithaca: Cornell University Press, 2008); David Armitage, *The Ideological Origins of the British Empire* (Cambridge: Cambridge University Press, 2000); Susan Staves, *Players' Scepters: Fictions of Authority in the Restoration* (Lincoln: University of Nebraska Press, 1979); J. A. W. Gunn, *Beyond Liberty and Property: The Process of Self-Recognition in Eighteenth-Century Political Thought* (Kingston and Montreal: McGill-Queen's University Press, 1983); Steven N. Zwicker, *Lines of Authority: Politics and English Literary Culture, 1649–1689* (Ithaca: Cornell University Press, 1993); and Michael Mendle, "Parliamentary Sovereignty: A Very English Absolutism," in *Political Discourse in Early Modern Britain*, ed. Nicholas Phillipson and Quentin Skinner, 97–119 (Cambridge: Cambridge University Press, 1993).

6. These terms, particularly the word *savage*, of course encode a myriad of ethnocentric and racist assumptions. I have declined to enclose these terms within quotation marks in this book, but I wish to underscore that a savage is always a fictional construct and is never to be taken as referring to real historical inhabitants of lands beyond Europe. I should also note that I am taking into account not only savages derived from accounts of the Americas and West Africa but also Asia and Europe, as I discuss later.

7. For a discussion of *war* as a signifier, see Marc Redfield, *The Rhetoric of Terror: Reflections on 9/11 and the War on Terror* (New York: Fordham University Press, 2009), 66.

8. Richard Hakluyt, *The Principal Navigations, Voyages, Traffiques & Discoveries of the English Nation Made by Sea or Over-land to the Remote and Farthest Distant Quarters of the Earth at Any Time within the Compasse of These 1600 Yeeres*, 12 vols. (London, 1598–1600; repr., Glasgow: J. MacLehose and Sons, 1903–5); Samuel Purchas, *Hakluytus Posthumus; or Purchas His Pilgrimes; Contayning a History of the World in Sea Voyages and Lande Travells by Englishmen and Others*, 20 vols. (London, 1625; repr., Glasgow: J. MacLehose and Sons, 1905–7); John Churchill and Awnsham Churchill, eds., *A Collection of Voyages and Travels, Some Now First Printed from Original Manuscripts; Others Translated Out of Foreign Languages, and Now First Published in English; To Which Are Added Some*

Few That Have Formerly Appear'd in English, but Do Now for Their Excellency and Scarceness Deserve to Be Reprinted; In Four Volumes, with a General Preface, Giving an Account of the Progress of Navigation, from Its First Beginning . . . the Whole Illustrated with a Great Number of Useful Maps, and Cuts, All Engraven on Copper, 4 vols. (London, 1704). For an excellent overview of recent scholarship on Hakluyt, see Daniel Carey and Claire Jowitt, introduction to *Richard Hakluyt and Travel Writing in Early Modern Europe*, ed. Daniel Carey and Claire Jowitt, 1–10, Hakluyt Society Extra Series 47 (Burlington, VT: Ashgate, 2012).

9. Daniel Defoe, *A New Voyage Round the World*, ed. John McVeagh, vol. 10 of *The Novels of Daniel Defoe* (London: Pickering & Chatto, 2009),127.

10. Ibid., 127.

11. Bartolomé de las Casas, *An Account of the First Voyages and Discoveries Made by the Spaniards in America: Containing the Most Exact Relation Hitherto Publish'd, of Their Unparallel'd Cruelties on the Indians, in the Destruction of Above Forty Millions of People; with the Propositions Offer'd to the King of Spain to Prevent the Further Ruin of the West-Indies / by Don Bartholomew De Las Casas, Bishop of Chiapa, Who Was an Eye-witness of Their Cruelties; Illustrated with Cuts; to Which Is Added, The Art of Travelling, Shewing How a Man May Dispose His Travels to the Best Advantage* (London, 1699).

12. Robert Boyle, *Some Considerations Touching the Usefulness of Experimental Natural Philosophy: Propos'd in a Familiar Discourse to a Friend, by Way of Invitation to the Study of It* (Oxford, UK, 1664), 6–7.

13. Charles Blount, *An Appeal from the Country to the City for the Preservation of His Majesties Person, Liberty, Property, and the Protestant Religion* ([London?], 1679), 2.

14. On the Tower of London as a royal and Norman institution long associated with tyranny, see Sir Laurence Gomme, *The Making of London* (Oxford, UK: Clarendon, 1912), 134–36, 158–60.

15. My discussion of natural law draws heavily on Richard Tuck, *Natural Rights Theories: Their Origin and Development* (Cambridge: Cambridge University Press, 1982); Tuck, *The Rights of War and Peace: Political Thought and the International Order from Grotius to Kant* (Oxford: Oxford University Press, 1999); and Skinner, *Foundations of Modern Political Thought*.

16. William Connolly, *The Ethos of Pluralization* (Minneapolis: University of Minnesota Press, 1995), 137–39.

17. Jean-Jacques Rousseau, *Rousseau: "The Social Contract" and Other Later Political Writings*, ed. Victor Gourevitch, Cambridge Texts in the History of Political Thought (Cambridge: Cambridge University Press,

1997), 71. See also the discussion in Bonnie Honig, *Emergency Politics: Paradox, Law, Democracy* (Princeton: Princeton University Press, 2009), 17–28.

18. Kahn, *Wayward Contracts*, 2.

19. For a brief summary of some forces behind this development, see Colin Gordon, "Governmental Rationality: An Introduction," in *The Foucault Effect: Studies in Governmentality*, ed. Graham Burchell, Colin Gordon, and Peter Miller, 1–52 (Chicago: University of Chicago Press, 1991), 12–13. Gordon is addressing an earlier period in Europe and is, of course, generalizing about a very long and complex transformation, but many of the trends he cites are applicable to the seventeenth- and eighteenth-century British Isles. See also E. P. Thompson, "Patrician Society, Plebeian Culture," *Journal of Social History* 7, no. 4 (1974): 382–405; Robert Shoemaker, *The London Mob: Violence and Disorder in Eighteenth-Century London* (London: Hambledon and London, 2004).

20. On this point, see Michel Foucault, "Governmentality," in Burchell, Gordon, and Miller, *Foucault Effect*, 87–104. In this lecture and elsewhere in his later work, Foucault modifies the claims developed in his *Discipline and Punish: The Birth of the Prison*, trans. Alan Sheridan (New York: Vintage Books, 1995). For a more traditional summation of liberalism's origins in this period, see Alan Ryan, *The Making of Modern Liberalism* (Princeton: Princeton University Press, 2012). For discussions of the social background, see A. L. Beier, *Masterless Men: The Vagrancy Problem in Britain, 1560–1640* (London: Methuen, 1985). Beier's account leaves off roughly where mine begins; his argument concludes that vagrancy and masterlessness cease to be problems during the century that followed, largely due to new settlement laws and increased emigration to the colonies. However, the idea of the wandering, undisciplined, unsettled, or uncivilized person is the persistent problem of Restoration and early eighteenth-century political writing. Roger B. Manning provides a fascinating discussion of the use of extralegal and emergency measures against vagrants in earlier periods in *Village Revolts: Social Protest and Popular Disturbances in England, 1509–1640* (Oxford, UK: Clarendon, 1988), 157–85. On the importance of vagrancy law to the regulation of British labor markets in the eighteenth century, see Nicholas Rogers, "Vagrancy, Impressment and the Regulation of Labour in Eighteenth-Century Britain," *Slavery & Abolition* 15, no. 2 (1994): 102–13.

21. Carole Pateman, *The Sexual Contract* (Stanford: Stanford University Press, 1988), 1–75. Connolly notes Rousseau's similar subjection of women in *The Ethos of Pluralization*, 138–39.

22. Foucault, "Governmentality."

23. On liberalism and power, see Gordon, "Governmental Rationality." Exemplary studies emphasizing Foucauldian, distributed modes of power in the eighteenth century include John Bender, *Imagining the Penitentiary: Fiction and the Architecture of Mind in Eighteenth-Century England* (Chicago: University of Chicago Press, 1987); Erin Mackie, *Market à la Mode: Fashion, Commodity, and Gender in "The Tatler" and "The Spectator"* (Baltimore: Johns Hopkins University Press, 1997).

24. "Sovereign is he who decides on the exception." Carl Schmitt, *Political Theology: Four Chapters on the Concept of Sovereignty*, trans. George Schwab (Cambridge: MIT Press, 1985), 5. Schmitt's sovereign, whether an individual or an institution, is charged with making the decision about whether a given situation can be managed within the framework of norms and laws, or whether it requires the suspension of those norms. Schmitt argues that this decision must be, at bottom, groundless, in the sense that it cannot be completely derived or deduced from norms or from law. Schmitt's definition has spawned a great deal of commentary, much of which is addressed later in this introduction or in the chapters that follow. For an indispensible commentary on the role of exception and emergency in the context of Schmitt's thought and career, see Gopal Balakrishnan, *The Enemy: An Intellectual Portrait of Carl Schmitt* (London: Verso, 2000), 42–52.

25. Moira Fradinger, *Binding Violence: Literary Visions of Political Origins* (Stanford: Stanford University Press, 2010), 11.

26. For discussion of this trial, its circulation in print, and its contribution to the development of radical political cultures, see Visconsi, *Lines of Equity*, 148–54; Annabel M. Patterson, *Early Modern Liberalism* (Cambridge: Cambridge University Press, 1997), 129–52. Both these sources hereafter cited parenthetically in the text.

27. Jonathan Scott, *Algernon Sidney and the Restoration Crisis, 1677–1683* (Cambridge: Cambridge University Press, 1991), 212.

28. Algernon Sidney, *Discourses Concerning Government*, ed. Thomas G. West (Indianapolis: Liberty Fund, 1996), 2.1, 83. Hereafter cited parenthetically in the text by volume, chapter, and page number in this edition.

29. Laura Doyle, *Freedom's Empire: Race and the Rise of the Novel in Atlantic Modernity, 1640–1940* (Durham: Duke University Press, 2008), 27–56.

30. Scott, *Algernon Sidney and the Restoration Crisis*; Patterson, *Early Modern Liberalism*; Visconsi, *Lines of Equity*.

31. James Tyrrell, *Bibliotheca Politica; or, An Enquiry into the Ancient Constitution of the English Government: Both in Respect to the Just Ex-*

tent of Regal Power, and the Rights and Liberties of the Subject (London, 1694), n.p.

32. Daniel Defoe, *The Original Power of the Collective Body of the People of England, Examined and Asserted* (London, 1701), 10, 20. Defoe never abandons this stance, which features prominently in his major political poem *Jure Divino* (London, 1706). Defoe's restricted definition of "the people" is hardly unusual in liberal and republican writing from this period. For synthetic commentary, see Doyle, *Freedom's Empire*, 1–23; Domenico Losurdo, *Liberalism: A Counter-history*, trans. Gregory Elliott (London: Verso, 2011), 1–65. The degree of egalitarianism endorsed by republican writers varied widely and is not always entirely clear. Machiavelli's republican writings can be interpreted in multiple ways; some contemporary critics see in him a radical democrat, but his intellectual heirs in England generally did not fit that profile. For contrasting views on Machiavelli, see John P. McCormick, *Machiavellian Democracy* (Cambridge: Cambridge University Press, 2011), 1–12; and Vickie B. Sullivan, *Machiavelli, Hobbes, and the Formation of a Liberal Republicanism in England* (Cambridge: Cambridge University Press, 2006), 31–79. On landownership and the franchise, see H. T. Dickinson, "The Representation of the People in Eighteenth-Century Britain," in *Realities of Representation: State Building in Early Modern Europe and European America*, ed. Maija Jansson, 19–44 (New York: Palgrave Macmillan, 2007), 19–24.

33. Daniel Defoe, *A Collection of the Writings of the Author of "The True-Born English-man"* (London, 1703), lines 2.211–18. Hereafter cited parenthetically in the text by part and line numbers.

34. Wolfram Schmidgen suggests that Defoe here attempts to ground English institutions in natural law. Wolfram Schmidgen, *Eighteenth-Century Fiction and the Law of Property* (Cambridge: Cambridge University Press, 2002), 50–51.

35. Daniel Defoe, *Hymn to the Mob* (1715), in *The True-Born Englishman and Other Poems*, vol. 1 of *Satire, Fantasy, and Writings on the Supernatural*, ed. W. R. Owen and Philip Nicholas Furbank (London: Pickering & Chatto, 2003). Maximillian Novak has argued that Defoe recognized the mob as a de facto authority despite his wish to restrict franchise to the landed. Novak's point is well taken, but it is also clear that Defoe sees the legitimacy of the mob as limited; its chaotic energy must be given shape and direction by an outside force. Novak, "Defoe and the Disordered City," *PMLA* 92, no. 2 (1977): 241–52. Cf. Lee Horsley, "'Vox Populi' in the Political Literature of 1710," *Huntington Library Quarterly* 38, no. 4 (1975): 335–53.

36. I am briefly summarizing here a large body of criticism; for recent work that underscores the realist novel's engagement with questions of liberal individualism and the nation, see Srinivas Aravamudan, "In the Wake of the Novel: The Oriental Tale as National Allegory," *NOVEL: A Forum on Fiction* 33, no. 1 (1999): 5–31; Aravamudan, *Enlightenment Orientalism: Resisting the Rise of the Novel* (Chicago: University of Chicago Press, 2011), 1–75; Doyle, *Freedom's Empire*, 16–21.

37. Jonathan Elmer, *On Lingering and Being Last: Race and Sovereignty in the New World* (New York: Fordham University Press, 2008), 7.

38. Elaine McGirr, among others, closely associates heroic tragedy with absolutist and patriarchal ideologies; its aesthetic seeks to astonish the viewer into reverence for the monarchy in a way not unlike the effect of the first gunshot on savages. McGirr, *Heroic Mode and Political Crisis, 1660–1745* (Cranbury, NJ: Associated University Presses, 2009). Visconsi, however, argues that a more complex aesthetic is at work in these texts; he demonstrates the similarities between the equitable procedures encouraged by Dryden's sophisticated tragedies and narrative fiction. Visconsi, *Lines of Equity*, 40–48.

39. Charles Leslie, *The Finishing Stroke: Being a Vindication of the Patriarchal Scheme of Government in Defence of the Rehearsals . . .* (London, 1711), 125–233.

40. Staves, *Players' Scepters*, 111–98. As Staves notes, this analogy was under pressure from two directions, as the legacies of the civil war had challenged the authority of monarchs and of husbands alike.

41. Mary Astell, "Reflections upon Marriage," in *Astell: Political Writings*, ed. Patricia Springborg (Cambridge: Cambridge University Press, 1996), 18, 57.

42. Richard Helgerson, *Forms of Nationhood: The Elizabethan Writing of England* (Chicago: University of Chicago Press, 1992); Elliott Visconsi, "A Degenerate Race: English Barbarism in Aphra Behn's *Oroonoko* and *The Widow Ranter*," *ELH* 69, no. 3 (2002): 673–701; Visconsi, *Lines of Equity*; Debora Shuger, "Irishmen, Aristocrats, and Other White Barbarians," *Renaissance Quarterly* 50, no. 2 (1997): 494–525.

43. Bernard Mandeville, *The Fable of the Bees: Or, Private Vices, Publick Benefits*, ed. Frederick Benjamin Kaye, 2 vols. (Oxford, UK: Clarendon, 1924), 2:264. For a discussion of Mandeville's use of the idea of savagery, see E. J. Hundert, *The Enlightenment's Fable: Bernard Mandeville and the Discovery of Society* (Cambridge: Cambridge University Press, 2005), 41–44, 62–70.

44. Giorgio Agamben, *State of Exception*, trans. Kevin Attell (Chicago: University of Chicago Press, 2005). See also David Bates on Gabriel Naudé, discussed in more detail later: *States of War*, 49–50.

45. Daniel Defoe, *Serious Reflections during the Life and Surprising Adventures of Robinson Crusoe: With His Vision of the Angelick World* (London, 1720), 129.

46. Samuel Johnson, *A Dictionary of the English Language: In Which the Words Are Deduced from Their Originals, and Illustrated in Their Different Significations by Examples from the Best Writers; To Which Are Prefixed, a History of the Language, and an English Grammar*, 2 vols. (London, 1755), vol. 1, s.v. "civil"; Agamben, *Homo Sacer*, 104–105.

47. The classic treatment of this form of civility is Norbert Elias, *The Civilizing Process*, trans. Edmund Jephcott (Oxford, UK: Blackwell, 1994). This conception of civility, as Roxann Wheeler notes, originates in courtly contexts as a way to mediate and soften hostility and violence; this form is readily exported to moments of intercultural contact. Wheeler, *Complexion of Race*, 102–3, 110. See also Bernard W. Sheehan, *Savagism and Civility: Indians and Englishmen in Colonial Virginia* (Cambridge: Cambridge University Press, 1980); and Anthony Pagden, *European Encounters with the New World: From Renaissance to Romanticism* (New Haven: Yale University Press, 1994), 117–40.

48. Johnson, *Dictionary*, vol. 1, s.v. "civilize." See, for more discussion of the early modern savage who informs these texts, Anthony Pagden, *The Fall of Natural Man: The American Indian and the Origins of Comparative Ethnology*, Cambridge Iberian and Latin American Studies (Cambridge: Cambridge University Press, 1982), 16–25.

49. For a discussion of stadial theory's origins and development, see Karen O'Brien, *Narratives of Enlightenment: Cosmopolitan History from Voltaire to Gibbon* (Cambridge: Cambridge University Press, 1997), 132–36.

50. Of the traits associated with savagery, cannibalism has received the most critical attention as a key marker of the most profoundly debased and inhuman forms of savagery. For discussion, see Philip P. Boucher, *Cannibal Encounters: Europeans and Island Caribs, 1492–1763* (Baltimore: Johns Hopkins University Press, 1992); Markman Ellis, "Crusoe, Cannibalism and Empire," *Robinson Crusoe: Myths and Metamorphoses*, ed. Lieve Spaas and Brian Stimpson, 45–61 (New York: St. Martin's, 1996); and the essays in Francis Barker, Peter Hulme, and Margaret Iversen, eds., *Cannibalism and the Colonial World* (Cambridge: Cambridge University Press, 1998).

51. Mandeville, *Fable of the Bees*, 2:199.

52. Gemelli Careri, "A Voyage Round the World," in Churchill and Churchill, *Collection of Voyages and Travels*, 4:510.

53. Pietro Martire d'Anghiera, *De Nouo Orbe, or the Historie of the West Indies, Contayning the Actes and Adventures of the Spanyardes, Which Haue Conquered and Peopled Those Countries, Inriched with Varietie of Pleasant Relation of the Manners, Ceremonies, Lawes, Gouernments, and Warres of the Indians; Comprised in Eight Decades; Written by Peter Martyr, a Millanoise of Angleria . . . Whereof Three, Have Beene Formerly Translated into English, by R. Eden, Whereunto the Other Five, Are Newly Added by the Industrie, and Painefull Trauaile of M. Lok Gent* (London, 1612). See also Peter Hulme, *Colonial Encounters: Europe and the Native Caribbean, 1492–1797* (London: Methuen, 1986).

54. John Smith, "A Map of Virginia: With a Description of the Countrey, the Commodities, People, Government and Religion," in *The Complete Works of Captain John Smith (1580–1631)*, ed. Philip L. Barbour, vol. 1 (Chapel Hill: University of North Carolina Press, 1986), 168.

55. John Atkins, *A Voyage to Guinea, Brasil, and the West-Indies; in His Majesty's Ships the Swallow and Weymouth* (London, 1735), 102–3.

56. Keith Thomas, *Religion and the Decline of Magic* (New York: Charles Scribner's Sons, 1971), 123.

57. Sarah Ellenzweig, *The Fringes of Belief: English Literature, Ancient Heresy, and the Politics of Freethinking, 1660–1760* (Stanford: Stanford University Press, 2008).

58. William Pietz, "The Problem of the Fetish, II: The Origin of the Fetish," *Res* 13 (1987): 40. See also the other two essays in this series: Pietz, "The Problem of the Fetish, I," *Res* 9 (1985): 5–17; Pietz, "The Problem of the Fetish, IIIa: Bosman's Guinea and the Enlightenment Theory of Fetishism," *Res* 16 (1988): 105–23, as well as Pietz, "Bosman's Guinea: The Intercultural Roots of an Enlightenment Discourse," *Comparative Civilizations Review*, Fall 1982, 1–22.

59. Atkins, *A Voyage to Guinea, Brasil, and the West-Indies*, 84.

60. Michael Gaudio, *Engraving the Savage: The New World and Techniques of Civilization* (Minneapolis: University of Minnesota Press, 2008), xxi.

61. Pietz, "Problem of the Fetish, IIIa," 106.

62. O'Brien, *Narratives of Enlightenment*, 159.

63. William McNeill, *The Pursuit of Power: Technology, Armed Force, and Society since A.D. 1000* (Chicago: University of Chicago Press, 1984), 81–94.

64. Jeremy Black, *European Warfare, 1453–1815* (New York: St. Martin's, 1999), 37.

65. John Evelyn, *The Diary of John Evelyn*, ed. Austin Dobson, 4 vols. (London: Macmillan, 1906), 3:218.

66. This motto was chosen by Cardinal Richelieu in 1628 and appeared on all French-manufactured artillery until 1774. Maj. Gen. Jonathan B. A. Bailey, *Field Artillery and Firepower*, 2nd ed. (Annapolis, MD: Naval Institute Press, 2004), 160.

67. For an indispensible discussion of gunpowder's cultural significance, see Claude Rawson, *Satire and Sentiment, 1660–1830: Stress Points in the English Augustan Tradition* (Cambridge: Cambridge University Press, 1994), 29–97. Rawson's interest here is primarily in the great Tory satirists, but his arguments have much wider application. See also Roy Wolper, "The Rhetoric of Gunpowder and the Idea of Progress," *Journal of the History of Ideas* 31, no. 4 (1970): 589–98.

68. Francis Bacon, *The New Organon and Related Writings*, ed. Fulton H. Anderson (New York: Liberal Arts Press, 1960), 118. For discussion of the significance of gunpowder to European history and its relationship to the rest of the globe, see Carlo M. Cipolla, *Guns, Sails, and Empires: Technological Innovation and the Early Phases of European Expansion, 1400–1700* (Manhattan, KS: Sunflower University Press, 1985); McNeill, *Pursuit of Power*, 81–94; and J. R. Partington, *A History of Greek Fire and Gunpowder* (Baltimore: Johns Hopkins University Press, 1999).

69. Cadamosto comments that Africans believe his ship's guns must be "an invention of the devil's"; they also cite the great ship as evidence that the Venetians must be "great wizards, almost the equal of the devil." In Pietz, "Problem of the Fetish, II," 41. On the use of technology in these contexts more generally, see Michael Adas, *Machines as the Measure of Men: Science, Technology, and Ideologies of Western Dominance* (Ithaca: Cornell University Press, 1989), 112–25. See also Aravamudan, *Tropicopolitans*, 400n.

70. "True Relation of Waymouth's Voyage, 1605," in *Early English and French Voyages, Chiefly from Hakluyt*, ed. Henry S. Burrage (New York: Charles Scribner's Sons, 1906), 369. Recent scholarship has emphasized that the practical advantages guns gave to explorers and colonists was not necessarily decisive. See, for example, Joyce E. Chaplin, *Subject Matter: Technology, the Body, and Science on the Anglo-American Frontier, 1500–1676* (Cambridge: Harvard University Press, 2001). Chaplin's account persuasively contends that for American colonists by the second half of the seventeenth century, the distinction between gun wielder and bow user was hardly firm; many settlers would have hunted with bows, and most indigenous nations possessed at least some guns. Chaplin's argument highlights the fact that guns play a role

in colonial encounters that is more symbolic than practical; the gun appears more powerfully in colonial fiction than in the historical colony. For a contrary account of the importance of guns to colonization, see Jared M. Diamond, *Guns, Germs, and Steel: The Fates of Human Societies* (New York: Norton, 1997).

71. "True Relation of Waymouth's Voyage," 371.

72. Thomas Harriot, *A Briefe and True Report of the New Found Land of Virginia of the Commodities and of the Nature and Manners of the Naturall Inhabitants: Discouered by the English Colon There Seated by Sir Richard Greinuile Knight in the Eere 1585; Which Remained vnder the Gouernement of Twelue Monethes, at the Speciall Charge . . . of the Honourable Sir Walter Raleigh Knight* (London, 1590).

73. My reading here is partially indebted to that of Stephen Greenblatt, *Shakespearean Negotiations: The Circulation of Social Energy in Renaissance England* (Berkeley: University of California Press, 1988), 27. For a slightly different reading of these encounters, see William M. Hamlin, "Imagined Apotheoses: Drake, Harriot, and Raleigh in the Americas," *Journal of the History of Ideas* 57, no. 3 (1996): 405–28.

74. Isabel Rivers, *Joseph Priestley, Scientist, Philosopher, and Theologian* (Oxford: Oxford University Press, 2008).

75. J. R. Hale, "Gunpowder and the Renaissance: An Essay in the History of Ideas," in *From the Renaissance to the Counter-Reformation: Essays in Honor of Garrett Mattingly*, ed. Charles H. Carter, 113–44 (New York: Random House, 1965), 115.

76. Sir Walter Raleigh cites gunpowder's origins in China in his *The History of the World*, (London, 1614), Book 4, 207–8. A useful introduction to the history and chemistry of gunpowder may be found in Jack Kelly, *Gunpowder: Alchemy, Bombards, and Pyrotechnics: The History of the Explosive That Changed the World* (New York: Basic Books, 2004). See also D. L. Simms, "Archimedes and the Invention of Artillery and Gunpowder," *Technology and Culture* 28 (1987): 77.

77. Ben Johnson, "Execration upon Vulcan," in *The Complete Poems*, ed. George A. E. Parfitt (New Haven: Yale University Press, 1982), lines 202–3; John Milton, *Paradise Lost*, ed. Scott Elledge (New York: Norton, 1975), Bk. 6, lines 567–608.

78. Jonathan Sawday, *Engines of the Imagination: Renaissance Culture and the Rise of the Machine* (London: Routledge, 2007), 266–72; Blair Worden, "Milton's Republicanism and the Tyranny of Heaven," in *Machiavelli and Republicanism*, ed. Gisela Bock, Quentin Skinner, and Maurizio Viroli, 225–45, Ideas in Context 18 (Cambridge: Cambridge University Press, 1990).

79. Thomas, *Religion and the Decline of Magic*.

80. John Henry, "The Fragmentation of Renaissance Occultism and the Decline of Magic," *History of Science* 46, no. 1 (2008): 1–48.

81. Sir William Temple, "An Essay upon the Ancient and Modern Learning," in *The Works of Sir William Temple, Bart.*, vol. 1, 151–69 (London, 1731), 162.

82. For some recent reconsiderations and adaptations of Thomas's thesis, see Alan Macfarlane, "Civility and the Decline of Magic," in *Civil Histories: Essays Presented to Sir Keith Thomas*, edited by Peter Burke, Brian Harrison, and Paul Slack, 145–59 (Oxford: Oxford University Press, 2000); Ian Bostridge, "Music, Reason, and Politeness: Magic and Witchcraft in the Career of George Frideric Handel," in Burke, Harrison, and Slack, *Civil Histories*, 251–63; Michael Hunter, "Witchcraft and the Decline of Belief," *Eighteenth-Century Life* 22, no. 2 (1998): 139–47; Brian Copenhaver, "Magic," in *The Cambridge History of Science*, vol. 3, *Early Modern Science*, ed. Katharine Park and Lorraine Daston, 518–40 (Cambridge: Cambridge University Press, 2006); Martha Kaplan, "The Magical Power of the (Printed) Word," in *Magic and Modernity: Interfaces of Revelation and Concealment*, ed. Birgit Meyer and Peter Pels, 183–99 (Stanford: Stanford University Press, 2003). More generally, see Barbara Maria Stafford and Frances Terpak, *Devices of Wonder: From the World in a Box to Images on a Screen* (Los Angeles: Getty Research Institute, 2001); Lorraine Daston and Katharine Park, *Wonders and the Order of Nature, 1150–1750* (Brooklyn, NY: Zone Books, 1998).

83. James R. Jacob, "Opera and Obedience: Thomas Hobbes and *A Proposition for Advancement of Moralitie* by Sir William Davenant," *Seventeenth Century* 6, no. 2 (1991): 223.

84. Joseph Addison, *Spectator*, no. 419 (July 1, 1712), in Joseph Addison and Richard Steele, *The Spectator*, ed. Donald F. Bond, 5 vols. (Oxford, UK: Clarendon, 1965), 3:572.

85. Thomas, *Religion and the Decline of Magic*, 162–65.

86. *The Execution, Last Speeches & Confessions, of the Thirteen Prisoners That Suffered on Friday the 24th of October, 1679* . . . ([London?], 1679), 2.

87. Thomas Gordon and John Trenchard, *Cato's Letters or Essays on Liberty, Civil and Religious, and Other Important Subjects*, ed. Ronald Hamowy, vol. 2 (Indianapolis: Liberty Fund, 1995), 926–27.

88. Gabriel Naudé, *The History of Magick by Way of Apology, for All the Wise Men Who Have Unjustly Been Reputed Magicians, from the Creation, to the Present Age: Written in French, by G. Naudæus Late Library-keeper to Cardinal Mazarin; Englished by J. Davies* (London, 1657); Naudé, *Political Considerations upon Refin'd Politicks, and the Master-strokes of State, as Practis'd by the Ancients and Moderns: Written*

by Gabriel Naudé, and Inscrib'd to the Cardinal Bagni; Translated into English by Dr. King., trans. William King (London, 1711). Behn's translation of Fontanelle alludes generally to Naudé; William King was a well-known writer of Tory sensibilities and Irish connections. James V. Rice, *Gabriel Naudé: 1600–1653*, Johns Hopkins Studies in Romance Literatures and Languages 35 (Baltimore: Johns Hopkins University Press, 1939), 71; William King, *The Original Works of William King, L.L.D.* (London, 1776), 6–26. For a general discussion of Naudé and his relationship to Machiavellianism, see Peter S. Donaldson, *Machiavelli and Mystery of State* (Cambridge: Cambridge University Press, 1988), 142–67.

89. Naudé, *Political Considerations*, 58–59.

90. Ibid., 161. This incident was widely known; for one version, see Hans Sloane, *A Voyage to the Islands Madera, Barbados, Nieves, S. Christophers and Jamaica* (London, 1707), iv.

91. See, for example, Juliette Merritt, *Beyond Spectacle: Eliza Haywood's Female Spectators* (Toronto: University of Toronto Press, 2004).

1. ENCHANTING THE SAVAGE: THE POLITICS OF PYROTECHNICS IN THE CAVENDISH CIRCLE

1. Margaret Cavendish, "Assaulted and Pursued Chastity," in *Natures Picture Drawn by Fancies Pencil to the Life: Being Several Feigned Stories, Comical, Tragical, Tragi-comical, Poetical, Romancical, Philosophical, Historical, and Moral; Some in Verse, Some in Prose; Some Mixt, and Some by Dialogues* (London, 1671), 394–514. The first edition appeared in 1656; hereafter cited parenthetically in the text by page numbers in the second edition of 1671. Travellia is also here disguised as a boy; Cavendish refers to the cross-dressed character with the male pronoun.

2. Cavendish draws most directly, I believe, on the English translation of Peter Martyr's account of the Columbian encounter with the New World. Among other details that link her account to that text is her description of the cannibal nation's purple skin—an attribute that seems peculiar until we recall that this term refers, in Cavendish's day, to a color closer to what we would now call red. Martyr's translator describes West Indians as "altogether in generall either purple or tawny, like unto sodd Quinces, or of the colour of Chesnuttes or Olives." Pietro Martire d'Anghiera, *De Nouo Orbe, or the Historie of the West Indies, Contayning the Actes and Adventures of the Spanyardes, Which Have Conquered and Peopled Those Countries, Inriched with Varietie of Pleasant Relation of the Manners, Ceremonies, Lawes, Gouernments, and Warres of the Indians;*

Comprised in Eight Decades; Written by Peter Martyr a Millanoise of Angleria . . . Whereof Three, Have Beene Formerly Translated into English, by R. Eden, Whereunto the Other Five, Are Newly Added by the Industrie, and Painefull Travaile of M. Lok Gent (London, 1612), 4. For an important discussion of Cavendish's use of racial imagery and skin color, see Sujata Iyengar, *Shades of Difference: Mythologies of Skin Color in Early Modern England* (Philadelphia: University of Pennsylvania Press, 2004), 226–31. Iyengar does not mention Peter Martyr or the shift in color terminology, however.

3. Marina Leslie, "Evading Rape and Embracing Empire: Margaret Cavendish's *Assaulted and Pursued Chastity*," in *Menacing Virgins: Representing Virginity in the Middle Ages and the Renaissance*, ed. Kathleen Coyne Kelly and Marina Leslie, 179–97 (Newark: University of Delaware Press, 1999), 192. Several critics have identified the heroine's chastity as a marker or enabler of agency; see, for instance, Kathryn Schwarz, "Chastity, Militant and Married: Cavendish's Romance, Milton's Masque," *PMLA: Publications of the Modern Language Association of America* 118, no. 2 (2003): 270–85.

4. Thomas Hobbes, *The Elements of Law, Natural and Politic*, ed. Ferdinand Tönnies, 2nd ed. (New York: Barnes & Noble, 1969); Hobbes, *On the Citizen [De Cive]*, ed. Richard Tuck, trans. Michael Silverthorne, Cambridge Texts in the History of Political Thought (Cambridge: Cambridge University Press, 1998); Hobbes, *Leviathan*, ed. C. B. Macpherson (London: Penguin Books, 1978). Hereafter both these sources cited parenthetically in the text by page numbers in these editions, with *On the Citizen* cited as DC and *Leviathan* as L.

5. I will hereafter follow conventions from recent biographies of these two figures by referring to Margaret Cavendish as "Cavendish" and William, Lord Newcastle, as "Newcastle." Their circle of acquaintance also included René Descartes and the natural philosopher Pierre Gassendi.

6. Hobbes's connection with Cavendish has received only minimal critical attention. In an important essay, Anna Battigelli identifies Hobbes as a decisive influence on Cavendish's quietist version of feminism and notes their social connections. Battigelli, "Political Thought / Political Action: Margaret Cavendish's Hobbesian Dilemma," in *Women Writers and the Early Modern British Political Tradition*, ed. Hilda L. Smith, 40–55 (Cambridge: Cambridge University Press, 1998). Victoria Kahn and Deborah Boyle have also noted Cavendish's obvious familiarity with Hobbes's thought. Victoria Kahn, *Wayward Contracts: The Crisis of Political Obligation in England, 1640–1674* (Princeton:

Princeton University Press, 2004), 177; Deborah Boyle, "Fame, Virtue, and Government: Margaret Cavendish on Ethics and Politics," *Journal of the History of Ideas* 67, no. 2 (2006): 251–89.

7. Hobbes's most developed form of this theory is found in *Leviathan*, 223–88. An earlier, less formalized version appears in *De Cive*.

8. See, e.g., C. B. Macpherson, *The Political Theory of Possessive Individualism: Hobbes to Locke* (Oxford University Press, 1964), 20–21. Srinivas Aravamudan, however, underscores the significance of the New World as a model and testing ground for new theorizations of sovereignty and the state. Aravamudan, "Hobbes and America," in *The Postcolonial Enlightenment: Eighteenth-Century Colonialism and Postcolonial Theory*, ed. Lynn Festa and Daniel Carey, 37–70 (Oxford: Oxford University Press, 2009).

9. For discussion, see Kahn, *Wayward Contracts*, 164–66; Michel Foucault, *"Society Must Be Defended": Lectures at the Collège de France, 1975–76*, ed. Mauro Bertani, Alessandro Fontana, and François Ewald, trans. David Macey (New York: Picador, 2003), 94–97.

10. Richard H. Popkin, *The Third Force in Seventeenth Century Thought* (Leiden: Brill, 1992), 25; Noel Malcolm, *Aspects of Hobbes* (Oxford: Oxford University Press, 2004), 504.

11. For discussion of Hobbes's thinking about the historical evolution of sovereignty, see Robert P. Kraynak, "Hobbes on Barbarism and Civilization," *Journal of Politics* 45, no. 1 (1983): 86–109.

12. Jacques Derrida, "The Force of Law: The 'Mystical Foundation of Authority,'" *Cordoza Law Review* 11 (1990): 943. See also Derrida, *Rogues: Two Essays on Reason*, trans. Pascale-Anne Brault and Michael Naas (Stanford: Stanford University Press, 2005), 12; and Derrida, *The Beast and the Sovereign, Volume I*, ed. Michel Lisse, Marie-Louise Mallet, and Ginette Michaud, trans. Geoffrey Bennington (Chicago: University of Chicago Press, 2009).

13. Treatments of this issue are not common in the literature on Hobbes. For one discussion, see Christopher Pye, *The Regal Phantasm: Shakespeare and the Politics of Spectacle* (London: Routledge, 1990), 43–81. Pye locates a common root for Hobbesian and pre-Hobbesian fantasies of sovereign power in the Lacanian conception of the gaze: the sovereign makes the practice of seeing itself possible, entangling the subject in the gaze by revealing the source of the gaze itself in the sovereign. This analysis, rooted in new historicist appropriations of psychoanalytic theory, now reads as somewhat dated, but it raises important questions about the way the visual field constitutes the absolute sovereign. See also on this point Geoffrey M. Vaughan,

Behemoth Teaches Leviathan: Thomas Hobbes on Political Education (Lanham, MD: Lexington Books, 2002), 42. Vaughan reads Hobbes's late work *Behemoth* as a model for a political education that relies on the power of nonviolent rhetoric rather than force on the one hand or full-throated philosophical justification on the other. Quentin Skinner discusses *Leviathan* itself as a rhetorical work that deploys eloquence in the service of rational truth. Skinner, *Reason and Rhetoric in the Philosophy of Hobbes* (Cambridge: Cambridge University Press, 1996), 334. See also Kraynak, "Hobbes on Barbarism and Civilization," 107–8; and Todd Butler, *Imagination and Politics in Seventeenth-Century England* (Aldershot, UK: Ashgate, 2008), 139–79.

14. Giorgio Agamben, *Homo Sacer: Sovereign Power and Bare Life*, trans. Daniel Heller-Roazin (Stanford: Stanford University Press, 1998), 36–38.

15. Leslie, "Evading Rape and Embracing Empire," 179, 192; Kahn, *Wayward Contracts*, 172–94.

16. Marina Leslie points out that Travellia's virginity might have had very specific associations with sovereignty and royal power. Charles I's white coronation gowns explicitly associated sovereignty with a preternatural innocence and chastity. Leslie, "Evading Rape and Embracing Empire."

17. Margaret Cavendish, *The Worlds Olio* (London, 1655), 73.

18. Emma L. E. Rees, "A Well-Spun Yarn: Margaret Cavendish, and Homer's Penelope," in *A Princely Brave Woman: Essays on Margaret Cavendish, Duchess of Newcastle*, edited by Stephen Clucas, 171–81 (Aldershot, UK: Ashgate, 2003). See also Emma L. E. Rees, *Margaret Cavendish: Gender, Genre, Exile* (Manchester: Manchester University Press, 2003), 104–33.

19. Margaret Cavendish, *Sociable Letters*, ed. James Fitzmaurice (New York: Routledge, 2004), 25.

20. Sara Mendelson and Patricia Crawford, *Women in Early Modern England, 1550–1720* (Oxford, UK: Clarendon, 1998), 54.

21. Duke of Newcastle (William Cavendish), *Ideology and Politics on the Eve of Restoration: Newcastle's Advice to Charles II*, ed. Thomas P. Slaughter (Philadelphia: American Philosophical Society, 1984), 45. Hereafter cited parenthetically in the text by page numbers in this edition.

22. Cavendish, *Worlds Olio*, 51.

23. Samuel Purchas, *Hakluytus Posthumus; or Purchas His Pilgrimes; Contayning a History of the World in Sea Voyages and Lande Travells by Englishmen and Others*, 20 vols. (Glasgow: J. MacLehose and Sons, 1905), 18:497–98.

24. William Davenant, "Preface to *Gondibert*," in *Critical Essays of the Seventeenth Century*, ed. J. E. Spingarn, vol. 2, 1–53 (Oxford, UK: Clarendon, 1908). Hereafter cited parenthetically in the text.

25. Visconsi discusses the preface in *Lines of Equity*. My reading builds on his analysis but attends to certain aspects of the text that complicate his interpretation. Elliott Visconsi, *Lines of Equity: Literature and the Origins of Law in Later Stuart England* (Ithaca: Cornell University Press, 2008), 29–33.

26. Charles II (King of England), *A True Copy of a Commission, from the Late Kings Eldest Sonne, to Mr. William Davenant, Concerning Maryland, Etc. (Given at Our Court in Jersey, the 16th Day of February, 16 50/49)* (London, 1653).

27. Steven N. Zwicker, *Lines of Authority: Politics and English Literary Culture, 1649–1689* (Ithaca: Cornell University Press, 1993), 17–26.

28. William Davenant, *A Proposition for Advancement of Morality, by a New Way of Entertainment of the People* (London, 1656); reprinted in James R. Jacob, "Opera and Obedience: Thomas Hobbes and *A Proposition for Advancement of Moralitie* by Sir William Davenant," *Seventeenth Century* 6, no. 2 (1991), 205–50; Davenant's tract is reprinted on 242–48. Hereafter cited parenthetically in the text by page numbers in Jacob's edition.

29. Mary Edmond, *Rare Sir William Davenant: Poet Laureate, Playwright, Civil War General, Restoration Theatre Manager* (Manchester: Manchester University Press, 1987), 56.

30. For discussion of masquing and its relationship to representations and practices of sovereign power, see Martin Butler, "Courtly Negotiations," in *The Politics of the Stuart Court Masque*, ed. David Bevington and Peter Holbrook, 20–40 (Cambridge: Cambridge University Press, 1998); Nancy E. Wright, "Civic and Courtly Ceremonies in Jacobean London," in ibid., 197–217; David Bevington and Peter Holbrook, introduction to *The Politics of the Stuart Court Masque*, 1–19; Stephen Orgel, "Marginal Jonson," in ibid., 144–75; Dawn Lewcock, *Sir William Davenant, the Court Masque, and the English Seventeenth-Century Scenic Stage, c. 1605–c. 1700* (Amherst, NY: Cambria, 2008); Stephen Orgel, *The Illusion of Power* (Berkeley: University of California Press, 1975); Jonathan Goldberg, *James I and the Politics of Literature* (Stanford University Press, 1989).

31. See Stephen Orgel and Roy Strong, *Inigo Jones: The Theatre of the Stuart Court, Including the Complete Designs for Productions at Court for the Most Part in the Collection of the Duke of Devonshire Together with Their Texts and Historical Documentation* (London: Sotheby Parke

Bernet, 1973). Jones did not leave behind theoretical justifications for his spectacular effects; the theories have been ably explicated by Orgel and others. But Davenant took this aesthetics of spectacular display and altered it in significant ways in his justifications of theater and of heroic poetry. For whether the masque is understood primarily as a mode for representing sovereign power to itself—a production specifically for the king—or whether it is understood as a more complex working out of tensions within the courtly audience, it is nevertheless a phenomenon centered on the court.

32. Orgel and Strong, *Inigo Jones*, 731; Douglas Brooks-Davies, *The Mercurian Monarch: Magical Politics from Spencer to Pope* (Manchester: Manchester University Press, 1983), 108–12.

33. William Davenant, *Salmacida Spolia: A Masque Presented by the King and Queenes Majesties, at White-Hall, on Tuesday the 21 Day of January 1639* (London, 1639), 5.

34. Ibid., 731.

35. William Davenant, *Britannia Triumphans* (London, 1638), 11.

36. For more discussion of this theme, see Paula R. Backscheider, *Spectacular Politics: Theatrical Power and Mass Culture in Early Modern England* (Baltimore: Johns Hopkins University Press, 1993), 3–30.

37. Cavendish, *Worlds Olio*, 39.

38. Margaret Cavendish, *The Blazing World and Other Writings*, ed. Kate Lilley (London: William Pickering, 1992). Hereafter cited parenthetically in the text by page numbers in this edition. Relatively little criticism examines the politics of *The Blazing World*, though Susan James understands the text primarily as a political allegory (introduction to *Margaret Cavendish: Political Writings*, ed. Susan James, ix–xxix [Cambridge: Cambridge University Press, 2003]). More common are readings examining the text for insights into genre and constructions of gender: Nicole Pohl, "'Of Mixt Natures': Questions of Genre in Margaret Cavendish's *The Blazing World*," in Clucas, *Princely Brave Woman*, 51–68; Eve Keller, "Producing Petty Gods: Margaret Cavendish's Critique of Experimental Science," *ELH* 64, no. 2 (1997): 447–71; Oddvar Holmesland, "Margaret Cavendish's *The Blazing World*: Natural Art and the Body Politic," *Studies in Philology* 96, no. 4 (1999): 457–79; Jonathan Goldberg, "Margaret Cavendish, Scribe," *GLQ: A Journal of Lesbian and Gay Studies* 10, no. 3 (2004): 433–52.

39. Margaret Cavendish, *Philosophical Letters: Or, Modest Reflections upon Some Opinions in Natural Philosophy* (London, 1664), 47. She justifies her neglect by arguing that causality does not logically allow a creation of humankind to govern humankind; that is, sovereignty is a human practice and is ultimately controlled by human agency, rather

than shaping human agency in the name of a transcendent value: "Nature doth not rule God, nor Man Nature, nor Politick Government Man; for the Effect cannot rule the Cause, but the Cause doth rule the Effect.... The truth is, Man rules an artificial Government, and not the Government Man, just like as a watch-maker rules his Watch, and not the watch the Watch-maker" (ibid., 47–48). In this treatment, there is little room for human sovereignty, much less for treatises theorizing it. Nature, or human nature, determines the ordering of political arrangements. Yet Cavendish's writings repeatedly engage with very specific Hobbesian ideas, even mirroring his language. Some of her orators, as the military debates what government to institute in place of the deposed king, affirm that the worst condition of all is anarchy. The orators invoke Hobbes in all but name: without government, there can be "neither Tillage nor Trade," and thus no food nor money—"for, where there is no Government, there can be no Assurance; and who will take pains for that, they are not sure to keep, or rather I may say, they are sure to lose?" Cavendish, *Orations of Divers Sorts, Accommodated to Divers Places*, 2nd ed. (London: Printed by A. Maxwell, 1668), 294–95. This is a very close echo of Hobbes's famous argument (cited earlier) about the state of nature. Despite Cavendish's earlier disclaimers, then, her familiarity with Hobbes is not limited to his scientific inquiries.

40. Catherine Gallagher, "Embracing the Absolute: The Politics of the Female Subject in Seventeenth-Century England," *Genders* 1 (Spring 1988): 24–39. Michael McKeon capitalizes on this mobility of absolutism in *The Secret History of Domesticity: Public, Private, and the Division of Knowledge* (Baltimore: Johns Hopkins University Press, 2005), 3–48, 150–52.

41. Margaret Cavendish, *Orations of Divers Sorts, Accommodated to Divers Places*, 2nd ed. (London, Printed by A. Maxwell, 1668), 1–2. Hereafter cited parenthetically in the text by page numbers in this edition.

42. The *Orations* are discussed briefly in Battigelli, "Political Thought / Political Action."

43. On Hobbes, see J. G. A Pocock, "Time, History, and Eschatology in the Thought of Thomas Hobbes," in *Politics, Language, and Time: Essays on Political Thought and History*, 2nd rev. ed., 148–201 (Chicago: University of Chicago Press, 1971).

44. This might be read as suggesting that the government of the Blazing World return to its monotheistic but non-Christian origins; I think the text points most directly to the disputing societies of natural philosophers, but the point is ambiguous. Anna Battigelli argues that this moment casts doubt on the Erastian politics of these churches and

their institution. Anna Battigelli, *Margaret Cavendish and the Exiles of the Mind* (Lexington: University Press of Kentucky, 1998), 81–82. But the Empress's actions in the second part of the narrative point toward an ongoing belief in the efficacy of sovereign violence and sovereign performance. Battigelli has argued that *The Blazing World* offers a "political quietism." Reading the Empress's churches as a refiguration of Henrietta Maria's own efforts to convert England to Roman Catholicism, she concludes that the Empress acknowledges the limits of this approach in her conversations with the diagetic version of Cavendish, who advises her to restore "the same form of Government again, which had been before" (Ibid., 81; Cavendish, *Blazing World*, 201). There is no necessary connection, however, between the religious conversion and the political reforms the Empress acquiesces to.

45. EFSI is presumably an acronym for England, France, Scotland, and Ireland.

46. Sylvia Bowerbank and Sara Mendelson, introduction to *Paper Bodies: A Margaret Cavendish Reader*, 9–34 (Peterborough, ON: Broadview, 2000), 18–19.

47. Claude Rawson, *Satire and Sentiment, 1660–1830: Stress Points in the English Augustan Tradition* (Cambridge: Cambridge University Press, 1994), 65–71.

2. FIRE AND SWORD: APHRA BEHN AND THE MATERIALS OF AUTHORITY

1. Aphra Behn, *Abdelazer; or, The Moor's Revenge* (London, 1677), 2.1.

2. Aphra Behn, *Oroonoko*, in *The Fair Jilt and Other Short Stories*, vol. 3 of *The Works of Aphra Behn*, ed. Janet Todd (Columbus: Ohio State University Press, 1995), 98–99. Hereafter cited parenthetically in the text by page numbers in this edition.

3. The tigers in this sequence have received much critical attention, particularly for the ambiguity of their gender, which is referred to with alternating masculine and feminine pronouns, and, more recently, for their associations with Asia. See, for example, Margaret W. Ferguson, *Dido's Daughters: Literacy, Gender, and Empire in Early Modern England and France* (Chicago: University of Chicago Press, 2003), 366; Chi-ming Yang, "Asia Out of Place: The Aesthetics of Incorruptibility in Behn's *Oroonoko*," *Eighteenth-Century Studies* 42, no. 2 (2009): 246–49. Ferguson associates Oroonoko and other romantic characters with these tigers and with styles of narration inadequate to the harsh conditions of

modernity. Srinivas Aravamudan has similarly understood the tiger hunt as a feminized activity, characteristic of Oroonoko's status as a pet. Aravamudan, *Tropicopolitans: Colonialism and Agency, 1688–1804* (Durham: Duke University Press, 1999), 39. I build on these insights to insist on the importance of objects and props in these performances and styles of narration.

4. Throughout this chapter, my discussion draws on William Pietz's discussion of fetishism, cited in the introduction. Behn, I suggest, is also part of the development of the concept of fetishism in ways that anticipate and prefigure the work of Enlightenment thinkers.

5. Richard Frohock, "Violence and Awe: The Foundations of Government in Aphra Behn's New World Settings," *Eighteenth-Century Fiction* 8, no. 4 (1996): 437–52.

6. I use the term *memento* in part to avoid the more specific religious connotations of the term *relic*. A memento, in Behn's day, was beginning to shift its signification from the idea of a reminder—as in a *memento mori*—toward its now-dominant meaning of an embodiment of memory, even nostalgia. My use of the term is influenced by Susan Stewart's discussion of souvenirs; see *On Longing: Narratives of the Miniature, the Gigantic, the Souvenir, the Collection* (Durham: Duke University Press, 1993), 138–39.

7. For influential readings of *Oroonoko* as, in part, an allegory of a Stuart king, see Richard Kroll, " 'Tales of Love and Gallantry': The Politics of *Oroonoko*," *Huntington Library Quarterly* 67, no. 4 (2004): 573–605, 691; Laura Brown, "The Romance of Empire: *Oroonoko* and the Trade in Slaves," in *The New Eighteenth Century: Theory, Politics, English Literature*, ed. Laura Brown and Felicity Nussbaum, 41–61 (New York: Methuen, 1987); Catherine Gallagher, *Nobody's Story: The Vanishing Acts of Women Writers in the Marketplace, 1670–1820* (Berkeley: University of California Press, 1994), 49–87; George Robert Guffey, "Aphra Behn's *Oroonoko*: Occasion and Accomplishment," in *Two English Novelists: Aphra Behn and Anthony Trollope; Papers Read at a Clark Library Seminar, May 11, 1974*, by George Robert Guffey and Andrew H. Wright, 1–41 (Los Angeles: William Andrews Clark Memorial Library, UCLA, 1975); Laura Doyle, *Freedom's Empire: Race and the Rise of the Novel in Atlantic Modernity, 1640–1940* (Durham: Duke University Press, 2008), 97–114.

8. It perhaps goes without saying that this "givenness" of obedience is itself a fantasy of Behn's—the history of English governance is hardly free from unruliness.

9. For exemplary arguments, see Margaret Ferguson, "Juggling the Categories of Race, Class and Gender: Aphra Behn's *Oroonoko*," *Women's*

Studies 19 (1991): 159–81; Brown, "Romance of Empire"; Stephanie Athey and Daniel Cooper Alarcón, "*Oroonoko*'s Gendered Economies of Honor/Horror: Reframing Colonial Discourse Studies in the Americas," *American Literature* 65, no. 3 (1993): 415–43.

10. Cassius Dio, *Dio's Roman History*, trans. Earnest Cary, vol. 2 (London: William Heinemann, 1914), 171–73n. Cary's edition somewhat confusingly interpolates Tzetzes's version into the lacuna in Dio's text. Behn certainly knew of Dio's history; it is cited in her translation of Bernard le Bovier de Fontenelle's *History of Oracles*, in *Seneca Unmasqued and Other Prose Translations*, vol. 4 of *The Works of Aphra Behn*, ed. Janet Todd (Columbus: Ohio State University Press, 1993), 255.

11. D. L. Simms, "Archimedes and Burning Mirrors," *Physics Education* 10 (November 1975): 517–21. As Simms notes, the story is referenced in several other classical sources, including Diodorus Siculus, Lucian, Dion, Zonaras, Galen, Anthemius, and Eustathias. It appears, too, in a few texts from late antiquity, including John Tzetzes's *Chiliades* and John Zonaras's *Epitome ton Istorion*. For a discussion of scientific interest in testing this feat in the eighteenth century, see W. E. Knowles Middleton, "Archimedes, Kircher, Buffon, and the Burning-Mirrors," *Isis* 52 (December 1961): 533–43.

12. Robert Baron, *Mirza: A Tragedie, Really Acted in Persia, in the Last Age: Illustrated with Historicall Annotations* (London, 1647), 208. The incident is not dramatized but is mentioned in Baron's extensive notes on the military history of Byzantium.

13. John Dunton, *The Young-Students-Library: Containing Extracts and Abridgments of the Most Valuable Books Printed in England, and in the Forreign Journals, from the Year Sixty Five, to This Time; To Which Is Added a New Essay upon All Sorts of Learning* (London, 1692), xi.

14. Adam Olearius, *The Voyages and Travels of the Ambassadors Sent by Frederick, Duke of Holstein, to the Great Duke of Muscovy and the King of Persia*, 2nd ed., trans. John Davies (London, 1669), 280–81.

15. For an erudite discussion of Carib, Arawak, and other political organization in this period, see Neil L. Whitehead, "Native Peoples Confront Colonial Regimes in Northeastern South America (c. 1500–1900)," in *The Cambridge History of the Native Peoples of the Americas*, vol. 3, *South America*, part 2, ed. Frank Salomon and Stuart B. Schwartz, 382–442 (Cambridge: Cambridge University Press, 1999). Whitehead underscores the agency of indigenous responses to and manipulations of colonial settlement and occupation.

16. Tales of the king's ability to heal date at least from the reign of Edward I (the Confessor; 1005–1066). For a description of this practice from Edward's own century, see *The Life of King Edward, Who Rests at*

Westminster: Attributed to a Monk of Saint Bertin, ed. and trans. Frank Barlow (Oxford, UK: Clarendon, 1992), 93–95. Barlow notes that the practice of touching probably dates from the time of Henry III (1216–72) and that it did not end until the Hanoverian Succession in 1714. See Barlow, *The Norman Conquest and Beyond* (London: Hambledon, 1983), 44–46.

17. On this point, see Robert L. Chibka, "'Oh! Do Not Fear a Woman's Invention': Truth, Falsehood, and Fiction in Aphra Behn's *Oroonoko*," *Texas Studies in Literature and Language* 30, no. 4 (1988): 522–25; Ferguson, *Dido's Daughters*, 359; Doyle, *Freedom's Empire*, 113–14.

18. Keith Thomas, *Religion and the Decline of Magic* (New York: Charles Scribner's Sons, 1971), 178–80.

19. For detailed discussions of the Restoration crowd, in addition to the works cited in the introduction, see Tim Harris, *London Crowds in the Reign of Charles II: Propaganda and Politics from the Restoration until the Exclusion Crisis* (Cambridge: Cambridge University Press, 1987); Harris, "Perceptions of the Crowd in Later Stuart London," in *Imagining Early Modern London: Perceptions and Portrayals of the City from Stow to Strype*, ed. J. F. Merritt, 250–72 (Cambridge: Cambridge University Press, 2001); and David Underdown, *Revel, Riot and Rebellion: Popular Politics and Culture in England, 1603–1660* (Oxford: Oxford University Press, 1987), 270–75.

20. Aphra Behn, *The Second Part of the Rover*, in *Plays, 1678–1682*, vol. 6 of *The Works of Aphra Behn*, ed. Janet M. Todd (Columbus: Ohio State University Press, 1996), 228 (emphasis in original).

21. Aphra Behn, *The Fair Jilt*, in *Works of Aphra Behn*, vol. 3, 45–46.

22. Melissa Mowry sees Bacon instantiating Behn's hostility to collectivity and advocacy for a principle of sovereign singularity guaranteed by personal honor: "'Past Remembrance or History': Aphra Behn's *The Widdow Ranter*, or, How the Collective Lost Its Honor," *ELH* 79, no. 3 (2012): 597–621. Mowry's reading is compelling; I hope to suggest, however, that Behn's interests in this play include honor's hazards as well as its virtues.

23. I adopt the term "Tory triumphalism" from Susan J. Owen, "'Suspect My Loyalty When I Lose My Virtue': Sexual Politics and Party in Aphra Behn's Plays of the Exclusion Crisis, 1678–83," *Restoration: Studies in English Literary Culture, 1660–1700* 18, no. 1 (1994): 37–47. For an account of the political and social history of this period, see Annabel Patterson, *The Long Parliament of Charles II* (New Haven: Yale University Press, 2008), 209–30.

24. See Kimberly Latta, "Aphra Behn and the Roundheads," *Journal for Early Modern Cultural Studies* 4, no. 1 (2004): 1–36; Anita Pacheco,

"Reading Toryism in Aphra Behn's Cit-Cuckolding Comedies," *Review of English Studies* 55 (2004): 696–700; Susan J. Owen, "Suspect My Loyalty When I Lose My Virtue," 37–47; and Elizabeth Bennett Kubek, "'Night Mares of the Commonwealth': Royalist Passion and Female Ambition in Aphra Behn's *The Roundheads*," *Restoration: Studies in English Literary Culture, 1660–1700* 17 (1993): 39–52. These essays highlight Behn's complex inspection of the role of female authority and its relationship to royalism and popular power in the play. See also Derek Hughes, *The Theatre of Aphra Behn* (New York: Palgrave, 2001), 139–47.

25. Aphra Behn, *The Roundheads*, in *Works of Aphra Behn*, vol. 6, 357–424. Hereafter cited parenthetically in the text by act, scene, and line number. For a concentrated discussion of the turbulent politics of this period, see Ruth E. Mayers, *1659—The Crisis of the Commonwealth* (Woodbridge, UK: Boydell & Brewer, 2004).

26. John Lambert was Oliver Cromwell's close ally during the wars and his rival afterward. Lambert had opposed moves during the Protectorate to centralize a monarchical or quasi-monarchical power, preferring to maintain a strong role for the military in the government. Dismissed by Cromwell, Lambert reemerged as an important player in the confused reign of Richard Cromwell; he played a crucial role in putting down the uprising under George Booth in 1659. His forces eventually dispersed due, largely, to the lack of money, and he surrendered to Thomas Fairfax in 1660. Committed to the Tower, Lambert escaped and attempted once more to rally forces against the Restoration, but his efforts failed miserably. He remained very much alive, though imprisoned on St. Nicholas Island, during the staging of Behn's play; he died in 1684. D. N. Farr, "Lambert, John (bap. 1619, d. 1684)," in *Oxford Dictionary of National Biography*, ed. H. C. G. Matthew and Brian Harrison (Oxford: Oxford University Press, 2004). Charles Fleetwood was also a highly placed military leader, but Behn's portrait of him emphasizes his commitment to godliness and religious reform, which is accurate enough. For an excellent summary of the complex political maneuverings of this period, see Ronald Hutton, *The Restoration: A Political and Religious History of England and Wales, 1658–1667* (Oxford, UK: Clarendon, 1985), 85–118.

27. Note that the pike is the weapon of a common soldier, not an officer, emphasizing the dangerous power of the armed rabble. See John Childs, *The Army of Charles II* (London: Routledge and Kegan Paul, 1976), 61.

28. Behn, *Second Part of the Rover*, 229.

29. For details on Monck's critical role in bringing about Charles's restoration, see Maurice Ashley, *General Monck* (London: J. Cape, 1977), 180–218.

30. We should note here that the rabble are more unambiguously satirized in Tatham's *The Rump*, in which we lack the centering presence of the Cavaliers to endorse the often dubious activities of the apprentices. At one point in Tatham's drama, the captain of the apprentices relates the assassination of a random army officer. John Tatham, *The Rump*, in *The Broadview Anthology of Restoration and Early Eighteenth-Century Drama*, ed. J. Douglas Canfield and Maja-Lisa von Sneidern, 1596–1641 (Peterborough, ON: Broadview, 2001), 1623.

31. Sarah Ellenzweig, *The Fringes of Belief: English Literature, Ancient Heresy, and the Politics of Freethinking, 1660–1760* (Stanford: Stanford University Press, 2008), 58–77.

32. Aphra Behn, "A Pindarick Poem on the Happy Coronation of His Most Sacred Majesty James II," in *Poetry*, vol. 1 of *The Works of Aphra Behn*, ed. Janet Todd (Columbus: Ohio State University, 1992), 216–18.

33. For a discussion of the coronation as a crucial ritual of authority in an earlier period, see Alice Hunt, *The Drama of Coronation: Medieval Ceremony in Early Modern England* (Cambridge: Cambridge University Press, 2008). See also Roy Strong, *Art and Power: Renaissance Festivals, 1450–1650* (Berkeley: University of California Press, 1984); and Strong, *Coronation: From the 8th to the 21st Century* (London: HarperCollins, 2007). Bruce Lenman provides an important discussion of symbolic and sacral qualities of the regalia in "The Exiled Stuarts and the Precious Symbols of Sovereignty," *Eighteenth-Century Life* 25, no. 2 (2001): 185–200.

34. Hughes, *Theatre of Aphra Behn*, 141. Latta argues that Lady Lambert's lust in effect rescues her from the false pleasures of usurpation. Latta, "Aphra Behn and the Roundheads," 23–25.

35. Robert Markley, "'Be Impudent, Be Saucy, Forward, Bold, Touzing, and Leud': The Politics of Masculine Sexuality and Feminine Desire in Behn's Tory Comedies," in *Cultural Readings of Restoration and Eighteenth-Century English Theater*, ed. J. Douglas Canfield and Deborah C. Payne, 114–40 (Athens: University of Georgia Press, 1995).

36. Paula R. Backscheider, *Spectacular Politics: Theatrical Power and Mass Culture in Early Modern England* (Baltimore: Johns Hopkins University Press, 1993), 14–21.

37. Aphra Behn, *The Widdow Ranter*, in *Plays 1682–1696*, vol. 7 of *The Works of Aphra Behn*, ed. Janet M. Todd, 357–424 (Columbus: Ohio State University Press, 1996). Hereafter cited parenthetically in the text by act, scene, and line number.

38. Adam Beach has underscored what he calls the "pro-colonist" stance of the plot, which does not treat all "Virginians" as equally

slothful and callow. Peter Herman similarly sees Virginia as embodying a more liberated space that embodies the future, in contrast to what Behn saw as the collapsing cultural and political systems of England. Beach and Herman are certainly right that the plot distinguishes among colonists of different sorts, but I think both downplay the degree to which the colony is an unstable space where the weakness of institutions and traditions creates opportunities for dangerous vainglory and inglorious usurpers as well as for social regeneration. Beach, "Anti-Colonist Discourse, Tragicomedy, and the 'American' Behn," *Comparative Drama* 38, nos. 2–3 (2004): 213–33; Herman, "'We All Smoke Here': Behn's *The Widdow Ranter* and the Invention of American Identity," in *Envisioning an English Empire: Jamestown and the Making of the North Atlantic World*, ed. John Wood Sweet and Robert Appelbaum, 254–74 (Philadelphia: University of Pennsylvania Press, 2005).

39. Kathleen M. Brown, *Good Wives, Nasty Wenches, and Anxious Patriarchs: Gender, Race, and Power in Colonial Virginia* (Chapel Hill: University of North Carolina Press, 1996), 161.

40. Melissa Mowry traces many of these alterations in "Past Remembrance or History," 609–12.

41. Melinda S. Zook, "The Political Poetry of Aphra Behn," in *The Cambridge Companion to Aphra Behn*, ed. Derek Hughes and Janet Todd, 46–67 (Cambridge: Cambridge University Press, 2004), 49–55.

42. Eliot Visconsi discusses the social anomie of Virginia in *Lines of Equity: Literature and the Origins of Law in Later Stuart England* (Ithaca: Cornell University Press, 2008), 155–84. Aspasia Velissariou underscores the drama's denial of popular power and its endorsement of Bacon's ethic of honor, in "''Tis Pity That When Laws Are Faulty They Should Not Be Mended or Abolisht': Authority, Legitimations, and Honor in Aphra Behn's *The Widdow Ranter*," *Papers on Language and Literature* 38, no. 2 (2002): 137–66. Janet Todd, in her biography of Behn, also makes the explicitly synecdochical qualities of the Virginia colony clear: "Everywhere was America" in Behn's rapidly modernizing world. Todd, *The Secret Life of Aphra Behn* (New Brunswick: Rutgers University Press, 1997), 411. Cf. Jonathan Elmer, *On Lingering and Being Last: Race and Sovereignty in the New World* (New York: Fordham University Press, 2008), 21–49.

43. The play is, in fact, a tragicomedy and includes a comic plot that equals that of Bacon's tragedy in weight. That plot, concerning the courting and marriage of the eponymous widow, is beyond the scope of my argument.

44. Janet Todd, "Notes," in *Oroonoko, The Rover, and Other Works*, by Aphra Behn, ed. Janet Todd (London: Penguin Books, 1992), 375n87.

45. Edmund Hickeringill, *Jamaica Viewed with All the Ports, Harbours, and Their Several Soundings, Towns, and Settlements Thereunto Belonging Together, with the Nature of Its Climate, Fruitfulnesse of the Soile, and Its Suitableness to English Complexions: With Several Other Collateral Observations and Reflexions upon the Island* (London, 1661), 59. The term appears to have arrived in English by way of a Spanish adaptation of a Haitian term; however, the *OED* notes its apparent relationship with the term *babracot*, used among the indigenous population of Guyana. Andrew Warnes discusses this etymology in detail in *Savage Barbecue: Race, Culture, and the Invention of America's First Food* (Athens: University of Georgia Press, 2008), 57–64.

46. Hughes, *Theatre of Aphra Behn*, 185–86.

47. The "Oriental despot" is a figure common to writings about Persia, China, and the Ottoman Empire. Montesquieu provides the most developed formulation of this figure, but the idea was available in more inchoate form well before this time, as Behn's writings demonstrate. We might compare her depiction of Coramantien with Montesquieu's description of despotic government: "In despotic states the nature of the government requires extreme obedience, and the prince's will, once known, should produce its effect as infallibly as does one ball thrown against another." Montesquieu, *The Spirit of Laws*, ed. and trans. Anne M. Cohler, Basia Carolyn Miller, and Harold Samuel Stone (Cambridge: Cambridge University Press, 1989), 29. See also Ros Ballaster, *Fabulous Orients: Fictions of the East in England, 1662–1785* (Oxford: Oxford University Press, 2005), 73–79.

48. Visconsi, *Lines of Equity*, 1–3.

49. Corrinne Harol, "The Passion of *Oroonoko*: Passive Obedience, the Royal Slave, and Aphra Behn's Baroque Realism," *ELH* 79, no. 2 (2012): 447–75.

50. Victoria Kahn, *Wayward Contracts: The Crisis of Political Obligation in England, 1640–1674* (Princeton: Princeton University Press, 2004), 141–47.

51. Harol, "Passion of *Oroonoko*," 460–61.

52. Marcus Tullius Cicero, *De Inventione, De Optimo Genere Oratorum, Topica*, trans. H. M. Hubbell, Loeb Classical Library (1949; repr., Cambridge: Harvard University Press, 1968), I.ii. 5–7.

53. Cicero, *De Inventione*, I.ii.3. For discussion of Cicero's significance in the civic sciences of the sixteenth and seventeenth centuries, see Quentin Skinner, *Reason and Rhetoric in the Philosophy of Hobbes* (Cambridge: Cambridge University Press, 1996), 93–99. Tudor and

Stuart rhetoricians echoed this point; Henry Peacham, for example, saw oratory blended with wisdom as having "made savage nations civil, wild people tame, and cruell tyrants not only to become meek, but likewise mercifull." Peacham, *Garden of Eloquence* (London, 1593), iii.

54. Aphra Behn, "To the Unknown Daphnis on His Excellent Translation of Lucretius," in *Works of Aphra Behn*, vol. 1, 25–29.

55. Oddvar Holmesland similarly argues that *Oroonoko* is an effort to resolve tensions between a receding aristocratic ideology and an emergent progressive individualism. I concur, but while Holmesland finds in Oroonoko a transitional figure between aristocratic romance and realist individualism, I read this transition from romance to realism as pointedly unsuccessful. Holmesland, "Aphra Behn's *Oroonoko*: Cultural Dialectics and the Novel," *ELH* 68, no. 1 (2001): 57–79.

56. See, especially, Susan B. Iwanisziw, "Behn's Novel Investment in *Oroonoko*: Kingship, Slavery, and Tobacco in English Colonialism," *South Atlantic Review* 63, no. 2 (1998): 75–98. As Iwanisziw and others have pointed out, "Oroonoko" is among other things a name for a species of tobacco.

57. Thomas Hobbes, *Tracts of Sir Thomas Hobbs of Malmsbury* (London, 1682), 33–34.

58. *The Roundheads* had already gestured toward the punishment for treason, since its joiner is probably a stand-in for Stephen Colledge, a carpenter and radical Whig executed for treason in 1681. Melinda S. Zook, *Radical Whigs and Conspiratorial Politics in Late Stuart England* (University Park: Pennsylvania State University Press, 1999), 90. Zook also notes a specific reference to Sidney's treason trial in *The Widdow Ranter*, when the dullard Dullman comments that only a single witness is necessary in treason trials (4.3). Zook, "Contextualizing Aphra Behn," in *Women Writers and the Early Modern British Political Tradition*, ed. Hilda L. Smith, 75–93 (Cambridge: Cambridge University Press, 1998), 90–91.

59. Peter Earle, *Monmouth's Rebels: The Road to Sedgemoor, 1685* (London: Weidenfeld and Nicolson, 1977), 172. That this form of torture and execution was not rare in cases of treason or insurrection suggests that Richard Kroll is misguided in seeking sources for Oroonoko's fate in the anti-Dutch portraits of Amboyna. See Kroll, "Tales of Love and Gallantry," 596–601.

60. For treason in English law, see George Keaton, *The Norman Conquest and the Common Law* (London: Ernest Benn, 1966), 76–77; Sarah Covington, *Wounds, Flesh, and Metaphor in Seventeenth-Century England* (New York: Palgrave Macmillan, 2009), 58–81; and John Bellamy, *The Tudor Law of Treason: An Introduction* (London: Routledge &

Kegan Paul, 1979). Quartering was also associated with treason in Europe; see Foucault's famous introduction to *Discipline and Punish*, as well as Richard J. Evans, *Rituals of Retribution: Capital Punishment in Germany, 1600–1987* (Oxford: Oxford University Press, 1996), 31, 86–89, 135. The sentence was still on the books in Britain in the early nineteenth century. As late as the 1780s, David Tyrie was convicted of illegal correspondence with the French during the American Revolutionary War; he was executed and quartered. The punishment remained legal and could be executed by the pleasure of the king until the Forfeiture Act of 1870.

61. Earle, *Monmouth's Rebels*, 176–77. The precise number of executions is not certain. See E. S. de Beer, "Executions Following the 'Bloody Assize,'" *Bulletin of the Institute of Historical Research* 4, no. 10 (1926): 36–39.

62. See Melinda S. Zook, "Violence, Martyrdom, and Radical Politics: Rethinking the Glorious Revolution," in *Politics and the Political Imagination in Later Stuart Britain: Essays Presented to Lois Green Schwoerer*, ed. Howard Nenner, 75–95 (Rochester, NY: University of Rochester Press, 1997).

63. Charlotte Sussman, "The Other Problem with Woman: Reproduction and Slave Culture in Aphra Behn's *Oroonoko*," in *Rereading Aphra Behn: History, Theory, and Criticism*, ed. Heidi Hunter, 212–33 (Charlottesville: University of Virginia Press, 1993). Harol, similarly, refers to Oroonoko's "auto-cesarean." Harol, "Passion of *Oroonoko*," 463.

64. Harol persuasively argues that Oroonoko's body here becomes a marker of human limitation more generally; transformed from a sovereign to a *homo sacer*, Oroonoko's vulnerability becomes a figure for a universal precariousness that the body cannot overcome (Harol, "Passion of *Oroonoko*," 462–64). This reading is tempting, but the specific relationship of his execution to treason and to usurped sovereign power leads me to see a different politics at work here.

65. Cf. Suvir Kaul's suggestion that Behn's narrative delocalizes violence, making it common to decaying feudalism, savagery, and colonialism alike. Kaul, "Reading Literary Symptoms: Colonial Pathologies and the Oroonoko Fictions of Behn, Southerne, and Hawkesworth," *Eighteenth-Century Life* 18, no. 3 (1994): 83.

66. Albert J. Rivero, "Aphra Behn's *Oroonoko* and the 'Blank Spaces' of Colonial Fictions," *SEL Studies in English Literature 1500–1900* 39, no. 3 (1999): 447–48.

3. TALKING GUNS AND SAVAGE SPACES: DANIEL DEFOE'S CIVILIZING TECHNOLOGIES

1. Daniel Defoe, *Robinson Crusoe* (1719), ed. J. Donald Crowley (Oxford: Oxford University Press, 1983), 212. Hereafter cited parenthetically in the text by page numbers in this edition.

2. The classic account of Defoe's novels as individualist manifestoes is of course Ian Watt, *The Rise of the Novel: Studies in Defoe, Richardson, and Fielding* (Berkeley: University of California Press, 2001), 60–92.

3. Mary Poovey, *A History of the Modern Fact: Problems of Knowledge in the Sciences of Wealth and Society* (Chicago: University of Chicago Press, 1998), 157–70.

4. Everett Zimmerman, "Robinson Crusoe and No Man's Land," *Journal of English and Germanic Philology* 102, no. 4 (2003): 506–29.

5. This chapter focuses primarily on Defoe's fiction, which offers a more complex and nuanced portrait of Britain's modernizing politics than is usually found in his journalism and poetry. Defoe's poetry is famously political in content and typically offers what appear to be straightforward arguments on behalf of a limited constitutional monarchy with strong powers to control the mob. This body of writing has not received the attention it deserves, but a full treatment of these poems is outside the scope of this chapter. For a recent discussion of Defoe's poetry that attends very carefully to their political contexts, see Andreas Mueller, *A Critical Study of Daniel Defoe's Verse: Recovering the Neglected Corpus of His Poetic Work* (Lewiston, NY: Edwin Mellen, 2010).

6. On Sacheverell's trial, see Geoffrey Holmes, *The Trial of Doctor Sacheverell* (London: Eyre Methuen, 1973), 123–206, esp. 141–42, 181–83. For a discussion of the suppression of the term *conquest* in relation to the Glorious Revolution, see M. P. Thompson, "The Idea of Conquest in Controversies of the 1688 Revolution," *Journal of the History of Ideas* 38, no. 1 (1977): 33–46. For contemporary political writing that addresses these issues, see the Sacheverell materials cited in Holmes; see also James Tyrrell's set of Whiggish dialogues, the *Bibliotheca Politica; or, An Enquiry into the Ancient Constitution of the English Government; Both in Respect to the Just Extent of Regal Power, and the Rights and Liberties of the Subject* (London, 1694), 128, 715.

7. Numerous pamphlets in the wake of the 1715 Jacobite uprising address the legitimacy of conquest and force; see, for example, the debate between Francis Atterbury and Joseph Addison regarding punishment of the Jacobite rebels: Atterbury, *An Argument to Prove the Affections of the People of England to Be the Best Security of the Government; Humbly Offer'd to the Consideration of the Patrons of Severity, and Applied to the*

Present Juncture of Affairs ([London], 1716); and Addison, *An Answer to a Pamphlet Entituled, An Argument to Prove the Affections of the People of England to Be the Best Security of the Government* (Edinburgh, 1716).

8. Kathleen Wilson, *The Sense of the People: Politics, Culture, and Imperialism in England, 1715–1785* (Cambridge: Cambridge University Press, 1995), 87–90, 98–101. As Wilson points out, the Whig regime's elevated rhetoric of political liberty coincides precisely with its suspension of habeas corpus, house arrests of Catholics, and violent assaults on political demonstrators. The Riot Act of 1714 effectively authorized the use of military force against rioters, indemnifying magistrates and officers in the event that they injured or killed rioters while attempting to disperse them. The act also notoriously made failure to disperse a capital offense. Nicholas Rogers, "Popular Protest in Early Hanoverian London," *Past & Present* 79 (May 1, 1978): 75.

9. Mark Goldie briefly summarizes these issues in "The English System of Liberty," in *The Cambridge History of Eighteenth-Century Political Thought*, ed. Mark Goldie and Robert Wokler, 40–78 (Cambridge: Cambridge University Press, 2006), 42–45. See also John Kenyon, "The Revolution of 1688: Resistance and Contract," in *Historical Perspectives: Studies in English Thought and Society in Honour of J. H. Plumb*, ed. Neil McKendrick, 43–69 (London: Europa, 1974).

10. A thorough review of political readings of *Crusoe* would run to many pages. Most helpful to the arguments presented in this chapter have been these: Manuel Schonhorn, *Defoe's Politics: Parliament, Power, Kingship, and Robinson Crusoe* (Cambridge: Cambridge University Press, 1991), 141–64; Carol Kay, *Political Constructions: Defoe, Richardson, and Sterne in Relation to Hobbes, Hume, and Burke* (Ithaca: Cornell University Press, 1988), 75–92; Peter Hulme, *Colonial Encounters: Europe and the Native Caribbean, 1492–1797* (London: Methuen, 1986), 175–222; Maximillian E. Novak, *Defoe and the Nature of Man* (Oxford: Oxford University Press, 1963); Roxann Wheeler, *The Complexion of Race: Categories of Difference in Eighteenth-Century British Culture* (Philadelphia: University of Pennsylvania Press, 2000); Wolfram Schmidgen, *Eighteenth-Century Fiction and the Law of Property* (Cambridge: Cambridge University Press, 2002), 32–62. Dennis Todd has recently highlighted the kinship between Carib and European that justified colonial activity, in *Defoe's America* (Cambridge: Cambridge University Press, 2010), 41–45.

11. Michel Foucault, *Discipline and Punish: The Birth of the Prison*, trans. Alan Sheridan (New York: Vintage Books, 1995), 49.

12. Two images from the later eighteenth century illustrate this tension. In William Lanne's 1790 edition of the novel, an engraving by

J. Barlow emphasizes Crusoe's role as a beneficent savior; this illustration pushes the violent context to the side, excluding it from the frame. In this fanciful frame, Barlow depicts Crusoe as offering gifts of grapes and bread, emblematic symbols of Christian rituals of communion. This presentation emphasizes Crusoe's conversion of Friday to Christianity as a gift. Conversely, Mather Brown's frontispiece to the 1785 edition of J. Walter highlights Crusoe's ambiguous position as wild man, savior, and warrior and emphasizes Friday's necessary choice between two scenes in the background—Crusoe's enclosure and a cannibal feast. The peculiar depiction of Crusoe here makes it difficult to unambiguously associate him with the former choice. See David Blewett, *The Illustration of* Robinson Crusoe: *1719–1920* (Gerrards Cross, UK: Colin Smythe, 1995), 60–63.

13. This scene has frequently been read in Providential and allegorical terms; see, for example, J. Paul Hunter, *The Reluctant Pilgrim: Defoe's Emblematic Method and Quest for Form in "Robinson Crusoe"* (Baltimore: Johns Hopkins University Press, 1966), 182–88. In this reading, the arrival of Friday offers Crusoe an opportunity to test, demonstrate, and propagate his faith; in converting Friday, he achieves a spiritual deliverance. My argument here does not necessarily contest this reading but rather calls attention to the violence that this narrative of spiritual progress appears to require.

14. Henry Louis Gates, Jr., *The Signifying Monkey: A Theory of Afro-American Literary Criticism* (New York: Oxford University Press, 1988), 131–32.

15. Olaudah Equiano, *The Interesting Narrative of the Life of Olaudah Equiano, or Gustavus Vassa, the African, Written by Himself*, ed. Werner Sollors (1789; repr., New York: Norton, 2001), 48.

16. Ibid., 44.

17. Gates, *Signifying Monkey*, 156.

18. Ibid.

19. Carol Kay describes the selling of Xury as "not heartless," depending as it does on Xury's consent (*Political Constructions*, 82). I suggest that Defoe, consciously or not, encourages the reader to meditate on the kinds of consent that might be available to Xury, cut off from his nation and surrounded by men with guns.

20. Hugo Grotius, *The Rights of War and Peace*, ed. Richard Tuck, vol. 1 (Indianapolis: Liberty Fund, 2005), 1022.

21. Daniel Defoe, *The Political History of the Devil*, ed. John Mullan, vol. 6 of *Satire, Fantasy, and Writings on the Supernatural*, ed. W. R. Owen and Philip Nicholas Furbank (London: Pickering & Chatto, 2005), 269–70. The most comprehensive treatment of Defoe's writings on

demonology and magic is still Rodney M. Baine, *Daniel Defoe and the Supernatural*, (Athens: University of Georgia Press, 1969).

22. Adam Lifshey hints at a similar reading, pointing to the parallels between the "slaughter [of] the undomesticated" in the Caribbean and in Europe. Lifshey, *Specters of Conquest: Indigenous Absence in Transatlantic Literatures* (New York: Fordham University Press, 2010), 86. Carol Houlihan Flynn similarly suggests that Defoe uses Friday to comment on Crusoe's "rage for order." Flynn, *The Body in Swift and Defoe* (Cambridge: Cambridge University Press, 1990), 158–59. Phillip Armstrong argues that this sequence is characteristic of the commonplace cruelty to nondomesticated animals in Defoe's day but also notes the analogues between human relationships with animals and colonizers' relationships with savages. Armstrong, *What Animals Mean in the Fiction of Modernity* (London: Routledge, 2008), 42–45.

23. Homi Bhabha, "Signs Taken for Wonders," in *The Location of Culture* (London: Routledge, 1994), 107. See also Martin Calder, *Encounters with the Other: A Journey to the Limits of Language through Works by Rousseau, Defoe, Prévost and Graffigny* (Amsterdam: Rodopi, 2003), 172–73.

24. Jonathan Elmer, *On Lingering and Being Last: Race and Sovereignty in the New World* (New York: Fordham University Press, 2008), 24. In a different register, Coby Dowdell argues that Defoe's fiction registers a growing skepticism about mercantile self-interest as a force that can adequately regulate behavior. "'A Living Law to Himself and Others': Daniel Defoe, Algernon Sidney, and the Politics of Self-Interest in *Robinson Crusoe* and *Farther Adventures*," *Eighteenth-Century Fiction* 22, no. 3 (2010): 415–42.

25. Markley's interpretation points toward a shift in Defoe's thought away from self-sufficient individuality toward fantasies of "infinite profits" through trade. Markley, *The Far East and the English Imagination, 1600–1730* (Cambridge: Cambridge University Press, 2006), 85, 177–209.

26. Dutch efforts at settlement began in the late sixteenth century; Charles I had considered establishing a colony there in the 1630s and 1640s. In 1644, an English settlement was briefly established, but the settlers were massacred; only twelve survivors remained to return to England. French settlers had more success for a time, but they, too, were eventually pushed from the island. See Arne Bialuschewski, "Pirates, Slavers, and the Indigenous Population in Madagascar, c. 1690–1715," *International Journal of African Historical Studies* 38, no. 3 (2005): 401–25; Solofo Randrianja and Stephen Ellis, *Madagascar: A Short History* (Chicago: University of Chicago Press, 2009), 77–121. Gwyn

Campbell has argued that the history of the island must be seen as an integral part of the "Indian Ocean World." Campbell, *An Economic History of Imperial Madagascar, 1750–1895: The Rise and Fall of an Island Empire* (Cambridge: Cambridge University Press, 2005), 4–6.

27. Daniel Defoe, *The Farther Adventures of Robinson Crusoe; Being the Second and Last Part of His Life, and the Strange Surprising Accounts of His Travels Round Three Parts of the Globe* (London, 1719), 221–22. Hereafter cited parenthetically in the text.

28. Arthur Secord notes that Defoe drew this ethnographic detail on Madagascar from the "Voyages and Travels of J. Albert de Mandelslo," which appears in Adam Olearius's *Voyages & Travels of the Ambassadors Sent by Frederick Duke of Holstein, to the Great Duke of Muscovy, and the King of Persia Begun in the Year M.DC.XXXIII, and Finish'd in M.DC.XXXIX . . .*, trans. John Davies (London, 1662), 254. Defoe owned a copy of this work. It is significant that Mandelslo does not refer to any sort of spatial configuration created by the staff of peace. Rather, the Madagascans who meet Mandelslo merely "planted a great pole in the ground, as a mark of the Alliance they made" with the Europeans (254). The spatial politics created by the poles in this sequence is, as far as I can tell, entirely Defoe's creation.

29. Note here this language of genocide, provocatively discussed in a different context by Claude Rawson in *God, Gulliver, and Genocide: Barbarism and the European Imagination, 1492–1945* (Oxford: Oxford University Press, 2001). It is worth noting the presence of this language of genocide in this early novel; Rawson associates this topos closely with Swift and the satiric tradition. On the language of atrocity, see also John Richardson, "Atrocity in Mid-Eighteenth-Century War Literature," *Eighteenth-Century Life* 33, no. 2 (2009): 92–114.

30. For helpful discussions of this sequence and its relation to the anomic spaces of the non-European world, see Stephen H. Gregg, *Defoe's Writings and Manliness: Contrary Men* (Burlington, VT: Ashgate, 2009), 87; Markley, *Far East and the English Imagination*, 222–23; Zimmerman, "Robinson Crusoe and No Man's Land," 519–20.

31. Daniel Defoe, *Augusta Triumphans; or, The Way to Make London the Most Flourishing City in the Universe; First, by Establishing an University . . . Concluding with an Effectual Method to Prevent Street Robberies; and a Letter to Coll. Robinson, on Account of the Orphan's Tax* (London, 1728), 51–54.

32. Henri Lefebvre, *The Production of Space* (1974), trans. Donald Nicholson-Smith (Oxford, UK: Blackwell, 1991), 280.

33. A similar discourse is found regarding the Americas; at almost precisely the same historical moment, Experience Mayhew was writing of

fences and land use in the Massachusetts Bay Colony as characteristic of the transformation of Wampanoag culture from a space of savagery into one indicating civility. For Mayhew, as John Smolenski has argued, "space, culture, and sovereignty were isomorphic." I suggest that much the same may be said of spaces characterized by savagery—including European spaces—wherever that space may intrude. John Smolenski, "The Ordering of Authority in the Colonial Americas," in *New World Orders: Violence, Sanction, and Authority in the Colonial Americas*, ed. John Smolenski and Thomas J. Humphrey, 1–16 (Philadelphia: University of Pennsylvania Press, 2005), 1–2.

34. John Bender, *Imagining the Penitentiary: Fiction and the Architecture of Mind in Eighteenth-Century England* (Chicago: University of Chicago Press, 1987), 56. See also Schonhorn, *Defoe's Politics*, 143–46. Patricia Seed points to the centrality of enclosure to the English colonial tradition: *Ceremonies of Possession in Europe's Conquest of the New World, 1492–1640* (Cambridge: Cambridge University Press, 1995), 15–40.

35. See, for example, Bruce McLeod, *The Geography of Empire in English Literature, 1580–1745* (Cambridge: Cambridge University Press, 1999), 206–8.

36. K. G. Davies, *The Royal African Company* (New York: Longmans, Green, 1957), 240.

37. Willem Bosman, *A New and Accurate Description of the Coast of Guinea, Divided into the Gold, the Slave, and the Ivory Coasts* (London, 1705), 55. Some efforts were made by the Royal African Company to claim administrative authority over areas immediately adjacent to its forts—nascent dreams of sovereignty and conquest that came to nothing. See Davies, *Royal African Company*, 281–82.

38. Daniel Defoe, *Defoe's Review*, ed. Arthur Wellesley Secord, 22 vols., Facsimile Text Society, Publication 44 (New York: Columbia University Press, 1938). Hereafter cited parenthetically in the text by volume, book, and page number in this edition.

39. Davies, *Royal African Company*, 262–64. Tim Keirn offers an excellent overview of these debates in "Monopoly, Economic Thought, and the Royal African Company," in *Early Modern Conceptions of Property*, ed. John Brewer and Susan Staves, 427–66 (London: Routledge, 1996).

40. It goes without saying that Defoe's presentation of the West African coast as anarchic is a shocking distortion. His Dutch contemporary Bosman—an apologist for the slave trade and no lover of Africans—was careful to distinguish varying African polities into "monarchies and commonwealths," though he did confess that he found

their affairs muddled and disordered. Defoe's *Review*, on the other hand, aligns African political space with his conception of the savage. Peter Knox-Shaw has noted that the conception of African space as intrinsically "hostile to cultivation and civility" is closely associated in *Captain Singleton* with the African interior. Peter Knox-Shaw, "Defoe and the Politics of Representing the African Interior," *Modern Language Review* 96, no. 4 (2001): 939." See also Wheeler's comments on this passage in *The Complexion of Race*, 114.

41. Daniel Defoe, *Memoirs of a Cavalier* (1720), ed. James T. Boulton (Oxford: Oxford University Press, 1991), 44–45.

42. Quoted in Chris J. Tabraham and Doreen Grove, *Fortress Scotland and the Jacobites*, (London: B. T. Batsford, 1995), 39.

43. Most recent critical treatments of Defoe do not discuss this sequence, choosing instead to focus on the relationship between Singleton and his companion and adviser William Walters, or investigating Singleton's ambiguous status as a pirate trader. See, for example, Stephen H. Gregg, "Male Friendship and Defoe's *Captain Singleton:* 'My Every Thing,'" *British Journal for Eighteenth-Century Studies* 27, no. 2 (2004): 203–18; Hans Turley, "Piracy, Identity, and Desire in *Captain Singleton*," *Eighteenth-Century Studies* 31, no. 2 (1997): 199–214; and Markley, *Far East and the English Imagination*, 210–35. Other important discussions of the novel primarily examine its first half, which takes place in Madagascar and on the African mainland. See especially Wheeler, *Complexion of Race*, 101–36; Knox-Shaw, "Defoe and the Politics of Representing the African Interior."

44. William Shakespeare, *King Richard II*, ed. Andrew Gurr, New Cambridge Shakespeare (Cambridge: Cambridge University Press, 2003), 2.1.43–49.

45. To be sure, Gaunt's speech is ironic, given that Richard's England was about to fall victim to an invasion and civil war led by the exiled Henry Bolingbroke. My point is not that Shakespeare endorses the idea; I use this quotation to illustrate the availability of this rhetoric by the late sixteenth century.

46. J. Bates, *Two (United) Are Better than One Alone: A Thanksgiving Sermon upon the Union of the Two Kingdoms of England and Scotland, Preach'd at Hackney, May 1, 1707* (London, 1707), 5.

47. Daniel Defoe, *An Essay at Removing National Prejudices against a Union with Scotland*, part 1 (London, 1706), 12.

48. Daniel Defoe, *Captain Singleton* (1720), ed. Shiv K. Kumar (Oxford: Oxford University Press, 1969), 99–100. Hereafter cited parenthetically in the text by page numbers in this edition.

49. Anna Neill discusses the importance of this hostility to trade in a different context in "Crusoe's Farther Adventures: Discovery, Trade, and the Law of Nations," *Eighteenth Century: Theory and Interpretation* 38, no. 3 (1997): 213–30.

50. See, for example, Hugo Grotius, *The Rights of War and Peace*, ed. Richard Tuck, vol. 2 (Indianapolis: Liberty Fund, 2005), 448.

51. Paul Kléber Monod, *Jacobitism and the English People* (Cambridge: Cambridge University Press, 1989), 71–73.

52. Mary Louise Pratt's conception of "anti-conquest" in a somewhat later period has influenced my thinking here. Pratt, *Imperial Eyes: Travel Writing and Transculturation* (London: Routledge, 1992), 38–68.

4. *DOCTRINES DÉTESTABLES*: JONATHAN SWIFT, DESPOTISM, AND VIRTUE

1. Jonathan Swift, *Gulliver's Travels*, vol. 11 of *The Prose Works of Jonathan Swift*, ed. Herbert Davis (1941; repr., Oxford, UK: Blackwell, 1959), 19. I follow the convention of referring to Swift's *Travels into Several Remote Nations in the World* as *Gulliver's Travels* throughout this chapter. Hereafter cited parenthetically in the text by page numbers in this edition.

2. Swift was well versed in the literature of travel and exploration. He refers directly to William Dampier (*Travels*, 5), and his library included editions of Hakluyt and Purchas; see Harold Williams, *Dean Swift's Library, with a Facsimile of the Original Sale Catalogue and Some Account of Two Manuscript Lists of His Books* (Cambridge: Cambridge University Press, 1932). For specific discussions of book 4's treatment of the "savagery" of the Yahoos, see R. W. Frantz, "Swift's Yahoos and the Voyagers," *Modern Philology* 29 (1931): 49–57.

3. For Swift as a Whig, see J. A. Downie, *Jonathan Swift, Political Writer* (London: Routledge & Kegan Paul, 1984). For Swift as a Tory, see F. P. Lock, *The Politics of Gulliver's Travels* (Oxford, UK: Clarendon, 1980); Lock, *Swift's Tory Politics* (Newark: University of Delaware Press, 1983); and Isaac Kramnick, *Bolingbroke and His Circle: The Politics of Nostalgia in the Age of Walpole* (Cambridge: Harvard University Press, 1968), 202–17. Ian Higgins offers a suggestive, if inconclusive, argument that Swift's writing expresses Jacobite "velleities," if not a fully committed Jacobitism, in *Swift's Politics: A Study in Disaffection* (Cambridge: Cambridge University Press, 1994).

4. See, for example, J. G. A Pocock, *The Machiavellian Moment: Florentine Political Thought and the Atlantic Republican Tradition* (Princeton: Princeton University Press, 1975), 423–61.

5. Warren Montag, *The Unthinkable Swift: The Spontaneous Philosophy of a Church of England Man* (London: Verso, 1994), 86.

6. See, for example, Swift to Pope, Dublin, 10 Jan. 1721, in *The Correspondence of Jonathan Swift, D.D.*, ed. David Woolley, vol. 2 (New York: P. Lang, 1999), 362–63.

7. There has been surprisingly little attention to questions of exemplarity in Swift's writing. Much of the literature on exemplarity focuses on exemplary lives and the genres of biography and autobiography, but Swift's writings as the Drapier are more invested in the way virtue and patriotism roll downhill from the highest levels of society to the lowest. For a useful general discussion, see Geoffrey Cubitt, "Introduction: Heroic Reputations and Exemplarity," in *Heroic Reputations and Exemplary Lives*, ed. Geoffrey Cubitt and Warren Allen, 1–26 (Manchester: Manchester University Press, 2000).

8. Jonathan Swift, "Marginalia," in *Miscellaneous and Autobiographical Pieces, Fragments, and Marginalia*, vol. 5 of *The Prose Works of Jonathan Swift*, ed. Herbert Davis, 239–320 (Oxford, UK: Blackwell, 1962), 245.

9. Ibid. Swift's note is in French: "et qui fiera à un tel roy?" The translation is my own.

10. Carol Flynn, *The Body in Swift and Defoe* (Cambridge: Cambridge University Press, 1990), 179–80. Swift's ambivalent stances on the repellent body and on sovereignty converge in the figure of Henry VIII, whose bodily excesses are metonymically associated with his tyrannical power.

11. Jonathan Swift, *A Discourse of the Contests and Dissentions between the Nobles and the Commons in Athens and Rome*, in *A Tale of a Tub, with Other Early Works, 1696–1707*, vol. 1 of *The Prose Works of Jonathan Swift*, ed. Herbert Davis, 191–236 (1938; repr., Oxford, UK: Blackwell, 1957). Hereafter cited parenthetically in the text by page numbers in this edition.

12. Mark Goldie lucidly sets out this context in "Situating Swift's Politics in 1701," in *Politics and Literature in the Age of Swift: English and Irish Perspectives*, ed. Claude Rawson, 31–51 (Cambridge: Cambridge University Press, 2010). See also the historical introduction to Frank H. Ellis's edition of the *Discourse* (Oxford, UK: Clarendon, 1967), 1–79; the concise account in David Ogg, *England in the Reigns of James II and William III* (Oxford, UK: Clarendon, 1955), 461–63; and Downie, *Jonathan Swift*, 75–78.

13. Ellis, introduction to *Discourse*, 55.

14. Polybius, *The Histories*, trans. W. R. Paton, vol. 3 (London: William Heinemann, 1923), book 6, 11–18, 295–311. For Hobbes's attack

on Polybian notions about the balanced constitution, see *Leviathan*, ed. C. B. Macpherson (London: Penguin Books, 1978), 368–70.

15. Lock, *Swift's Tory Politics*, 153. Goldie argues that it is the nobility who hold the scales in this figure, but this seems unlikely; the contest, in this case, is between two parliamentary institutions, whom it is the task of the monarch to balance ("Situating Swift's Politics," 43). This is why the tactics adopted by the Tories in the Commons are so dangerous; they not only attack the nobility but also encroach on the monarch's prerogative, "cramping the Hand that holds the Balance" (Swift, *Discourse*, 236). These attacks on the king are one reason that the English people threaten to rise against their representatives, seeing that their king "hath, in many things, been Hardly used" (235).

16. Jonathan Swift, *Sentiments of a Church of England Man*, in *Bickerstaff Papers and Pamphlets on the Church*, vol. 2 of *The Prose Works of Jonathan Swift*, ed. Herbert Davis, 1–25 (Oxford, UK: Blackwell, 1939). Hereafter cited parenthetically in the text by page numbers in this edition. Unlike the *Discourse*, *Sentiments*' date of composition and the purpose of its publication remain uncertain. Irvin Ehrenpreis persuasively dates its composition to 1708 or earlier, but it did not appear in print until the publication of Swift's *Miscellanies in Prose and Verse* (London, 1711). See Ehrenpreis, *Dr. Swift*, vol. 2 of *Swift: The Man, His Works, and the Age* (Cambridge: Harvard University Press, 1967), 124–31. Montag follows Ehrenpreis's line, suggesting that the *Sentiments* are written during a period when Swift was wavering between Whig and Tory philosophies and mark an "attempt to situate himself beyond 'the rage of party'" (*Unthinkable Swift*, 13). Lock dissents, suggesting that the essay reflects his position in 1711 and not that of 1708 (*Swift's Tory Politics*, 95).

17. Marcus Tullius Cicero, *De Officiis*, trans. Walter Miller (London: William Heinemann, 1913), III, 29. The famous quotation from Cicero—*hostis humani generis*—is often said to refer to pirates, though Cicero actually used the term with reference to any gang of criminals ("praedones"). See Alfred Rubin, *The Law of Piracy* (New York: Transnational, 1998), 20.

18. Claude Rawson, *Satire and Sentiment, 1660–1830: Stress Points in the English Augustan Tradition* (Cambridge: Cambridge University Press, 1994), 70–73.

19. Watches as luxury goods and exemplars of foppish display are discussed in Stuart Sherman, *Telling Time: Clocks, Diaries, and English Diurnal Form, 1660–1785* (Chicago: University of Chicago Press, 1996), 83–85. Sherman notes that watches tended to become more functional and less ornamental over the later seventeenth and early eighteenth

centuries, but the pocket watch continues to surface as an index of foppishness and luxury in poetry and drama in this period. Michael Adas discusses timepieces as objects of wonder in *Machines as the Measure of Men: Science, Technology, and Ideologies of Western Dominance* (Ithaca: Cornell University Press, 1989), 60–62.

20. For background on the plot and its commemoration, see James Sharpe, *Remember, Remember: A Cultural History of Guy Fawkes Day* (Cambridge: Harvard University Press, 2005), esp. 93–112.

21. Clement Hawes notes that Gulliver's malleability parodies the topos of assimilation. Hawes, *The British Eighteenth Century and Global Critique* (New York: Palgrave Macmillan, 2005), 146.

22. For discussions of the role of the militia in Country ideology or neo-Harringtonianism, see Pocock, *Machiavellian Moment*, 410–22; and Lois G. Schwoerer, *"No Standing Armies!" The Antiarmy Ideology in Seventeenth-Century England* (Baltimore: Johns Hopkins University Press, 1974), 13–14, 36.

23. Numerous critics have noted the complexity of Swift's relationship to Irish nationalism and his ambivalent identification as a Protestant Irishman. See, for example, Louis A. Landa, *Swift and the Church of Ireland* (Oxford, UK: Clarendon, 1954); Carole Fabricant, *Swift's Landscape* (Notre Dame: University of Notre Dame Press, 1995); Fabricant, "Speaking for the Irish Nation: The Drapier, the Bishop, and the Problems of Colonial Representation," *ELH* 66, no. 2 (1999): 337–72; Sean D. Moore, *Swift, the Book, and the Irish Financial Revolution: Satire and Sovereignty in Colonial Ireland* (Baltimore: Johns Hopkins University Press, 2010).

24. Jonathan Swift, *The Drapier's Letters and Other Works, 1724–1725*, vol. 10 of *The Prose Works of Jonathan Swift*, ed. Herbert Davis (1941; repr., Oxford, UK: Blackwell, 1959). Hereafter cited parenthetically in the text by page numbers in this edition.

25. For a discussion of Swift's dislike of Irish dialect, see Irvin Ehrenpreis, *Dean Swift*, vol. 3 of *Swift: The Man, His Works, and the Age* (Cambridge: Harvard University Press, 1983), 133.

26. Moore, *Swift, the Book, and the Irish Financial Revolution*, 152.

27. Jonathan Swift to Dean John Brandreth, 30 June 1732, in *The Correspondence of Jonathan Swift*, ed. Harold Herbert Williams, vol. 4 (Oxford, UK: Clarendon, 1965).

28. For the size of the Irish military establishment, see J. A. Houlding, *Fit for Service: The Training of the British Army, 1715–1795* (Oxford, UK: Clarendon, 1981), 45–46. See also comments in Ehrenpreis, *Dean Swift*, 152–53; Moore, *Swift, the Book, and the Irish Financial Revolution*, 159.

29. Jonathan Swift, *Proposal for the Universal Use of Irish Manufacture*, in *Irish Tracts 1720–1723*, vol. 9 of *The Prose Works of Jonathan Swift*, ed. Herbert Davis, 13–22 (1948; repr., Oxford, UK: Blackwell, 1963), 17. Hereafter cited parenthetically in the text by page numbers in this edition.

30. For an important recent discussion of this event, see Moore, *Swift, the Book, and the Irish Financial Revolution*, 134–67. Moore identifies the crisis not only with an assertion of Irish rights but also with developments in a specifically Irish print culture.

31. Jan Hogendorn and Marion Johnson, *The Shell Money of the Slave Trade* (Cambridge: Cambridge University Press, 1986), 47. Defoe in 1728 gloatingly commented on the ability of English traders in Africa to purchase "*Slaves, Teeth*, and *Gold*" from childlike "Savages" who desired only "Trifles, and Toys, such as Knives and Sissars, Kettles and Clouts, Glass Beads, and Cowries." Daniel Defoe, *A Plan of the English Commerce: Being a Compleat Prospect of the Trade of This Nation, as Well the Home Trade as the Foreign; In Three Parts* (London, 1728), 328–29.

32. The complete paragraph, not quoted by Swift, is printed in Ehrenpreis, *Dean Swift*, 249.

33. Rawson discusses this moment in the tract in "The Injured Lady and the Drapier: A Reading of Swift's Irish Tracts," *Prose Studies* 3, no. 1 (1980): 27. He links this imagery both to the perverse literalism of the experimenters in the Academy of Lagado and to the cannibalism imagery of *A Modest Proposal* (1728). Rawson's larger point is that Swift's contempt in his Irish writings is not limited to the English but extends to the Irish—or at least some Irish—as well.

34. Jonathan Swift, *A Proposal That All the Ladies and Women of Ireland Should Appear Constantly in Irish Manufacture*, in *Irish Tracts, 1728–1733*, vol. 12 of *The Prose Works of Jonathan Swift*, ed. Herbert Davis (1955; repr., Oxford, UK: Blackwell, 1964), 26.

35. Harriet Guest discusses this location of national failure in the shopping woman in *Small Change: Women, Learning, Patriotism, 1750–1810* (Chicago: University of Chicago Press, 2000), 70–75.

36. See Claude Rawson, *God, Gulliver, and Genocide: Barbarism and the European Imagination, 1492–1945* (Oxford: Oxford University Press, 2001), 237–45.

37. Jonathan Swift, *A Modest Proposal for Preventing the Children of Poor People from Being a Burden to Their Parents or the Country, and for Making Them Beneficial to the Public*, in *Prose Works of Jonathan Swift*, vol. 12, 111. Hereafter cited parenthetically in the text by page numbers in this edition. Hawes notes that this passage may have been suggested by

the visit of the Iroquois kings to London in 1711 (*British Eighteenth Century and Global Critique*, 164).

38. My association of Laputa with Lana-Terzi is partly suggested by Marjorie Hope Nicolson and Nora Mohler, "The Scientific Background of Swift's *Voyage to Laputa*," *Annals of Science* 2 (1937): 299–334; and Nicolson and Mohler, "Swift's 'Flying Island' in the *Voyage to Laputa*," *Annals of Science* 2 (1937): 405–30.

39. Srinivas Aravamudan, *Tropicopolitans: Colonialism and Agency, 1688–1804* (Durham: Duke University Press, 1999), 209.

40. Robert Hooke, *Philosophical Collections*, vol. 1 (London, 1679). This publication was begun while the *Philosophical Collections* of the Royal Society were on hiatus. Hereafter cited parenthetically in the text.

41. Lana-Terzi's invention suggested very different possibilities to Joseph Galien, who in 1757 proposed an alternative design for an airship—one which he hoped would be capable of colonizing Africa. Mi Gyung Kim, "'Public' Science: Hydrogen Balloons and Lavoisier's Decomposition of Water," *Annals of Science* 63, no. 3 (2006): 296.

42. Joseph Addison and Richard Steele, *The Guardian*, ed. John Calhoun Stephens (Lexington: University Press of Kentucky, 1982), 383–85. Hereafter cited parenthetically in the text by page numbers in this edition. Although Richard Steele was the driving force behind the *Guardian*, Addison penned a series of essays for the journal during the summer of 1713, including this one. See Stephens, introduction to *The Guardian*, 18–19. Swift would not likely have seen this essay at the time of its initial publication, since he was in Ireland to claim his deanship and handle other obligations from June through August (Ehrenpreis, *Dr. Swift*, 636–70). However, given Swift's sometime closeness to Addison and his lifelong interest in his work, we have reason to believe that he may have read this essay, though my argument here does not depend on his having done so.

43. This passage, like Swift's *Modest Proposal*, may allude to the visit of the Mohawk "kings" to London in 1711. See Stephens's notes to *The Guardian*, 704n. 4. Cf. Joseph Roach, *Cities of the Dead: Circum-Atlantic Performance* (New York: Columbia University Press, 1996), 118–22.

44. Laura Brown, *Ends of Empire: Women and Ideology in Early Eighteenth-Century English Literature* (Ithaca: Cornell University Press, 1993), 18–19.

45. The possibility that Anglo-Irish relations are represented here finds support in Swift's comment in *A Proposal for the Universal Use of Irish Manufacture*: "some ministries ... were apt, from their *high* elevation, to look *down* upon this kingdom as if it had been one of their *colonies* of *outcasts* in America" (21).

46. Montag points out that this scene, too, directly parodies *Robinson Crusoe*; the island on which Gulliver is marooned is entirely unlike Crusoe's, barren and incapable of supporting human life. Montag suggests that this is part of Swift's project to deflate theories of government that imagine a state of nature (*Unthinkable Swift*, 135–36), though he fails to account for the implicit theories of just such a state in some of Swift's earlier writings, as noted earlier. Cf. the similar account of this passage, not cited by Montag, in Dennis Todd, "Laputa, the Whore of Babylon, and the Idols of Science," *Studies in Philology* 75, no. 1 (1978): 100–104.

47. For classic discussions of these sequences, see Nicolson and Mohler, "Scientific Background"; for a more recent treatment, see Robert P. Fitzgerald, "Science and Politics in Swift's Voyage to Laputa," *Journal of English and Germanic Philology* 87 (Spring 1988): 213–29; Paul Korshin, "The Intellectual Contexts of Swift's Flying Island," *Philological Quarterly* 50 (1978): 630–46; and Todd, "Laputa, the Whore of Babylon, and the Idols of Science."

48. See the famously ludicrous projects of the Lagadan Academy (176–78).

49. See Lock, *Politics of "Gulliver's Travels,"* 100–101, for a skeptical reading of this interpretation. Lock's contention—an extreme one—is that the scene "contains nothing and no one that can stand for either the Drapier, Wood, the Halfpence, or the Duchess of Kendall."

50. It remained a treasonable offense to so much as imagine the death of the king, as Swift knew well. Cf. John Barrell, *Imagining the King's Death: Figurative Treason, Fantasies of Regicide, 1793–1796* (Oxford: Oxford University Press, 2000).

51. This is not the place to restage the antiquated disputations of the "hard" and "soft" schools of Houyhnhnm criticism. For a description of the various opinions on this spectrum, see James Lowry Clifford, "Gulliver's Fourth Voyage: 'Hard' and 'Soft' Schools of Interpretation," in *Quick Springs of Sense: Studies in the Eighteenth Century*, ed. Larry S. Champion (Athens: University of Georgia Press, 1974), 33–49. My position, in brief, is that the Houyhnhnms, like Gulliver, are defined relative to whatever Swift's text needs them to be at any given moment. They are certainly objects of satire at times—particularly in their egregious inability to experience the playfulness and slipperiness of language. But it can hardly be denied that at times they embody virtues sorely lacking in Europe. We ought not say that Gulliver's wish for a Houyhnhnm colonization of Britain represents a Swiftian dream, but the language does express a velleity of that sort: a half wish or a fantasy that contains elements of a nightmare.

5. SAVAGE VISION: VIOLENCE, REASON, AND SURVEILLANCE IN ELIZA HAYWOOD

1. John Atkins, *A Voyage to Guinea, Brasil, and the West-Indies; in His Majesty's Ships the Swallow and Weymouth* (London, 1735), 102–3.

2. Many critics follow Foucault in arguing that regimes of surveillance and normalization tend to supplant sovereignty over the course of the eighteenth century. Foucault's later work tends to subsume these practices under the larger rubric of governmentality, as we have seen. In addition to the works cited earlier, see Michel Foucault, *Discipline and Punish: The Birth of the Prison*, trans. Alan Sheridan (New York: Vintage Books, 1995), 195–228, 293–308. For studies of the *Spectator* that leverage Foucault, see Erin Mackie, *Market à la Mode: Fashion, Commodity, and Gender in* The Tatler *and* The Spectator (Baltimore: Johns Hopkins University Press, 1997); and Shawn Lisa Maurer, *Proposing Men: Dialectics of Gender and Class in the Eighteenth-Century English Periodical* (Stanford: Stanford University Press, 1998). Scott Paul Gordon offers a limited critique of these approaches, as discussed later, in *The Power of the Passive Self in English Literature, 1640–1770* (Cambridge: Cambridge University Press, 2002), 86–118.

3. Foucault himself returned to questions of sovereignty later in his career. For a helpful discussion, see Brian C. J. Singer and Lorna Weir, "Sovereignty, Governance and the Political: The Problematic of Foucault," *Thesis Eleven* 94, no. 1 (2008): 49–71.

4. Manushag N. Powell, "See No Evil, Hear No Evil, Speak No Evil: Spectation and the Eighteenth-Century Public Sphere," *Eighteenth-Century Studies* 45, no. 2 (2012): 255–76; Gordon, *Power of the Passive Self in English Literature*, 86–118.

5. See, for example, the essays collected in Lynn Marie Wright and Donald J. Newman, eds., *The Fair Philosopher: Eliza Haywood and "The Female Spectator"* (Lewisburg, PA: Bucknell University Press, 2006).

6. There is a growing body of writing on Haywood's political commitments, beginning with Paula Backscheider's pioneering essay "The Shadow of an Author: Eliza Haywood," *Eighteenth-Century Fiction* 18, no. 1 (1998): 79–102. For an important assessment of the evidence regarding Haywood's political activities in the 1740s, see Kathryn R. King, "Patriot or Opportunist? Eliza Haywood and the Politics of *The Female Spectator*," in Wright and Newman, *Fair Philosopher*, 104–21; King, *A Political Biography of Eliza Haywood*, Eighteenth-Century Political Biographies 9 (London: Pickering & Chatto, 2012). Catherine Ingrassia offers intriguing speculations about Haywood's possible political sympathies and affiliations, though her primary interest is in

Haywood's position within the book trade and economies of credit: *Authorship, Commerce, and Gender in Early Eighteenth-Century England: A Culture of Paper Credit* (Cambridge: Cambridge University Press, 1998), 116–27. Elizabeth Kubek situates Haywood's text in the political context of the 1730s in "The Key to Stowe: Toward a Patriot Whig Reading of Eliza Haywood's *Eovaai*," in *Presenting Gender: Changing Sex in Early-Modern Culture*, ed. Chris Mounsey, 225–54 (Lewisburg, PA: Bucknell University Press, 2001).

7. Discussions of the generic complications of *Eovaai* are found in three important essays: Earla A. Wilputte, "The Textual Architecture of Eliza Haywood's *Adventures of Eovaai*," *Essays in Literature* 22 (Spring 1995): 31–44; Srinivas Aravamudan, "In the Wake of the Novel: The Oriental Tale as National Allegory," *NOVEL: A Forum on Fiction* 33, no. 1 (1999): 5–31; and Ros Ballaster, "A Gender of Opposition: Eliza Haywood's Scandal Fiction," in *The Passionate Fictions of Eliza Haywood*, ed. Kirsten T. Saxton and Rebecca P. Bocchicchio, 143–67 (Lexington: University Press of Kentucky, 2000). Wilputte's pathbreaking essay offers an important assessment of *Eovaai*'s formal complexities and multiple layers of narration. Aravamudan explores the genre of the oriental tale using *Eovaai* as a case study, concluding that the oriental romance contests notions of a hegemonic realism constitutive of British fiction. Ballaster trenchantly examines the complex layering of voices and unreliability of narration and translation, supplementing her briefer treatment in *Fabulous Orients: Fictions of the East in England, 1662–1785* (Oxford: Oxford University Press, 2005), 223–25.

8. Eliza Haywood, *The Adventures of Eovaai*, ed. Earla Wilputte (Peterborough, ON: Broadview, 1999), 94. Hereafter cited parenthetically in the text by page numbers in this edition.

9. See Margaret Cavendish, *Sociable Letters*, ed. James Fitzmaurice (New York: Routledge, 2004), 25, discussed in chapter 1. For a discussion of European conceptions of lawlessness in the New World, see, for example, Carl Schmitt, *The Nomos of the Earth in the International Law of the Jus Publicum Europaeum*, trans. G. L. Ulmen (New York: Telos, 2003), 92–96.

10. My thinking on this point is influenced by Carole Pateman, *The Sexual Contract* (Stanford: Stanford University Press, 1988). Shea Stuart notes the difficulty of accommodating women to developing notions about the original political contract, in "Subversive Didacticism in Eliza Haywood's *Betsy Thoughtless*," *SEL Studies in English Literature 1500–1900* 42, no. 3 (2002): 563.

11. Cf. the discussion of romance heroism in the preface to *The Secret History, of Queen Zarah, and the Zarazians, Being a Looking-Glass for*

——————— *in the Kingdom of Albigion*, by [Delarivier?] Manley (London, 1705): "The Heroes in the Ancient *Romances* have nothing in them that is Natural; all is unlimited in their Character; all their Advantages have Something Prodigious, and all their Actions Something that's Marvellous; in short, they are not Men.... The Heroes of the Modern Romances are better Characteriz'd, they give them Passions, Vertues or Vices, which resemble Humanity" (ix–x). The preface praises the ability to distinguish a complex of passions within a character; Haywood takes this principle farther, depicting conflicting passions within the princess that contrast sharply with the more monochromatic portraits of the major male characters. *The Secret History of Queen Zarah* is traditionally attributed to Delarivier Manley, but this attribution is disputed; see J. A. Downie, "What If Delarivier Manley Did Not Write *The Secret History of Queen Zarah*?" *Library* 5, no. 3 (2004): 247–64. Aravamudan notes that this preface is an unacknowledged translation from the French of Sieur Du Plaisir's commentary on Madame de Lafayette's *Princesse de Clèves*, in *Enlightenment Orientalism: Resisting the Rise of the Novel* (Chicago: University of Chicago Press, 2011), 26. See also Ros Ballaster's discussion in *Seductive Forms: Women's Amatory Fiction from 1684 to 1740* (Oxford, UK: Clarendon, 1992), 50–52. Victoria Kahn emphasizes Hobbes's association of the heroic and pastoral romance with absolutist Stuart politics; *Eovaai* extends those associations to encompass Britain's constitutional monarchy. Kahn, *Wayward Contracts: The Crisis of Political Obligation in England, 1640–1674* (Princeton: Princeton University Press, 2004), 141–47.

12. The reference to the "real state of emergency" is from Walter Benjamin, "Theses on the Philosophy of History," in *Illuminations*, ed. Hannah Arendt, 253–64 (New York: Schocken Books, 1968), 257.

13. A full discussion of the term *romance* is of course beyond the scope of this chapter. In the eighteenth century and today, it is often deployed by writers and critics as the antithesis of other forms of writing—historical, veridical, or "probable." See, for example, Michael McKeon, *The Origins of the English Novel, 1600–1740*, rev. ed. (Baltimore: Johns Hopkins University Press, 2002), 25–64, 212–55. Haywood, however, is not interested in dispassionately evaluating genres but rather in strategic manipulations of convention; the comingling of romance and "true history" or scandal chronicle in *Eovaai* is not an accidental hybridization but rather a pointed incongruity. For discussions of the seventeenth-century romance and its politics, see Annabel Patterson, *Censorship and Interpretation: The Conditions of Writing and Reading in Early Modern England* (Madison: University of Wisconsin Press, 1984); Paul Salzman, *English Prose Fiction, 1588–1700: A Critical History*

(Oxford, UK: Clarendon, 1985); and Steve Mentz, *Romance for Sale in Early Modern England: The Rise of Prose Fiction* (Aldershot, UK: Ashgate, 2006).

14. Kubek similarly argues that *Eovaai* describes the "natural" role of sexual desire and ambition in the development of an "autonomous and mature" female self ("Key to Stowe," 232).

15. Backscheider cites this section as characteristic of the "advice to princes" genre ("Shadow of an Author," 91).

16. For discussion of the figure of the Patriot King in the 1730s, see Christine Gerrard, *The Patriot Opposition to Walpole: Politics, Poetry, and National Myth, 1725–1742* (Oxford, UK: Clarendon, 1994), 194–223.

17. The text might be taken to imply that all the preceding monarchs were male, though this is not explicitly stated.

18. The distinction between despot and sovereign is fundamentally one of legitimacy: Hobbes's sovereign is authorized by liberal subjects through contractual agreement from which the sovereign is structurally excluded. The despot, or usurper, operates without contract, seizing power that is legally granted to a legitimate sovereign. Yet both are similar in that neither is answerable to any other legal authority; both stand outside the legally constituted order. Thomas Hobbes, *Leviathan*, ed. C. B. Macpherson (London: Penguin Books, 1978), 265–66; Giorgio Agamben, *Homo Sacer: Sovereign Power and Bare Life*, trans. Daniel Heller-Roazin (Stanford: Stanford University Press, 1998), 104–6.

19. Gerrard, *Patriot Opposition to Walpole*, 187. Bolingbroke may be represented in the text by the figure of Alhahuza, whose praise for virtuous monarchy and critique of luxury echoes Bolingbroke's writings (Kubek, "Key to Stowe," 230–31, 244–45).

20. On the importance of curiosity in Haywood's fiction and in the emergence of fictional categories more generally, see Kathryn R. King, "Spying upon the Conjurer: Haywood, Curiosity, and 'The Novel' in the 1720s," *Studies in the Novel* 30, no. 2 (1998): 178–93. King's remarks, which anticipated a reinvigorated inquiry into Haywood's sophistication as a self-reflexive author, note the sense of play and ironic indeterminacy in her earlier writings—traits characteristic of *Eovaai* as well.

21. Giorgio Agamben, *State of Exception*, trans. Kevin Attell (Chicago: University of Chicago Press, 2005), 48.

22. Haywood idiosyncratically uses the spelling "genii" as both singular and plural; I have retained her practice.

23. To be sure, the arbitrary command is a common romance trope, and not always given to women; see, for example, the Green Knight's command to Sir Gawain in *Sir Gawain and the Green Knight*, in Malcolm Andrew and Ronald Waldron, eds., *The Poems of the Pearl Manu-*

script, 208–300 (Berkeley: University of California Press, 1979). I am indebted to Manushag Powell for pointing out this example to me. Haywood's use of this topos, however, is decidedly gendered.

24. Wilputte notes in her edition that "the Leviathan" was a satirical epithet for Walpole; see, for example, the 1729 ballad "The Honest Jury, or, Caleb Triumphant," which celebrates Bolingbroke's victory in his libel trial. Nicholas Amhearst, ed., *A Collection of Poems on Several Occasions; Publish'd in the Craftsman* (London, 1731), 67–70. This association perhaps conflates the Leviathan as an image of Hobbesian absolutism with a somewhat older usage of the term that describes a man of vast power and wealth. *Oxford English Dictionary*, 2nd ed., 20 vols. (Oxford: Oxford University Press, 1989), s.v. "Leviathan n^1."

25. Kubek instead reads the (female) genii as a complex condensation of Patriot Whig iconography and motherly power ("Key to Stowe," 238–40). Kubek's argument is powerful but misses interesting valences of the sequence that are illuminated by the narrative's debt to the colonial archive.

26. Eovaai's magical telescope is perhaps also inspired by a similar instrument belonging to Prince Ali in Prince Ahmed's tale; see *Arabian Nights' Entertainments*, ed. Robert Mack (Oxford: Oxford University Press, 1995), 826–30. However, the functions of the two glasses in their respective tales are quite different, as Ali's telescope neither transforms nor enlightens him.

27. *Parrot* 7 (1746); reprinted in *Selected Works of Eliza Haywood*, ed. Christine Blouch, Alexander Pettit, and Rebecca Sayers Hanson, series 2, vol. 1 (London: Pickering & Chatto, 2000–2001), 270. Hereafter cited parenthetically in the text by page numbers in this edition.

28. The passage suggests but does not explicitly state that the young woman is a slave herself.

29. Mary Astell, "Reflections upon Marriage," in *Astell: Political Writings*, ed. Patricia Springborg, 1–80 (Cambridge: Cambridge University Press, 1996), 61–75.

30. See Manushag Powell, "Parroting and the Periodical: Women's Speech, Haywood's *Parrot*, and Its Antecedents," *Tulsa Studies in Women's Literature* 27, no. 1 (2008): 63–91.

31. The figural connection between optical technologies and reason is of long standing. Cf. Margaret Cavendish, *The Worlds Olio* (London, 1655), 100: "The Brain is like a Perspective-glass, and the Understanding is the Eye to discover the Truth, Follies, and Falsehood in the World." Haywood advocates the use of optical technology as part of female education. For discussion of optics in relation to gendered gazes and

female subject formation, see Juliette Merritt, *Beyond Spectacle: Eliza Haywood's Female Spectators* (Toronto: University of Toronto Press, 2004); for an incisive discussion of optics in another crucial Haywood text, see Rivka Swenson, "Optics, Gender, and the Eighteenth-Century Gaze: Looking at Eliza Haywood's *Anti-Pamela*," *Eighteenth Century: Theory and Interpretation* 51, nos. 1–2 (2010): 27–43. For a discussion of the complex gendered valences of the microscope, see Deborah Needleman Armintor, "The Sexual Politics of Microscopy in Brobdingnag," *SEL Studies in English Literature 1500–1900* 47, no. 3 (2007): 619–40.

32. Haywood's literary corpus does not always emphasize male physical power. Nicola Graves has suggested that Haywood is in sympathy with Hobbes in perceiving a fundamental equality between men and women in the state of nature, citing Haywood's revenge narratives as evidence that violence is a zone of "equality between the sexes that has ... the potential to be the foundation for new relations between men and women." Graves, "'Injury for Injury'; or, 'The Lady's Revenge': Female Vengeance in Eliza Haywoood's *Female Spectator*," in Newman and Wright, *Fair Philosopher*, 159. In *Eovaai*, however, women's capacity for violence is nowhere on display, and women remain vulnerable to masculine force.

33. Viscount Bolingbroke (Henry St. John), "The Idea of a Patriot King" (1738), in *Political Writings*, ed. David Armitage, 217–94 (Cambridge: Cambridge University Press, 1997), 257.

34. For a comment on the republicanism of this sequence, see Frank Palmeri, *Satire, History, Novel: Narrative Forms, 1665–1815* (Newark: University of Delaware Press, 2003), 224.

35. For numerous examples of this rhetoric, see Gerrard, *Patriot Opposition to Walpole*, as well as Bertrand A. Goldgar, *Walpole and the Wits: The Relation of Politics to Literature, 1722–1742* (Lincoln: University of Nebraska Press, 1976).

36. For discussion of the concept of the balance of power, see the previous chapter. The formulation of Haywood's republican is intriguing for its omission of the other estate—the aristocracy, or the "few," often seen as a key balance against potential alliances of demagogic tyrants and the servile multitude.

37. Ballaster suggests that *Eovaai* links republicanism and misogyny through the figure of the commentator Hahehahotu, who expresses sympathy for both extreme republican and misogynist traditions. This is surely correct, but I think the more remarkable feature of the passage is the cogency of the republican's critique of other political systems without any proper explanation of how his own functions. Ballaster, "Gender of Opposition," 159.

38. Haywood very possibly had pro-Jacobite sympathies in the wake of the 1745 uprising, but *Eovaai* provides only thin justification for any Jacobitism at this early stage. Kathryn King treats the question of Haywood's Jacobite affiliations comprehensively in *A Political Biography of Eliza Haywood*, 177–91. For a note on Haywood's arrest for pro-Jacobite sedition in the late 1740s, see Catherine Ingrassia, "Additional Information about Eliza Haywood's 1749 Arrest for Seditious Libel," *Notes and Queries* 42, no. 2 (1997): 202–3. We might observe, however, that the Walpole figure, Ochihatou, commits suicide by bashing his head into an oak tree—the oak being one of Jacobitism's most salient icons. See also Powell, "Parroting," 65; and Rachel Carnell, "The Very Scandal of Her Tea Table: Eliza Haywood's Response to the Whig Public Sphere," in Mounsey, *Presenting Gender*, 255–73. Marta Kvande offers a distinctive treatment of Haywood's political fiction in "The Outsider Narrator in Eliza Haywood's Political Novels," *SEL Studies in English Literature 1500–1900* 43, no. 3 (2003): 625–43. Kvande is perceptive in seeing the category of the outside or the exterior as crucial to Haywood's political writing, but I would argue that she misses the mark in seeing Haywood's narrator in this text, at least, as being clearly distinct from the contaminated values of the diagetic world of the fiction.

39. It thus seems not quite correct to say with Backscheider that the reader is well-versed in Eovaai's and Adelhu's "theory and practice of government" by the narrative's end ("Shadow," 92). The political views and practices of these characters are more slippery than at first appears. Kubek notes that the "fairy-tale" qualities of the narrative's end are in accord with Lord Bolingbroke's own mythology of the "patriot king," but does not consider the possibility that this echoing might have a satiric bent ("Key," 230–32).

40. Eliza Haywood, *The Invisible Spy*, 4 vols. (London, 1755), 1:20. Hereafter cited parenthetically in the text by volume and pages numbers in this edition, unless otherwise noted.

41. The most thorough account of *The Invisible Spy* is found in Anthony Pollock, *Gender and the Fictions of the Public Sphere, 1690–1755* (New York: Routledge, 2009), 147–83. Pollock's argument has profoundly influenced my thinking in this section, but I hope to use his analysis to make more specific connections to the politics of magical objects and narratives of civility that I have been discussing.

42. For discussion of the Marriage Act and population, see Eve Tavor Bannet, "The Marriage Act of 1753: 'A Most Cruel Law for the Fair Sex,'" *Eighteenth-Century Studies* 30, no. 3 (1997): 233–54. The Jewish Naturalization Act is discussed in relation to nationhood in Todd M. Endelman, *The Jews of Britain, 1656 to 2000* (Berkeley: University of

California Press, 2002), 69–76; Dana Y. Rabin, "The Jew Bill of 1753: Masculinity, Virility, and the Nation," *Eighteenth-Century Studies* 39, no. 2 (2006): 157–71. The rhetoric of anti-Semitism in Great Britain in this period could at times collapse distinctions between Jews and other, more "savage" races; Jews are compared to "Negroes" in J. E., *Some Considerations on the Naturalization of the Jews; and How Far the Publick Will Benefit from This Hopeful Race of Israelites* (London, 1753), quoted in James Shapiro, *Shakespeare and the Jews* (New York: Columbia University Press, 1996), 197. Haywood does use anti-Semitic stereotyping elsewhere in *The Invisible Spy*, as S. Vida Muse notes; the implications of these racist gestures are beyond the scope of this chapter, however. Muse, "Eliza Haywood and the Jew Bill," *Notes and Queries* 57 (2010): 105–8.

43. Delarivier Manley, *The New Atlantis*, ed. Rosalind Ballaster (London: Pickering & Chatto, 1991), 9; Eliza Haywood, *Memoirs of a Certain Island Adjacent to the Kingdom of Utopia* (London, 1725; facsimile edition, New York: Garland, 1972), 243.

44. As Marc Shell notes, earlier versions of this story describe Gyges as an aristocrat. Shell, "The Ring of Gyges," *Mississippi Review* 17, nos. 1–2 (1989): 34.

45. Plato, *The Republic of Plato: An Ideal Commonwealth*, trans. Benjamin Jowett, rev. ed. (1901; repr., New York: Modern Library, 1941), 47–50. The tale is related in similar terms by Cicero in *De Officiis*; most eighteenth-century readers would be more familiar with this text.

46. Plato, *Republic*, 48.

47. Gyges's ring is also referenced by Addison in *The Tatler*, no. 243 (October 28, 1710), in Joseph Addison and Richard Steele, *The Tatler: Selected Essays*, ed. Alex Charles Ewald (London: Frederick Warne, 1888), 407–10. Addison's Isaac Bickerstaff uses the ring to spy on various foibles of the town, joking at the end of the essay that he ought to gift the ring to "the author of the 'Atalantis'" (410).

48. Keith Thomas has noted that English magical practices of the seventeenth century and earlier used at times the bodies of virgin children in tandem with talismans to act as clairvoyants and crystal gazers. Thomas, *Religion and the Decline of Magic* (New York: Charles Scribner's Sons, 1971), 215.

49. Pollock, *Gender and the Fictions of the Public Sphere*, 170.

50. The most detailed discussion of this aspect of the text is found in ibid., 147–83. Kathryn King also notes the way that Exploralibus's dependence on the girl suggests a masculine dependence on a "perverse" ideal of feminine innocence, which is in turn suggestive of "the ambiguous interplay of sexual virtue and artistic creativity" (*Political Biography of Eliza Haywood*, 196).

51. Frances E. Dolan, *Marriage and Violence: The Early Modern Legacy* (Philadelphia: University of Pennsylvania Press, 2009).
52. King, *Political Biography of Eliza Haywood*, 197.
53. Pollock, *Gender and the Fictions of the Public Sphere*, 175–76.
54. Sara Suleri has argued that imperial rhetoric often follows this pattern of exposure and evasion—the turning away from an atrocity that one recognizes. Suleri, *The Rhetoric of English India* (Chicago: University of Chicago Press, 1993), 62.
55. The relevant sections appear in *The Invisible Spy* (London, 1759), 2:288–90; and *The Invisible Spy* (Dublin, 1768), 2:324–27. These are not the only changes to the posthumous editions; while some sections and chapters were probably cut in order to compress the text into two volumes, one passage discusses Catholicism and Jacobitism, suggesting thematic as well as logistical reasons for the edits.
56. King, *Political Biography of Eliza Haywood*, 9.

CODA: ENEMIES

1. Carl Schmitt, *The Concept of the Political*, trans. George Schwab (Chicago: University of Chicago Press, 1996), 26.
2. *The Onion*, February 5, 2013, http://www.theonion.com/articles/american-citizens-split-on-doj-memo-authorizing-go,31207/.
3. *Beauty's Triumph; or, The Superiority of the Fair Sex Invincibly Proved; Wherein the Arguments for the Natural Right of Man to a Sovereign Authority over the Woman Are Fairly Urged, and Undeniably Refuted; and the Undoubted Title of the Ladies, Even to a Superiority over the Men Both in Head and Heart, Is Clearly Evinced; Shewing Their Minds to Be as Much More Beautiful than the Mens as Their Bodies; and That, If They Had the Same Advantages of Education, They Would Excel Their Tyrants as Much in Sense as They Do in Virtue; in Three Parts, the Whole Interspers'd with a Delightful Variety of Characters, Which Some of the Most Celebrated Heroes and Heroines of the Present Time Have Had the Goodness to Sit For* (London, 1751), 37.
4. Mary Poovey, *A History of the Modern Fact: Problems of Knowledge in the Sciences of Wealth and Society* (Chicago: University of Chicago Press, 1998), 218–48.
5. Giorgio Agamben, *State of Exception*, trans. Kevin Attell (Chicago: University of Chicago Press, 2005); Judith Butler, *Precarious Life: The Powers of Mourning and Violence* (London: Verso, 2004), 50–100; Marc Redfield, *The Rhetoric of Terror: Reflections on 9/11 and the War on Terror* (New York: Fordham University Press, 2009), 69.

6. Schmitt, *Concept of the Political*, 32, 46–48.

7. Ibid., 79; William Rasch, "Lines in the Sand: Enmity as a Structuring Principle," *South Atlantic Quarterly* 104, no. 2 (2005): 253–62.

8. "Were the target of a lethal operation a U.S. citizen who may have rights under the Due Process Clause and the Fourth Amendment, that individual's citizenship would not immunize him [*sic*] from a lethal operation." United States Department of Justice, *Lawfulness of a Lethal Operation Directed against a U.S. Citizen Who Is a Senior Operational Leader of Al-Qa'ida or an Associated Force*, white paper, 2012, 2, available online at http://msnbcmedia.msn.com/i/msnbc/sections/news/020413_DOJ_White_Paper.pdf (accessed February 9, 2012).

9. Achille Mbembe, "Necropolitics," *Public Culture* 15, no. 1 (2003): 11–12.

10. Ian Baucom, "The Disasters of War: On Inimical Life," *Polygraph* 18 (2006): 166–90; Baucom, "Cicero's Ghost: The Atlantic, the Enemy, and the Laws of War," in *States of Emergency: The Object of American Studies*, ed. Russ Castronovo and Susan Gillman, 124–42 (Chapel Hill: University of North Carolina Press, 2009).

11. Hugo Grotius, *The Rights of War and Peace*, ed. Richard Tuck, 3 vols. (Indianapolis: Liberty Fund, 2005), 2:1021–24. Hereafter cited parenthetically in the text to volume and page numbers in this edition.

12. David William Bates, *States of War: Enlightenment Origins of the Political* (New York: Columbia University Press, 2012), 125–30. See also Benjamin A. Kleinerman, "Can the Prince Really Be Tamed? Executive Prerogative, Popular Apathy, and the Constitutional Frame in Locke's *Second Treatise*," *American Political Science Review* 101, no. 2 (2007): 209–22.

13. John Locke, *Two Treatises of Government*, ed. Peter Laslett, 2nd ed. (Cambridge: Cambridge University Press, 1967), 292.

14. William Rasch, "Human Rights as Geopolitics: Carl Schmitt and the Legal Form of American Supremacy," *Cultural Critique* 54, no. 1 (2003): 136–37.

15. For a discussion of bills of attainder as a key marker of Parliamentary sovereignty, see Robert J. Frankle, "Parliament's Right to Do Wrong: The Parliamentary Debate on the Bill of Attainder against Sir John Fenwick, 1696," *Parliamentary History* 4, no. 1 (1985): 71–85. Fenwick, a Jacobite conspirator, was convicted of treason by Parliamentary fiat after it became clear that a legal proceeding against him would be unlikely to yield a conviction. He was beheaded in 1697.

16. Richard West, *A Discourse Concerning Treasons and Bills of Attainder* (London, 1716).

17. For details on the Popish Plot and in particular the treason trials, see John Kenyon, *The Popish Plot* (London: William Heinemann, 1972).

18. *The History of the Rise, Progress, and Extinction of the Late Rebellion in Scotland* (Edinburgh, 1759), 147; Josiah Owen, *The Humourist; or, An Entertaining Display of the Absurdities of the Roman Catholicks and Nonjurors* (London, 1752), 11.

19. George Masters, *A Poem Humbly Inscribed to His Royal Highness the Duke of Cumberland, on His Defeat of the Rebels at Culloden, April 16, 1746* (London, 1747), 25.

20. Geoffrey Plank, *Rebellion and Savagery: The Jacobite Rising of 1745 and the British Empire*, Early American Studies (Philadelphia: University of Pennsylvania Press, 2006), 63 (Chesterfield's comments), 70 (exterminationist rhetoric).

21. Ibid., 175–80.

22. Chantal Mouffe, "Carl Schmitt and the Paradox of Liberal Democracy," in *The Challenge of Carl Schmitt*, ed. Chantal Mouffe, 38–53 (London: Verso, 1999), 43–44.

23. Barry Unsworth, *Sacred Hunger* (New York: Norton, 1993). Hereafter cited parenthetically in the text.

24. Daniel Defoe, *Robinson Crusoe* (1719), ed. J. Donald Crowley (Oxford: Oxford University Press, 1983), 53.

25. Redfield, *Rhetoric of Terror*, 95.

26. Butler, *Precarious Life*, 19–49.

Bibliography

Sources marked ECCO refer to Eighteenth-Century Collections Online, Gale Group; sources marked EEBO refer to Early English Books Online, Chadwick, ProQuest.

Acuña, Cristóbal de, du Biscay Acarete, and Jean Grillet. *Voyages and Discoveries in South-America: The First Up the River of Amazons to Quito in Peru, and Back Again to Brazil, . . . the Whole Illustrated with Notes and Maps.* London, 1698.

Adas, Michael. *Machines as the Measure of Men: Science, Technology, and Ideologies of Western Dominance.* Ithaca: Cornell University Press, 1989.

Addison, Joseph. *An Answer to a Pamphlet Entituled, An Argument to Prove the Affections of the People of England to Be the Best Security of the Government.* Edinburgh, 1716.

Addison, Joseph, and Richard Steele. *The Guardian.* Edited by John Calhoun Stephens. Lexington: University Press of Kentucky, 1982.

———. *The Spectator.* Edited by Donald F. Bond. 5 vols. Oxford, UK: Clarendon, 1965.

———. *The Tatler: Selected Essays.* Edited by Alex Charles Ewald. London: Frederick Warne, 1888.

Africanus, Leo. *A Geographical Historie of Africa . . . Before Which, Out of the Best Ancient and Moderne Writers, Is Prefixed a Generall Description of Africa, and Also a Particular Treatise of All the Maine Lands and Isles Undescribed by Iohn Leo.* Translated by John Pory. London, 1600.

Agamben, Giorgio. *Homo Sacer: Sovereign Power and Bare Life.* Translated by Daniel Heller-Roazin. Stanford: Stanford University Press, 1998.

———. *State of Exception.* Translated by Kevin Attell. Chicago: University of Chicago Press, 2005.

Agnew, John A., and Stuart Corbridge. *Mastering Space: Hegemony, Territory and International Political Economy.* London: Routledge, 1995.

Amhearst, Nicholas, ed. *A Collection of Poems on Several Occasions; Publish'd in the Craftsman.* London, 1731.

Andrew, Malcolm, and Ronald Waldron, eds. *The Poems of the Pearl Manuscript.* Berkeley: University of California Press, 1979.

Anghiera, Pietro Martire d'. *De Novo Orbe, or the Historie of the West Indies, Contayning the Actes and Adventures of the Spanyardes, Which Have Conquered and Peopled Those Countries, Inriched with Varietie of Pleasant Relation of the Manners, Ceremonies, Lawes, Governments, and Warres of the Indians; Comprised in Eight Decades; Written by Peter Martyr a Millanoise of Angleria . . . Whereof Three, Have Beene Formerly Translated into English, by R. Eden, Whereunto the Other Five, Are Newly Added by the Industrie, and Painefull Travaile of M. Lok Gent.* London, 1612.

Arabian Nights' Entertainments. Edited by Robert L. Mack. Oxford: Oxford University Press, 1995.

Aravamudan, Srinivas. *Enlightenment Orientalism: Resisting the Rise of the Novel.* Chicago: University of Chicago Press, 2011.

———. "Hobbes and America." In *The Postcolonial Enlightenment: Eighteenth-Century Colonialism and Postcolonial Theory*, edited by Lynn Festa and Daniel Carey, 37–70. Oxford: Oxford University Press, 2009.

———. "In the Wake of the Novel: The Oriental Tale as National Allegory." *NOVEL: A Forum on Fiction* 33, no. 1 (1999): 5–31.

———. "Subjects/Sovereigns/Rogues." *Eighteenth-Century Studies* 40, no. 3 (2007): 457–65.

———. *Tropicopolitans: Colonialism and Agency, 1688–1804.* Durham: Duke University Press, 1999.

———. "'The Unity of the Representer': Reading *Leviathan* against the Grain." *South Atlantic Quarterly* 104, no. 4 (2005): 631–53.

Armintor, Deborah Needleman. "The Sexual Politics of Microscopy in Brobdingnag." *SEL Studies in English Literature 1500–1900* 47, no. 3 (2007): 619–40.

Armitage, David. *The Ideological Origins of the British Empire.* Cambridge: Cambridge University Press, 2000.

Armstrong, Philip. *What Animals Mean in the Fiction of Modernity.* London: Routledge, 2008.

Arneil, Barbara. "The Wild Indian's Venison: Locke's Theory of Property and English Colonialism in America." *Political Studies* 44 (1996): 60–74.

Ashley, Maurice. *General Monck*. London: J. Cape, 1977.
Astell, Mary. "Reflections upon Marriage." In *Astell: Political Writings*, edited by Patricia Springborg, 1–80. Cambridge: Cambridge University Press, 1996.
Athey, Stephanie, and Daniel Cooper Alarcón. "*Oroonoko*'s Gendered Economies of Honor/Horror: Reframing Colonial Discourse Studies in the Americas." *American Literature* 65, no. 3 (1993): 415–43.
Atkins, John. *A Voyage to Guinea, Brasil, and the West-Indies; in His Majesty's Ships the Swallow and Weymouth*. London, 1735.
Atterbury, Francis. *An Argument to Prove the Affections of the People of England to Be the Best Security of the Government; Humbly Offer'd to the Consideration of the Patrons of Severity, and Applied to the Present Juncture of Affairs*. [London], 1716.
Backscheider, Paula R. "The Shadow of an Author: Eliza Haywood." *Eighteenth-Century Fiction* 11, no. 1 (1998): 79–102.
———. *Spectacular Politics: Theatrical Power and Mass Culture in Early Modern England*. Baltimore: Johns Hopkins University Press, 1993.
Bacon, Francis. *The New Organon and Related Writings*. Edited by Fulton H. Anderson. New York: Liberal Arts Press, 1960.
Bailey, Maj. Gen. Jonathan B. A. *Field Artillery and Firepower*. 2nd ed. Annapolis, MD: Naval Institute Press, 2004.
Baine, Rodney M. *Daniel Defoe and the Supernatural*. Athens: University of Georgia Press, 1969.
Balakrishnan, Gopal. *The Enemy: An Intellectual Portrait of Carl Schmitt*. London: Verso, 2000.
Ballaster, Ros. *Fabulous Orients: Fictions of the East in England, 1662–1785*. Oxford: Oxford University Press, 2005.
———. "A Gender of Opposition: Eliza Haywood's Scandal Fiction." In *The Passionate Fictions of Eliza Haywood*, edited by Kirsten T. Saxton and Rebecca P. Bocchicchio, 143–67. Lexington: University Press of Kentucky, 2000.
———. *Seductive Forms: Women's Amatory Fiction from 1684 to 1740*. Oxford, UK: Clarendon, 1992.
Bannet, Eve Tavor. "The Marriage Act of 1753: 'A Most Cruel Law for the Fair Sex.'" *Eighteenth-Century Studies* 30, no. 3 (1997): 233–54.
Barker, Francis, Peter Hulme, and Margaret Iversen, eds. *Cannibalism and the Colonial World*. Cambridge: Cambridge University Press, 1998.
Barlow, Frank. *The Norman Conquest and Beyond*. London: Hambledon, 1983.
Baron, Robert. *Mirza: A Tragedie, Really Acted in Persia, in the Last Age: Illustrated with Historicall Annotations*. London, 1647. EEBO.

Barrell, John. *Imagining the King's Death: Figurative Treason, Fantasies of Regicide, 1793–1796*. Oxford: Oxford University Press, 2000.
Bates, David William. *States of War: Enlightenment Origins of the Political*. New York: Columbia University Press, 2012.
Bates, J. *Two (United) Are Better than One Alone: A Thanksgiving Sermon upon the Union of the Two Kingdoms of England and Scotland, Preach'd at Hackney, May 1, 1707*. London, 1707.
Battigelli, Anna. *Margaret Cavendish and the Exiles of the Mind*. Lexington: University Press of Kentucky, 1998.
———. "Political Thought / Political Action: Margaret Cavendish's Hobbesian Dilemma." In *Women Writers and the Early Modern British Political Tradition*, edited by Hilda L. Smith, 40–55. Cambridge: Cambridge University Press, 1998.
Baucom, Ian. "Cicero's Ghost: The Atlantic, the Enemy, and the Laws of War." In *States of Emergency: The Object of American Studies*, edited by Russ Castronovo and Susan Gillman, 124–42. Chapel Hill: University of North Carolina Press, 2009.
———. "The Disasters of War: On Inimical Life." *Polygraph* 18 (2006): 166–90.
Beach, Adam R. "Anti-Colonist Discourse, Tragicomedy, and the 'American' Behn." *Comparative Drama* 38, nos. 2–3 (2004): 213–33.
Beasley-Murray, Jon. "The Common Enemy: Tyrants and Pirates." *South Atlantic Quarterly* 104, no. 2 (2005): 217–25.
Beauty's Triumph; or, The Superiority of the Fair Sex Invincibly Proved; Wherein the Arguments for the Natural Right of Man to a Sovereign Authority over the Woman Are Fairly Urged, and Undeniably Refuted; and the Undoubted Title of the Ladies, Even to a Superiority over the Men Both in Head and Heart, Is Clearly Evinced; Shewing Their Minds to Be as Much More Beautiful than the Mens as Their Bodies; and That, If They Had the Same Advantages of Education, They Would Excel Their Tyrants as Much in Sense as They Do in Virtue; in Three Parts, the Whole Interspers'd with a Delightful Variety of Characters, Which Some of the Most Celebrated Heroes and Heroines of the Present Time Have Had the Goodness to Sit For. London, 1751.
Behn, Aphra. *Abedelazer; or, The Moor's Revenge*. London, 1677.
———. *The Works of Aphra Behn*. Edited by Janet Todd. 7 vols. Columbus: Ohio State University Press, 1992–96.
Beier, A. L. *Masterless Men: The Vagrancy Problem in Britain, 1560–1640*. London: Methuen, 1985.
Bellamy, John. *The Tudor Law of Treason: An Introduction*. London: Routledge & Kegan Paul, 1979.

Bender, John. *Imagining the Penitentiary: Fiction and the Architecture of Mind in Eighteenth-Century England*. Chicago: University of Chicago Press, 1987.
Benjamin, Walter. "Critique of Violence." In *Walter Benjamin: Selected Writings Volume I, 1913–1926*, 5th ed., edited by Marcus Bullock and Michael W. Jennings, 236–52. Cambridge: Belknap Press of Harvard University Press, 1996.
———. "Theses on the Philosophy of History." In *Illuminations*, edited by Hannah Arendt, 253–64. New York: Schocken Books, 1968.
Bevington, David M., and Peter Holbrook. Introduction to *The Politics of the Stuart Court Masque*, edited by David M. Bevington and Peter Holbrook, 1–19. Cambridge: Cambridge University Press, 1998.
Bhabha, Homi. *The Location of Culture*. London: Routledge, 1994.
Bialuschewski, Arne. "Pirates, Slavers, and the Indigenous Population in Madagascar, c. 1690–1715." *International Journal of African Historical Studies* 38, no. 3 (2005): 401–25.
Black, Jeremy. *European Warfare, 1453–1815*. New York: St. Martin's, 1999.
———. *European Warfare, 1660–1815*. New Haven: Yale University Press, 1994.
Blewett, David. *The Illustration of "Robinson Crusoe": 1719–1920*. Gerrards Cross, UK: Colin Smythe, 1995.
Blount, Charles. *An Appeal from the Country to the City for the Preservation of His Majesties Person, Liberty, Property, and the Protestant Religion*. [London?], 1679.
Bodin, Jean. *On Sovereignty: Four Chapters from Six Books on the Commonwealth*. Edited and translated by Julian H. Franklin. Cambridge: Cambridge University Press, 1992.
Bolingbroke, Viscount (Henry St. John). *Political Writings*. Edited by David Armitage. Cambridge: Cambridge University Press, 1997.
Bosman, Willem. *A New and Accurate Description of the Coast of Guinea, Divided into the Gold, the Slave, and the Ivory Coasts*. London, 1705.
Bostridge, Ian. "Music, Reason, and Politeness: Magic and Witchcraft in the Career of George Frideric Handel." In *Civil Histories: Essays Presented to Sir Keith Thomas*, edited by Peter Burke, Brian Harrison, and Paul Slack, 251–63. Oxford: Oxford University Press, 2000.
Boucher, Philip P. *Cannibal Encounters: Europeans and Island Caribs, 1492–1763*. Baltimore: Johns Hopkins University Press, 1992.
Bowerbank, Sylvia, and Sara Mendelson. Introduction to *Paper Bodies: A Margaret Cavendish Reader*, 9–34. Peterborough, ON: Broadview, 2000.

Boyle, Deborah. "Fame, Virtue, and Government: Margaret Cavendish on Ethics and Politics." *Journal of the History of Ideas* 67, no. 2 (2006): 251–89.

Boyle, Robert. *Some Considerations Touching the Usefulness of Experimental Natural Philosophy: Propos'd in a Familiar Discourse to a Friend, by Way of Invitation to the Study of It.* Oxford, UK, 1664.

Brewer, John, and Susan Staves, eds. *Early Modern Conceptions of Property.* London: Routledge, 1996.

Brooks-Davies, Douglas. *The Mercurian Monarch: Magical Politics from Spencer to Pope.* Manchester: Manchester University Press, 1983.

Brown, Kathleen M. *Good Wives, Nasty Wenches, and Anxious Patriarchs: Gender, Race, and Power in Colonial Virginia.* Chapel Hill: University of North Carolina Press, 1996.

Brown, Laura. *Ends of Empire: Women and Ideology in Early Eighteenth-Century English Literature.* Ithaca: Cornell University Press, 1993.

———. *Fables of Modernity: Literature and Culture in the English Eighteenth Century.* Ithaca: Cornell University Press, 2001.

———. "The Romance of Empire: *Oroonoko* and the Trade in Slaves." In *The New Eighteenth Century: Theory, Politics, English Literature,* edited by Laura Brown and Felicity Nussbaum, 41–61. New York: Methuen, 1987.

Burrage, Henry S., ed. *Early English and French Voyages, Chiefly from Hakluyt.* New York: Charles Scribner's Sons, 1906.

Butler, Judith. *Precarious Life: The Powers of Mourning and Violence.* London: Verso, 2004.

Butler, Martin. "Courtly Negotiations." In *The Politics of the Stuart Court Masque,* edited by David Bevington and Peter Holbrook, 20–40. Cambridge: Cambridge University Press, 1998.

Butler, Todd. *Imagination and Politics in Seventeenth-Century England.* Aldershot, UK: Ashgate, 2008.

Calder, Martin. *Encounters with the Other: A Journey to the Limits of Language through Works by Rousseau, Defoe, Prévost and Graffigny.* Amsterdam: Rodopi, 2003.

Campbell, Gwyn. *An Economic History of Imperial Madagascar, 1750–1895: The Rise and Fall of an Island Empire.* Cambridge: Cambridge University Press, 2005.

Canfield, J. Douglas, and Maja-Lisa von Sneidern, eds. *The Broadview Anthology of Restoration and Early Eighteenth-Century Drama.* Peterborough, ON: Broadview, 2001.

Carey, Daniel. "Reading Contrapuntally: *Robinson Crusoe,* Slavery, and Postcolonial Theory." In *Postcolonial Enlightenment: Eighteenth-*

Century Colonialism and Postcolonial Theory, edited by Daniel Carey and Lynn Festa, 105–36. Oxford: Oxford University Press, 2009.

Carey, Daniel, and Lynn Festa, eds. *The Postcolonial Enlightenment: Eighteenth-Century Colonialism and Postcolonial Theory*. Oxford: Oxford University Press, 2009.

Carey, Daniel, and Claire Jowitt. Introduction to *Richard Hakluyt and Travel Writing in Early Modern Europe*, edited by Daniel Carey and Claire Jowitt, 1–10. Hakluyt Society Extra Series 47. Burlington, VT: Ashgate, 2012.

Carnell, Rachel. "The Very Scandal of Her Tea Table: Eliza Haywood's Response to the Whig Public Sphere." In *Presenting Gender: Changing Sex in Early-Modern Culture*, edited by Chris Mounsey, 255–73. Lewisburg, PA: Bucknell University Press, 2001.

Casas, Bartolomé de las. *An Account of the First Voyages and Discoveries Made by the Spaniards in America; Containing the Most Exact Relation Hitherto Publish'd, of Their Unparallel'd Cruelties on the Indians, in the Destruction of Above Forty Millions of People; with the Propositions Offer'd to the King of Spain to Prevent the Further Ruin of the West-Indies / by Don Bartholomew De Las Casas, Bishop of Chiapa, Who Was an Eye-witness of Their Cruelties; Illustrated with Cuts; to Which Is Added, The Art of Travelling, Shewing How a Man May Dispose His Travels to the Best Advantage*. London, 1699. EEBO.

———. *Popery and Slavery Display'd; Containing the Character of Popery, and a Relation of Popish Cruelties, Including, the Spanish Butcheries on the Native Indians; the Persecution of the Waldenses, and Albigenses; of the Protestants in Bohemia, Other Parts of Germany, and in the Low-Countries, and Piedmont. . . .* London, 1699. EEBO.

Cavendish, Margaret. *The Blazing World and Other Writings*. Edited by Kate Lilley. London: William Pickering, 1992.

———. *Natures Picture Drawn by Fancies Pencil to the Life: Being Several Feigned Stories, Comical, Tragical, Tragi-comical, Poetical, Romantical, Philosophical, Historical, and Moral; Some in Verse, Some in Prose; Some Mixt, and Some by Dialogues*. London, 1671.

———. *Orations of Divers Sorts, Accommodated to Divers Places*. 2nd ed. London: Printed by A. Maxwell, 1668.

———. *Philosophical Letters: Or, Modest Reflections upon Some Opinions in Natural Philosophy*. London, 1664.

———. *Margaret Cavendish: Political Writings*. Edited by Susan James. Cambridge: Cambridge University Press, 2003.

———. *Sociable Letters*. Edited by James Fitzmaurice. New York: Routledge, 2004.

———. *The World's Olio*. London, 1655.

Chaplin, Joyce E. *Subject Matter: Technology, the Body, and Science on the Anglo-American Frontier, 1500–1676.* Cambridge: Harvard University Press, 2001.

Charles II. *A True Copy of a Commission, from the Late Kings Eldest Sonne, to Mr. William Davenant, Concerning Maryland, Etc.* (Given at Our Court in Jersey, the 16th Day of February, 16 50/49). London, 1653.

Chibka, Robert L. "'Oh! Do Not Fear a Woman's Invention': Truth, Falsehood, and Fiction in Aphra Behn's *Oroonoko.*" *Texas Studies in Literature and Language* 30, no. 4 (1988): 510–37.

Childs, John. *The Army of Charles II.* London: Routledge & Kegan Paul, 1976.

Churchill, John, and Awnsham Churchill, eds. *A Collection of Voyages and Travels, Some Now First Printed from Original Manuscripts; Others Translated Out of Foreign Languages, and Now First Publish'd in English; To Which Are Added Some Few That Have Formerly Appear'd in English, but Do Now for Their Excellency and Scarceness Deserve to Be Reprinted; In Four Volumes, with a General Preface, Giving an Account of the Progress of Navigation, from Its First Beginning . . . the Whole Illustrated with a Great Number of Useful Maps, and Cuts, All Engraven on Copper.* 4 vols. London, 1704.

———. *A Collection of Voyages and Travels, Some Now First Printed from Original Manuscripts, Others Now First Published in English; with a General Preface, Giving an Account of the Progress of Navigation, from Its First Beginning.* Rev. ed. 6 vols. London, 1732.

Cicero, Marcus Tullius. *De Inventione, De Optimo Genere Oratorum, Topica.* Translated by H. M. Hubbell. Loeb Classical Library. 1949. Reprint, Cambridge: Harvard University Press, 1968.

———. *De Officiis.* Translated by Walter Miller. London: William Heinemann, 1913.

Cipolla, Carlo M. *Guns, Sails, and Empires: Technological Innovation and the Early Phases of European Expansion, 1400–1700.* Manhattan, KS: Sunflower University Press, 1985.

Clifford, James Lowry. "Gulliver's Fourth Voyage: 'Hard' and 'Soft' Schools of Interpretation." In *Quick Springs of Sense: Studies in the Eighteenth Century,* edited by Larry S. Champion. Athens: University of Georgia Press, 1974.

Clucas, Stephen, ed. *A Princely Brave Woman: Essays on Margaret Cavendish, Duchess of Newcastle.* Aldershot, UK: Ashgate, 2003.

Connolly, William. *The Ethos of Pluralization.* Minneapolis: University of Minnesota Press, 1995.

Copenhaver, Brian. "Magic." In *The Cambridge History of Science*, vol. 3, *Early Modern Science*, edited by Katharine Park and Lorraine Daston, 518–40. Cambridge: Cambridge University Press, 2006.

Covington, Sarah. *Wounds, Flesh, and Metaphor in Seventeenth-Century England*. New York: Palgrave Macmillan, 2009.

Crone, G. R., Antonio Malfante, Diogo Gomes, João de Barros, and Alvise Cadamosto. *The Voyages of Cadamosto and Other Documents on Western Africa in the Second Half of the Fifteenth Century*. Nendeln, Liechtenstein: Kraus Reprint, 1967.

Cubitt, Geoffrey. "Introduction: Heroic Reputations and Exemplarity." In *Heroic Reputations and Exemplary Lives*, edited by Geoffrey Cubitt and Warren Allen, 1–26. Manchester: Manchester University Press, 2000.

Daston, Lorraine, and Katharine Park. *Wonders and the Order of Nature, 1150–1750*. Brooklyn, NY: Zone Books, 1998.

Davenant, William. *Britannia Triumphans: A Masque, Presented at White Hall, by the Kings Majestie and His Lords, on the Sunday after Twelfth-Night, 1637; by Inigo Iones Surveyor of His Majesties Workes, and William Davenant Her Majesties Servant*. London, 1638.

———. "Preface to *Gondibert*." In *Critical Essays of the Seventeenth Century*, edited by J. E. Spingarn, vol. 2, 1–53. Oxford, UK: Clarendon, 1908.

———. *A Proposition for Advancement of Morality, by a New Way of Entertainment of the People*. London, 1656.

———. *Salmacida Spolia: A Masque Presented by the King and Queenes Majesties, at White-Hall, on Tuesday the 21 Day of January 1639*. London, 1639. EEBO.

Davies, K. G. *The Royal African Company*. London: Longmans, Green, 1957.

de Beer, E. S. "Executions Following the 'Bloody Assize.'" *Bulletin of the Institute of Historical Research* 4, no. 10 (1926): 36–39.

Defoe, Daniel. *Augusta Triumphans; or, The Way to Make London the Most Flourishing City in the Universe; First, by Establishing an University . . . Concluding with an Effectual Method to Prevent Street Robberies; and a Letter to Coll. Robinson, on Account of the Orphan's Tax*. London, 1728. ECCO.

———. *Captain Singleton*. 1920. Edited by Shiv K. Kumar. Oxford: Oxford University Press, 1969.

———. *A Collection of the Writings of the Author of "The True-Born English-man."* London, 1703.

———. *Defoe's Review*. Edited by Arthur Wellesley Secord. 22 vols. Facsimile Text Society. Publication 44. New York: Columbia University Press, 1938.

———. *An Essay at Removing National Prejudices against a Union with Scotland*. London, 1706.

———. *An Essay upon the Trade to Africa, in Order to Set the Merits of That Cause in a True Light and Bring the Disputes between the African Company and the Separate Traders into a Narrower Compass*. London, 1711. ECCO.

———. *The Farther Adventures of Robinson Crusoe; Being the Second and Last Part of His Life, and the Strange Surprising Accounts of His Travels Round Three Parts of the Globe*. London, 1719.

———. *Jure Divino: A Satyr; in Twelve Books*. London, 1706.

———. *Memoirs of a Cavalier*. 1720. Edited by James T. Boulton. Oxford: Oxford University Press, 1991.

———. *A New Voyage Round the World*. Edited by John McVeagh. Vol. 10 of *The Novels of Daniel Defoe*. London: Pickering & Chatto, 2009.

———. *The Original Power of the Collective Body of the People of England, Examined and Asserted*. London, 1701.

———. *A Plan of the English Commerce: Being a Compleat Prospect of the Trade of This Nation, as Well the Home Trade as the Foreign; In Three Parts*. London, 1728.

———. *Political and Economic Writings of Daniel Defoe*. Edited by W. R. Owens and Philip Nicholas Furbank. 8 vols. London: Pickering & Chatto, 2000.

———. *Robinson Crusoe*. 1719. Edited by J. Donald Crowley. Oxford: Oxford University Press, 1983.

———. *Satire, Fantasy, and Writings on the Supernatural*. Edited by W. R. Owens and Philip Nicholas Furbank. 8 vols. London: Pickering & Chatto, 2003–2005.

———. *Serious Reflections during the Life and Surprising Adventures of Robinson Crusoe: With His Vision of the Angelick World*. London, 1720.

Derrida, Jacques. *The Beast and the Sovereign, Volume I*. Edited by Michel Lisse, Marie-Louise Mallet, and Ginette Michaud. Translated by Geoffrey Bennington. Chicago: University of Chicago Press, 2009.

———. "The Force of Law: The 'Mystical Foundation of Authority.'" *Cordoza Law Review* 11 (1990): 920–1045.

———. *Rogues: Two Essays on Reason*. Translated by Pascale-Anne Brault and Michael Naas. Stanford: Stanford University Press, 2005.

Diamond, Jared M. *Guns, Germs, and Steel: The Fates of Human Societies*. New York: Norton, 1997.

Dickinson, H. T. "The Representation of the People in Eighteenth-Century Britain." In *Realities of Representation: State Building in Early Modern Europe and European America*, edited by Maija Jansson, 19–44. New York: Palgrave Macmillan, 2007.

Dio, Cassius. *Dio's Roman History*. Translated by Earnest Cary. 9 vols. London: William Heinemann, 1914.

Dolan, Frances E. *Marriage and Violence: The Early Modern Legacy*. Philadelphia: University of Pennsylvania Press, 2009.

Donaldson, Peter S. *Machiavelli and Mystery of State*. Cambridge: Cambridge University Press, 1988.

Dowdell, Coby. "'A Living Law to Himself and Others': Daniel Defoe, Algernon Sidney, and the Politics of Self-Interest in *Robinson Crusoe* and *Farther Adventures*." *Eighteenth-Century Fiction* 22, no. 3 (2010): 415–42.

Downie, J. A. *Jonathan Swift, Political Writer*. London: Routledge & Kegan Paul, 1984.

———. "Swift and Jacobitism." *ELH* 64, no. 4 (1997): 887–901.

———. "What If Delarivier Manley Did Not Write *The Secret History of Queen Zarah*?" *Library* 5, no. 3 (2004): 247–64.

Doyle, Laura. *Freedom's Empire: Race and the Rise of the Novel in Atlantic Modernity, 1640–1940*. Durham: Duke University Press, 2008.

Dudley, Edward, and Maximillian E. Novak, eds. *The Wild Man Within: An Image in Western Thought from the Renaissance to Romanticism*. Pittsburgh: University of Pittsburgh Press, 1972.

Dunton, John. *The Young-Students-Library: Containing Extracts and Abridgments of the Most Valuable Books Printed in England, and in the Forreign Journals, from the Year Sixty Five, to This Time; To Which Is Added a New Essay upon All Sorts of Learning*. London, 1692.

Earle, Peter. *Monmouth's Rebels: The Road to Sedgemoor, 1685*. London: Weidenfeld and Nicolson, 1977.

Edie, Carolyn A. "The Public Face of Royal Ritual: Sermons, Medals, and Civic Ceremony in Later Stuart Coronations." *Huntington Library Quarterly* 53, no. 4 (1990): 311–36.

Edmond, Mary. *Rare Sir William Davenant: Poet Laureate, Playwright, Civil War General, Restoration Theatre Manager*. Manchester: Manchester University Press, 1987.

Ehrenpreis, Irvin. *Dean Swift*. Vol. 3 of *Swift: The Man, His Works, and the Age*. Cambridge: Harvard University Press, 1983.

———. *Dr. Swift*. Vol. 2 of *Swift: The Man, His Works, and the Age*. Cambridge: Harvard University Press, 1967.

Elias, Norbert. *The Civilizing Process.* Translated by Edmund Jephcott. Oxford, UK: Blackwell, 1994.

Ellenzweig, Sarah. *The Fringes of Belief: English Literature, Ancient Heresy, and the Politics of Freethinking, 1660–1760.* Stanford: Stanford University Press, 2008.

Ellis, Frank. Introduction to *A Discourse of the Contests and Dissentions between the Nobles and the Commons in Athens and Rome,* by Jonathan Swift, 1–79. Oxford, UK: Clarendon, 1967.

Ellis, Markman. "Crusoe, Cannibalism and Empire." In *Robinson Crusoe: Myths and Metamorphoses,* edited by Lieve Spaas and Brian Stimpson, 45–61. New York: St. Martin's, 1996.

Elmer, Jonathan. *On Lingering and Being Last: Race and Sovereignty in the New World.* New York: Fordham University Press, 2008.

Endelman, Todd M. *The Jews of Britain, 1656 to 2000.* Berkeley: University of California Press, 2002.

Equiano, Olaudah. *The Interesting Narrative of the Life of Olaudah Equiano, or Gustavus Vassa, the African, Written by Himself.* Edited by Werner Sollors. 1789. Reprint, New York: Norton, 2001.

Evans, Richard J. *Rituals of Retribution: Capital Punishment in Germany, 1600–1987.* Oxford: Oxford University Press, 1996.

Evelyn, John, *The Diary of John Evelyn.* Edited by Austin Dobson. 3 vols. London: Macmillan, 1906.

Execution, Last Speeches & Confessions, of the Thirteen Prisoners That Suffered on Friday the 24th of October, 1679, The. [London?], 1679.

Fabricant, Carole. "Speaking for the Irish Nation: The Drapier, the Bishop, and the Problems of Colonial Representation." *ELH* 66, no. 2 (1999): 337–72.

———. *Swift's Landscape.* Notre Dame: University of Notre Dame Press, 1995.

Ferguson, Adam. *An Essay on the History of Civil Society.* Edited by Fania Oz-Salzberger. Cambridge: Cambridge University Press, 1995.

Ferguson, Margaret. *Dido's Daughters: Literacy, Gender, and Empire in Early Modern England and France.* Chicago: University of Chicago Press, 2003.

———. "Feathers and Flies: Aphra Behn and the Seventeenth-Century Trade in Exotica." In *Subject and Object in Renaissance Culture,* edited by Peter Stallybrass, Magreta de Grazia, and Maureen Quilligan, 235–59. Cambridge: Cambridge University Press, 1996.

———. "Juggling the Categories of Race, Class and Gender: Aphra Behn's *Oroonoko.*" *Women's Studies* 19 (1991): 159–81.

Festa, Lynn. *Sentimental Figures of Empire in Eighteenth-Century Britain and France.* Baltimore: Johns Hopkins University Press, 2006.

Festa, Lynn, and Daniel Carey. "Introduction: Some Answers to the Question: 'What Is Postcolonial Enlightenment?'" In *The Postcolonial Enlightenment: Eighteenth-Century Colonialism and Postcolonial Theory*, edited by Daniel Carey and Lynn Festa, 1–33. Oxford: Oxford University Press, 2009.

Fitzgerald, Robert P. "Science and Politics in Swift's Voyage to Laputa." *Journal of English and Germanic Philology* 87 (Spring 1988): 213–29.

Flynn, Carol Houlihan. *The Body in Swift and Defoe*. Cambridge: Cambridge University Press, 1990.

Foucault, Michel. *Discipline and Punish: The Birth of the Prison*. Translated by Alan Sheridan. New York: Vintage Books, 1995.

———. "Governmentality." In *The Foucault Effect: Studies in Governmentality*. edited by Graham Burchell, Colin Gordon, and Peter Miller, 87–104. Chicago: University of Chicago Press, 1991.

———. *"Society Must Be Defended": Lectures at the Collège de France, 1975–76*. Edited by Mauro Bertani, Alessandro Fontana, and François Ewald. Translated by David Macey. New York: Picador, 2003.

Fradinger, Moira. *Binding Violence: Literary Visions of Political Origins*. Stanford: Stanford University Press, 2010.

Frankle, Robert J. "Parliament's Right to Do Wrong: The Parliamentary Debate on the Bill of Attainder against Sir John Fenwick, 1696." *Parliamentary History* 4, no. 1 (1985): 71–85.

Franklin, Julian H. *John Locke and the Theory of Sovereignty: Mixed Monarchy and the Right of Resistance in the Political Thought of the English Revolution*. Cambridge: Cambridge University Press, 1978.

Frantz, R. W. "Swift's Yahoos and the Voyagers." *Modern Philology* 29 (1931): 49–57.

Frohock, Richard. "Violence and Awe: The Foundations of Government in Aphra Behn's New World Settings." *Eighteenth-Century Fiction* 8, no. 4 (1996): 437–52.

Furbank, Philip Nicholas, and W. R. Owens. *A Political Biography of Daniel Defoe*. London: Pickering & Chatto, 2006.

Gallagher, Catherine. "Embracing the Absolute: The Politics of the Female Subject in Seventeenth-Century England." *Genders* 1 (Spring 1988): 24–39.

———. *Nobody's Story: The Vanishing Acts of Women Writers in the Marketplace, 1670–1820*. Berkeley: University of California Press, 1994.

Gates, Henry Louis, Jr. *The Signifying Monkey: A Theory of Afro-American Literary Criticism*. Oxford: Oxford University Press, 1988.

Gaudio, Michael. *Engraving the Savage: The New World and Techniques of Civilization*. Minneapolis: University of Minnesota Press, 2008.

Gerrard, Christine. *The Patriot Opposition to Walpole: Politics, Poetry, and National Myth, 1725–1742*. Oxford, UK: Clarendon, 1994.

Goldberg, Jonathan. *James I and the Politics of Literature*. Stanford: Stanford University Press, 1989.

———. "Margaret Cavendish, Scribe." *GLQ: A Journal of Lesbian and Gay Studies* 10, no. 3 (2004): 433–52.

Goldgar, Bertrand A. *Walpole and the Wits: The Relation of Politics to Literature, 1722–1742*. Lincoln: University of Nebraska Press, 1976.

Goldie, Mark. "The English System of Liberty." In *The Cambridge History of Eighteenth-Century Political Thought*, edited by Mark Goldie and Robert Wokler, 40–78. Cambridge: Cambridge University Press, 2006.

———. "Situating Swift's Politics in 1701." In *Politics and Literature in the Age of Swift: English and Irish Perspectives*, edited by Claude Rawson, 31–51. Cambridge: Cambridge University Press, 2010.

Goldie, Mark, and Robert Wokler, eds. *The Cambridge History of Eighteenth-Century Political Thought*. Cambridge: Cambridge University Press, 2006.

Gomme, Sir Laurence. *The Making of London*. Oxford, UK: Clarendon, 1912.

Gordon, Colin. "Governmental Rationality: An Introduction." In *The Foucault Effect: Studies in Governmentality*, edited by Graham Burchell, Colin Gordon, and Peter Miller, 1–52. Chicago: University of Chicago Press, 1991.

Gordon, Scott Paul. *The Power of the Passive Self in English Literature, 1640–1770*. Cambridge: Cambridge University Press, 2002.

Gordon, Thomas, and John Trenchard. *Cato's Letters or Essays on Liberty, Civil and Religious, and Other Important Subjects*. Edited by Ronald Hamowy. Vol. 2. Indianapolis: Liberty Fund, 1995.

Graves, Nicola. "'Injury for Injury'; or, 'The Lady's Revenge': Female Vengeance in Eliza Haywood's *Female Spectator*." In *The Fair Philosopher: Eliza Haywood and "The Female Spectator,"* edited by Donald J. Newman and Lynn Marie Wright, 157–75. Lewisburg, PA: Bucknell University Press, 2006.

Greenblatt, Stephen. *Shakespearean Negotiations: The Circulation of Social Energy in Renaissance England*. Berkeley: University of California Press, 1988.

Gregg, Stephen H. *Defoe's Writings and Manliness: Contrary Men*. Burlington, VT: Ashgate, 2009.

———. "Male Friendship and Defoe's *Captain Singleton*: 'My Every Thing.'" *British Journal for Eighteenth-Century Studies* 27, no. 2 (2004): 203–18.

Grotius, Hugo. *The Rights of War and Peace*. Edited by Richard Tuck. 3 vols. Indianapolis: Liberty Fund, 2005.

Guest, Harriet. *Empire, Barbarism, and Civilisation: James Cook, William Hodges, and the Return to the Pacific*. Cambridge: Cambridge University Press, 2007.

———. *Small Change: Women, Learning, Patriotism, 1750–1810*. Chicago: University of Chicago Press, 2000.

Guffey, George Robert. "Aphra Behn's *Oroonoko*: Occasion and Accomplishment." In *Two English Novelists: Aphra Behn and Anthony Trollope; Papers Read at a Clark Library Seminar, May 11, 1974*, by George Robert Guffey and Andrew H. Wright, 1–41. Los Angeles: William Andrews Clark Memorial Library, UCLA, 1975.

Gunn, J. A. W. *Beyond Liberty and Property: The Process of Self-Recognition in Eighteenth-Century Political Thought*. Kingston and Montreal: McGill-Queen's University Press, 1983.

Hakluyt, Richard. *The Principal Navigations, Voyages, Traffiques & Discoveries of the English Nation Made by Sea or Over-land to the Remote and Farthest Distant Quarters of the Earth at Any Time within the Compasse of These 1600 Yeeres*. London, 1598–1600. Reprint, 12 vols., Glasgow: J. MacLehose and Sons, 1903–5.

Hale, J. R. "Gunpowder and the Renaissance: An Essay in the History of Ideas." In *From the Renaissance to the Counter-Reformation: Essays in Honor of Garrett Mattingly*, edited by Charles H. Carter, 113–44. New York: Random House, 1965.

Hale, Matthew. *The History of the Common Law of England*. Edited by Charles M. Gray. Chicago: University of Chicago Press, 1971.

Hamlin, William M. "Imagined Apotheoses: Drake, Harriot, and Raleigh in the Americas." *Journal of the History of Ideas* 57, no. 3 (1996): 405–28.

Harol, Corrinne. "The Passion of *Oroonoko*: Passive Obedience, the Royal Slave, and Aphra Behn's Baroque Realism." *ELH* 79, no. 2 (2012): 447–75.

Harriot, Thomas. *A Briefe and True Report of the New Found Land of Virginia of the Commodities and of the Nature and Manners of the Naturall Inhabitants: Discouered by the English Colon There Seated by Sir Richard Greinuile Knight in the Eere 1585; Which Remained vnder the Gouernement of Twelue Monethes, at the Speciall Charge . . . of the Honourable Sir Walter Raleigh Knight*. London, 1590. EEBO.

Harris, Tim. *London Crowds in the Reign of Charles II: Propaganda and Politics from the Restoration until the Exclusion Crisis*. Cambridge: Cambridge University Press, 1987.

———. "Perceptions of the Crowd in Later Stuart London." In *Imagining Early Modern London: Perceptions and Portrayals of the City from Stow to Strype*, edited by J. F. Merritt, 250–72. Cambridge: Cambridge University Press, 2001.
———. *Restoration: Charles II and His Kingdoms, 1660–1685*. London: Allen Lane, 2005.
Hawes, Clement. *The British Eighteenth Century and Global Critique*. New York: Palgrave Macmillan, 2005.
Haywood, Eliza. *The Adventures of Eovaai*. Edited by Earla Wilputte. Peterborough, ON: Broadview, 1999.
———. *The Invisible Spy*. London, 1755.
———. *The Invisible Spy*. London, 1759.
———. *The Invisible Spy*. Dublin, 1768.
———. *Memoirs of a Certain Island Adjacent to the Kingdom of Utopia*. London, 1725. Facsimile edition, New York: Garland, 1972.
———. *The Parrot, with a Compendium of the Times*. In *The Selected Works of Eliza Haywood*, edited by Christine Blouch, Alexander Pettit, and Rebecca Sayers Hanson, series 2, vol. 1. London: Pickering & Chatto, 2000–2001.
Helgerson, Richard. *Forms of Nationhood: The Elizabethan Writing of England*. Chicago: University of Chicago Press, 1992.
Henry, John. "The Fragmentation of Renaissance Occultism and the Decline of Magic." *History of Science* 46, no. 1 (2008): 1–48.
Herman, Peter C. "'We All Smoke Here': Behn's *The Widdow Ranter* and the Invention of American Identity." In *Envisioning an English Empire: Jamestown and the Making of the North Atlantic World*, edited by John Wood Sweet and Robert Appelbaum, 254–74. Philadelphia: University of Pennsylvania Press, 2005.
Hickeringill, Edmund. *Jamaica Viewed with All the Ports, Harbours, and Their Several Soundings, Towns, and Settlements Thereunto Belonging Together, with the Nature of Its Climate, Fruitfulness of the Soile, and Its Suitableness to English Complexions: With Several Other Collateral Observations and Reflexions upon the Island*. London, 1661.
Higgins, Ian. *Swift's Politics: A Study in Disaffection*. Cambridge: Cambridge University Press, 1994.
History of the Rise, Progress, and Extinction of the Late Rebellion in Scotland, The. Edinburgh, 1759. ECCO.
Hobbes, Thomas. *Behemoth*. Edited by Ferdinand Tönnies. Reprinted with a new introduction by Stephen Holmes. Chicago: University of Chicago Press, 1990.
———. *The Elements of Law, Natural and Politic*. Edited by Ferdinand Tönnies. 2nd ed. New York: Barnes & Noble, 1969.

———. *Leviathan*. Edited by C. B. Macpherson. London: Penguin Books, 1978.
———. *On the Citizen*. Edited by Richard Tuck. Translated by Michael Silverthorne. Cambridge Texts in the History of Political Thought. Cambridge: Cambridge University Press, 1998.
———. *Tracts of Sir Thomas Hobbs of Malmsbury*. London, 1682.
Hogendorn, Jan, and Marion Johnson. *The Shell Money of the Slave Trade*. Cambridge: Cambridge University Press, 1986.
Holmes, Geoffrey. *The Trial of Doctor Sacheverell*. London: Eyre Methuen, 1973.
Holmesland, Oddvar. "Aphra Behn's *Oroonoko*: Cultural Dialectics and the Novel." *ELH* 68, no. 1 (2001): 57–79.
———. "Margaret Cavendish's *The Blazing World*: Natural Art and the Body Politic." *Studies in Philology* 96, no. 4 (1999): 457–79.
Honig, Bonnie. *Emergency Politics: Paradox, Law, Democracy*. Princeton: Princeton University Press, 2009.
Hooke, Robert. *Philosophical Collections*. 6 vols. London, 1679.
Horsley, Lee. "'Vox Populi' in the Political Literature of 1710." *Huntington Library Quarterly* 38, no. 4 (1975): 335–53.
Houlding, J. A. *Fit for Service: The Training of the British Army, 1715–1795*. Oxford, UK: Clarendon, 1981.
Hughes, Derek. *The Theatre of Aphra Behn*. New York: Palgrave, 2001.
Hulme, Peter. *Colonial Encounters: Europe and the Native Caribbean, 1492–1797*. London: Methuen, 1986.
Hundert, E. J. *The Enlightenment's Fable: Bernard Mandeville and the Discovery of Society*. Cambridge: Cambridge University Press, 2005.
Hunt, Alice. *The Drama of Coronation: Medieval Ceremony in Early Modern England*. Cambridge: Cambridge University Press, 2008.
Hunter, J. Paul. *The Reluctant Pilgrim: Defoe's Emblematic Method and Quest for Form in* Robinson Crusoe. Baltimore: Johns Hopkins University Press, 1966.
Hunter, Michael. "Witchcraft and the Decline of Belief." *Eighteenth-Century Life* 22, no. 2 (1998): 139–47.
Hutton, Ronald. *The Restoration: A Political and Religious History of England and Wales, 1658–1667*. Oxford, UK: Clarendon, 1985.
Ingrassia, Catherine. "Additional Information about Eliza Haywood's 1749 Arrest for Seditious Libel." *Notes and Queries* 42, no. 2 (1997): 202–3.
———. *Authorship, Commerce, and Gender in Early Eighteenth-Century England: A Culture of Paper Credit*. Cambridge: Cambridge University Press, 1998.

Iwanisziw, Susan B. "Behn's Novel Investment in *Oroonoko*: Kingship, Slavery, and Tobacco in English Colonialism." *South Atlantic Review* 63, no. 2 (1998): 75–98.

Iyengar, Sujata. *Shades of Difference: Mythologies of Skin Color in Early Modern England*. Philadelphia: University of Pennsylvania Press, 2004.

Jacob, James R. "Opera and Obedience: Thomas Hobbes and *A Proposition for Advancement of Moralitie* by Sir William Davenant." *Seventeenth Century* 6, no. 2 (1991): 205–50.

James, Susan. Introduction to *Margaret Cavendish: Political Writings*, edited by Susan James, ix–xxix. Cambridge: Cambridge University Press, 2003.

———. "The Philosophical Innovations of Margaret Cavendish." *British Journal for the History of Philosophy* 7, no. 2 (1999): 219–44.

Jameson, Fredric. "Notes on the *Nomos*." *South Atlantic Quarterly* 104, no. 2 (2005): 199–204.

Jansson, Maija. "Introduction: Realities of Representation: State Building in Early Modern Europe and European America." In *Realities of Representation: State Building in Early Modern Europe and European America*, edited by Maija Jansson, 1–17. New York: Palgrave Macmillan, 2007.

J. E. *Some Considerations on the Naturalization of the Jews; and How Far the Publick Will Benefit from This Hopeful Race of Israelites*. London, 1753.

Johnson, Ben. *The Complete Poems*. Edited by George A. E. Parfitt. New Haven: Yale University Press, 1982.

Johnson, Samuel. *A Dictionary of the English language: In Which the Words Are Deduced from Their Originals, and Illustrated in Their Different Significations by Examples from the Best Writers; To Which Are Prefixed, a History of the Language, and an English Grammar*. 2 vols. London, 1755.

Jones, Inigo, and William D'Avenant. *Britannia Triumphans: A Masque, Presented at White Hall, by the Kings Majestie and His Lords, on the Sunday after Twelfth-Night, 1637*. London, 1637.

Kahn, Paul W. *Political Theology: Four New Chapters on the Concept of Sovereignty*. New York: Columbia University Press, 2011.

———. *Sacred Violence: Torture, Terror, and Sovereignty*. Ann Arbor: University of Michigan Press, 2008.

Kahn, Victoria. *Wayward Contracts: The Crisis of Political Obligation in England, 1640–1674*. Princeton: Princeton University Press, 2004.

Kaplan, Martha. "The Magical Power of the (Printed) Word." In *Magic and Modernity: Interfaces of Revelation and Concealment*, edited by

Birgit Meyer and Peter Pels, 183–99. Stanford: Stanford University Press, 2003.

Kaul, Suvir. *Poems of Nation, Anthems of Empire: English Verse in the Long Eighteenth Century*. Charlottesville: University of Virginia Press, 2000.

———. "Reading Literary Symptoms: Colonial Pathologies and the Oroonoko Fictions of Behn, Southerne, and Hawkesworth." *Eighteenth-Century Life* 18, no. 3 (1994): 80–96.

Kay, Carol. *Political Constructions: Defoe, Richardson, and Sterne in Relation to Hobbes, Hume, and Burke*. Ithaca: Cornell University Press, 1988.

Keaton, George. *The Norman Conquest and the Common Law*. London: Ernest Benn, 1966.

Keirn, Tim. "Monopoly, Economic Thought, and the Royal African Company." In *Early Modern Conceptions of Property*, edited by John Brewer and Susan Staves, 427–66. London: Routledge, 1996.

Keller, Eve. "Producing Petty Gods: Margaret Cavendish's Critique of Experimental Science." *ELH* 64, no. 2 (1997): 447–71.

Kelly, Jack. *Gunpowder: Alchemy, Bombards, and Pyrotechnics: The History of the Explosive That Changed the World*. New York: Basic Books, 2004.

Kenyon, John. *The Popish Plot*. London: William Heinemann, 1972.

———. "The Revolution of 1688: Resistance and Contract." In *Historical Perspectives: Studies in English Thought and Society in Honour of J. H. Plumb*, edited by Neil McKendrick, 43–69. London: Europa, 1974.

Kim, Mi Gyung. "'Public' Science: Hydrogen Balloons and Lavoisier's Decomposition of Water." *Annals of Science* 63, no. 3 (2006): 291–318.

King, Kathryn R. "Patriot or Opportunist? Eliza Haywood and the Politics of *The Female Spectator*." In *The Fair Philosopher: Eliza Haywood and "The Female Spectator*," edited by Donald J. Newman and Lynn Marie Wright, 104–21. Lewisburg, PA: Bucknell University Press, 2006.

———. *A Political Biography of Eliza Haywood*. Eighteenth-Century Political Biographies 9. London: Pickering & Chatto, 2012.

———. "Spying upon the Conjurer: Haywood, Curiosity, and 'The Novel' in the 1720s." *Studies in the Novel* 30, no. 2 (1998): 178–93.

King, William. *The Original Works of William King, L.L.D.* London, 1776.

Kleinerman, Benjamin A. "Can the Prince Really Be Tamed? Executive Prerogative, Popular Apathy, and the Constitutional Frame in Locke's *Second Treatise*." *American Political Science Review* 101, no. 2 (2007): 209–22.

Knox-Shaw, Peter. "Defoe and the Politics of Representing the African Interior." *Modern Language Review* 96, no. 4 (2001): 937–51.
Korshin, Paul. "The Intellectual Contexts of Swift's Flying Island." *Philological Quarterly* 50 (1978): 630–46.
Kramnick, Isaac. *Bolingbroke and His Circle: The Politics of Nostalgia in the Age of Walpole*. Cambridge: Harvard University Press, 1968.
Kraynak, Robert P. "Hobbes on Barbarism and Civilization." *Journal of Politics* 45, no. 1 (1983): 86–109.
Kroll, Richard. "'Tales of Love and Gallantry': The Politics of *Oroonoko*." *Huntington Library Quarterly* 67, no. 4 (2004): 573–605, 691.
Kubek, Elizabeth Bennett. "The Key to Stowe: Toward a Patriot Whig Reading of Eliza Haywood's *Eovaai*." In *Presenting Gender: Changing Sex in Early-Modern Culture*, edited by Chris Mounsey, 225–54. Lewisburg, PA: Bucknell University Press, 2001.
———. "'Night Mares of the Commonwealth': Royalist Passion and Female Ambition in Aphra Behn's *The Roundheads*." *Restoration: Studies in English Literary Culture, 1660–1700* 7 (1993): 39–52.
Kvande, Marta. "The Outsider Narrator in Eliza Haywood's Political Novels." *SEL Studies in English Literature 1500–1900* 43, no. 3 (2003): 625–43.
Landa, Louis A. *Swift and the Church of Ireland*. Oxford, UK: Clarendon, 1954.
Latta, Kimberly. "Aphra Behn and the Roundheads." *Journal for Early Modern Cultural Studies* 4, no. 1 (2004): 1–36.
Lefebvre, Henri. *The Production of Space*. 1974. Translated by Donald Nicholson-Smith. Oxford, UK: Blackwell, 1991.
Lenman, Bruce. "The Exiled Stuarts and the Precious Symbols of Sovereignty." *Eighteenth-Century Life* 25, no. 2 (2001): 185–200.
Leslie, Charles. *The Finishing Stroke: Being a Vindication of the Patriarchal Scheme of Government in Defence of the Rehearsals. . . .* London, 1711.
Leslie, Marina. "Evading Rape and Embracing Empire: Margaret Cavendish's *Assaulted and Pursued Chastity*." In *Menacing Virgins: Representing Virginity in the Middle Ages and the Renaissance*, edited by Kathleen Coyne Kelly and Marina Leslie, 179–97. Newark: University of Delaware Press, 1999.
Lewcock, Dawn. *Sir William Davenant, the Court Masque, and the English Seventeenth-Century Scenic Stage, c. 1605–c. 1700*. Amherst, NY: Cambria, 2008.
Life of King Edward, Who Rests at Westminster: Attributed to a Monk of Saint Bertin, The. Edited and translated by Frank Barlow. Oxford, UK: Clarendon, 1992.

Lifshey, Adam. *Specters of Conquest: Indigenous Absence in Transatlantic Literatures*. New York: Fordham University Press, 2010.
Lindqvist, Sven. *A History of Bombing*. Translated by Linda Rugg. New York: New Press, 2001.
Lock, F. P. *The Politics of* Gulliver's Travels. Oxford, UK: Clarendon, 1980.
———. *Swift's Tory Politics*. Newark: University of Delaware Press, 1983.
Locke, John. *Two Treatises of Government*. Edited by Peter Laslett. 2nd ed. Cambridge: Cambridge University Press, 1967.
Losurdo, Domenico. *Liberalism: A Counter-history*. Translated by Gregory Elliott. London: Verso, 2011.
Loughlin, Martin. "Constituent Power Subverted: From English Constitutional Argument to British Constitutional Practice." In *The Paradox of Constitutionalism: Constituent Power and Constitutional Form*, edited by Martin Loughlin and Neil Walker, 27–48. Oxford: Oxford University Press, 2007.
Loughlin, Martin, and Neil Walker, eds. *The Paradox of Constitutionalism: Constituent Power and Constitutional Form*. Oxford: Oxford University Press, 2007.
Macfarlane, Alan. "Civility and the Decline of Magic." In *Civil Histories: Essays Presented to Sir Keith Thomas*, edited by Peter Burke, Brian Harrison, and Paul Slack, 145–59. Oxford: Oxford University Press, 2000.
Machiavelli, Niccolò. *The Works of the Famous Nicholas Machiavel, Citizen and Secretary of Florence: Written Originally in Italian, and from Thence Newly and Faithfully Translated into English*. Translated by Henry Neville. London: Printed for John Starkey, Charles Harper, and John Amery, at the Miter, the Flower-de-Luce, and the Peacock, in Fleetstreet, 1680.
Mackie, Erin. *Market à la Mode: Fashion, Commodity, and Gender in* The Tatler *and* The Spectator. Baltimore: Johns Hopkins University Press, 1997.
Macpherson, C. B. *The Political Theory of Possessive Individualism: Hobbes to Locke*. Oxford: Oxford University Press, 1964.
Malcolm, Noel. *Aspects of Hobbes*. Oxford: Oxford University Press, 2004.
Mandeville, Bernard. *The Fable of the Bees: Or, Private Vices, Publick Benefits*. Edited by Frederick Benjamin Kaye. 2 vols. Oxford, UK: Clarendon, 1924.
Manley, Delarivier. *The New Atlantis*. 1709. Edited by Rosalind Ballaster. London: Pickering & Chatto, 1991.

———. *The Secret History, of Queen Zarah, and the Zarazians, Being a Looking-Glass for —————— in the Kingdom of Albigion*. London, 1705. ECCO.

Manning, Roger B. *Village Revolts: Social Protest and Popular Disturbances in England, 1509–1640*. Oxford, UK: Clarendon, 1988.

Markley, Robert. "'Be Impudent, Be Saucy, Forward, Bold, Touzing, and Leud': The Politics of Masculine Sexuality and Feminine Desire in Behn's Tory Comedies." In *Cultural Readings of Restoration and Eighteenth-Century English Theater*, edited by J. Douglas Canfield and Deborah C. Payne, 114–40. Athens: University of Georgia Press, 1995.

———. *The Far East and the English Imagination, 1600–1730*. Cambridge: Cambridge University Press, 2006.

Masters, George. *A Poem Humbly Inscribed to His Royal Highness the Duke of Cumberland, on His Defeat of the Rebels at Culloden, April 16, 1746*. London, 1747.

Maurer, Shawn Lisa. *Proposing Men: Dialectics of Gender and Class in the Eighteenth-Century English Periodical*. Stanford: Stanford University Press, 1998.

Mayers, Ruth E. *1659—The Crisis of the Commonwealth*. Woodbridge, UK: Boydell & Brewer, 2004.

Mbembe, Achille. "Necropolitics." *Public Culture* 15, no. 1 (2003): 11–40.

McCormick, John P. *Machiavellian Democracy*. Cambridge: Cambridge University Press, 2011.

McGirr, Elaine M. *Heroic Mode and Political Crisis, 1660–1745*. Cranbury, NJ: Associated University Presses, 2009.

McKeon, Michael. *The Origins of the English Novel, 1600–1740*. Rev. ed. Baltimore: Johns Hopkins University Press, 2002.

———. *The Secret History of Domesticity: Public, Private, and the Division of Knowledge*. Baltimore: Johns Hopkins University Press, 2005.

McLeod, Bruce. *The Geography of Empire in English Literature, 1580–1745*. Cambridge: Cambridge University Press, 1999.

McNeill, William. *The Pursuit of Power: Technology, Armed Force, and Society since A.D. 1000*. Chicago: University of Chicago Press, 1984.

Mendelson, Sara, and Patricia Crawford. *Women in Early Modern England, 1550–1720*. Oxford, UK: Clarendon, 1998.

Mendle, Michael. "Parliamentary Sovereignty: A Very English Absolutism." In *Political Discourse in Early Modern Britain*, edited by Nicholas Phillipson and Quentin Skinner, 97–119. Cambridge: Cambridge University Press, 1993.

Mentz, Steve. *Romance for Sale in Early Modern England: The Rise of Prose Fiction*. Aldershot, UK: Ashgate, 2006.
Merritt, Juliette. *Beyond Spectacle: Eliza Haywood's Female Spectators*. Toronto: University of Toronto Press, 2004.
Meyer, Birgit, and Peter Pels, eds. *Magic and Modernity: Interfaces of Revelation and Concealment*. Stanford: Stanford University Press, 2003.
Middleton, W. E. Knowles. "Archimedes, Kircher, Buffon, and the Burning-Mirrors." *Isis* 52 (December 1961): 533–43.
Milton, John. *Paradise Lost*. Edited by Scott Elledge. New York: Norton, 1975.
Mocquet, Jean. *Travels and Voyages into Africa, Asia, and America, the East and West-Indies; Syria, Jerusalem, and the Holy-Land*. Translated by Nathaniel Pullen. London, 1696.
Monod, Paul Kléber. *Jacobitism and the English People*. Cambridge: Cambridge University Press, 1989.
———. *The Power of Kings: Monarchy and Religion in Europe, 1589–1715*. New Haven: Yale University Press, 2001.
Montag, Warren. *The Unthinkable Swift: The Spontaneous Philosophy of a Church of England Man*. London: Verso, 1994.
Montesquieu. *The Spirit of Laws*. Edited and translated by Anne M. Cohler, Basia Carolyn Miller, and Harold Samuel Stone. Cambridge: Cambridge University Press, 1989.
Moore, Sean D. *Swift, the Book, and the Irish Financial Revolution: Satire and Sovereignty in Colonial Ireland*. Baltimore: Johns Hopkins University Press, 2010.
Mouffe, Chantal. "Carl Schmitt and the Paradox of Liberal Democracy." In *The Challenge of Carl Schmitt*, edited by Chantal Mouffe, 38–53. London: Verso, 1999.
Mowry, Melissa. " 'Past Remembrance or History': Aphra Behn's *The Widdow Ranter*, or, How the Collective Lost Its Honor." *ELH* 79, no. 3 (2012): 597–621.
Mueller, Andreas. *A Critical Study of Daniel Defoe's Verse: Recovering the Neglected Corpus of His Poetic Work*. Lewiston, NY: Edwin Mellen, 2010.
Muse, S. Vida. "Eliza Haywood and the Jew Bill." *Notes and Queries* 57 (2010): 105–8.
Nash, Richard. *Wild Enlightenment: The Borders of Human Identity in the Eighteenth Century*. Charlottesville: University of Virginia Press, 2003.
Naudé, Gabriel. *The History of Magick by Way of Apology, for All the Wise Men Who Have Unjustly Been Reputed Magicians, from the Creation,*

to the Present Age: Written in French, by G. Naudæus Late Library-keeper to Cardinal Mazarin; Englished by J. Davies. London, 1657.

———. Political Considerations upon Refin'd Politicks, and the Masterstrokes of State, as Practis'd by the Ancients and Moderns: Written by Gabriel Naudé, and Inscrib'd to the Cardinal Bagni; Translated into English by Dr. King. Translated by William King. London, 1711.

Negri, Antonio. Insurgencies: Constituent Power and the Modern State. Translated by Maurizia Boscagli. 2nd rev. ed.. Minneapolis: University of Minnesota Press, 2009.

Neill, Anna. "Crusoe's Farther Adventures: Discovery, Trade, and the Law of Nations." Eighteenth Century: Theory and Interpretation 38, no. 3 (1997): 213–30.

Newcastle, Duke of (William Cavendish). Ideology and Politics on the Eve of Restoration: Newcastle's Advice to Charles II. Edited by Thomas P. Slaughter. Philadelphia: American Philosophical Society, 1984.

Nicolson, Marjorie Hope, and Nora Mohler. "The Scientific Background of Swift's Voyage to Laputa." Annals of Science 2 (1937): 299–334.

———. "Swift's 'Flying Island' in the Voyage to Laputa." Annals of Science 2 (1937): 405–30.

Novak, Maximillian E. "The Cave and the Grotto: Realist Form and Robinson Crusoe's Imagined Interiors." Eighteenth-Century Fiction 20, no. 3 (2008): 445–68.

———. Daniel Defoe: Master of Fictions: His Life and Ideas. Oxford: Oxford University Press, 2001.

———. "Defoe and the Art of War." Philological Quarterly 75, no. 2 (1996): 197–214.

———. "Defoe and the Disordered City." PMLA 92, no. 2 (1977): 241–52.

———. Defoe and the Nature of Man. Oxford: Oxford University Press, 1963.

Nussbaum, Felicity. Torrid Zones: Maternity, Sexuality, and Empire in Eighteenth-Century English Narratives. Baltimore: Johns Hopkins University Press, 1995.

Oakleaf, David. A Political Biography of Jonathan Swift. London: Pickering & Chatto, 2008.

O'Brien, Karen. Narratives of Enlightenment: Cosmopolitan History from Voltaire to Gibbon. Cambridge: Cambridge University Press, 1997.

Ogg, David. England in the Reigns of James II and William III. Oxford, UK: Clarendon, 1955.

Ogilby, John. Africa: Being an Accurate Description of the Regions of Aegypt, Barbary, Lybia, and Billedulgerid, the Land of Negroes,

Guinee, Aethiopia, and the Abyssines, with All the Adjacent Islands. . . . London, 1670.

———. *The Entertainment of His Most Excellent Majestie Charles II in His Passage through the City of London to His Coronation.* Facsimile edition with an introduction by Ronald Knowles. Binghamton, NY: Medieval & Renaissance Texts & Studies, 1988.

Olearius, Adam. *The Voyages & Travels of the Ambassadors Sent by Frederick Duke of Holstein, to the Great Duke of Muscovy, and the King of Persia Begun in the Year M.DC.XXXIII, and Finish'd in M. DC.XXXIX. . . .* Translated by John Davies. London, 1662. EEBO.

———. *The Voyages and Travels of the Ambassadors Sent by Frederick, Duke of Holstein, to the Great Duke of Muscovy and the King of Persia.* 2nd ed. Translated John Davies. London, 1669. EEBO.

Orgel, Stephen. *The Illusion of Power.* Berkeley: University of California Press, 1975.

———. "Marginal Jonson." In *The Politics of the Stuart Court Masque*, edited by David Bevington and Peter Holbrook, 144–75. Cambridge: Cambridge University Press, 1998.

Orgel, Stephen, and Roy Strong. *Inigo Jones: The Theatre of the Stuart Court, Including the Complete Designs for Productions at Court for the Most Part in the Collection of the Duke of Devonshire Together with Their Texts and Historical Documentation.* London: Sotheby Parke Bernet, 1973.

Owen, Josiah. *The Humourist; or, An Entertaining Display of the Absurdities of the Roman Catholicks and Nonjurors.* London, 1752.

Owen, Susan J. "'Suspect My Loyalty When I Lose My Virtue': Sexual Politics and Party in Aphra Behn's Plays of the Exclusion Crisis, 1678–83." *Restoration: Studies in English Literary Culture, 1660–1700* 18, no. 1 (1994): 37–47.

Pacheco, Anita. "Reading Toryism in Aphra Behn's Cit-Cuckolding Comedies." *Review of English Studies* 55 (2004): 690–708.

Pagden, Anthony. *European Encounters with the New World: From Renaissance to Romanticism.* New Haven: Yale University Press, 1994.

———. *The Fall of Natural Man: The American Indian and the Origins of Comparative Ethnology.* Cambridge Iberian and Latin American Studies. Cambridge: Cambridge University Press, 1982.

———. *Lords of All the World: Ideologies of Empire in Spain, Britain and France c. 1500–c. 1800.* New Haven: Yale University Press, 1995.

Palmeri, Frank. *Satire, History, Novel: Narrative Forms, 1665–1815.* Newark: University of Delaware Press, 2003.

Partington, J. R. *A History of Greek Fire and Gunpowder.* Baltimore: Johns Hopkins University Press, 1999.

Pateman, Carole. *The Sexual Contract*. Stanford: Stanford University Press, 1988.
Patterson, Annabel M. *Censorship and Interpretation: The Conditions of Writing and Reading in Early Modern England*. Madison: University of Wisconsin Press, 1984.
———. *Early Modern Liberalism*. Cambridge: Cambridge University Press, 1997.
———. *The Long Parliament of Charles II*. New Haven: Yale University Press, 2008.
Peacham, Henry. *Garden of Eloquence*. London, 1593.
Pietz, William. "Bosman's Guinea: The Intercultural Roots of an Enlightenment Discourse." *Comparative Civilizations Review*, Fall 1982, 1–22.
———. "The Problem of the Fetish, I." *Res* 9 (1985): 5–17.
———. "The Problem of the Fetish, II: The Origin of the Fetish." *Res* 13 (1987): 23–45.
———. "The Problem of the Fetish, IIIa: Bosman's Guinea and the Enlightenment Theory of Fetishism." *Res* 16 (1988): 105–23.
Pincus, Steve. *1688: The First Modern Revolution*. New Haven: Yale University Press, 2009.
Pinto, Fernão Mendes. *The Voyages and Adventures of Ferdinand Mendez Pinto, a Portugal: During His Travels for the Space of One and Twenty Years in the Kingdoms of Ethiopia, China, Tartaria, Cauchinchina, Calaminham, Siam, Pegu, Japan, and a Great Part of the East-Indies*. Translated by Henry Cogan. London, 1692.
Plank, Geoffrey. *Rebellion and Savagery: The Jacobite Rising of 1745 and the British Empire*. Early American Studies. Philadelphia: University of Pennsylvania Press, 2006.
Plato. *The Republic of Plato: An Ideal Commonwealth*. Translated by Benjamin Jowett. Rev. ed. 1901. Reprint, New York: Modern Library, 1941.
Pocock, J. G. A. *The Ancient Constitution and the Feudal Law: A Study of English Historical Thought in the Seventeenth Century*. New York: Norton, 1967.
———. *The Machiavellian Moment: Florentine Political Thought and the Atlantic Republican Tradition*. Princeton: Princeton University Press, 1975.
———. "Time, History, and Eschatology in the Thought of Thomas Hobbes." In *Politics, Language, and Time: Essays on Political Thought and History*, 2nd rev. ed., 148–201. Chicago: University of Chicago Press, 1971.

Pohl, Nicole. "'Of Mixt Natures': Questions of Genre in Margaret Cavendish's *The Blazing World*." In *A Princely Brave Woman: Essays on Margaret Cavendish, Duchess of Newcastle*, edited by Stephen Clucas, 51–68. Aldershot, UK: Ashgate, 2003.

Pollock, Anthony. *Gender and the Fictions of the Public Sphere, 1690–1755*. New York: Routledge, 2009.

Polybius. *The Histories*. Translated by W. R. Paton. 6 vols. London: William Heinemann, 1923.

Poovey, Mary. *A History of the Modern Fact: Problems of Knowledge in the Sciences of Wealth and Society*. Chicago: University of Chicago Press, 1998.

Popkin, Richard H. *The Third Force in Seventeenth Century Thought*. Leiden: Brill, 1992.

Powell, Manushag N. "Parroting and the Periodical: Women's Speech, Haywood's *Parrot*, and Its Antecedents." *Tulsa Studies in Women's Literature* 27, no. 1 (2008): 63–91.

———. "See No Evil, Hear No Evil, Speak No Evil: Spectation and the Eighteenth-Century Public Sphere." *Eighteenth-Century Studies* 45, no. 2 (2012): 255–76.

Pratt, Mary Louise. *Imperial Eyes: Travel Writing and Transculturation*. London: Routledge, 1992.

Purchas, Samuel. *Hakluytus Posthumus; or Purchas His Pilgrimes; Contayning a History of the World in Sea Voyages and Lande Travells by Englishmen and Others*. 20 vols. London, 1625. Reprint, 20 vols., Glasgow: J. MacLehose and Sons, 1905–7.

Pye, Christopher. *The Regal Phantasm: Shakespeare and the Politics of Spectacle*. London: Routledge, 1990.

Rabin, Dana Y. "The Jew Bill of 1753: Masculinity, Virility, and the Nation." *Eighteenth-Century Studies* 39, no. 2 (2006): 157–71.

Raleigh, Sir Walter. *The History of the World*. London, 1614. EEBO.

Randrianja, Solofo, and Stephen Ellis. *Madagascar: A Short History*. Chicago: University of Chicago Press, 2009.

Rasch, William. "From Sovereign Ban to Banning Sovereignty." In *Giorgio Agamben: Sovereignty and Life*, edited by Matthew Calarco and Steven DeCaroli, 92–108. Stanford: Stanford University Press, 2007.

———. "Human Rights as Geopolitics: Carl Schmitt and the Legal Form of American Supremacy." *Cultural Critique* 54, no. 1 (2003): 120–47.

———. "Lines in the Sand: Enmity as a Structuring Principle." *South Atlantic Quarterly* 104, no. 2 (2005): 253–62.

Rawson, Claude. *God, Gulliver, and Genocide: Barbarism and the European Imagination, 1492–1945*. Oxford: Oxford University Press, 2001.

———. "The Injured Lady and the Drapier: A Reading of Swift's Irish Tracts." *Prose Studies* 3, no. 1 (1980): 15–43.

———, ed. *Politics and Literature in the Age of Swift: English and Irish Perspectives*. Cambridge: Cambridge University Press, 2010.

———. *Satire and Sentiment, 1660–1830: Stress Points in the English Augustan Tradition*. Cambridge: Cambridge University Press, 1994.

Redfield, Marc. *The Rhetoric of Terror: Reflections on 9/11 and the War on Terror*. New York: Fordham University Press, 2009.

Rees, Emma L. E. *Margaret Cavendish: Gender, Genre, Exile*. Manchester: Manchester University Press, 2003.

———. "A Well-Spun Yarn: Margaret Cavendish, and Homer's Penelope." In *A Princely Brave Woman: Essays on Margaret Cavendish, Duchess of Newcastle*, edited by Stephen Clucas, 171–81. Aldershot, UK: Ashgate, 2003.

Rice, James V. *Gabriel Naudé: 1600–1653*. Johns Hopkins Studies in Romance Literatures and Languages 35. Baltimore: Johns Hopkins University Press, 1939.

Richardson, John. "Atrocity in Mid-Eighteenth-Century War Literature." *Eighteenth-Century Life* 33, no. 2 (2009): 92–114.

Richetti, John J. *Defoe's Narratives: Situations and Structures*. Oxford, UK: Clarendon, 1975.

Rivero, Albert J. "Aphra Behn's *Oroonoko* and the 'Blank Spaces' of Colonial Fictions." *SEL Studies in English Literature 1500–1900* 39, no. 3 (1999): 443–62.

Rivers, Isabel. *Joseph Priestley, Scientist, Philosopher, and Theologian*. Oxford: Oxford University Press, 2008.

Roach, Joseph R. *Cities of the Dead: Circum-Atlantic Performance*. New York: Columbia University Press, 1996.

Rogers, Nicholas. "Caribbean Borderland: Empire, Ethnicity, and the Exotic on the Mosquito Coast." *Eighteenth-Century Life* 26, no. 3 (2002): 117–38.

———. *Crowd, Culture, and Politics in Georgian Britain*. Oxford, UK: Clarendon, 1998.

———. "Popular Protest in Early Hanoverian London." *Past & Present* 79 (May 1, 1978): 70–100.

———. "Vagrancy, Impressment and the Regulation of Labour in Eighteenth-Century Britain." *Slavery & Abolition* 15, no. 2 (1994): 102–13.

Rousseau, Jean-Jacques. *Rousseau: "The Social Contract" and Other Later Political Writings*. Edited by Victor Gourevitch. Cambridge Texts in the History of Political Thought. Cambridge: Cambridge University Press, 1997.

Royal African Company. *An Account of the Number of Forts and Castles, Necessary to Be Kept Up and Maintained on the Coast of Africa, for Preserving and Securing to Great Britain the Trade to Those Parts*. [London?], 1730.

Rubin, Alfred P. *The Law of Piracy*. New York: Transnational, 1998.

Ryan, Alan. *The Making of Modern Liberalism*. Princeton: Princeton University Press, 2012.

Salzman, Paul. *English Prose Fiction, 1558–1700: A Critical History*. Oxford, UK: Clarendon, 1985.

Sawday, Jonathan. *Engines of the Imagination: Renaissance Culture and the Rise of the Machine*. London: Routledge, 2007.

Schmidgen, Wolfram. *Eighteenth-Century Fiction and the Law of Property*. Cambridge: Cambridge University Press, 2002.

Schmitt, Carl. *The Concept of the Political*. Translated by George Schwab. Chicago: University of Chicago Press, 1996.

———. *The Nomos of the Earth in the International Law of the Jus Publicum Europaeum*. Translated by G. L. Ulmen. New York: Telos, 2003.

———. *Political Theology: Four Chapters on the Concept of Sovereignty*. Translated by George Schwab. Cambridge: MIT Press, 1985.

Schonhorn, Manuel. *Defoe's Politics: Parliament, Power, Kingship, and Robinson Crusoe*. Cambridge: Cambridge University Press, 1991.

Schwarz, Kathryn. "Chastity, Militant and Married: Cavendish's Romance, Milton's Masque." *PMLA: Publications of the Modern Language Association of America* 118, no. 2 (2003): 270–85.

Schwoerer, Lois G. *"No Standing Armies!" The Antiarmy Ideology in Seventeenth-Century England*. Baltimore: Johns Hopkins University Press, 1974.

Scott, Jonathan. *Algernon Sidney and the Restoration Crisis, 1677–1683*. Cambridge: Cambridge University Press, 1991.

Seed, Patricia. *Ceremonies of Possession in Europe's Conquest of the New World, 1492–1640*. Cambridge: Cambridge University Press, 1995.

Shakespeare, William. *King Richard II*. Edited by Andrew Gurr. New Cambridge Shakespeare. Cambridge: Cambridge University Press, 2003.

Shapiro, James. *Shakespeare and the Jews*. New York: Columbia University Press, 1996.

Sharpe, James. *Remember, Remember: A Cultural History of Guy Fawkes Day*. Cambridge: Harvard University Press, 2005.

Sheehan, Bernard W. *Savagism and Civility: Indians and Englishmen in Colonial Virginia*. Cambridge: Cambridge University Press, 1980.

Shell, Marc. "The Ring of Gyges." *Mississippi Review* 17, nos. 1–2 (1989): 21–84.

Sherman, Stuart. *Telling Time: Clocks, Diaries, and English Diurnal Form, 1660–1785*. Chicago: University of Chicago Press, 1996.

Shoemaker, Robert. *The London Mob: Violence and Disorder in Eighteenth-Century London*. London: Hambledon and London, 2004.

Shuger, Debora. "Irishmen, Aristocrats, and Other White Barbarians." *Renaissance Quarterly* 50, no. 2 (1997): 494–525.

Sidney, Algernon. *Discourses Concerning Government*. Edited by Thomas G. West. Indianapolis: Liberty Fund, 1996.

Sieyès, Emmanuel Joseph, comte. "What Is the Third Estate?" In *Political Writings: Including the Debate between Sieyès and Tom Paine in 1791*, edited and translated by Michael Sonenscher. Indianapolis: Hackett, 2003.

Simms, D. L. "Archimedes and Burning Mirrors." *Physics Education* 10 (November 1975): 517–21.

———. "Archimedes and the Invention of Artillery and Gunpowder." *Technology and Culture* 28, no. 1 (1987): 67–79.

Singer, Brian C. J., and Lorna Weir. "Sovereignty, Governance and the Political: The Problematic of Foucault." *Thesis Eleven* 94, no. 1 (2008): 49–71.

Skinner, Quentin. *The Foundations of Modern Political Thought*. 2 vols. Cambridge: Cambridge University Press, 1978.

———. *Reason and Rhetoric in the Philosophy of Hobbes*. Cambridge: Cambridge University Press, 1996.

Sloane, Hans. *A Voyage to the Islands Madera, Barbados, Nieves, S. Christophers and Jamaica with the Natural History of the Herbs, and Trees, Four-Footed Beasts, Fishes, Birds, Insects, Reptiles &c. of the Last of Those Islands: To Which Is Prefix'd an Introduction Wherein Is an Account of the Inhabitants, Air, Waters, Diseases, Trade, &c of that Place, with Some Relations concerning the Neighbouring Continent, and Islands of America; Illustrated with the Figures of the Things Described Which Have Not Been Heretofore Engraved; in Large Copper-Plates as Big as the Life*. London, 1707.

Smith, John. *The Complete Works of Captain John Smith (1580–1631)*. Edited by Philip L. Barbour. Chapel Hill: University of North Carolina Press, 1986.

Smolenski, John. "The Ordering of Authority in the Colonial Americas." In *New World Orders: Violence, Sanction, and Authority in the Colonial Americas*, edited by John Smolenski and Thomas J. Humphrey, 1–16. Philadelphia: University of Pennsylvania Press, 2005.

Spedding, Patrick. *A Bibliography of Eliza Haywood*. London: Pickering & Chatto, 2004.

Stafford, Barbara Maria, and Frances Terpak. *Devices of Wonder: From the World in a Box to Images on a Screen*. Los Angeles: Getty Research Institute, 2001.

Staves, Susan. *Players' Scepters: Fictions of Authority in the Restoration*. Lincoln: University of Nebraska Press, 1979.

Stephens, John Calhoun. Introduction to *The Guardian*, by Joseph Addison and Richard Steele, 1–36. Lexington: University Press of Kentucky, 1982.

Stewart, Susan. *On Longing: Narratives of the Miniature, the Gigantic, the Souvenir, the Collection*. Durham: Duke University Press, 1993.

Strachey, William. *A True Reportory of the Wracke, and Redemption of Sir Thomas Gates Knight; upon, and from the Ilands of the Bermudas*. 1610. In *Hakluytus Posthumus; or Purchas His Pilgrimes; Contayning a History of the World in Sea Voyages and Lande Travells by Englishmen and Others*, by Samuel Purchas, vol. 19, 5–72. London, 1625. Reprint, Glasgow: J. MacLehose and Sons, 1905–7.

Strong, Roy. *Art and Power: Renaissance Festivals, 1450–1650*. Berkeley: University of California Press, 1984.

———. *Coronation: From the 8th to the 21st Century*. London: HarperCollins, 2007.

Stuart, Shea. "Subversive Didacticism in Eliza Haywood's *Betsy Thoughtless*." *SEL Studies in English Literature 1500–1900* 42, no. 3 (2002): 559–75.

Suleri, Sara. *The Rhetoric of English India*. Chicago: University of Chicago Press, 1993.

Sullivan, Vickie B. *Machiavelli, Hobbes, and the Formation of a Liberal Republicanism in England*. Cambridge: Cambridge University Press, 2006.

Sussman, Charlotte. "The Other Problem with Woman: Reproduction and Slave Culture in Aphra Behn's *Oroonoko*." In *Rereading Aphra Behn: History, Theory, and Criticism*, edited by Heidi Hunter, 212–33. Charlottesville: University of Virginia Press, 1993.

Swenson, Rivka. "Optics, Gender, and the Eighteenth-Century Gaze: Looking at Eliza Haywood's *Anti-Pamela*." *Eighteenth Century: Theory and Interpretation* 51, nos. 1–2 (2010): 27–43.

Swift, Jonathan. *The Correspondence of Jonathan Swift*. Edited by Harold Herbert Williams. 5 vols. Oxford, UK: Clarendon, 1963–65.

———. *The Correspondence of Jonathan Swift, D.D.* 2 vols. Edited by David Woolley. New York: P. Lang, 1999.

———. *The Prose Works of Jonathan Swift*. Edited by Herbert Davis. 14 vols. Oxford, UK: Blackwell, 1939–1968.

Tabraham, Chris J., and Doreen Grove. *Fortress Scotland and the Jacobites*. London: B. T. Batsford, 1995.

Tatham, John. *The Rump*. In *The Broadview Anthology of Restoration and Early Eighteenth-Century Drama*, edited by J. Douglas Canfield and Maja-Lisa von Sneidern, 1596–1641. Peterborough, ON: Broadview, 2001.

Temple, Sir William. "An Essay upon the Ancient and Modern Learning." In *The Works of Sir William Temple, Bart.*, vol. 1, 151–69. London, 1731.

Thomas, Keith. *Religion and the Decline of Magic*. New York: Charles Scribner's Sons, 1971.

Thompson, E. P. "Patrician Society, Plebeian Culture." *Journal of Social History* 7, no. 4 (1974): 382–405.

———. *Whigs and Hunters: The Origin of the Black Act*. New York: Pantheon, 1976.

Thompson, M. P. "The Idea of Conquest in Controversies of the 1688 Revolution." *Journal of the History of Ideas* 38, no. 1 (1977): 33–46.

Todd, Dennis. *Defoe's America*. Cambridge: Cambridge University Press, 2010.

———. "Laputa, the Whore of Babylon, and the Idols of Science." *Studies in Philology* 75, no. 1 (1978): 93–120.

Todd, Janet. *The Secret Life of Aphra Behn*. New Brunswick: Rutgers University Press, 1997.

Tuck, Richard. *Natural Rights Theories: Their Origin and Development*. Cambridge: Cambridge University Press, 1982.

———. *The Rights of War and Peace: Political Thought and the International Order from Grotius to Kant*. Oxford: Oxford University Press, 1999.

Turley, Hans. "Piracy, Identity, and Desire in *Captain Singleton*." *Eighteenth-Century Studies* 31, no. 2 (1997): 199–214.

———. *Rum, Sodomy, and the Lash: Piracy, Sexuality, and Masculine Identity*. New York: NYU Press, 1999.

Tutchin, John. *A New Martyrology; or, The Bloody Assizes; Now Exactly Methodizing in One Volume*. London, 1689.

———. *The Protestant Martyrs; or, The Bloody Assizes. . . .* London, 1688.

Tyrrell, James. *Bibliotheca Politica; or, An Enquiry into the Ancient Constitution of the English Government; Both in Respect to the Just Extent of Regal Power, and the Rights and Liberties of the Subject.* London, 1694.

———. *Patriarcha Non Monarcha.* London, 1681.

Underdown, David. *Revel, Riot and Rebellion: Popular Politics and Culture in England, 1603–1660.* Oxford: Oxford University Press, 1987.

United States Department of Justice. *Lawfulness of a Lethal Operation Directed against a U.S. Citizen Who Is a Senior Operational Leader of Al-Qa'ida or an Associated Force.* White paper, 2012. Available online at http://msnbcmedia.msn.com/i/msnbc/sections/news/020413_DOJ_White_Paper.pdf (accessed February 9, 2012).

Unsworth, Barry. *Sacred Hunger.* New York: Norton, 1993.

Vaughan, Geoffrey M. *Behemoth Teaches Leviathan: Thomas Hobbes on Political Education.* Lanham, MD: Lexington Books, 2002.

Velissariou, Aspasia. "''Tis Pity That When Laws Are Faulty They Should Not Be Mended or Abolisht': Authority, Legitimations, and Honor in Aphra Behn's *The Widdow Ranter.*" *Papers on Language and Literature* 38, no. 2 (2002): 137–66.

Visconsi, Elliott. "A Degenerate Race: English Barbarism in Aphra Behn's *Oroonoko* and *The Widow Ranter.*" *ELH* 69, no. 3 (2002): 673–701.

———. *Lines of Equity: Literature and the Origins of Law in Later Stuart England.* Ithaca: Cornell University Press, 2008.

Warnes, Andrew. *Savage Barbecue: Race, Culture, and the Invention of America's First Food.* Athens: University of Georgia Press, 2008.

Watt, Ian. *The Rise of the Novel: Studies in Defoe, Richardson, and Fielding.* Berkeley: University of California Press, 2001.

West, Richard. *A Discourse Concerning Treasons and Bills of Attainder.* London, 1716.

Wheeler, Roxann. *The Complexion of Race: Categories of Difference in Eighteenth-Century British Culture.* Philadelphia: University of Pennsylvania Press, 2000.

White, Hayden V. "The Noble Savage Theme as Fetish." In *Tropics of Discourse: Essays in Cultural Criticism*, 183–96. Baltimore: Johns Hopkins University Press, 1978.

Whitehead, Neil L. "Native Peoples Confront Colonial Regimes in Northeastern South America (c. 1500–1900)." In *The Cambridge History of the Native Peoples of the Americas*, vol. 3, *South America*, part 2, edited by Frank Salomon and Stuart B. Schwartz, 382–442. Cambridge: Cambridge University Press, 1999.

Williams, Harold Herbert. *Dean Swift's Library, with a Facsimile of the Original Sale Catalogue and Some Account of Two Manuscript Lists of His Books.* Cambridge: Cambridge University Press, 1932.

Wilputte, Earla A. "The Textual Architecture of Eliza Haywood's *Adventures of Eovaai.*" *Essays in Literature* 22 (Spring 1995): 31–44.

Wilson, Kathleen. *The Sense of the People: Politics, Culture, and Imperialism in England, 1715–1785.* Cambridge: Cambridge University Press, 1995.

Wolper, Roy. "The Rhetoric of Gunpowder and the Idea of Progress." *Journal of the History of Ideas* 31, no. 4 (1970): 589–98.

Worden, Blair. "Milton's Republicanism and the Tyranny of Heaven." In *Machiavelli and Republicanism*, edited by Gisela Bock, Quentin Skinner, and Maurizio Viroli, 225–45. Ideas in Context 18. Cambridge: Cambridge University Press, 1990.

Wright, Lynn Marie, and Donald J. Newman, eds. *Fair Philosopher: Eliza Haywood and "The Female Spectator."* Lewisburg, PA: Bucknell University Press, 2006.

Wright, Nancy E. "Civic and Courtly Ceremonies in Jacobean London." In *The Politics of the Stuart Court Masque*, edited by David Bevington and Peter Holbrook, 197–217. Cambridge: Cambridge University Press, 1998.

Yang, Chi-ming. "Asia Out of Place: The Aesthetics of Incorruptibility in Behn's *Oroonoko.*" *Eighteenth-Century Studies* 42, no. 2 (2009): 235–53.

Zimmerman, Everett. "Robinson Crusoe and No Man's Land." *Journal of English and Germanic Philology* 102, no. 4 (2003): 506–29.

Zook, Melinda S. "Contextualizing Aphra Behn." In *Women Writers and the Early Modern British Political Tradition*, edited by Hilda L. Smith, 75–93. Cambridge: Cambridge University Press, 1998.

———. "The Political Poetry of Aphra Behn." In *The Cambridge Companion to Aphra Behn*, edited by Derek Hughes and Janet Todd, 46–67. Cambridge: Cambridge University Press, 2004.

———. *Radical Whigs and Conspiratorial Politics in Late Stuart England.* University Park: Pennsylvania State University Press, 1999.

———. "Violence, Martyrdom, and Radical Politics: Rethinking the Glorious Revolution." In *Politics and the Political Imagination in Later Stuart Britain: Essays Presented to Lois Green Schwoerer*, edited by Howard Nenner, 75–95. Rochester, NY: University of Rochester Press, 1997.

Zwicker, Steven N. *Lines of Authority: Politics and English Literary Culture, 1649–1689.* Ithaca: Cornell University Press, 1993.

Index

'15, The (Jacobite invasion and uprising), 30, 106

'45, The (Jacobite invasion and uprising), 224–25

Act of Union (1707), 30, 106, 133, 223
Addison, Joseph: on flight, 171–73, 271n42; and invisibility, 280n47; and Jacobitism, 259–60n7; on superstition, 25
Africa, 15, 163, 264–65n40; in Behn, 93–95; in Defoe, 111–14, 128–31; and fetishism, 18–20, 181; fortifications in, 128–31, 134, 264n37; in Unsworth, 226–27
Agamben, Giorgio, 17, 44, 192, 220, 222, 230n3
animals, 66–67, 113–14, 118–20, 134, 250n3, 262n22
Anne (Queen of Great Britain), 19, 143
Arabian Nights' Entertainments, 277n26
Aravamudan, Srinivas, 170, 229n1, 230n3, 236n36, 244n8, 250n3
Archimedes, 72–75
Armintor, Deborah Needleman, 278
Armitage, David, 231n5
artillery, 21, 158–59
assimilation, 269n21
Astell, Mary, 15, 196
Atkins, John, 18–20, 181
atrocity: associated with sovereignty, 7, 175–78, 263n29; evasion of, 281n54; and gunpowder, 22, 168. *See also* massacre

Backscheider, Paula R., 86, 182, 273n6, 276n15, 279n39
Bacon, Francis, 22
Bacon, Nathaniel, 77–78, 87–89; Bacon's Rebellion, 87–88
Balakrishnan, Gopal, 234n24
barbecue, 90, 97, 256n45
Baron, Robert (author of *Mirza*), 73
Bates, David, 222, 231n5
Battigelli, Anna, 243n6, 248–49n44
Baucom, Ian, 220–21
Beach, Adam, 254–55n38
Behn, Aphra, 26, 29–30, 66–69; *Fair Jilt, The*, 77; *Oroonoko*, 29, 66–68, 92–103; *Roundheads*, 77, 83–87; *Second Part of the Rover*, 76, 81; *Widdow Ranter, The*, 77, 87–91, 252n22
Beier, A. L., 233n20
Bender, John, 128, 234n23
Benjamin, Walter, 186–87
Berkeley, William, 87–89
Bhabha, Homi, 119
bills of attainder, 223, 282n15
Blaine, Rodney M., 261–62n21
Blewett, David, 261n12
Bloody Assizes, 29–30, 97–100
Blount, Charles, 6–7, 106
Bodin, Jean, 145, 229n2

Bolingbroke, Henry St. John, Viscount, 189, 190, 199
borders, national, 133, 220
Bosman, Willem, 128–29, 264n40
Boyle, Robert, 6
Brown, Kathleen, 87–88
Brown, Laura, 173, 229n1, 250n7
burning glasses, 23, 29, 67–68, 72–75, 102–3
Butler, Judith, 283n26

Cadamosto, Alvise, 22, 239n69
cannibalism, 221, 237n50; in Behn, 87–91, 97; in Cavendish, 33–34, 37–39, 44; in Defoe, 114–16, 127–28; and Scotland, 223–24; in Swift, 165–67
Careri, Gemelli, 18
Carey, Daniel, 229n1, 232n8
Caribs, 251n15; in Behn, 67, 70–76, 90, 97; in Defoe, 114–20, 260n10
Carnell, Rachel, 279n38
Casas, Bartolomé de las, 6
Catholicism, 6–7, 161, 166, 223, 249n44, 281n55
Cavendish, Margaret: "Assaulted and Pursued Chastity," 33–35, 37–38, 39, 43–47, 58; *Blazing World, The*, 58, 61–65; intellectual circle of, 36–37; *Orations of Divers Sorts*, 59–60, 247–48n39; *Philosophical Letters*, 58, 247–48n39; *Sociable Letters*, 47
Cavendish, William, Duke of Newcastle, 36–37, 48–50, 131
Chaplin, Joyce E., 239–40n70
Christianity, 19, 25, 221, 248–49n44; in Cavendish, 62–63; in Defoe, 108, 114, 117, 261nn12–13; in Swift, 148
Churchill, John and Awnsham, 18
Cicero, 95–96, 153, 256–57n53, 268n17, 280n45
civic humanism, 95–96, 159–60
civility, 1–2, 4–7, 16–19, 28–29, 217, 221–22; in Addison, 171–73; in Behn, 89–90, 96–97, 101–2; in Cavendish, 33–36, 61, 63–65; in Davenant, 54–57; in Defoe, 106–7, 110–11, 117–19, 120–22, 125–26, 127–31, 132, 134–35; in Haywood, 182–84, 185–86, 195–98, 203–4; in Hobbes, 37–43; in Swift, 143–46, 146–49, 152–54, 160, 162–66, 178–80
Columbus, Christopher, 27, 40, 242n2
command, 51, 59, 82, 155, 183, 191–93, 205–6, 210–11, 276–77n23
commerce, 8–9, 205, 222; in Addison, 171–72; in Behn, 75–76; in Defoe, 106–7, 110–14, 119–20, 122, 127–30, 135
Connolly, William; 8, 233n21
conquest, 1, 6, 12, 259n6; in Behn, 67–70; in Cavendish, 43, 58–61; in Defoe, 106–7, 128–29; in Hobbes, 39–41; in Swift, 147, 154, 161, 170, 178–79
constituent power, 3–5, 12–13, 37, 152–53, 163, 204–5, 230n3
constitutional monarchy, 186, 187–92, 199–201, 259n5
contract, 8, 14–15, 276n18; in Behn, 76; in Haywood, 185–86, 190, 195, 211; in Hobbes, 35–41
Convention Parliament (1660), 79
Convention Parliament, Scottish (1689), 131–32
coronation, 85–86, 245n16, 254n33,
Creech, Thomas, 96
Cromwell, Oliver, 24, 59, 123, 136–37, 202, 253n26
crowds. *See* mob; rabble
Crown Jewels, 84–87, 254n33
curiosity, 139–40, 204, 207, 276n20

Davenant, William, 28, 50–57; *Brittania Triumphans*, 55; on marriage, 51–52; and masques, 54–55; *Preface to Gondibert*, 50–54; *Proposition for the Advancement of Moralitie, A*, 54–57; *Salmacida Spolia*, 55; on wit, 53
Defoe, Daniel: *Captain Singleton*, 132–41; *Hymn to the Mob*, 13–14;

illustrations of novels, 260–61n12; and individualism, 105, 125–26; *Jure Divino*, 235n32; *New Voyage Round the World* (1724), 1, 5–6; *Original Power of the Collective Body of the People of England, Examined and Asserted, The*, 235n32; poetry of, 12–13, 259n5; *Political History of the Devil*, 117; political views, 104–5; *Review*, 129–30; *Robinson Crusoe*, 104–20; *Tour Through the Whole Island of Great Britain*, 128; *True-Born Englishman, The*, 12–13; and violence, 9

democracy, 152–53, 225–28, 235n32
Derrida, Jacques, 41
Descartes, René, 73, 243n5
despotism, 20, 59, 92–94, 170, 189, 199, 202, 256n47, 276n18
deterritorialization, 120
Dickinson, H. T., 235n32
Dolan, Frances, 281n51
Doyle, Laura, 11
drawing and quartering, 98–102, 258n60
Dunton, John, 73

Edward I, 251–52n16
Ehrenpreis, Irvin, 268n16, 269n25
Elias, Norbert, 237n47
Elmer, Jonathan, 14, 120
emergency: in Britain, 107, 150, 233n20; and constitutionality, 186–87, 198, 275n12; and republicanism, 201–2; and sovereignty, 2–3, 5, 10, 13, 16, 30, 234n24
Equiano, Olaudah, 109–11, 156
equity, 94, 96, 101
Evelyn, John, 21
executive power, 222
exemplarity, 31, 141–42, 156–58, 161–67, 267n7

femininity, 34, 45–48, 50, 65, 70, 165, 186–91, 196, 218–19
Fenwick, John, 282n15

Ferguson, Margaret, 249n3, 250–51n9
Festa, Lynn, 229n1
fetishism, 19–22, 56; in Behn, 66–69, 75–76, 84–86, 98–103; in Defoe, 109–10, 125, 137; in Swift, 156, 164, 184–85; in Unsworth, 226
first gunshot topos, 4–6, 34, 184–85, 227, 236n38
Fleetwood, Charles, 253n26
flight, 168–78
fortifications and fortresses, 21, 49, 124–25, 127–35, 137–41; and aerial warfare, 169–76; in Scotland, 224–25. *See also* space
Foucault, Michel, 9–10, 13, 181–83, 233n19, 233n20, 258n60, 273n2, 273n3
Fradinger, Moira, 10
Frederick, Prince of Wales, 187
Frohock, Richard, 68

Galien, Joseph, 271n41
Gallagher, Catherine, 58–59, 65
Gardner, Thomas, 214
Gassendi, Pierre, 243n5
Gates, Henry Louis, Jr., 109–11
Gaudio, Michael, 20
gaze, 244n13
genocide, 263n29. *See also* atrocity, massacre
George II (King of Great Britain), 186, 199
Glorious Revolution, 87, 105, 223, 230–31n5, 259n6
Gordon, Colin, 233n19
Gordon, Scott Paul, 273n2,
Gordon, Thomas, 26
governmentality, 4, 9–10, 14, 16, 36, 218–19, 222, 233n29, 234n23, 273n2. *See also* Foucault, Michel
Graves, Nicola, 278n32
Grotius, Hugo, 7–8, 38, 115–16, 221–22
Guest, Harriet, 229n1
Gunn, J. A. W., 231n5

gunpowder: and atrocity, 6, 136–41, 177–78; connotations, of, 21–24, 53–54; and despotism, 154–60; as miraculous, 104–6, 106–10; as modern, 2, 4–6, 14, 21–22, 239n68, 239–40n70
Gunpowder Plot, 6, 157, 177–78
guns. *See* gunpowder

Hakluyt, Richard, 5, 22, 231–32n8; and Jonathan Swift, 266n2
Harol, Corrinne, 94–95, 258n63
Harriot, Thomas, 22–23, 64, 70, 73, 185, 192
Hawes, Clement, 269n21, 270n37
Haywood, Eliza, 31–32, 181–84, 217–18, 222; *Eovaai*, 182–203, 274n7; *Invisible Spy, The*, 182, 184, 203–15, 281n55; as Jacobite, 279n38; *Parrot, The*, 195–96; political views and activity, 273–74n6
Helgerson, Richard, 15
Henry VIII (King of England), 267n10
Henry, John, 25
Herman, Peter, 255n38
Hobbes, Thomas: and Cavendish, 28, 35–36, 59–60; and Haywood, 193, 248n39; *Leviathan*, 1, 35–36, 37–43, 278n32; and natural law, 7–8; *Philosophical Problems*, 97–98; and romance, 94; and savages, 15, 222
homo sacer, 17, 44, 215, 218, 220–21, 258n64. *See also* Agamben, Giorgio
Honig, Bonnie, 233n17
Hooke, Robert, 170–71

individualism, 8–9, 236n36; in Behn, 257n55; in Defoe, 104–6, 122–23, 126, 132, 262n25; and invisibility, 208
Ingrassia, Catherine, 182, 273n6, 279n38
invisibility, 206–9
Ireland, 148–49, 161–67, 169, 178, 269n23
Iyengar, Sujata, 243n2

Jacobitism: and the '15, 106–7, 259–60n7; and the '45, 224–25; and bills of attainder, 282n15; and Boscabel Oak, 134–40; and Haywood, 279n38, 281n55; and mobs, 13
James II (King of England), 7, 69–71, 76, 78, 85, 93, 97–102
James, Duke of Monmouth, 99
Jewish Naturalization Act (1753), 204–5, 279–80n42
Johnson, Samuel, 17
Jonson, Ben, 23

Kahn, Paul, 230n5
Kahn, Victoria, 8, 44, 231n5, 275n11
Kaul, Suvir, 229n1, 258n65
Kepler, Johannes, 72–73
King, Kathryn, 212, 215, 276n20, 279n38, 280n50
king's evil, touching for, 74
Kroll, Richard, 102, 257n59
Kvande, Marta, 279n38

Lambert, John, 253n26
Lana-Terzi, Francesco, 170–71
Leslie, Charles, 15
Leslie, Marina, 35, 44, 245n16
Locke, John, 7–8, 15, 135, 222–23
Loughlin, Martin, 230n3, 235n32, 242n88
luxury, 31, 57, 114, 144–46, 164–65, 167, 171–72, 191, 268–69n19, 276n19

Machiavelli, Nicolai, 235n32
Mackie, Erin, 234n23
Madagascar, 120–25, 130, 132, 134, 262–63n26, 263n28
magic, 1–2, 19, 24–26, 27–28; in Behn, 67–70, 75; in Davenant, 54–55; in Defoe, 105–7, 112, 116–17, 263n28; Equiano and, 110; gunpowder as, 22–24, 35, 45; in Haywood, 184–98, 204–10, 214, 277n26, 280n48; Hobbes and, 40–43
Mandelslo, John Albert de, 263n28

Mandeville, Bernard, 16, 18
Manley, Delarivier, 207, 274–75n11
Manning, Roger B., 233n20
Markley, Robert, 121, 262n25
marriage, 47, 50, 212–15
Marriage Act (1753), 204–5, 279–80n42
Martyr, Peter, 242n2
masques, 54–56, 63–64, 246–47n31
massacre: in Defoe, 104–5, 115–16, 121–26, 129–32; in Haywood, 194; in Naudé, 26; in Swift, 147, 169, 175–78
Mayhew, Experience, 263–64n33
Mbembe, Achille, 282n9
McCormick, John P., 235n32
McGirr, Elaine, 236n38
Mendle, Michael, 231n5
Merritt, Juliette, 278n31
militias, 159–60
Milton, John, 24
miracles, 26–27, 39–40
mob, 13, 235n35, 252n19. *See also* rabble
Mohawk kings, visit of, 271n43
monarchy, 2, 19, 29–30, 84–87, 102–3, 181–82, 268n15; and conquest, 59; constitutional, 186–87, 188–92, 199–201, 203, 259n5; and heroism, 81, 102, 151–53, 236n38; and Jacobitism, 134–35; and masques, 54–56
Monck, George, 79, 82–83, 87, 253n29
money, 163–67, 270n31
Monmouth, Duke of. *See* James, Duke of Monmouth
Monmouth's Rebellion, 97–100
Montag, Warren, 143, 174, 268n16, 272n46
Montesquieu, Charles-Louis de Secondat, Baron de, 256n47
Mouffe, Chantal, 225–26
Muse, S. Vida, 280n42

Nash, Richard, 229n1
Naudé, Gabriel, 26–27, 40
Negri, Antonio, 230n3
Novak, Maximillian, 235n35

Novelists' Magazine, The (1788), 214
Nussbaum, Felicity, 229n1

O'Brien, Karen, 237n49
objects, magical, 2, 20–21, 66–67, 183–84, 192–94, 206–10, 213
Olearius, Adam, 73
opera, 55–57
optics, 277–78n31. *See also* telescopes
oratory, 59–61, 92, 95–97, 247–48n39, 256–57n53
oriental despotism, 92–94, 170, 189, 256n47
oriental tales, 182, 184, 236n36, 277n26

Pagden, Anthony, 237n47, 237n48
Paris Massacre, 26–27
Parliament, British, 10, 106–7, 149–52, 205, 268n15, 282n15; and Royal African Company, 129. *See also* Convention Parliament (1660); Convention Parliament, Scottish (1689); Parliament, Irish
Parliament, Irish, 164–65
Pateman, Carole, 8, 274n10
Patterson, Annabel, 11, 234n26, 252n23, 275n13
Peacham, Henry, 257n53
performance, 19, 22, 24; in Behn, 67, 80–82, 84–87, 102; in Cavendish, 33–34, 63; in Defoe, 104–5, 117–20
periodicals, 181–84, 203–6
Pietz, William, 19–20, 250n4
Pincus, Steve, 230–31n5
Plato, 208–9
Pocock, J. G. A., 230n4, 248n43, 266n4, 269n22
political community, 1–5, 7, 10–18, 26, 106, 150–51, 162, 204–5, 218–28
Pollock, Anthony, 210, 213, 279n41
Popish Plot, 6–7, 78, 99, 283n17
Poullain de la Barre, François, 218
Powell, Manushag, 277n23, 279n38
privacy, 19, 181–83, 204–6, 212–13, 215, 217

Proclus, 72–73
Purchas, Samuel, xiii, 1, 11–12, 22, 50, 231n8; volumes owned by Swift, 266n2
Pye, Christopher, 244n13

rabble, 3, 8, 26; in Behn, 67–68, 74–75, 76–78, 78–83, 87, 89–91, 95, 98, 100, 102–3, 254n30; in Cavendish, 35; in Defoe, 235n35; in Lord Newcastle, 50
Raleigh, Sir Walter, 22–23, 240n76
rape, 44–45, 51, 122, 194, 195
Rasch, William, 222–23
Rawson, Claude, 64–65, 155, 165, 239n67, 263n29, 270n33
Redfield, Marc, 228, 231n7
republicanism, 10–11, 24, 235n32; in Haywood, 199–202, 278n36, 278n37
rhetoric, 59, 61, 81, 83, 95–96, 152, 245n1. *See also* oratory
Riot Act (1714), 260n8
Rogers, Nicholas, 233n20, 260n8
romance: and Behn, 66–67, 91–92, 94, 102–3, 257n55; and Cavendish, 34, 44–45, 59; and Davenant, 52; and Haywood, 185–94, 198–99, 201–3, 274n7, 274–75n11, 275–76n13
Rousseau, Jean-Jacques, 8, 233n21
Royal African Company, 128–30, 364n37
Royal Ordnance, 24, 36
Ryan, Alan, 233n20

Sacheverell, Henry, 106; Sacheverell Riots (1710), 30
satire, 155, 165–66, 183, 188
savagery, xiii, 1–2, 3–4, 6–7, 14–18, 19–21, 22–23, 50, 231n6; and anti-semitism, 280n42; in Behn, 67–76, 87, 89–90, 95–97; and cannibalism, 33–34, 90, 114–16, 127, 167, 221, 224, 237n50; in Cavendish, 33–34, 65; and criminality, 25–26; in Davenant, 37, 51, 53–54, 54–56; in Defoe, 30, 104, 108–109, 112–18, 119, 120–22, 125–26, 127–30, 131–32, 135–41 ; and enmity, 220–22, 226, 228; and femininity, 217–18; in Haywood, 31–32, 182, 185, 186–87, 195–99, 209; in Hobbes, 28, 37–39, 40–41; and materialism, 23–24, 56; and Scottish Highlanders,131–32, 224–25; and superstition, 24–25, 40; in Swift, 31, 143, 144, 146, 153–54, 163, 166–67, 170
Sawday, Jonathan, 24
Schmidgen, Wolfram, 235n34
Schmitt, Carl, 9, 217–221, 225, 227, 234n24, 274n9
Scotland, 106, 131–33, 223–25. *See also* Act of Union (1707)
Seneca, 221
sensation, 24–25, 56–57, 183
senses. *See* sensation
Shakespeare, William, 132–33
Sheehan, Bernard W., 237n47
Shell, Marc, 280n44
ships, 18, 22
Shuger, Debora, 15
Sidney, Algernon, 10–12, 15, 257n58
Sieyès, Emmanuel Joseph, 230n3
Skinner, Quentin, 229n2, 245n13
slavery: and absolutism, 59; in Behn, 95–97, 100–1; in Defoe, 261n19; and Equiano, 109–12; and savagery, 34; in Swift, 153–54; in Unsworth, 226–28; and women, 15
slave trade, 128–30, 163
Smith, Hilda, 15
Smolenski, John, 264n33
sovereignty, 17; absolute, 59–60, 153, 157; and anarchy, 132; and bills of attainder, 282n15; and biopower, 204–205, 207; colonial, 244n8; and constituent power, 12–13, 230n3; and contract, 7–9; and custom, 122–24, 136–41; defined by Hobbes, 38–39, 40–43, 244n11; and divine right, 190; and exceptions, 151–52, 234n24; and exemplarity, 143–44; and fetishism,

19–21, 25–27, 68–75, 78–87, 254n33; and force, 47–49, 104–5, 106–8, 110–11, 119, 147, 157–59, 163–64, 168–70, 174–78, 183–84, 202–3, 248–49n44; fragmentation of, 120–21; and friend/enemy distinction, 219–28; and gender, 51–52, 58–59, 217–19; and governmentality, 9–10, 182–84, 273nn2–3; and gunpowder, 4–7, 24; as human construct, 248n39; and invisibility, 208–9; and Ireland, 161–67; and magic, 54–55, 39–40, 206–7; and money, 163; and nature, 132–135, 140–41; as origin of law, 89, 154; as outside of law, 100–1; and performance, 49–50, 54–55, 63, 74–76, 91, 246n30, 248–49n44; and punishment, 43, 101–2, 109, 115; and republican critiques, 199–202; and savagery, 2–4, 16, 146, 153; and space, 127–41, 263–64n33, 264n37; and Algernon Sidney, 11–12; and surveillance, 181–84, 214; Swift, fascination with, 145; and violence, 61–62, 64–65, 71, 150–51, 157–59; and visibility, 244n13. *See also* emergency

space: as customary, 120–26; and fortification, 127–41; as lawless, 30, 43–44, 87, 105; as private, 204; in Swift, 168–70, 171, 173, 174, 175–78; in Unsworth, 227

Spain, 115

St. John, Henry. *See* Bolingbroke, Henry St. John, Viscount.

stadial theory, 17, 237n49

Statute of Treasons. *See* Treason Act (1351)

Staves, Susan, 231n5

Steele, Richard, 181, 271n42

Stewart, Susan, 250n6

Suleri, Sara, 281n54

Sullivan, Vickie B., 235n32

surveillance, 31, 170, 207, 210, 213, 273n2; and fetishism, 181

Sussman, Charlotte, 100

Swenson, Rivka, 278n31

Swift, Jonathan, 31, 142–80; *Discourse of the Contests and Dissentions between the Nobles and the Commons in Athens and Rome*, 149–52, 268n15; *Drapier's Letters*, 161–65; *Gulliver's Travels*, 142–49, 154–61, 168–80, 272n51; *Modest Proposal, A*, 165–67; political views and activities, 142, 266n3, 268n15; and *Robinson Crusoe*, 272n46; *Sentiments of a Church-of-England Man*, 152–54, 268n16

Tatham, John (author of *The Rump*), 78, 254n30

technology, 2, 4–5, 35, 47, 135–39, 239n69. *See also* fortification; gunpowder; ships

telescopes, 31–32, 184–85, 192, 194–97, 277n26

Temple, Sir William, 25, 143

theater, 54–57, 246–47n31

Thomas, Keith, 24, 241n82

tigers, 249–50n3

tobacco, 257n56

Tower of London, 7

tragedy, 14, 66, 94, 236n38

tragicomedy, 255n43

treason, 98, 99–100, 223, 257n58. *See also* drawing and quartering

Treason Act (1351), 99

tyranny. *See* despotism

Tyrrell, James, 12, 259n6

Unsworth, Barry, 226–28

violence: and civility, 3; and display, 3–4, 118–20. *See also* atrocity; conquest; gunpowder; Gunpowder Plot; *homo sacer*; massacre; rape; sovereignty; vulnerability

Virginia, 22–23, 52–53, 73, 87–91, 254–55n38, 255n42

virginity, 43–45, 209, 211–12, 243n3, 280n48
Visconsi, Elliott, 11, 14, 15, 94, 234n26, 236n38, 246n25, 255n42
vulnerability, 228

Walpole, Robert, 163, 173, 187; in Cavendish, 58–61, 65; in Davenant, 53; in Defoe, 123, 131; in Haywood, 186, 198; in Hobbes, 38, 42; as "Leviathan," 277n24; in Swift, 144, 150–52, 163–64, 178–80; war; 5, 10, 12–13, 219–20, 224
watches, 109–10, 155–56, 268–69n19
West, Richard, 223
Wheeler, Roxann, 229n1, 237n47

William III (King of England), 106, 132, 149–50
Wilputte, Earla A., 274n7
Wilson, Kathleen, 107
women, 8, 12, 34, 45–46, 86, 182; as outside of law, 29, 34, 47, 65, 185; as rational agents, 183–85, 186–87, 190–93, 196, 211–12; as savages, 15, 96; and sexual desire, 193–94, 197, 209; as slaves, 15; violence against, 214–15, 217–19. *See also* femininity; virginity
Worden, Blair, 24

Zimmerman, Everett, 105
Zwicker, Steven N., 231n5